STILL NOT EQUAL

PETER LANG
New York • Washington, D.C./Baltimore • Bern
Frankfurt am Main • Berlin • Brussels • Vienna • Oxford

STILL NOT EQUAL

Expanding Educational Opportunity in Society

Edited by M. Christopher Brown II
with assistance from RoSusan D. Bartee
Foreword by Michael L. Lomax

PETER LANG
New York • Washington, D.C./Baltimore • Bern
Frankfurt am Main • Berlin • Brussels • Vienna • Oxford

Library of Congress Cataloging-in-Publication Data

Still not equal: expanding educational opportunity in society /
edited by M. Christopher Brown II.
p. cm.
Includes bibliographical references.
1. Educational equalization—United States. 2. Discrimination in education—
United States. 3. Educational equalization. I. Brown, M. Christopher.
LC213.2.S75   379.1′58—dc22   2007003223
ISBN 978-0-8204-9727-3 (hardcover)
ISBN 978-0-8204-9522-4 (paperback)

Bibliographic information published by **Die Deutsche Bibliothek**.
Die Deutsche Bibliothek lists this publication in the "Deutsche
Nationalbibliografie"; detailed bibliographic data is available
on the Internet at http://dnb.ddb.de/.

Cover image courtesy of the United Negro College Fund, Inc.
Cover design by George Holton

The paper in this book meets the guidelines for permanence and durability
of the Committee on Production Guidelines for Book Longevity
of the Council of Library Resources.

© 2007 Peter Lang Publishing, Inc., New York
29 Broadway, 18th floor, New York, NY 10006
www.peterlang.com

All rights reserved.
Reprint or reproduction, even partially, in all forms such as microfilm,
xerography, microfiche, microcard, and offset strictly prohibited.

Printed in the United States of America

Contents

Foreword	xi
Acknowledgments	xv
Introduction	1
M. Christopher Brown II and RoSusan D. Bartee	

Part One: Racial Inequalities

Chapter One
African American College Enrollment and Completion:
A Decade of Progress — 7
M. Christopher Brown II, Tazewell V. Hurst III,
RoSusan D. Bartee, and Trimika M. Yates

Chapter Two
Accommodation or Immediacy? The Role of African Americans
in the Quest for Education and Equality in the Evolution
of American Education — 19
David Boers

Chapter Three
Closing the Racial/Ethnic Gaps 29
LISA MARIE MARTINEZ AND DON ANTHONY WOODS

Chapter Four
Navigating the River: Environmental Scanning to Enable Diversity Programs and Initiatives to Withstand Internal and External Challenges 39
M. COOKIE NEWSOM AND ARCHIE ERVIN

Chapter Five
Historical and Contemporary Dilemmas Facing Urban Black Male Students Today: Focusing on the Past to Correct Present and Future Deficits 49
THEODORE LOUIS THOMPSON III

Chapter Six
Racial Profiling: A Never-Ending Problem for America's Minorities 65
SHARON J. CHAMBERS

Chapter Seven
Equalizing Educational Opportunities for African American Students: The Evaluation and Evolution of Teacher Education 85
RENEE WHITE-CLARK, GRACE LAPPIN, AND ODESA WEATHERFORD-JACOBS

Part Two: Student Performance and Assessment

Chapter Eight
The Brown Decision and Its Impact on African Americans: Examining Teacher Education, the Sociology of Education, and Agricultural Education 103
PATRICIA J. LARKE, ALVIN LARKE JR., AND EVANGELINE M. CASTLE

Chapter Nine
The LEAP for Accountability? Ideology and Practice of Testing in a Louisiana Urban Elementary School 111
JIM HORN

Chapter Ten
The Use of Jigsawing in Second Language Acquisition Among Third- and Fourth-Grade Hispanic Migrant Students in Kansas 145
RUDOLPH BUSTOS

Contents

Chapter Eleven
Achieving Success: Voices of Successful African American Mathematics Students — 167
ANGILINE POWELL AND ROBERT Q. BERRY III

Chapter Twelve
Reasons African American Men Persist to Degree Completion in Institutions of Higher Education — 177
JOHN P. HAMILTON

Chapter Thirteen
Moving Beyond National Standards and Assessment — 197
BOYCE C. WILLIAMS

Part Three: Legal Issues and Black Colleges

Chapter Fourteen
Blacks Still Not Equal Even After the Civil Rights Act of 1964 — 217
OTIS D. ALEXANDER

Chapter Fifteen
Curriculum Violence: The New Civil Rights Issue—How Efforts at Standardization Impact the Academic Achievement of African Americans — 229
ERHABOR IGHODARO

Chapter Sixteen
The Use of Corporal Punishment on Minorities in the Public Schools — 239
CYNTHIA NORTHINGTON

Chapter Seventeen
Historically Black Colleges and Universities: An Opportunity for Leadership in the Twenty-First Century — 245
LOUIS A. CASTENELL JR.

Chapter Eighteen
Vyuo vya Weusi (Black colleges): Their Future, Use, and Survival in a White Country — 259
BARUTI I. KATEMBO

Part Four: School and Community

Chapter Nineteen
Community Uplift Theory for Positive Change of African Americans in Urban Schools — 269
FLOYD D. BEACHUM, FESTUS OBIAKOR, AND CARLOS R. MCCRAY

Chapter Twenty
Mentoring Across Social Class Boundaries: Empirical Lessons   279
FRED MUSKAL

Chapter Twenty-One
Discourse(s) of Local Literacy Practices in Adolescent Jail Classrooms: Cultural Mediation Through Critical Race Theory   297
BRETT ELIZABETH BLAKE

Chapter Twenty-Two
An Industry's Delight: The Messages, Implications, and Uses of Positive Rap and Hip-Hop Media   315
LISA D. HORTON AND RODNEY WASHINGTON

Chapter Twenty-Three
Still Unequal: A Critical Exploration of Early Literacy Instruction with Primary Teachers and Implications for Policy   339
DENEESE L. JONES, SHERRY POWERS, ANTONY NORMAN, WILLIAM BINTZ, ANGELA COX, MARGARET DAVIS, YVONNE GREENWALT, PATRICIA HIGGINS, AND FAYE NEWSON

Chapter Twenty-Four
A Thing Most Brutish: The Calibanization of the African American Male   355
JAMES RICHARDSON

Chapter Twenty-Five
African American College Students' Attitudes Toward Mental Health Treatment   367
MAVIS MITCHELL, MALCOLM CORT, GEORGE YOUNG, AND LORNA ROBERTS

Part Five: Global Perspectives

Chapter Twenty-Six
Education Enhances Equality and Fairness: Where Do People of Color Fit in Global Educational Systems?   381
JAMES MBUVA

Chapter Twenty-Seven
Obstacles to Equal Opportunity for African Refugees in the United States   393
ELAVIE NDURA AND OMIUNOTA NELLY UKPOKODU

Chapter Twenty-Eight
Counseling for Global Citizenship Education as Innovation in South Nations — 409
    RICHARD IRIKEFE OKORODUDU

Chapter Twenty-Nine
Provision of Sports Facilities and Coaching for University Undergraduates in Southern Africa: A Comparative Study of Students with and without Disabilities — 425
    I. U. ONYEWADUME AND H. S. DHALIWAL

Chapter Thirty
Equality or Inequality: Physical Education for the Children of Africa, Problems and Way Forward — 443
    I. U. ONYEWADUME

Foreword

MICHAEL L. LOMAX, PH.D.

The year 2004 marked the 60th anniversary of the founding of the United Negro College Fund (UNCF). Sharing this milestone year were the 50th anniversary of *Brown v. Board of Education* (1954) and the 40th anniversary of the Civil Rights Act of 1964. In commemoration of these historic events, UNCF hosted a conference of more than 600 attendees and 200 sessions. The 2004 Patterson Research Conference was designed to reaffirm UNCF's mission of providing educational opportunities by identifying the most critical issues impacting the education and social experiences of people of color.

The conference theme, "Still Not Equal: Expanding Opportunities in Global Societies," embraces the mission that UNCF has pursued throughout its 60-year history. In the twenty-first century, the need for an educated society and workforce has become more critical than ever before. As a result, UNCF must work to ensure even more bright and talented individuals have the ability to expand their own opportunities through higher education, so that they can make significant contributions in the communities where they will one day work and live.

This was a very important conference not only because of the subject we are considering here a half century after the Brown decision, but also the recognition that educational opportunity is still in many ways separate and unequal in this country. Fifty years after *Brown*, the importance of educational attainment in the lives of individuals and in the life of this nation is as great an issue as it was a half century ago.

One of the individuals whose name now means so much more to me than it has over the 40-plus years since I have known of him is Frederick Patterson. Having lived in Tuskegee, I knew of Dr. Patterson, the visionary president of Tuskegee Institute in the 1940s whose idea it was to form the UNCF fund-raising initiative 60 years ago, but it's really only from the close association now with the College Fund that I'm reminded that the UNCF fund-raising initiative raised $750,000 in its first year and has raised $2.3 billion over 60 years.

Dr. Patterson had the foresight to recognize the power of combining efforts in order to achieve a greater goal that would ultimately benefit so many. And now, six decades and over $2 billion later, Dr. Patterson's vision is evident. UNCF has become the nation's largest African American charity, supporting more than 65,000 students and 38 member colleges and universities.

Sixty years ago, UNCF was an idea whose time had come. Today, the College Fund is a mature institution serving a vital role at a time when higher education is more important than ever before. Sixty years ago, a high school diploma was, first of all, difficult for African Americans to earn because there were not accredited high schools for African Americans in every community in which we resided, certainly not in the South. But a high school diploma ensured a good job and a competitive wage. Today, it guarantees little more than an entry-level job and a poverty wage.

College attainment is an educational necessity that increasingly has to be viewed as one of the benchmarks against which we will judge the health and vitality of the African American community. And we must ensure that more Black Americans are college graduates because, as we at the UNCF constantly remind the nation: A mind is terrible thing to waste.

UNCF has expanded educational opportunities for thousands of students, but there remains much more to be done to ensure such opportunities for all children in this nation and beyond. Our focus at this conference upon "still not equal" opportunities extends to global societies, as we acknowledge that this is not just a US domestic issue—it is an international issue.

If we commit ourselves to this greater cause, maybe sometime in the not-so-distant future we can reflect on what we have achieved on behalf of generations yet unborn. As one who vividly remembers what the *Brown* ruling meant, and the subsequent challenges, I know that it will be because of the efforts of individuals who recognize our responsibilities and stand up to meet them that we will make the changes that will help us realize the dream of *Brown* here in this country and extend that vision of equal access to educational opportunity abroad.

It is critically important that all of us focus on closing the gaps. Unfortunately, the challenge of doing that is greater than any single decision by any court. We are not going to suggest that there are not still opportunities for impactful court decisions to be made, but there really is tremendous work yet to be done.

I think it is important that the Patterson Institute, a division of the UNCF that was founded a decade before the *Brown* decision, be an active and engaged participant in the continuing work. The 38 member institutions, 60,000 students, and 5,000 students who are receiving scholarships from the fund clearly play a more robust role than we even could have contemplated 60 years ago when Dr. Patterson challenged the independent member presidents to join in a UNCF fund-raising campaign, which in its first year raised three-quarters of a million dollars and during the 60 years since its founding has raised more than $2.3 billion.

Even with as magnificent and ambitious a record as that, the gaps remain, the challenges remain, and the College Fund, like all who participated in this conference, struggles with how to have impact, how to achieve the dream, the promise, of equal educational opportunity in this nation.

Participants in the conference worked to identify some of the most critical educational and social issues impacting the educational attainment levels of African Americans. Many of the issues that were discussed and debated are central to the work of the College Fund, which strives to increase African American college enrollment, strengthen historically Black colleges and universities, and increase access to education for deserving young men and women. While UNCF has broadened educational opportunities for thousands of students over the last 60 years, there is still much work to be done to ensure that all children have an equal chance. What follows in this volume are selected research findings, conceptualizations, and initiatives by the dedicated educators, researchers, and professionals who joined in that historic meeting in September 2004. Each chapter presented identifies challenges, develops strategies for eliminating barriers, and/or introduces ideas for creating an educational environment that is truly equal for everyone.

I hope you find this book both challenging and stimulating. Further, I hope that you will keep in your consciousness the very simple but powerful message that we keep before us at the College Fund every day in all the work that we do: *A mind is a terrible thing to waste.*

Michael L. Lomax, Ph.D.
President and CEO, United Negro College Fund

Acknowledgments

The Frederick D. Patterson Research Institute of the United Negro College Fund gratefully acknowledges the generous support of both the AT&T Foundation and TIAA-CREF. These two entities provided significant financial resources toward the planning, execution, and dissemination of the conference research. Further, both provided staff assistance in order to assure the success of all phases of the initiative. Also central to this effort was the support of The Pew Charitable Trusts and National Education Association.

Other supporters of this initiative include the Goldman Sachs Foundation, Longue Vue House and Gardens Foundation, Lumina Foundation for Education, the National Alliance of Black School Educators, the National Council for the Accreditation of Teacher Education, the National Opinion Research Council, Peter Lang Publishing, Stylus Publishing, Bowie State University, Dillard University, Howard University, Pennsylvania State University, and the University of Michigan.

Introduction

M. Christopher Brown II and RoSusan D. Bartee

This book, *Still Not Equal: Expanding Educational Opportunity in Society*, addresses the successes and failures of *Brown v. Board of Education* and the Civil Rights Act of 1964, as well as the continuing challenge of expanding educational opportunity in the United States and across the Black diaspora. The educational, political, and social influence resulting from *Brown*, the Civil Rights Act, and their progeny have shaped the dynamics of the collective educational and social experiences of people of color. Notwithstanding, the obstacles, barriers, and enablers of educational, occupational, and economic status outcomes impact the formation and interpretation of public policy, specifically, and public perception, generally, about racialized notions of schooling and learning. The pursuit of educational access, attendance, and attainment is intertwined with the implications of academic research and public policy to improve local practices in school settings. Inasmuch as a diverse research agenda, priorities, and activities become situated to critically address status and attainment outcomes in education from preschool through adulthood for African Americans in the United States and abroad, the resulting complexities in education and other settings will continue to behave in ways that cross racial lines.

This book focuses on the implications of racial inequalities in school and societal settings. Racial inequalities impede the processes by which institutions of higher education develop human potential and talent. The effects of racial inequalities represent an unfinished quest to secure equality in educational settings at large. Rallying *to* and *behind* the call is imperative. Given the demands of the diverse nature of schools and other settings, it is also necessary to conceptualize policies and implement practices that promote opportunity, access, and hopefulness. Racial inequalities interrupt the ability to create an academic continuum that seeks to be inclusive rather than exclusive. The context of an academic continuum must necessarily be forged in order to provide cultural sensitivity and awareness of the challenges that the racial divide creates.

This book engages various perspectives related to student performance and assessment in education. Student performance levels for African Americans are becoming increasingly linked to the quality of "the teacher" and "the teaching." How teachers are prepared in teacher education programs impacts the ways in which their students learn in school classrooms. Standardized assessments must be developed in concert with the school's curriculum and pedagogy. The use of traditional forms of curriculum and pedagogy can no longer be accepted without question. As all children can learn, it is our civic responsibility to develop to the highest capacity all of our human capital. The time has come to close the achievement gaps, to place all children on the same college preparatory curricular track, and to provide the resources necessary to acquire the best learning facilitators, school environments, and scholastic materials.

This book examines the legal implications and ramifications of *Brown v. Board of Education* in the arenas of public and higher education. While the Civil Rights Act of 1964 sought to eliminate the external impact of segregation, the vestiges of segregation denied African Americans full participation in society and produced a de facto apartheid within America's proclaimed democratic society. Segregation systematically reproduced inequalities between racial groups, and it evoked feelings of inferiority among students within the schools (as do practices such as classroom tracking and ability grouping). Historically, a two-tiered system of higher education emerged as a result of these vestiges—one for African Americans and one for Whites. Today, historically Black colleges and universities (HBCUs) provide African Americans with quality education and training that consistently and statistically adequately prepares them for viable professions and positions that contribute to this society's productivity. HBCUs are meeting national standards as afforded by accrediting agencies as well as surviving the political battles that periodically question their existence. The challenge now remains securing the future of HBCUs, particularly given the competitiveness of traditionally White institutions (TWIs) that are attracting increased numbers of African American students, the rising costs of tuition at HBCUs, and the fiscal challenges of maintaining the operations at HBCUs.

This book exposes the role of the school and the community in creating environments for learning. It is important to have community involvement within the processes of educational settings. The community can provide a certain type of input that has practical and applicable value. Such input is critical to preparing the families of school-age children to be able to parent in ways that are transferable within school contexts. Literacy does not begin and end in the school. Literacy is required in both the home and school environments in order for children to do well in academic activities. Both males and females must have the kind of educational preparedness that speaks to their individual needs without generalizing based on gender.

The full spectrum of educational change in the 50 years since *Brown* was illuminated by and for diverse, multinational participants over the 4-day course of the United Negro College Fund's (UNCF's) 2004 Patterson Research Conference. Panelists and participants jointly addressed the global impact of the Supreme Court's ruling from every aspect. Over 200 concurrent sessions focused on post-*Brown* educational issues from early childhood to college teaching and learning, and from adult education to doctoral studies. Their approaches and perspectives ranged from local to national to international. Additionally, several keynote speakers sparked intensive reflection and speculation about the factors leading to the 50-year-old Supreme Court decision, as well as the programs and policies—both successful and failed—resulting from it. The speakers included such noted educator-researchers as Goldman Sachs Foundation President Stephanie Bell-Rose; theologian James H. Cone; urban education specialist Asa G. Hilliard III; psychologist Edwin J. Nichols; South African physician and anthropologist Mamphela A. Ramphele; NAACP Legal and Defense and Education Fund President Theodore M. Shaw; National Education Association President Reg Weaver; Bush administration appointee Grover J. (Russ) Whitehurst; poet Nikki Giovanni, now a professor at Virginia Tech; and astronaut-turned-technology-entrepreneur Mae C. Jemison.

The chapters included in this volume represent the most instructive and innovative ideas to emerge from this historic meeting. *Still Not Equal: Expanding Educational Opportunity in Society* acknowledges that the commitment of time, effort, and academic preparation is necessary for the process of lifelong educational attainment. This volume highlights the global dimensions of both education and school. Attaining higher levels of performance for all persons at all levels in all sectors is critical to global participation and productivity. What is becoming increasingly clear is that the skills students need to be successful in college go beyond K–12 academic preparation. Without prior academic development and financial aid materials, students may suffer from disparate educational attainment across their lifespan. This phenomenon remains unacceptable and requires continued attention to the details of what it truly means to leave no one behind. More importantly, it highlights the continued inequality across myriad contexts and invites everyone to assist in expanding opportunity throughout society.

Part One
Racial Inequalities

CHAPTER ONE

African American College Enrollment and Completion

A Decade of Progress

M. Christopher Brown II, Tazewell V. Hurst III, RoSusan D. Bartee, and Trimika M. Yates

Introduction

African American collegiate trends at the dawning of the twentieth century reveal promising yet disparate findings. Analysis of the decade between 1990 and 2000 shows that African Americans made proportionately great strides in their abilities to enroll in higher education and fare well in degree attainment. Such progress is largely a function of increased access to educational settings. The evidence reveals that African Americans took standardized college entrance exams, attended institutions of higher learning, and fulfilled the academic demands for degree conferment at the highest rates in the nation's history. These academic achievements, however, do not alleviate the continued presence of incongruence between African Americans and White Americans in terms of their respective levels of college enrollment and college completion. The nature of this gap is attributed to Black and White students' access to college and their ability to navigate the academic pathway. The relationship between external and internal factors and their impact upon the educational attainment process warrants serious examination.

Historical and Theoretical Perspectives on Collegiate Trends

Since the Emancipation era, educational attainment as a means for economic and social advancement has been prevalent in the African American community. The common sentiment among African Americans has long been that if a person can obtain a "good education" then he or she will have the opportunity to advance beyond his or her present condition. Direct links can be found between the progress of African Americans in the United States economy and in society as a whole and African American gains in educational attainment since the early 1900s (Smith & Welch, 1989).

Prior to the mid-1970s, the majority of African American college students attended historically Black colleges and universities (HBCUs). Established as formal education centers to educate freed Blacks, these institutions began with a curriculum that stressed basic reading and math as well as agricultural and mechanical training. HBCUs educated numerous African Americans who initially were barred from predominantly White institutions (PWIs) due to segregation. After the mid-1970s, affirmative action policies created more opportunities for African Americans to obtain a postsecondary education. For instance, in 1976, African American student enrollment at four-year colleges and universities nationwide totaled 603,700 students, with 206,676 students or 34% attending HBCUs. By 2000, 773,765 African American students were enrolled at four-year colleges and universities, with four-year HBCUs accounting for 24% of African American student enrollment. HBCUs continue to produce a large share of the nation's African American graduates in the field of medicine, engineering, technology, law, and education.

Educational attainment beyond high school can include on-the-job training, trade/technical school, college, or graduate school. From a socioeconomic perspective, a common conclusion is that individuals will attend college when they believe they will be better off socially and economically in the long term than they would had they not attended college. Human capital theory states that educational attainment is the outcome of individual choice informed by perceptions of the future wage returns on investments in education (Morgan, 1996). Higher education serves as a socializing agent for both insiders and outsiders to gain status and wealth in society. In standard human capital models, variations in education attainment arise mainly from changes in the opportunity costs of time and the direct costs of education such as tuition, discount rates, and educational premiums.

The human capital model emphasizes the degree to which earnings may be expected to rise as a result of greater schooling (Charles & Luoh, 2002). In other words, high school graduates will invest in higher education if the benefits, such as higher future wages, outweigh the costs to attend college. For instance, a high school graduate considering college has, in some broad sense, a choice between two streams of earnings over his or her lifetime. He or she can select from the following options: (A) Choose not to go to college and enter directly into the labor force; (B) forgo immediate earnings and invest in higher education. Assuming option B yields higher lifetime labor market earnings, the likelihood increases that high school graduates with the resources and ability will choose it over option A.

Secondary and Postsecondary Enrollment and Completion Rates

The proportion of 18- to 24-year-old high school graduates in the United States annually by race since 1990 as calculated using Current Population Survey (CPS) methodology. The percentage of White and Black high school graduates remained consistent over the decade between 1990 and 2000 while the proportion of Hispanic American high school graduates peaked at 62% in 1997 and declined to 60% in 2000. The Black–White differential was 5% in 1990 and 2000, with the greatest differential of 9% evidenced in 1992. The Hispanic–White differential in high school completion was 28% in 1990; however, the gap narrowed to 23% in 2000.

College attendance of White high school graduates between the ages of 18- and 24-years-old increased steadily between 1990 and 1998, but declined to 43% in 2000. College enrollment rates for Black high school graduates fluctuated between 1990 and 1994, peaking at 39% in 1998. From 1991 to 1993 the college enrollment rates for Hispanic high school graduates exceeded the enrollment rates of African Americans.

The postsecondary enrollment of African Americans between the ages of 18 and 24 years increased between 1990 and 2000 (*Status and Trends in the Education of Blacks*, 2003). In 1990, only 25% of college-age African Americans attended tertiary institutions, and by the end of that decade 31% of all college-age African Americans were enrolled at that level. Steady enrollment trends suggest that African Americans' access to colleges and universities is becoming more attainable. Blacks also have enrolled at increased rates as direct-to-college high school completers. While African American enrollment percentages were 33% in 1990, those percentages increased to 39% in 2000. By comparison, Whites comprised 40% of total enrollments in 1990, with later increases to 44% in 2000. These rates infer that the pool of African Americans who receive their diploma and enroll immediately into colleges and universities is expanding.

Research has consistently revealed that individuals with more education receive higher wages (Ashenfelter, 1991; Card, 1998; Card & Krueger,

1994, 1996; Mincer, 1974; Park, 1994). In theory, individuals choose their number of years of schooling by comparing average earnings corresponding to different levels of education. The difference in earnings is directly attributed to educational attainment. It is interesting to note that between 1990 and 2000, earnings increased for Blacks and Whites at all levels of education; however, the earnings disparity increased at a greater rate.

Opportunity-cost studies have tended to focus on Black–White differences in higher education attainment (Dawkins & Kinloch, 1981; Morgan, 1996). In attempting to explain enrollment rates among African Americans, studies have focused on the roles of direct tuition costs, parental education (Kane, 1994), and financial aid (Dynarski, 1999) as explanations for enrollment trends. More specifically, these studies find that African Americans are not only enrolling in colleges and universities across the land, but they are also graduating and attaining degrees.

In 1990, African Americans received 4.2% of the awarded doctoral degrees; in 2000, they received 5.0% of that total. Notably, African Americans were earning twice as many of their doctoral degrees in educational fields and religious vocations. African Americans received 5.5% of the awarded master's degrees in 1990. Ten years later, African Americans were awarded 7.8% of the nation's master's degrees. African Americans overwhelming received master's degrees in education, public administration, and service-related fields. According to *Status and Trends in the Education of Blacks* (2003), 34% of African Americans received education degrees compared to 27% of all other racial/ethnic groups. African Americans also received 11% of the Master's in Public Administration (MPA) and other service degrees in comparison to 6% of the nation's total.

African Americans received 6.2% of the nation's bachelor's degrees in 1990. By 2000, that percentage had increased by 2.5%, as African Americans received 8.7% of the total awarded bachelor's degrees. Many of the bachelor's degrees awarded to African Americans were in the fields of business, social science/history, psychology, and health-related sciences. African Americans received 8.3% of the nation's associate degrees in 1990 and 10.7% of those awarded degrees in 2000. The increase during the 10-year span was a little more than 2% for the bachelor's and associate degrees, respectively. In 2000, African Americans aged 25 years and older were more likely than Hispanic Americans, but less likely than White Americans, to have earned an associate's, bachelor's, or master's degree.

Status and Trends in the Education of Blacks (2003) highlights even more significant data about the degrees conferred during the 1990s. For instance, the completion rates of African Americans in colleges and universities remained disproportionate to the overall completion rates of Whites.

Although White males received more degrees in their respective group compared to their counterparts, African American females receive more postsecondary degrees in their respective racial/ethnic group. No differences emerged in the college completion rates of African American males and females. African Americans received a lower percentage of their bachelor's degrees in education, engineering, and biological and life sciences than did other groups. This finding is particularly interesting, given that African Americans were receiving primarily master's and doctoral degrees in the field of education in previous decades. Evidently, African Americans are transitioning into different career pathways upon the completion of the bachelor's degree.

Enrollment and Degree Attainment at HBCUs

HBCUs are assuming a critical role in the collegiate enrollment and degree attainment processes of African Americans. Between 1976 and 1996, the number of African American undergraduates attending four-year HBCUs increased by 9% (from 174,922 to 191,158), compared to 51% at four-year TWIs (from 353,114 to 532,168). Further, between 1976 and 1996, African American undergraduate enrollment increased by 48% at public TWIs (from 245,222 to 362,767), 57% at private four-year TWIs (from 107,892 to 169,401), 7% at public HBCUs (from 121,615 to 130,177), and 14% at private HBCUs (from 53,307 to 60,891) (Nettles et al., 1996).

These findings highlight some interesting aspects related to the type of college selections that increasingly are being made by African Americans. Notably, African Americans are attending TWIs—and more specifically, private TWIs—at higher rates than they are attending HBCUs. Among African Americans who are attending HBCUs, most are choosing to attend those that are private. Juxtaposing the earlier data from the Nettles et al. (1996) study and the more recent data presented in the *Status and Trends in the Education of Blacks* (2003) study, these findings suggest that while African Americans are attending private TWIs at increased rates, they are not completing their degrees at those institutions at a rate proportionate or comparative rate to that of African Americans attending HBCUs. In effect, HBCUs continue to play an important role in the degree completion or graduation of African American students.

Table 1.1 shows the total number of African American undergraduates enrolled at all institutions, four-year institutions, HBCUs (four-year only), and the 39 UNCF (United Negro College Fund)-member institutions in fall 1990 and fall 2000. Between 1990 and 2000, the enrollment of African American undergraduates at all colleges and universities increased by

432,159 students, or 38% (from 1,147,200 in 1990 to 1,579,359 in 2000). At four-year institutions, African American undergraduate enrollment increased by 150,820 students, or 24%, between 1990 and 2000; while African American enrollment at four-year HBCUs decreased by 9,271 students, or 5%, during the same period.

Table 1.1 Number of African American Undergraduates Enrolled at All Institutions and at Four-Year Institutions, Four-Year HBCUs, and United Negro College Fund Institutions: Fall 1990 and Fall 2000

Number of African Americans attending	1990		2000	
	Number	Percent	Number	Percent
All institutions	1,147,200	100	1,579,359	100
College Fund Institutions	47,120	4	53,157	3
Four-year institutions	622,945	100	773,765	100
College Fund Institutions	47,120	8	53,157	7
HBCUs (four-year only)	197,857	100	188,586	100
College Fund Institutions	47,120	24	53,157	28

Source: *United Negro College Fund 2001 Statistical Report.* Fairfax, VA: Frederick D. Patterson Research Institute, 2002.

From a different perspective, the gender gap in college enrollment has become a growing concern among educators, college administrators, and researchers alike.

The nation's postsecondary institutions in general and HBCUs in particular are facing a gender gap insofar as African American male student enrollments are concerned. The disproportionate number of African American males attending US tertiary institutions has decreased significantly over the years. Scholarly research could offer insight into why there are few African American undergraduate and graduate males, and why accountability for reversing this dearth of Black males must be mandated to the public schools. Such research could further explain why reading comprehension is essential in the earlier stages of education for African American males.

According to King (2000), the number of women participating annually in higher education at all levels equals almost 8 million, while only 6.3 million men enroll. Prior to 1975 (except for a few periods which can be attributed to the Korean and Vietnam wars), African American men had higher college enrollment rates than did African American women; however, since 1976 African American females have consistently out numbered African American males in attending colleges and universities.

Specifically, Table 1.2 shows that women consistently represented at least 59% of the total African American student population at all US postsecondary institutions, including HBCUs, for the selected years of 1990, 1995, and 2000 (Hurst, 2002). In 2000, African American women attending all institutions represented 63% of the total African American student enrollment, and they represented 61% and 60% of African American enrollment at HBCUs and UNCF-member institutions, respectively.

Table 1.2 Enrollment of African American College Students at All Institutions and at HBCUs and United Negro College Fund Institutions, by Sex: Fall 1990, 1995, and 2000

African Americans attending	1990		1995		2000	
	Men	Women	Men	Women	Men	Women
All institutions						
Number	484,700	762,300	555,911	917,761	640,354	1,099,934
Percent	39	61	38	62	37	63
HBCUs						
Number	82,897	125,785	90,130	136,391	86,410	134,958
Percent	40	60	40	60	39	61
College Fund Institutions						
Number	20,484	29,375	20,143	31,069	23,066	35,121
Percent	41	59	39	61	40	60

Source: United Negro College Fund 2001 Statistical Report. Fairfax, VA: Frederick D. Patterson Research Institute, 2002.

One explanation for the continuing gender gap in African American college enrollments is that African American women are more likely to be financially independent with dependents of their own, and thus more in need of financial assistance than African American men (Cohen & Nee, 2000). Cohen and Nee also reported that African American women were more likely to receive financial aid from most institution types. Trent (1991) states that funding policies that constrict education overall are clearly more perverse for Blacks and most severe for Black males at the early degree levels. Thus, the cost of education may outweigh the benefits for African American men to enroll in higher education.

The postsecondary failure rate of many African American males also can be attributed partly to between and within classroom ability grouping, or tracking—an approach that fosters the development of a caste system that allows for downward but not upward mobility. Tracking increases the likelihood of failure for those who are placed in the lower groups, of whom the least is expected, taught, and encouraged. When children are tracked, they are deprived of the opportunity to develop the skills they will need to enter and find success in the labor force. When placed in tracks from which they rarely advance, many African American students respond by being truant or withdrawing mentally and emotionally from school. African American students placed in low-ability classroom tracks, in which they know they are perceived as low achievers, typically are not challenged to do their best. Given that higher order thinking skills are developed in higher ability groups and basic skills in lower ability groups, this system of sorting and labeling students increasingly contributes to a class-based society that could eventually become as rigid as any in the world.

The persistent phenomenon of ability grouping, conjoined with the decreased number of African American teachers, systematically has influenced and continues to influence the kind of opportunities and outcomes made available to African American students in these settings. Likewise, when incongruity exists between teaching and learning styles, African American children generally become less motivated and more likely to question their self-worth. When African American youth find learning difficult, they often blame themselves, develop animosity, or drop out of school. As a result, educational attainment for African American students, especially males, remains significantly lower than that of their compeers in elementary, secondary, and higher education. A better synthesis of the schooling needs of African American students must be achieved to address the challenges of attainment disparities.

Concluding Perspectives on Collegiate Trends

One critique of much of the literature on the gender gap has been the failure of researchers to disaggregate the data they have obtained by important variables such as age, race/ethnicity, and socioeconomic status. King (2000), for example, argues that when this is done, a very different picture of the gender gap emerges. Her argument contends that no generalized educational crisis exists among men; but African American, Hispanic American, and low-income males are being left behind their female peers in terms of educational attainment. King examined enrollment by race, gender, and income for undergraduates aged 24 and younger. Her data suggest that the gender gap is substantial for most groups of low-income students but as income increases, the gender gap disappears or reverses itself to favor males. Despite the rise in income, however, African American males still lag behind African American females in college enrollment.

Charles and Luoh (2002) have found the human capital predication to be an unlikely explanation for men, as future dispersions and uncertainty about future earnings evolve very differently over time for men and women. In a study examining returns to education and noncognitive skills as explanations for the gender gap, they found that higher returns from college and greater noncognitive skills among women accounted for nearly 90% of the gender gap in the sample. Opportunity-cost models further suggest that the gender gap ought to be greater in states with a strong construction or manufacturing base. According to Jacob (2002), point estimates for living in a rural area or in a state with a larger construction base were larger for boys than girls. Although these findings also present some evidence that men are simply taking on blue-collar jobs rather than pursuing higher education, more evidence points to the conclusion that this is not the entire explanation for the gender gap.

Given the steady decline in availability of the types of low-skilled, living-wage jobs African American men with little education traditionally have held, one might logically conclude that African American men would be more inclined to enroll in college. Yet, as the research data clearly indicate, this is not the case. Cohen and Nee (2000), for example, suggest that because the decline in the number of available low-skilled jobs occurred in concert with the decline in educational attainment in African American communities, Black high school students were not willingly forgoing college for greater employment opportunities.

In addition to the forgone earnings, tuition, and other costs of college, the benefits of higher education must clearly be worth the investment. Responsiveness to labor market incentives has been found to be a necessary component of any complete explanation of group differences and trends in educational expectations (Morgan, 1996). Several studies have shown that returns on college are higher for women, particularly among young workers (Murphy & Welch, 1992). Among African Americans, Kane (1994) reports that college earnings differentials in the 1980s rose faster for women than men, as did enrollment rates. Concurrently, uncertainty about future earnings for both education choices (college and no college) rose for men between the 1945 and 1972 cohort (Charles & Luoh, 2002).

Implications for Higher Educational Policies and Practices

College attendance and attainment rates of African American students have made steady progress during the last decade. These patterns are due to African Americans' increased levels of access to and opportunities in educational settings. Sustaining the "flow" within the academic pipeline of elementary and secondary education is critical to African American achievement of lifelong outcomes and possibilities in higher education and beyond. The educational policies and practices implemented in P–16 education have a substantial impact on the quality and quantity of African American students who complete high school, college, and/or enter the global workforce (Hodgkinson, 1985). More specifically, for African American students, the academic pipeline leading to higher education has the greatest importance (Brown & Davis, 2000).

The incongruent patterns of college enrollment and completion rates for African Americans are linked to the type of academic pathways. Although racial bias may not affect the academic performance of all African American students in identical ways, the continuing existence of institutionalized practices of discrimination prohibits the likelihood of their equitable educational outcomes. Moreover, the meritocracy, in its present form, does not consider group-based needs. The disproportionate representation of African American students in special education and vocational–technical classes demonstrates that the inequalities long present in the larger society are being systematically reproduced in its educational systems, thereby limiting access and opportunity for this group. For all too many African American students in the academic pipeline between primary, secondary, and higher education, security in these pathways has been wavering. Somewhere within that pipeline, a unique set of "clogs" and "leaks continue to disrupt the successful matriculation of these students, as indicated by the incongruence between African Americans and Whites in college enrollment and college completion.

Radical systemic change is required in order to move from the equality of educational opportunity promised by the 1954 *Brown v. Board of Education* ruling to the equity of educational outcomes demanded by the global economy. There is no one pathway to attainment of this goal. Merely placing multicolored bodies in classrooms, however, is not sufficient to guarantee lifelong success. In the 21st century, African American students must be provided the power and privileges that result from successful navigation of the P–16 academic pipeline.

Moving from an era focused on opportunity to one focused on outcomes requires the utilization of value-based ideologies. Infusing the values of equity, efficiency, community, security, and liberty into P–16 educational settings can potentially prevent African American students from unremittingly succumbing to academic failure. Employing value-based ideologies is only the first (although important) step in responding to the crises that many African American students face in educational settings. Acknowledging and embracing the educational system as a P–16 continuum will enable US educators to formulate a systemic remedy to the problems that hinder African American student success and prepare them for participation in the global workforce. The nation and the world will be the beneficiaries.

References

Ashenfelter, O. (1991). *How convincing is the evidence linking education and income?* Working Paper No. 292. Princeton, NJ: Industrial Relations Section, Princeton University.

Brown, M. C., & Davis, J. E. (Eds.). (2000). *Black sons to mothers: Compliments, critiques, and challenges for cultural workers in education.* New York: Peter Lang Publishing.

Brown v. Board of Education of Topeka, 347 US 483 (1954).

Card, D. (1998). *The casual effect of education on earnings* (Working Paper No. 2). Berkeley, CA: Center for Labor Economics, University of California-Berkeley.

Card, D., & Krueger, A. B. (1996). *Labor market effects of school quality: Theory and evidence* (Working Paper No. 545). New York: National Bureau of Economic Research.

———. (1994). *The economic return to school quality: A partial survey* (Working Paper No. 334). Princeton, NJ: Industrial Relations Section, Princeton University.

Charles, K. K., & Luoh, M.-C. (2002). *Gender differences in completed schooling* (Working Paper No. w9028). New York: National Bureau of Economic Research.

Cohen, C. J., & Nee, C. E. (2000). Educational attainment and sex differentials in African American communities. *American Behavioral Scientist 43*(7), 1159.

Dawkins, M. P., & Kinloch, G. C. (1981). Black students and the labor market: An analysis of occupational expectations. *Journal of Black Studies 12*(1), 107–16.

Dynarski, S. M. (1999). *Does aid matter? Measuring the effect of student aid on college attendance and completion.* Working Paper No. 7422. New York: National Bureau of Economic Research.

Hodgkinson, H. (1985). *All one system: Demographics of education, kindergarten through graduate school.* Washington, DC: The Institute for Educational Leadership.

Hurst, T. (2002). *United Negro College Fund 2001 statistical report.* Fairfax, VA: Frederick D. Patterson Research Institute.

Jacob, B. A. (2002). *Non-cognitive skills, returns to school and the gender gap in higher education* (Working Paper No. w8964). Cambridge, MA: National Bureau of Economic Research.

Kane, T. (1994). College entry by Blacks since 1970: The role of college costs, family background and the returns to education. *Journal of Political Economy 102*(5): 878–911.

King, J. E. (2000). *Gender equity in higher education: Are male students at a disadvantage?* Washington, DC: American Council on Education, Center for Policy Analysis.

Mincer, J. (1974). *Schooling, experience, and earnings.* New York: National Bureau of Economic Research.

Morgan, S. L. (1996). Trends in Black–White differences in educational expectations, 1980–1992. *Sociology of Education 69*, 308–19.

Murphy, K. M., & Welch, F. (1992). The structure of wages. *Quarterly Journal of Economics, 107*(3), 889–906.

Nettles, M. T., Perna, L. W., & Freeman, K. (1996). *Two decades of progress: African Americans moving forward in higher education.* Fairfax, VA: Frederick D. Patterson Research Institute.

Park, J. H. (1994). *Returns to schooling: A peculiar deviation from linearity.* Working Paper No. 335. Princeton, NJ: Industrial Relations Section, Princeton University.

Smith, J. P., & Welch, F. R. (1989, June). Black economic progress after Myrdal. *Journal of Economic Literature 27*, 519–63.

Hoffman, K., & Llagas, C. (2003). *Status and trends in the education of Blacks* (NCES 2003–034). Washington, DC: National Center for Education Statistics, US Department of Education.

Trent, W. T. (1991). Focus on equity: Race and gender differences in degree attainment 1975–1976, 1980–1981. In W. Allen, E. Epps, & N. Z. Hanif (Eds.), *College in Black and White: African American students in predominantly White and historically Black public universities.* Albany: State University of New York Press.

Chapter Two

Accommodation or Immediacy?

The Role of African Americans in the Quest for Education and Equality in the Evolution of American Education

David Boers

A turning point in American educational history occurred in 1895 when Booker T. Washington gave his famous speech at the opening of the Cotton States and International Exposition in Atlanta, Georgia. This brilliantly worded address has been a topic of interest to scholars. It has been alternately described as both the beginning of the end for segregated schooling in America and as a setback for the nation's desegregation efforts. After his address, Washington's followers redoubled their efforts to open and maintain segregated schools, but W. E. B. DuBois, who entered the debate in opposition to Washington, had more impact on the development of educational and social equality in the decades immediately following. DuBois escalated the criticism of Washington's ideas and pushed for full equality for African Americans in all aspects of American life. His demands for immediacy in the achievement of full constitutional rights for African Americans stood in direct opposition to Washington's calls for gradualism and a much slower pace in the march toward full equality. DuBois's emphasis on a liberal arts education for Black also contrasted with Washington's insistence that African Americans receive a "useful" education. The question thus is whose technique or stance was more effective, appropriate, or desirable in the quest to obtain both educational and social rights for African Americans? There is no definitive answer to this question.

Throughout the early history of American education, African Americans, and other minority populations, were neglected in many ways. The schools established in the American colonies from 1630 to 1775 served a select population that included few children other than male members of the dominant culture. Most people of African descent in the Americas of that period were considered slaves, and slaves, for a variety of reasons—mostly racist ones—were prevented from obtaining an education. After the Revolutionary War, two distinct populations of African Americans emerged in the educational arena. In the northern states, where slavery was not allowed, free African American men and women made numerous attempts to create educational opportunities for young and old. Their efforts were vastly different from those of their enslaved counterparts in the American South, who, prior to the Civil War, were denied an education by law. Between 1800 and 1835, the Southern states passed laws making it a crime to educate slaves (Spring, 2001). To counter this lack of institutional education, many enslaved African Americans, at great risk, secretly obtained books and taught themselves and others how to read. Thus, the process of education for African Americans in the South was slow, tedious, and dangerous. By the time the Civil War began in 1860, only 5% of the slave population knew how to read (Spring, 2001). Within a milieu of discrimination and segregation, and while developing a powerful oral tradition of songs and stories, they struggled to become literate. This tradition created an enduring legacy in African American culture that, as it evolved, would eventually aid Southern Blacks achieve the right of education and, much later, some degree of political and social rights.

African Americans in the northern states experienced a different struggle for educational opportunity. Prior to the Civil War, free Blacks in the North were becoming increasingly literate. This increase led to a push for knowledge that in turn led to an understanding of the American political system, which they effectively navigated using the courts to gain judicial decisions to help achieve educational opportunity. Evidence of northern Blacks' burgeoning political prowess can be witnessed in the aftermath of the passage of the Massachusetts Education Act of 1789, which required towns of 200 or more families to provide elementary and grammar schools for their young, regardless of race (Spring, 2001).

By the late 1700s, several different minority populations in the North, including the free Blacks, had established home or neighborhood private schools because, to put it gently, their children were receiving a less-than-friendly welcome at the White-dominated public schools. In 1798, a group of

African American adults asked the Boston School Committee to establish a separate system of schools for Black children. The committee refused this proposal and another one in 1800, so the Blacks, with funding from both Black and White donors, opened private schools to educate their children. In 1806, the Boston School Committee finally honored the request for segregated public schools, and by 1812 voted to fund and control the schools. By the 1820s, however, the segregated schools were generally recognized as inferior in terms of facilities, maintenance, materials, supplies, teachers, and, of course, funding inequities.

By 1849, the debate over the legality and appropriateness of separate-but-equal facilities for Blacks and Whites had been waging unresolved for 30 years. In that year, Benjamin Roberts lost his case to have his daughter attend the closer, majority-White public school. a Massachusetts court ruled that the separate all-Black school she was attending was equal to the Whites-only school, therefore she had to attend the former. In 1855, however, the Massachusetts legislature passed a law stating that no child could be denied admission to public schools based on religion or race. This law was countered in 1895, when the Supreme Court thwarted efforts toward racial equality and equal educational opportunity in the 1895 *Plessy v. Ferguson* case. With the African American desire for educational opportunity offset by the dominant culture's desire for discrimination and segregation, an uneasy system of segregated education accompanied America's entrance into the Industrial Age. The *Plessy* ruling and its subsequent upholding in 1896 came educational opportunity, especially for industrial education, but "separate" would be called "equal" for many years to come, even though everyone knew it was not. It would be another 100 years before the high court would rule in *Brown v. Board of Education of Topeka*, the 1954 case that would become the nation's greatest symbol of hope in the quest for an end to school discrimination and segregation.

Moving from an agrarian society to an industrial one created a new set of circumstances for the nation's public schools. To accommodate the number of new workers needed in American factories, schools were called upon to create and deliver education that would yield a skilled work force for the new American economy. In the North, powerful industrialists were demanding a qualified work force for their factories. In the South, would-be industrialists promoted industrial education for African Americans. By the 1890s, African Americans in both the North and the South generally conceded that the Black struggle for and the eventual attainment of educational opportunities would yield improvements in their economic, political, and social conditions. The link between educational rights and political, social, and civil rights was forged, first via the struggle for educational opportunity and then via the struggle for equal educational opportunity.

Washington's 1895 Atlanta Exposition speech marked a turning point in African American education. Washington was a Southern Black man who had been born into slavery and educated at Hampton Institute in Virginia. Hampton promoted the education of freed slaves to become teachers of proper work habits for other freed slaves. It was a school at which long, hard, manual work was viewed as essential to prepare African Americans to enter the dominant culture and reap the fruits of economic advantage. Political and social rights, on the other hand, were held as secondary by-products to be obtained in the distant future. Washington's Hampton experiences encouraged him to use it as a model for Tuskegee Normal and Industrial Institute, an historically Black institution of higher education that he established in Alabama in 1881. The "Tuskegee idea," which Washington wrote and spoke widely about, to both Black and White audiences, since the school's founding, was to provide practical education for African Americans so that they could find jobs.

An example of Washington's educational thinking is clearly evident in his 1885 article, "The Educational Outlook in the South" in which he states, "Brains, property, and character for the Negro will settle the question of civil right" (Johnson, 2002, p. 130). Later in the same article he states, " . . . any work looking towards the improvement of the Negro south, must have for one of its aims . . . to live . . . with his white neighbors both socially and politically" (Johnson, 2002, p. 131). This second passage, especially, seems to establish Washington's notion that education for employment is the pathway for Blacks to political and social and thus, civil equality. To further solidify his point, Washington (1901), in his book *Up from Slavery*, discounts traditional educational topics as French grammar and other "book learning" as a waste of time for African Americans (Spring, 2001, p. 223).

Attempting to convince his 1895 Atlanta audience of African Americans' economic value, Washington told a story of a ship lost at sea:

> A ship lost at sea for many days suddenly sighted a friendly vessel. From the mast of the unfortunate vessel was seen a signal: "Water, water; we die of thirst!" The answer from the friendly vessel at once came back: "Cast your bucket down where you are." A second time the signal, "Water, water; send us water!" ran up from the distressed vessel, and was answered: "Cast down your bucket where you are." And a third and a fourth signal for water was answered: "Cast down your bucket where you are." The captain of the distressed vessel, at last heeding the injunction, cast down his bucket, and it came up full of fresh, sparkling water from the mouth of the Amazon River.

> To those of my race who depend on bettering their condition in a foreign land, or who underestimate the importance of cultivating friendly relations with the Southern White man, who is their next door neighbor, I would say: "Cast down your bucket where you are"—cast it down making friends in every manly way of the people of all races by whom we are surrounded. (Johnson, 2002, p. 134)

In this passage, Washington is clearly telling the freed African Americans not to leave America for another land to seek work and imploring them to align themselves with the needs of the White American industrialists. He subsequently reviewed the vast experience and expertise in manual labor exhibited by African Americans, asserting that mastery of these skill should precede exposure to poetry and the fine arts.

Washington then used the same ship story to convince Whites to hire African Americans for the work force:

> To those of the white race who look to the incoming of those of foreign birth and strange tongue and habits for the prosperity of the South, were I permitted, I would repeat what I say to my own race, "Cast down your bucket where you are." Cast it down among the 8,000,000 Negroes whose habits you know, whose fidelity and love you have tested in days when to have proved treacherous meant the ruin of your firesides. Cast down your bucket among those people who have, without strikes and labor wars, tilled your fields, cleared your forests, . . . and helped make possible this magnificent representation of progress of the south. Casting down your bucket among my people, helping them and encouraging them as you are doing on these grounds, and, with education of head, hand, and heart, you will find that they will buy your surplus land, make blossom the waste places in your fields, and run your factories . . . we shall stand by you with a devotion that no foreigner can approach. . . . In all things that are purely social we can be as separate as the finger, yet one as the hand in all things essential to mutual progress. (Johnson, 2002, pp. 134–135)

The last sentence in this passage is the one that best captures the essence of what has been called Washington's "Southern Compromise"—that is, the key to convincing Southern Whites to provide industrial education and jobs for African Americans. Washington supports his point with another statement near the end of his speech. "The opportunity to earn a dollar in the factory just now," he claimed, "is worth infinitely more than the opportunity to spend a dollar in the opera house" (Johnson, 2002, p. 135).

Clearly, Washington believed in putting off political and social equality until African Americans had proven their value to White America by working to create the new industrial complex. However, in perhaps the least-discussed statement in his entire speech, Washington also noted his obvious belief that industrial education and industrial employment for Blacks would lead to

Black political and social equality later when he stated: "No race that has anything to contribute to the markets of the world is long in any degree ostracized" (Johnson, 2002, p. 135).

As the audience left the Cotton States and International Exposition that day in 1895, most no doubt interpreted Washington's ideas as a politically and socially safe means of creating an industrial work force in the South. Southern Whites agreed with Washington because he did not push for Black political, social, or civil rights. They saw his ideas as confirming the inferior status of African Americans, a status Southern Whites wanted and felt comfortable with. Whites from the North saw Washington's speech as a way to get the South back up and running economically. Washington, in their view, offered a solution for the 1890's labor problem that could help save the American economy. Both groups began immediately to press for the establishment of segregated schools and industrial education for African Americans.

The loudest response to Booker T. Washington's ideas came from W. E. B. DuBois, a Black northerner who had been educated at Fisk University, Harvard University, and the University of Berlin. A Ph.D. and a leading American sociologist, DuBois was an early leader in the struggles for civil rights for African Americans. He founded the National Association for the Advancement of Colored People (NAACP) in 1909, and served as editor of its magazine, *The Crisis*. In his book, *The Souls of Black Folk: Essays and Sketches*, DuBois (1903/1969) attacked Washington and his ideas. He began his criticism by stating that Washington was only interested in "work and money," and that he completely ignored "the higher aims of life" (Johnson, 2002, p. 136). DuBois further berated Washington for retreating from the gains Blacks had won during the Civil War:

> Again, in our own land, the reaction from the sentiment of war—time has given impetus to race-prejudice against Negroes, and Mr. Washington withdraws many of the high demands of Negroes as men and American citizens. In other periods of intensified prejudice all the Negro's tendency to self-assertion has been called forth; at this period a policy of submission is advocated. In the history of nearly all other races and peoples the doctrine preached at such crises has been that manly self-respect is worth more than lands and houses, and that a people who voluntarily surrender such respect, or cease striving for it, are not worth civilizing. (Johnson, 2002, p. 136)

DuBois viewed Washington as advocating submission to Whites at a time, after the Civil War, when what was needed was not submission, but rather an intensification of the assertion of citizenship rights. DuBois asserted that acquiring education only to buy material possessions was not enough.

Doing so created indignity in his view, and he deemed Washington old-fashioned in his attempt to appease and submit to the dominant culture. Indeed, DuBois was outraged at Washington's willingness to give in at a time when he believed acceleration in human rights should take place.

DuBois claimed that Washington was asking African Americans to give up their political power, cease their insistence on civil rights, and forsake the higher education of youth in order to "concentrate all their energies on industrial education, the accumulation of wealth, and the conciliation of the South" (Johnson, 2002, p. 136). Such a focus, DuBois maintained, was both superficial and over-conciliatory. He noted that while Washington had been preaching this philosophy for more than 15 years before the 1895 speech, he had only been successful in convincing others of it for the past 10 years. That influence, DuBois lamented, had a tremendously damaging effect on the advancement of African Americans in the post-Civil War period. The result, he explained, was threefold:

1. the disfranchisement of African Americans;
2. the legal creation of a distinct status of civil inferiority for African Americans; and
3. the steady withdrawal of aid from institutions for the higher training of African Americans. (Johnson, 2002, p. 137)

Thus, DuBois concluded, Washington's Southern Compromise could only end in a disaster for Black people, especially in the South. As he wrote in *The Souls of Black Folk*:

> The question then becomes: Is it possible, and probable, that nine millions of men can make effective progress in economic lines if they are deprived of political rights, made a servile caste, and allowed only the most meager chance for developing their exceptional men? If history and reason give any distinct answer to these questions, it is an emphatic *No*. And Mr. Washington thus faces the triple paradox of his career:
>
> 1. He is striving nobly to make Negro artisans businessmen and property-owners, but it is utterly impossible, under modern competitive methods, for workingmen and property-owners to defend their rights and exist without the right of suffrage.
> 2. He insists on thrift and self-respect, but at the same time counsels a silent submission to civic inferiority such as is bound to sap the manhood of any race in the long run.
> 3. He advocates common-school and industrial training, and deprecates institutions of higher learning; but neither the Negro common-schools, nor Tuskegee itself, could remain open a day were it not for teachers trained in Negro colleges, or trained by their graduates. (Johnson, 2002, p. 137)

Outraged by Washington's stance, DuBois demanded that Blacks instead fight for three goals: (1) the right to vote, (2) civil equality, and (3) education according to ability. He believed that all African Americans were and should be involved in a constant struggle, without compromise, to obtain equal rights as granted all citizens in the American Constitution. That struggle, in his view, would call for a much different type of education for African Americans than Washington had proposed.

In a short story in Chapter XIII of *The Souls of Black Folk*, entitled "Of the Coming of John," Spring (2001) asserts that DuBois described what he hoped African Americans would be able to accomplish through education. In this story, a Southern Black community raises money to send a young man named John to the North for an education. According to Spring:

> The community's hope is that he will return to teach in the local black school. After receiving his education in the North, John does return to teach. He goes to the house of the local white judge and, after making the mistake of knocking at the front door instead of the rear door, is ushered into the judge's dining room. The judge greets John with his philosophy of education: "In this country the Negro must remain subordinate, and can never expect to be the equal of white men." The judge describes two different ways in which blacks might be educated in the South. The first, which the judge favors, is to "teach the darkies to be faithful servants and laborers as your fathers were." The second way, the one supported by DuBois and most feared by white southerners, is described by the judge as putting "fool ideas of rising and equality into these folks' heads, and . . . making them discontent and unhappy." (p. 225)

Spring goes on to explain that DuBois favored an education that would make African Americans discontented with the status quo. He illustrates this point by relating more of DuBois' story, in which he describes a meeting between John and his sister:

> John, she said, "does it make everyone unhappy when they study and learn lots of things?"
>
> He paused and smiled. "I am afraid it does," he said.
>
> "And, John, are you glad you studied?"
>
> "Yes," came the answer slowly and positively.
>
> She watched the flickering lights upon the sea, and said thoughtfully, "I wish I was unhappy—and—and," putting both arms around his neck, "I think I am, a little, John." (Spring, 2001, p. 226)

Unhappiness was DuBois' goal for African Americans, Spring contends.

DuBois wanted African Americans to have an education that would advance and protect their political and social rights, and he wanted African American leaders in both the North and the South to promote this type of education.

By 1900, the majority of public expenditures for education went toward establishing and maintaining segregated schools for White children. Ironically, a disproportionate amount of Black citizens' taxes were used to pay for White segregated schools, since most African American school-aged children were sent to work, to perform menial labor in farmers' fields, rather than to school. It was not until the 1930s that African Americans in the South had a viable system of education, albeit a segregated one. Even then, inequalities in school funding, and in virtually every other area, including state and local tax support, persisted.

Washington spent the better part of 35 years attempting to establish the notion of gradualism and accommodation in his quest for equality. DuBois diametrically opposed Washington's ideas in an effort to promote immediate equality throughout political, social, and educational arenas. Nonetheless, private or segregated Southern Black schools that supported the Washington philosophy received funding from Blacks and wealthy Whites alike. For at least the next 60 years after Washington's Atlanta Exposition speech, many would say the next 108 years, segregated education was promoted as a means of providing industrial training—and only industrial training—to African Americans.

What DuBois hoped for African Americans to accomplish with regards to political and social equality has been analyzed and argued in relation and opposition to Washington's Southern Compromise for over a century. Although it may be said that DuBois' ideas became a reality within a segregated school system, it may also be said that segregated schools severely impeded the process of obtaining educational, political, and social equality. Indeed, the segregation of the nation's public schools resulted in the denial of education to large numbers of African Americans.

In the end it can be said without question that both Washington and DuBois had the same long-term goals for educational equality and civil rights even though they espoused two different plans to achieve them. Washington believed that Blacks had to start at the bottom of the work force and gradually work their way up to positions of leadership and responsibility as a path to equal citizenship. He accepted a temporary position of inferiority for Blacks. DuBois, on the other hand, wanted Blacks to have the same rights guaranteed Whites by the Constitution. Clearly, each man was striving for equality for his people in all aspects of American life and citizenry. No one can doubt the sincerity of each in his attempts to plot out the best course for his people and then to lead Blacks and Whites alike into believing his was indeed the best plan.

The question becomes: Whose technique was more effective and appropriate for the time? History reports that Washington's ideas won over during his lifetime. After his death in 1915, Washington's leadership and ideas were passed over in favor of the more militant views of DuBois, who, in his press for immediacy, would not submit to any compromise of rights or conciliatory accommodation. Had DuBois' ideas come to prominence sooner than they did, might they have resulted in more or faster political, social, and educational equality than Washington's ideas? Would DuBois' refusal to compromise have resulted in an entirely different experience for African Americans—and thus, for all Americans? Was DuBois, in the long run, more responsible than Washington for the passing of civil rights legislation and the success of the civil rights movement?

The answers to these questions for every individual lie in the personal assessment and analysis of the many and varied factors that interplay in the complexity of the very questions themselves and the plethora of personal, emotional, social, and intellectual elements therein. Despite their differing approaches, Washington and DuBois remain two very important inspirational thinkers who led the way for the transition of American culture.

References

DuBois, W. E. B. (1969). *The souls of Black folk: Essays and sketches.* New York: New American Library. (Original work published 1903).

Johnson, T. W. (2002). *Historical documents in American education.* Boston: Allyn & Bacon.

Spring, J. (2001). *The American school, 1642–2000.* Boston: McGraw-Hill.

Washington, B. T. (1901). *Up from slavery.* Garden City, New York: Doubleday & Company.

CHAPTER THREE

Closing the Racial/Ethnic Gaps

LISA MARIE MARTINEZ AND DON ANTHONY WOODS

Abstract

When most Americans think about racial or ethnic minorities, the two main groups that come to mind are African Americans and Hispanics. Throughout US history, the discrimination faced by these two groups has resulted in limited opportunity and little room for advancement. In this chapter, we intend to show why this has been the case and to discuss various educational issues of common significance to both groups, including affirmative action, disparities in higher education enrollments, lack of funding for education, and the impact of high incarceration rates on educational attainment. This chapter will also examine the political and economic importance for African Americans and Hispanics to work together to resolve these issues.

Introduction

Recent years have seen more African American and Hispanic educational organizations working together to resolve some of the prejudices and conflicts shared in common by the ethnic groups they represent. For example, one university recently hosted an open house for its Institute of Black Culture and its Institute of Hispanic and Latino Culture. This event, in the words of one attendee, provided the two minority groups with an opportunity to talk, share experiences, and learn from each other. The gathering was a success because people from both institute were able to communicate directly with each other and show their support" for each other's cause. According to the director of the Institute of Black Culture, it allowed all to see firsthand the dynamics of race relations and how they work *when they really work*. This event, which sought to develop relationships and promote dialogue among and between Black and Hispanic college students, is but one example of similar activities that increasingly have been taking place on campuses nationwide.

Where We Stand

African Americans and Hispanics today have a political advantage for working together. In Texas, for example, the two minority groups combined populate the majority of the state's three largest metropolitan areas—namely, Houston, Dallas, and San Antonio. This leaves Texas politicians little choice but to listen to the needs of their "minority majority" constituents (Tables 3.1 and 3.2).

Considered in combination, as the majority of the US population, African Americans and Hispanics—America's traditional minorities—are quickly realizing that their economic and political struggles can be lessened. They are just as quickly reminded, however,, that the top 10% of the population still retains the majority of the country's wealth, and arguably the bulk of its economic and political power. Thus, a great deal more work is required if African Americans and Hispanics want to make a better future for themselves and their children.

Table 3.1 Ten Largest US Cities, in Total Population and in Black or African American Population (2000)

Place, state	Total population		Black or African American alone		Black or African American alone or in combination		Total population (%)	
	Rank	Number	Rank	Number	Rank	Number	Black or African American alone	Black or African American alone or in combination
New York, NY	1	8,008,278	1	2,129,762	1	2,274,049	26.6	28.4
Los Angeles, CA	2	3,694,820	7	415,195	6	444,635	11.2	12.0
Chicago, IL	3	2,896,016	2	1,065,009	2	1,084,221	36.8	37.4

Table 3.1 continued

Houston, TX	4	1,953,631	5	494,496	5	505,101	25.3	25.9
Philadelphia, PA	5	1,517,550	4	655,824	4	672,162	43.2	44.3
Phoenix, AZ	6	1,321,045	60	67,416	53	76,065	5.1	5.8
San Diego, CA	7	1,223,400	36	96,216	32	109,470	7.9	8.9
Dallas, TX	8	1,188,580	11	307,957	11	314,678	25.9	26.5
San Antonio, TX	9	1,144,646	48	78,120	45	84,250	6.8	7.4
Detroit, MI	10	951,270	3	775,772	3	787,687	81.6	82.8
Baltimore, MD	17	651,154	6	418,951	7	424,449	64.3	65.2
Memphis, TN	18	650,100	8	399,208	8	402,367	61.4	61.9
Washington, DC	21	572,059	9	343,312	9	350,455	60.0	61.3
New Orleans, LA	31	484,674	10	325,947	10	329,171	67.3	67.9

Source: McKinnon, J. (2001, August). *The Black population: 2000.* Available from http://www.census.gov/prod/2001pubs/c2kbr01-5.pdf

Table 3.2 Ten Largest US Cities, in Total Population and in Hispanic Population (2000)

	Total population		Hispanic population		Hispanic of total
Place, state	*Number*	*Rank*	*Number*	*Rank*	population (%)
New York, NY	8,008,278	1	2,160,554	1	27.0
Los Angeles, CA	3,694,820	2	1,719,073	2	46.5
Chicago, IL	2,896,016	3	753,644	3	26.0
Houston, TX	1,953,631	4	730,865	4	37.4
Philadelphia, PA	1,517,550	5	128,928	24	8.5
Phoenix, AZ	1,321,045	6	449,972	6	34.1
San Diego, CA	1,223,400	7	310,752	9	25.4
Dallas, TX	1,188,580	8	422,587	8	35.6
San Antonio, TX	1,144,646	9	671,394	5	58.7
Detroit, MI	951,270	10	47,167	72	5.0
El Paso, TX	563,662	23	431,875	7	76.6
San Jose, CA	894,943	11	269,989	10	30.2

Guzman, B. (2001, May). *The Hispanic population: 2000.* Available from http://www.census.gov/prod/2001pubs/c2kbr01-3.pdf

Long Way to Go

In 1954, a landmark ruling was decided in one of the biggest cases in Supreme Court history, *Brown v. Board of Education of Topeka, Kansas.* This case was brought before the Court in an effort to obtain equal educational opportunities for *all* US citizens regardless of race, creed, or color. The case clearly helped African Americans, yet Hispanics also benefited from it. As Garcia (1999) maintains, Latinos were the target of discriminatory laws in the Southwest, where there was no significant concentration of African Americans. Like African Americans, Hispanics were stereotyped as disadvantaged because of their skin color. According to Gloria Sanders, Chair of the California Teachers Association's *Brown v. Board of Education* Commemoration Committee and President of Associated Chaffey Teachers, the ruling in the *Brown* case meant that people finally were afforded the opportunity to receive a better education. Sanders noted, however, that the situation was not ideal and needed improvement. This quest for improvement, Posnick-Goodwin (2004) asserts, is one reason why the civil rights movement occurred, yet, US minorities today must still struggle to improve their social status.

The civil rights movement was largely responsible for the integration of US society and for the policy of affirmative action. Although affirmative action has proven beneficial for its role in increasing the number of minorities in higher education, it has also been the subject of much controversy. Opponents of the policy decry that is unfair toward Whites, and that it discriminates against them "in reverse." Several White higher-education students have initiated reverse-discrimination lawsuits, such as *Regents of the University of California v. Bakke (1978)*. The Court's decision in the *Bakke* case yielded little judicial support for affirmative action. The validity of affirmative action was also challenged in the *Gratz v. Bollinger* and *Grutter v. Bollinger* cases. In both, the Supreme Court questioned and "ended the wholesale use of mechanical racial preferences favored by many elite schools," including the University of Michigan (Center for Individual Rights, 2004). These post-*Brown* rulings have jeopardized many universities' affirmative action programs and subsequently impeded many African Americans' and Hispanics' chances for educational advancement.

Some Hispanic advocacy groups focus on the Court's ruling in an uncelebrated case, *Hernandez v. Texas*, as a bellwether event in the Hispanic struggle for equal educational opportunity. The *Hernandez* case dealt with jury discrimination and set the restraint against group-based inequity. According to Lopez (2004),

> The question in *Hernandez*, unlike in *Brown*, was not whether the state's conduct was unconstitutional; it was whether the Constitution protected Mexican-Americans. But the dynamics of the case prevented the court from answering that question by reasoning that Mexican-Americans, like Blacks, constituted a racial minority.

In the aftermath of the Court's ruling, the US government created, through its policies, a schism between Blacks and Hispanics by classifying the two groups separately (i.e., US Census ethnicity and racial classifications). This schism fed into increasing conflicts over federal resources offered or dedicated to racial minority groups.

In 1974, the Supreme Court held in *Lau v. Nichols* that the San Francisco school system violated the Civil Rights Act of 1964 by denying non-English-speaking students of Chinese ancestry a meaningful opportunity to participate in the public educational program. *Lau v. Nichols*, by opening the door to bilingual education programs, provided educational advancement opportunities and eliminated language barriers for minorities. As the Court declared: "If English is the mainstream language of instruction, then measures have to be taken to ensure that English is taught to students who do not speak English or limited-English proficient in order to provide equal access to educational opportunities" (*Lau v. Nichols*, 1974).

New developments in the educational finance operations of the Texas school system have raised new challenges. Recently, an alliance of school districts in the State of Texas filed suit against their state, calling its school finance system "broken" and "unconstitutional" ("Texas School Finance Law Trial Opens Monday," 2004). The districts argued that Texas's current public education funding system, which requires wealthy districts to share local property tax revenue with poor districts, is illegal because it results in underfunding of schools in poor districts. This case made history because it was the first time any state has been sued by its own school districts.

Though the school districts may have a good argument, their lawsuit will have a negative impact on the citizens of Texas because it will result in raised taxes. According to Schlomach (2004), "What we have are 46 school districts (all taxpayer funded) suing the state (also taxpayer funded) for (you guessed it) more taxpayer money—and the lawyers are all paid with (get ready) taxpayer money" (p. 4). Nonetheless, on September 15, 2004, a state district judge declared the states' school funding system unconstitutional, claiming that Texas "faces a bleak future if it fails to spend more on public education" (Elliot, 2004). Due to this decision, the State of Texas will be required to provide more funding for its educational programs, and those costs will certainly be borne by its taxpaying residents.

Why Educational Equity Continues to Be Important

Americans generally claim to value educational equity and equal educational opportunities for everyone, yet they cannot seem to create legislation that provides this. Four factors must be considered when trying to improve education for African Americans and Hispanics:

1. the high representation of African Americans and Hispanics among the nation's prison population;
2. the high dropout rates and low secondary school and college graduation rates of African American and Hispanic students;
3. the persistence of an achievement gap between African Americans, Hispanics, and White Americans; and
4. the economic impact of failing to educate African Americans and Hispanics.

Many of the nation's prison inmates, the majority of whom are Black or Hispanic, are high school dropouts whose problems began early in life. The additional frustrations of confronting and/or trying to break through racial/ethnic and financial barriers have caused many minorities to become criminals. As Headley (2001) maintains, "Frustrated youths who are powerless to change the source of their frustration take advantage of the 'opportunities' afforded by street crime." Better education must be provided for America's inmates so that they will have a chance to re-establish themselves in society and decrease their likelihood of being re-incarcerated. Faith-based initiatives, such as those of the Wheeler Avenue Baptist Church in Houston, which has been successful in its efforts to educate inmates and give them a second chance to improve their lives, can play an important role in this regard. Blacks and Hispanics should urge the White House to support these kinds of programs at the federal, state, and local levels. Investment in faith-based programs for inmate populations may provide a viable alternative to the large amounts currently being spent on building new prisons.

Arguably, the high secondary school and college dropout rates among the nation's Hispanics have partly been a result of language barriers that cause Hispanic students to fall behind. Add to this the pressures of having to compete with English-proficient students and the frustrations of trying to break the "glass ceiling," and overcome the educational achievement gap. This latter obstacle is one that has existed for many years. Virtually everyone knows about it, and by now most generally accept it as a fact of life. According to Barton (2003), "Achievement differences in school among subgroups of the population have deep roots. They arrive early and stay late—beginning before the cradle and continuing through to graduation, if that happy outcome is obtained." Barton, is hopeful, however, noting that the recent passage of the No Child Left Behind Act demonstrates "a consensus commitment to the reduction, if not the elimination, of the achievement gap."

The educational attainment of children is affected by their parents' lifetime earnings. It is also affected by school funding levels. Low-level funding of minority-populated schools has contributed to the widespread failure to educate these children and youth. Given their schools' inadequate funding, minority students are usually placed in overcrowded classrooms with second-hand textbooks. As Executive Director of the Human Relations Commission of Topeka, Kansas, Elias Garcia (1999), recalls, during his childhood, "We [Hispanic students] were the ones whose school supplies, schoolbooks, teachers, and learning materials were nothing more than hand me downs or leftovers from other more affluent schools and neighborhoods." Other reasons fewer African Americans and Hispanics pursue a college education include the disproportionate minority high-school dropout rates, inability to afford college tuition, and lack of financial aid for minority students.

Where Do We Go from Here?

Resolution of the many educational issues presently faced by the nation's African American and Hispanic minorities will take concerted effort. The problems of poor education, high dropout rates, and the "brain drain" resulting from disproportionate numbers of Blacks and Hispanics serving time in prison instead of college can be resolved in large part by more federal and state funding for various programs targeted to benefit minorities (Rice & Arekere, 2004). Such actions, according to Cameron and Hickman (2001), are far more likely to improve the scholastic ability of African Americans and Hispanics in the long run and to alleviate measured educational differentials between these two groups and White Americans.

Resolution of these challenges will also require Blacks and Hispanics to reconsider their priorities, work together, and gain control of their involvements in the political, economical, and educational arenas. As Dr. Gabriela Lemus, Director of Policy and Legislation for the League of United Latin American Citizens, maintains:

> "We want to see both groups [African Americans and Hispanics] get access to education, we want to see less high school dropouts, stronger voter participation, and clout and representation in Congress and at the highest levels of government. We've been conscious that our communities are growing very fast for some time, but obviously we can do more together." ("Leaders Question Importance of Report of Hispanics Becoming Largest Minority," 2003)

These efforts, however, need to begin today, so that 10 years from now we will begin to see improvements in African American and Hispanic children's educational attainment and lives.

References

Barton, P. E. (2003, October). *Parsing the achievement gap: Baseline for tracking progress*. Available from http://www.ets.org/research/pic/parsing.pdf

Bowie, M. (1997, January 17). Open house unites Black, Hispanic groups. *Alligator Online*. Available from http://www.alligator.org/edit/issues/97spring/970117/b13ibc.htm

Cameron, S. V., & Heckman, J. J. (2001). The dynamics of educational attainment for Black, Hispanic and White males. *Journal of Political Economy 109*(3). Available from http://www.journals.uchicago.edu/JPE/journal/issues/v109n3/019204/019204

Center for Individual Rights. (2004, July 16). *Showdown in the Supreme Court: The lawsuits against the University of Michigan*. Available from http://www.cir-usa.org/recent_cases/michigan.html

Elliot, J. (2004, September 16). Judge overturns Robin Hood. *The Houston Chronicle 103*(339), A1.

Garcia, E. (1999). A Latino perspective: The impact of Brown v. Board of Education. *The Brown Quarterly 3*(2). Available from http://www.brownvboard.org/brwnqurt/03-2/03-2b.htm

Guiding federal court cases on equal educational opportunity (The English Language Learner Knowledge Base). (2004, August 26). Available from http://www.helpforschools.com/ELLKBase/legal/Court_Cases_Federal_Equa_Educ_Opp.shtml

Guzman, B. (2001, May). *The Hispanic population: 2000*. Available from http://www.census.gov/prod/2001pubs/c2kbr01-3.pdf

Headley, B. D. (2001). Race, class and powerlessness in world economy. *The Black Scholar 21*(3). Available from http://www.theblackscholar.org

Leaders question importance of report of Hispanics becoming largest minority. (2003, June 20). Available from http://www.bet.com/articles/0,clgb6638-7434,00.html

Lopez, I. H. (2004, May 22). Hernandez v. Brown. Available from http://www.virtualboricua.org/docs/nytimes10.htm

McKinnon, J. (2001, August). *The Black population: 2000*. Available from http://www.census.gov/prod/2001pubs/c2kbr01-5.pdf

Moore–Brown, B. (2004, September 16). *Case in point: The administrative predicament of special education funding—El Rancho Unified School District*. Available from http://csef.air.org/publications/related/jsel/moorebrown.html

Posnick–Goodwin, S. (2004, April). Remembering *Brown v. Board of Education*: Tearing down the walls that divide us. *California Educator 8*(7). Available from http://www.cta.org/CaliforniaEducator/v8i7/Feature_1.htm

Rice, M. F., & Arekere, D. M. (2004, April). *Education attainment and income gaps among African and Hispanic Americans* [Research brief]. College Station: Race and Ethnic Studies Institute, Texas A&M University.

Schlomach, B. (2004, August 15). *Suing ourselves will never suit: No matter who wins school finance lawsuit, taxpayers lose.* Available from http://www.texas policy.com/pdf/2004-08-15-sanbenito-suing.pdf

Texas school finance law trial opens Monday. (2004, August 9). Available from http://www.kxan.com/global/story.asp?s=2148903&ClientType=Printable

CHAPTER FOUR

Navigating the River

Environmental Scanning to Enable Diversity Programs and Initiatives to Withstand Internal and External Challenges

M. COOKIE NEWSOM AND ARCHIE ERVIN

In the early years of the twenty-first century, pitfalls, challenges, and, perhaps, opportunities face diversity workers on the nation's college and university campuses. Charged as they are with the recruitment, retention, and support of minority students, whose presence on those campuses in centuries past was hardly proportional, these workers have an increasingly important role to play in the future of American higher education.

Following the Civil Rights era of the 1950s and 1960s, recognition of the need for healing resulted in the movement of at least one minority group, African Americans, into the mainstream of American life. That struggle provided African Americans with opportunities, including educational opportunities, that previously had been denied to them (Bowen & Bok, 2004). It further propelled society to recognize and appreciate that the denial of educational opportunity to Blacks—from the ban on teaching slaves to read to the separate-but-(hardly)-equal schools established in the era of Jim Crow and perpetuated into the mid-twentieth century—was one of the most damaging effects of the system of discrimination that had flourished in the nation virtually unchecked until the 1960s. Wide acknowledgment of the reality that opportunities for Blacks to get a decent education in the United States had been limited at best, and absent at worst, gave way to improved educational opportunity for all Americans. The mind-set of American society seemed to be one of a resurging interest in social justice and in making the rhetoric of freedom and equality so often expressed in our government documents a reality. The nation, it appeared, was ready at last to address some of the inequities of its past and banish them from the future.

As a result of the ameliorative programs launched during this era, including programs such as affirmative action, the percentage of African Americans graduating from college in the United States rose from 5.4% in 1960 to 15.4% in 1995 (Bowen & Bok, 2004). In more recent years, however, the idea that certain other populations—generally viewed to include Indians, Asian Americans, and Latinos—still need specifically targeted programs for educational recruitment, retention, and support has faced a growing challenge. Apparently, many Americans believe that all the inequities in our society were eliminated by the Civil Rights Act of 1964 and the growth of the Black middle class. Racism, in the view of many segments of mainstream US society, is no longer a major threat to justice in this country. More and more is heard of the call for a so-called colorblind society, as if such a thing could actually exist. This has led some institutions of higher education in America to question not only their commitment to diversity, but also whether they should have such a commitment at all. As Wilson (1995) maintains, "The questions confronting the academy are whether diversity is a legitimate goal; whether achieving a diverse student [or faculty body] is an educational value; and what is the educational role and purpose of higher education" (p. 19).

In such a climate, the people charged with managing the recruitment, admissions, retention, and support of students of color increasingly find themselves confronting attitudes and practices antithetical to their mission. They may also encounter attitudes and responses to their work ranging from apathy to outright hostility and from episodic questions and challenges to organized resistance to the very idea of diversity. All of the issues and subcontexts university diversity workers must address today are rooted in the views different people hold of society. Are some animals, as George Orwell (1946) wrote, more equal than others? If so, to what does one attribute this superiority? Is it based on merit, opportunity, luck, individual effort? Gaither (1999) compares the different attitudes about diversity on college campuses to the philosophies of two former US presidents:

> It is no secret that a hot debate now rages across the United States about the role of remedial education, diversity, affirmative action, which students to recruit and educate, and the balance of public resources spent versus personal responsibility for education cost. As the new century dawns, it brings with it twin ver-

sions of egalitarianism that deeply divide our attitudes toward recruitment, retention and remediation. One version of egalitarianism, the Jeffersonian, believes in opportunity, gain, and growth on the basis of individual merit. They largely demand that the academy hold fast to its traditional roles, character, and mission. A second egalitarian theme in the American context is the Jacksonian levelers, who seek greater equality of result and condition. The Jacksonians are interested in closing the economic, social, and education gap between those at the top and those at the bottom, and they are willing to use the power of the state to accomplish these goals, using redistribution of income, whereas the Jeffersonians are suspicious of centralized power and state funding of social or remedial programs not based on clear individual merit. (p. 115)

Diversity actions evoke dichotomous reactions. Whereas one camp views equality only in terms of "clear individual merit" (unless one is talking about legacy issues, of course, which are entirely another matter), the other views the opportunity to succeed as the right of all people. The balancing act necessary to preserve targeted recruitment, retention, and support programs is readily apparent. Thus, when planning diversity programs, it is important to factor in as many of the arguments, barriers, and complaints one is bound to hear from one camp or the other, and develop strategies to address them. It is also important to be conversant with the literature of each side in order to discuss any position in context and with authority.

A battle currently is being waged in America over just what role race, ethnicity and other diversity factors should play in our society in general and in our colleges and universities in particular. The institution of higher education that successfully addresses equity issues is one that positions itself to stay abreast of the changing landscape and make plans to weather whatever shifts in policy, legal decisions, and institutional attitudes and policies occur. The question is, however, what does such positioning entail?

First, sufficient research must be conducted, compiled, and analyzed. What variables are in play, or potentially looming, that might influence the work of a college's or university's diversity officers? These variables can be organized into three categories: knowledge, behavior, and attitudes. In other words: What do diversity workers know about the diverse elements on campus, what do they do about these differences, and what do they think about them? In most cases, the answers to these questions must be considered at the national, state, and local community levels as well as that of the specific campus communities.

A large part of the knowledge component relies upon demographic data. What are the current demographic statistics for the campus? What will the future demographic picture look like? What is the demographic profile of the state and/or region in which the campus is located? How many students, by demographic category, graduate from high school in the state each year? Have any demographic shifts in the local or regional population occurred recently? What impact might those shifts have on the institution's potential students, faculty, and staff ? As if that were not enough, what about other "hidden" demographic groups such as faculty, staff, and students who are part of the LGBTQ (lesbian, gay, bisexual, transgendered, and queer) communities, religious minorities, those for whom English is a second language, and, in some instances, political conservatives or liberals? Knowing an institution's current and potential faculty, staff, and student demographics makes it easier for diversity workers to make a case for proposed equity programs. Identifying and becoming familiar with sources for accurate, current demographic information is a crucial part of any equity office's strategic planning through environmental scanning.

A second aspect of the knowledge component involves assessment of the legal climate. On any given day, numerous challenges to the quest for campus diversity arise all over this nation, any one of which could potentially wind up in the Supreme Court. For diversity workers on a college campus, knowing the legal landscape is one of the primary elements for conducting effective environmental scanning.

Various databases are available to help equity officers stay abreast of the legal climate. These databases provide searchable information on current and recent legal cases. Their use places college diversity officers in a position of making informed advocacy for their programs. The broader examinations they allow provide answers to the following questions: What litigation is either in process or being proposed that involves diversity issues, particularly those pertaining to recruitment, retention, and support of faculty, staff, and students? What positions are the challenges taking? Who is making the arguments, financing the charge? Are their arguments predicated on current law or are they trying to formulate new policies by offering alternate interpretations or attempting to make new law?

Recent court decisions have had an impact on the work of higher education equity officers. The 2001 *Grutter v. Bollinger, et al.* decision, for example, with its well-publicized arguments, amicus briefs, and public commentary on the issues, is one such case. The decision rendered in *Grutter* affected everyone from the president of a major university (the University of Michigan) to the average person. It also brought certain key phrases and practices into the world of achieving and managing diversity including, "critical mass," "educational benefit," and "compelling interest" (Proitz, Stensaker, & Harvey, 2004, p. 1).

Regarding behavior, a primary area of interest focuses on current practices in diversity management. What is being done on US campuses today to encourage and support diversity among their faculty, staff, and students? What is the public stance of the academy on the topic of diversity? How much support is evinced for diversity initiatives by the campus community, particularly upper-level administration? Even if legal counsel has given its opinion that certain college or university programs, initiatives, and procedures are free of language that would cause additional scrutiny or invite litigation, if a campus community is unwilling to embrace diversity—or to support the recruitment and retention efforts necessary to attract and retain a diverse mix of students, faculty, and staff—diversity will not happen. What a college or university says about diversity is important, but not as important as what it does about diversity.

One of the primary indicators of a college or university's commitment to diversity is its reporting hierarchy. Does the office for minority and/or multicultural affairs have access to decision makers at the top, or is that office buried under layer after layer of bureaucracy? In the latter case, diversity workers can be thwarted by the unwillingness of any one of their supervising offices. The amount and form of the resources allocated to such offices is another good indication of the true commitment of an institution to diversity. Valued programs and offices are given sufficient resources and the autonomy to allocate those resources as they see fit in the pursuit of creating an equitable and inclusive campus. Third, the degree to which an institution of higher education holds its various departments, schools, and divisions accountable for their management of diversity is a very important component of institutional behavior. Valued programs and initiatives are assessed on a regular schedule, provided suggestions for improvement, and permitted to make adjustments to facilitate those improvements. They are also allocated the resources needed to accomplish their goals. If the institution's commitment to diversity is tepid, it will be satisfied with vague, unfocused, and ineffective diversity management.

Finally yet importantly is the area of attitudes. The savvy equity office frequently "takes the temperature" of a wide variety of communities and constituencies, both those on campus and in wider communities, with regard to diversity issues. Knowing the political climate of the diversity landscape—locally, statewide and nationally—enables diversity workers to identify potential barriers to advocacy and undertake programmatic planning. How well is their office's mission woven into the mission of the institution? How well is diversity supported in campus extracurricular activities, symposia, conferences, and, of course, curricula? Does the college or university's mission statement include a commitment to diversity? Where can one find information about diversity initiatives and programs on the institution's website: is it on the main webpage or buried in obscure links?

The positioning of an office of minority/multicultural affairs to be successful regardless of legal, political, and institutional challenges is strongly linked to the ability of that office to understand the realities and assess the possibilities. Equity officers must keep abreast of both what is going on and what is coming up on the diversity horizon. Failure to complete environmental scanning consistently, to assess the state of diversity both externally and internally, invites marginalization or complete abandonment of higher education diversity offices. Those of us dedicated to the creation of equitable and inclusive campuses have a responsibility to see that this does not happen. A blueprint of the main elements necessary for such scanning is outlined below.

Environmental Scanning for Diversity Programs or Initiatives: Elements to Consider

1. Demographics
   (a) Existing populations of faculty, staff, and students on campus
   (b) Pipeline/available population
      (i) State
         - High school graduation rates for specific populations
         - Population by gender and race/ethnicity
      (ii) National
         - High school graduation rates for specific populations
         - Population by gender and race/ethnicity
2. Legal challenges/decisions/interpretations
   (a) *Grutter v. Bollinger, et al.*
      (i) Many institutions of higher education have chosen to interpret *Grutter* as a defeat and a signal to draw back or abandon their efforts at diversity recruiting
      (ii) The need for minority/multicultural affairs officers to have a good working knowledge of what the *Grutter* decision says and does not say
      (iii) Other relevant court cases in progress or recently decided
   (b) Institutional legal guidance/advice
      (i) How an institution supports or does not support diversity, in theory and practice, may be rooted in advice from legal counsel
   (c) Language for compliance with law
      (i) Certain terms and phrases are either illegal or unwise; thus, it is crucial for diversity workers to know what those terms and

phrases are, particularly as they relate to specific campuses
   (d) Other challenges
3. Institutional challenges
   (a) Reporting structure/chain of command
      (i) Positioning the minority/multicultural affairs office for easy access to decision makers
   (b) Support from president/chancellor
      (i) Ensuring a level of support and commitment for the minority/multicultural affairs office from the chief executive
   (c) Organized resistance
      (i) Organizations on campus or in the region that are hostile to diversity and/or organized to oppose it
   (d) Communications issues
      (i) Communicating the importance of diversity within and throughout the campus community
      (ii) Identifying resources are to help share information about diversity, diversity initiatives, programs, and collaborations
   (e) Establishment of common goals regarding diversity
      (i) Mission/vision statement
      (ii) Institutionwide consensus on the importance of and commitment to diversity
   (f) Objective evaluation of diversity issues
      (i) Assessment
      (ii) Diversity plan has a timeline, measurable outcomes, and periodic review
4. Politics
   (a) National
   (b) State
   (c) Local
   (d) Institutional

References

Bowen, W. G., & Bok, D. (2004). *The shape of the river: Long-term consequences of considering race in college and university admissions.* Princeton, NJ: Princeton University Press.

Gaither, G. H. (1999). What the future holds. *New directions for higher education* 108, 115–119.

Grutter v. Bollinger, et al. 137 F. Supp.2d 821, 851 (E.D. Mich. 2001).

Orwell, G. (1946). *Animal farm.* New York: Harcourt, Brace.

Proitz, T. S., Stensaker, B., & Harvey, L. (2004). Accreditation, standards and diversity: An analysis of EQUIS accreditation reports. *Assessment and Evaluation in Higher Education* 29(6), 735–751.

Wilson, R. (1995). *Affirmative action: Yesterday, today, and beyond.* Washington, DC: American Council on Education.

Further Reading

Brown, S. V. (1992). The shortage of Black faculty in higher education: Implications for student retention. In M. Lang & C. A. Ford (Eds.), *Strategies for retaining minority students in higher education* (pp. 133–147). Springfield, IL: Charles C. Thomas Publishers.

Christler Tourse, R. W. (1987). Recruiting and counseling people of color at western universities. *International Journal for the Advancement of Counseling* 10, 45–58.

Collins, M. (1990). Enrollment, recruitment, and retention of minority faculty and staff in institutions of higher education. *Action in Education* 12, 57–62.

Collison, M. N.-K. (1999). Achieving career satisfaction in the academy. *Black Issues in Higher Education* 16, 27–29.

Dumas-Hines, F. A., Cochran, L. L., & Williams, E. U. (2001). Promoting diversity: Recommendations for recruitment and retention of minorities in higher education. *College Student Journal* 35(3), 433–442.

Dyer, E. (2004). On the right path. *Black Issues in Higher Education* 21(3), 28–31.

Gardner, U. S., Keller, J. W., & Piotrowski, C. (1996). Retention issues as perceived by African-American university students. *Psychology: A Journal of Human Behavior* 33, 20–21.

Grieger, I., & D'Onofrio, A. (1996). Free your mind: A three-part sequential series of multicultural programs. *Journal of College Student Development* 37, 591–594.

Jacullo-Noto, J. (1991). Minority recruitment in teacher education: Problems and possibilities. *Urban Education* 26(2), 214–230.

Love, B. J. (1993). Issues and problems in the retention of Black students in predominantly White institutions of higher education. *Equity and Excellence in Education* 26(1), 27–36.

Matthews, Y. (1986). Painting with a detailed brush: A personalized minority student program. *Journal of College Student Personnel* 27, 76–77.

National Education Association. (1998). *American education statistics at a glance* [NEA research]. Available from www.wea.org/publiced/statsata.html

Perisco, C. F. (1990). Creating an institutional climate that honors diversity. In G. Stricker & E. Davis-Russell (Eds.), *Toward ethnic diversification in psychology education and training* (pp. 55–63). Washington, DC: American Psychological Association.

Pounds, A. W. (1987). Black students' needs on predominantly White campuses. In D. S. Wright (Ed.), *Responding to the needs of today's minority students* (pp. 23–38). San Francisco: Jossey-Bass.

Redmond, S. P. (1990). Mentoring and cultural diversity in academic settings. *American Behavioral Scientist* 34, 188–200.

Taylor, E., & Olswang, S. G. (1997). Crossing the color line: African Americans and predominantly White universities. *College Student Journal* 31, 11–18.

Turner, C. S. V., & Myers Jr., S. L. (2000). *Faculty of color in academe: Bittersweet success.* Needham Heights, MA: Allyn & Bacon.

CHAPTER FIVE

Historical and Contemporary Dilemmas Facing Urban Black Male Students Today

Focusing on the Past to Correct Present and Future Deficits

THEODORE LOUIS THOMPSON III

Abstract

This chapter provides a theoretical exploration of the primary issues surrounding the long-standing disparities noted in urban Black male student achievement. It discusses how the arduous social history of African-descended people in the New World has contributed, in the aggregate and over centuries, to the educational crises facing young Black males in today's urban school districts. The author maintains that if these students better understood the history of their forebears, especially those who long ago advocated African American political and cultural independence and separatism from mainstream American thought and culture, they would not sacrifice the multitude of opportunities they stand to gain by receiving an education. He suggests that curricula grounded and centered in the African American experience can help end the cycle of learned helplessness that many urban Black males experience in school and offer them a means of gaining educational focus and hope for school success.

Introduction

Since the dawn of American history, the acquisition of knowledge has been the defining means of advancement in our society. Today, education remains the dominant pathway to earning a viable living in the United States. Looking at the value of education from this perspective, one could easily infer that education is an essential part of being a productive citizen. As technology continues to advance, so too will the knowledge and information needed to operate and support the national infrastructure. That being the case, then all Americans should have the opportunity to obtain an education and prosper from it. Unfortunately, this is not necessarily happening for a large segment of American society, particularly its African American males.

Although the United States has been described as a melting pot of various cultures, European capitalistic values and traditions have dominated this mix since its inception, long supplanting the theocratic system imported to North America by the early settlers. The opportunity to make huge profits in the New World led colonial entrepreneurs to use any means necessary to exploit the vast untapped resources of their recently claimed land. This included using force to extract labor from unwilling participants. After a trial-and-error period with native American and indentured European workers, the "perfect" labor force for this harrowing task was identified on the African continent. Subsequently large numbers of Africans were brutally uprooted and shipped like cargo to strange lands hundreds of miles across the sea.

African slaves literally were worth their weight in gold to those intent on maximizing their profits without consideration of the toll such inhumanity would levy on their society, much less their souls. Given that they viewed and used Africans as chattel property, these "masters" did not see the need to educate Blacks beyond the common tasks they were forced to perform. Many of the colonies—for example, South Carolina in the late 1600s and Georgia in 1755—even passed slave codes which stated that under no circumstances were people of African descent to be taught to read or write (Franklin & Moss, 1994). Thus, from their earliest known arrival to these shores in 1661 to the 1954 *Brown v. Board of Education of Topeka, Kansas* ruling that overturned segregated schooling in America, African American males faced a conscious dilemma—that of being a commodity at worst and a second-class citizen at best. This dilemma differs in many respects from the unconscious dilemma that faces African American male students today. The latter challenge emanates from a lack of appreciation for the value of education, poor self–identity, a diminished sense of manhood, and encounters with covert and subtle racism.

Inner-City African American Male Youth: Conscious Versus Unconscious Dilemmas

Enslaved African males faced many obstacles. Viewed as chattel, they had no civil liberties and were thus afforded no human dignity. Even before their long journey across the Atlantic, systematic efforts were employed to purge them, physically and mentally, of the sense of freedom they once enjoyed. This was accomplished by a process called "seasoning," whereby slave men were emasculated, brutalized, demoralized, and generally made docile. Once the seasoning process was complete, they were shipped to the Americas and other places where slavery was legal. There, as former slave-turned-newspaperman, abolitionist, and statesman Fredrick Douglass explained in his article, "How to Make a Slave," slavery's proponents ruthlessly defined what little freedoms the dispossessed Africans could enjoy by instituting harsh social structures and restrictive codes for slaves at the national, state, local, and plantation levels (Akbar, 1996).

The enslaved Blacks were subject to extreme punishments and work expectations that were exploitive and unrealistic for any human being. Slave-owners also took steps to ensure that the African family unit was destroyed upon arrival in the "New World." Only White men were allowed the privilege of enjoying the union of family and the opportunity to provide for their progeny (Franklin & Moss, 1994).

The dilemma facing African American males during the colonial period intensified as some Black men obtained their freedom while others remained enslaved. The resulting free Black class emerged in mass after the American Revolution, thanks in part to Lord Dunmore, Governor of Virginia, who declared free any male slaves willing to fight for Britain. The Continental Congress later voted to use slave men as soldiers during the Revolutionary War, but did not waiver in its commitment to upholding slavery in the 13 colonies (Hine, Hine, & Harold, 2000). After the overthrow of the British and the establishment of an independent United States, enslaved Africans would see their dreams of freedom further deferred with the adoption of the American Constitution, which gave legal recognition to the institution of slavery. Many changes to the status of African American males followed in both the post-colonial North and South. The institution of restrictive "Black Codes" limited the freedom of the free Blacks, who continued to advocate for their enslaved brethren, but cautiously so, as their own rights were fragile and easily revocable.

In the years before the American Civil War, slavery decreased dramatically in the North, increased somewhat in the Upper South, and expanded greatly in the Lower South (see Table 5.1). Given their generally shorter lifespans, many slaves born in the southern states never lived to know freedom. Most knew, however, that Blacks "up North" were free, and large numbers attempted to escape and flee to the northern states and Canada.

Table 5.1 United States Slave Population, 1820 and 1860

	1820	1860
United States	1,538,125	3,953,760
North	19,108	64
South	1,519,017	3,953,696
Upper South	965,514	1,530,229
Delaware	4,509	1,798
Kentucky	127,732	225,483
Maryland	107,397	87,189
Missouri	10,222	114,931
North Carolina	205,017	331,059
Tennessee	80,107	275,719
Virginia	425,153	490,865
Washington, DC	6,377	3,185
Lower South	553,503	2,423,467
Alabama	41,879	435,080
Arkansas	1,617	111,115
Florida*	–	61,745
Georgia	149,654	462,198
Louisiana	69,064	331,726
Mississippi	328,114	436,631
South Carolina	258,475	402,406
Texas*	–	182,566

*Florida and Texas were not states in 1820.
Source: Berlin (1974).

The psychological conflict arising from the desire for freedom while enslaved was the conscious dilemma of the early African American male. To survive the multiple assaults upon their manhood, enslaved Black men had to develop many coping strategies. To withstand or escape the harshness of their condition, many no doubt turned within, creating for themselves an "alternative reality." Whether that alternative involved imagining freedom in the here and now or imagining a heaven beyond, African men in the Americas likely sought psychological release, refuge, or redemption from physical slavery in many ways. Some turned to music and songs that gave them strength to make it through arduous days. Others secretly learned how to read and write, thereby quietly empowering themselves with the knowledge publicly limited to their masters. Still others closely observed and emulated their captors, taking on what Hughes (1934) called "the ways of White folks."

Thus, a substantial component of many early African American males' concept of manhood was modeled upon that of their White counterparts and former enslavers. For those Black males, their quest was to prove that they were indeed men like, and to, White males (Cullen, 1992). Despite the multitude of obstacles placed before them, African American men were able to accomplish major achievements during the several decades from Reconstruction to the Civil Rights Movement; however, the role of violence in the separation of the Black male from his manhood or masculinity was clear. The willingness of an entire society and legal system to enforce brutalities such as lynching, castration, burnings, and other forms of abuse was a powerful force in this emasculation process (Booker, 1996). As a result, the assertion of Black manhood—as in, for example, protecting the virtue of Black women from pillaging slavers, resisting or fleeing enslavement, and finding ways to overcome the system of oppression—typically has involved bold acts of defiance toward a clearly identifiable oppressor.

Unfortunately, the ideological concept of manhood has been displaced in the Black communities of our nation today. Record numbers of African American males are finding it difficult to advance themselves and their families economically, politically, and socially. Black males are overrepresented in the nation's penal institutions and underrepresented in its academic institutions (Kunjufu, 1995, 2001). What has happened? Why are so many Black males finding it difficult to become responsible, reputable, and productive men?

Poverty and economic inequality play a tremendous role in this problem, but the disappearance of the Black male father figure and role model—through either incarceration or divorce or both—has been instrumental in breaking the social cycle of positive Black male youth development. To make matter worse, African American males traditionally have had little support to help them cope with life crises (Majors & Billson, 1992). Coupled with the resulting embittered perceptions of Black manhood held by some Black women, this absence has produced an imagined oppressive mentality among these young men, particularly those in the nation's inner cities, where the absence is greatest.

Additionally, the perception of a White male oppressor who is covertly or overtly preventing their social and economic advancement is misplaced but common among today's African American male youth. It is also intellectually and emotionally damaging, as Woodson (1933) maintains:

> . . . to handicap a student by teaching him that his black face is a curse and that his struggle to change his condition is hopeless is the worst sort of lynching. It kills one's aspirations and dooms him to vagabondage and crime. (p. 3)

Covert racism is racism not openly practiced but practiced just the same. The two forms of covert racism common to the experiences of today's inner-city Black male youth are institutionalized racism and inequitable hiring practices. These forms are manifested in a variety of ways, from discriminatory classroom tracking behaviors that inhibit Black male academic achievement to unfair employment practices that keep Black male youth out of the workforce or resign them to the lower rungs of it. As a result, many of these youth have come to perceive covert racism as overt racism. This perception leads them to retreat to the presumed safety of infantile intellectual states or to use misguided coping strategies.

The question, however, is why are so many of today's young African American males, who presently face few overt obstacles compared to those of their forebears, not achieving educationally? Although this question does not appear to have an easy answer, a focus on the psychological phenomenon of learned helplessness may prove useful in framing an explanation. Learned helplessness refers to the emotional numbing and maladaptive passivity that sometimes follows victimization (Peterson & Seligman, 1983). As Peterson and Seligman maintain, victims may learn during their victimization episodes that responding is futile. This learning results in an expectation of future-response outcome independence, or helplessness. Victims' subsequent casual interpretations of the episode affect the chronicity and generality of deficits resulting from this expectation as well as the loss of self-esteem.

Elkins (1968) describes the dependency of slave upon slavemaster as a form of learned helplessness, as typified in the "Sambo" stereotype. Sambo, a character originally postulated by Phillips (1918/1966), was depicted as the typical African American male plantation slave: docile but irresponsible, loyal but lazy and infantile, with speech patterns inflated by childish exaggeration. Elkins maintains that Sambo's learned helplessness was not only an attempt to appease his slavemaster but also a ruse to stave off physical abuse. He theorized that slavery (the victimization episode) forced enslaved males (the victims) to exist in an extremely difficult environment; hence, their helpless behavior was perceived as appropriate. Eventually, the Sambo character became a tool for, and a symbol of, the emasculation of African American males. As Boskin (1986) writes:

> Sambo was an extraordinary type of social control, once extremely subtle, devious, and encompassing. To exercise a high degree of control meant also to be able to manipulate the full range of humor; to create ultimately, an insidious type

of buffoon. To make the black male into an object of laughter and conversely, to force him to devise laughter, was to strip him of masculinity, dignity, and self-possession. Sambo was then, an illustration of humor as a device of oppression, and one of the most potent in American popular culture. The ultimate objective for whites was to effect mastery: to render the black male powerless as a potential warrior, as a sexual competitor, as an economic adversary. (pp. 13–14)

Today's Black male students have developed a similar dependency. Their learned helplessness is based upon their acceptance of their forefathers' perceptions that all aspects of the American social structure—educational, political, economic, and so forth—are closed to them. This leads them to behave in a submissive manner rather than actualize their intellectual potential. As a result, many Black male students today, especially those in the most challenging urban environments, believe themselves to be victims of and within this system. This has led them to adopt a defeatist disposition toward education. These young men enjoy many freedoms their predecessors never knew, yet because most of them are unaware of the history of their people in this country, they do not exercise those freedoms in the way their ancestors envisioned. They perceive covert racist tactics as overt and belittle the intellectual and political thought of independent-thinking, self-empowered African American men and women. This perception has rendered them helpless and, in many cases, doomed for failure.

Although the rabid racism of earlier eras is not as common now as before, many of today's young Black males continue to view themselves as victims of overt types of racism. Most often, however, these young men suffer more from the ravages of self-inflicted, internalized oppression. Many prefer to earn fast money, by any legal or illegal means necessary, while rebuffing the value and the importance of traditional work ethics and lifestyles. They exploit their female counterparts' physical and mental talents, thereby reducing the African American woman's function and purpose. They refuse to engage in inquiry processes that would heighten their awareness and place them on a direct path to understanding. Most troubling, as the overtly racist beliefs and tactics of the past have become covert, discreet, and often institutionalized, many young Black males do not see these more subtle forms of racism as problematic. They thus face an unconscious dilemma.

By studying the philosophies and ideologies of early African American scholars and activists who advocated African American political and cultural independence and separatism from mainstream American thought and culture, these students can find new ways to defeat the social chains they imagine have been placed on them. The lessons they can learn from these notable forebears can also provide them with a better understanding of the function and goals of capitalism and help them cease to devalue the importance of acquiring an education.

African American Men Making History for Themselves

A real understanding of the roles of independent-minded African American men in history is needed if today's Black male youth are to discard the defeatist decorum that renders them helpless to the covert racism that leads too many of them to physical and mental incarceration. Such as examination reveals Black men such as Marcus Garvey, who articulated a back-to-Africa message, stressed racial nationalism for people of African ancestry, and advocated the importance of establishing a separate Black nation within the borders of the United States (McCartney, 1992). Garvey's Universal Negro Improvement Association (UNIA) was a group with major influence during the early 1900s. After his exile in 1927, Black nationalism was expressed in subsequent movements: (1) the Counter-Communalist, (2) the Black Power Pluralist, and (3) the Black Power Separatist movements (McCartney, 1992). The Counter-Communalists, exemplified by the Black Panthers, sought to replace the values, interest, institutions, and beliefs of the American political system with different ones. The Black Power Pluralists believed that by working within the American system and by skillfully using the strategies and techniques sanctioned by it, African Americans could achieve the level of success that other US ethnic groups have attained. The Black Power Separatists viewed Black nationhood as the focus of the separatist struggle and argued that American culture is inimical to African American development (McCartney, 1992).

The meaning and significance of the Black Nationalist and Black Power movements for African American men have been poorly misrepresented by mainstream American history and media. These movements, however, were crowning achievements for the Black men who led in them and selflessly gave of themselves in an effort to change the dismissal outlook for African Americans. They also serve as powerful testaments to the intellectual capacity and dedication of African American men during the Jim Crow era and beyond.

The Historical Value of Education for African American Men

To ascertain the extent to which today's urban African American male students value education, one must first understand the value of education to the ruling White capitalist class in America. According to Bowles (1976), American education serves two main objectives: (1) to train a disciplined and skilled labor force that can take its place in the existing order and contribute (mainly its labor power) to the maintenance and expansion of the capitalist system; and (2) to indoctrinate the youth of the society in the ideas, beliefs, values, and practices that are important to maintaining the existing socioeconomic order. Before the trans-Atlantic slave trade, Africans were no strangers to education. The African continent was home to many institutions of higher learning, one of which, for example, was the University of Sankore at Timbuktu. During the early 1500s, Sankore was a renowned intellectual center to which scholars from all over Africa, Asia, and Europe came to study. Throughout most of Africa, it was common for boys and girls to be taught separately the practices and customs important for assuming the sex-role responsibilities of adults. The education to which African youth were exposed reflected the needs and mores of the various societies in which they lived. Rites of passage initiations were common features of traditional African educational process (Karenga, 1982).

In the Americas, however, slaveowners generally were tolerant only of work-related and religious training for their Black chattel. Many slaveowners believed that biblical training made their slaves more obedient, hardworking, and submissive (Blassingame, 1972). An educated slave was commonly viewed as dangerous and a direct contradiction to the slavery philosophy. Nonetheless, formal schools for African American children—slave and free—date back to the early 1700s in both the American North and South. Typically these schools were run by White clergy, missionaries, Quakers, or abolitionist societies. After the Revolutionary War, free African Americans established several schools to teach their own (Hine et al., 2000).

Despite the odds, many Black men in early America found ways to achieve forms of manhood, realizing dignity, purpose, and power in their lives. These men recognized the reality of their enchained status and worked within the interstices of American society to carve out niches of opportunity, comfort, and social status (Booker, 1996). For example, Jeremiah Asher, a free Black veteran of the Revolutionary War, recalled how his grandfather modeled manhood by instilling in him the ability to resist insults and defend himself against Whites physically, whenever necessary (Berry & Blassingame, 1982). In the post-Civil War era, African Americans actively sought education as a means of solidifying their newfound liberation, and they rallied behind the creation of tax-supported public educational systems (Watkins, 2001). Although every Black male during the colonial, Reconstruction, and Jim Crow eras was not successful in breaking the mental chains of slavery, many served as pioneers in setting the stage that would eventually destroy the physical forms of enslavement and allow every Black male the opportunity to advance in areas that were previously inaccessible to him.

African American scholars Booker T. Washington and W. E. B. DuBois would later set the tone and direction for African American educational pursuits. Washington, on one hand, stressed agricultural and industrial education as a means of progress for African Americans. He asserted that economic acceptance would eventually lead to Blacks' political and social acceptance. Conversely, DuBois (1935) believed that African Americans needed a liberal education to garner the competencies required to gain and exercise their political and civil rights. Despite their differences in approach, both men understood that without education, African Americans would find it extremely difficult to contribute to American society.

The twentieth-century civil rights movement sought to put an end to the racially discriminatory practices common to many American institutions. Initially, the primary focus of this movement was the area of education, specifically the inequitable and inadequate educational facilities, materials, and other resources available to African American students. The 1954 ruling in *Brown* was a major step toward challenging the segregationist practices of many southern educational institutions. Neither *Brown* nor *Brown II* (1955) eradicated the racist educational practices of the American South, but they did establish a legal precedent for African Americans to attempt to compete on an equal footing.

The Black Power movement that evolved out of the civil rights struggle also heavily valued education. Many of the students involved in that movement attended historically Black postsecondary institutions such as Howard University in Washington, D.C. Their involvement can be described as having two phases. The first phase involved attempts by students at Black colleges and universities in the South to speak out against social inequalities. The second and most prolific phase began when Black students began enrolling in and attending majority White institutions of higher learning. The students on those campuses began to demand courses in Black history, culture, and literature. Eventually, Black Studies departments were established at elite institutions like Harvard, Cornell, and Yale universities. Students and faculty in these departments sought to make the study of African-descended people throughout the African Diaspora—their culture, problems, world views, and spirituality—a serious scholarly endeavor with practical implications for improving the lives of Black people worldwide (Hine et al., 2000).

The passage of nationwide civil rights legislation in the 1960s (i.e., the Higher Education Act of 1965) did very little to alleviate the suffering of masses of inner-city Blacks. Poverty remained an ever-present reality for large percentages of African Americans, many of whom began to see their survival as increasingly bleak. The pacifist African American leader, Dr. Martin Luther

King, Jr. (1967), was also aware of how poverty was destroying urban Black communities, and he launched a Poor People's Campaign to aid them in obtaining economic equity. The Black Panther Party and other, more militant African American groups were also welcomed in inner-city communities (Carmichael & Hamilton, 1967). The Black Panthers' platform recognized full employment, decent housing, and education as essential to African Americans' continued survival (Foner, 1995).

For many poor, inner-city Black males of this era, joining the armed forces and fighting in Vietnam was viewed as a way out. Others turned to crime to meet their, while still others turned to drug and alcohol use to escape from the reality of poverty and discrimination. Higher education and, in many cases, the completion of secondary education requirements were luxuries they could not fathom. The military was a viable option for these males because it offered educational and vocational opportunities that were not available to them otherwise (Hine et al., 2000). After their discharge from service, however, many faced a still-uncertain future (Franklin & Moss, 1994). For the Black veterans returning from the Vietnamese war, urban America had become a battlefield. Racial tensions were at an all-time high, riots erupted frequently, and the depressed economic climate pushed many Black males into criminal activities. "Black-on-Black" crime, an expression of displaced anger in many cases, became commonplace (Wilson, 1990).

These myriad societal ills and failures took a tremendous toll on Black communities in the nation's inner cities and drained many urban Black males of any hope for success in the traditional structures of American society. Subsequently, many of today's inner-city Black male youth no longer gauge success by the ability to earn a respectable livelihood, but by how quickly one can acquire expensive goods. Cut off from meaningful participation in the social and economic life of the nation, disproportionate numbers of these young men pursue alternative paths that are too often fraught with gang warfare, drug addiction, and high rates of human immunodeficiency virus (HIV) infection (Hine et al., 2000). It is not surprising then, that education has lost its value among these youth. Education, in their view, is too slow a process for acquiring wealth.

The Present as Lack of Perspective: Current Conditions

The cycle of poverty into which too many urban Black male youth are locked has been perpetuated by the large numbers of single, female-headed households in today's inner-city Black communities. More than half of all African Americans under the age of 18 years live in families with only one parent (Hine et al., 2000). These households suffer disproportionately from limited earning capacity, meager public assistance, and poor housing conditions—conditions that can handicap children for the rest of their lives (Table 5.2).

Table 5.2 Poverty Status of Persons, Families, and Children Under 18 Years, Black Female-Headed Households 1959–1998

Year	Families with female householder,* no husband present. Number below poverty level, in thousands.	
	Total	Children under 18 years in female household
1959	2,416	1,475
1966	3,160	2,107
1970	3,656	2,383
1975	4,168	2,724
1980	4,984	2,944
1985	5,342	3,181
1990	6,005	3,543
1991	6,557	3,853
1992	6,799	3,967
1993	6,955	4,104
1994	6,489	3,935
1995	6,553	3,954
1996	6,123	3,619
1997	5,654	3,402
1998	5,629	3,366

*Abridged to include only African American females.
Source: US Department of Commerce, Bureau of the Census, Current Population Reports, Series P-60-198, "Poverty in the United States" and "Income, Poverty, and Valuation of Noncash Benefits," various years.

The high incarceration rates of urban Black males has further perpetuated this cycle because incarcerated men cannot contribute or provide economic relief to their families. A 2000 Justice Policy Institute study found 791,600 Black men behind bars, a number far exceeding the 603,000 who were enrolled on college campuses nationwide (Hacker, 1992). In 1970, these numbers were decidedly different, with 143,000 Black men in prison nationwide compared to 463,700 enrolled in higher education. It is interesting to note the racial makeup of the nation's prison inmates between the years of 1930 and 2000. As shown in Table 5.3, the incarceration rates for

Black men has been increasing steadily over those decades, while the rates for White men have shown a marked decrease from 76.7% to 36.1%. By 2000, the majority group, which outnumbers African Americans in the larger society by 10 to 1, is now in the minority in the nation's prisons.

Table 5.3 Racial Makeups of Prison Inmates (in %)

	1930	**1950**	**1970**	**2000**
White	76.7	69.1	60.5	36.1
Black	22.4	29.7	35.8	46.3
Other*	0.9	1.2	3.7	17.6

*Mainly Hispanic.
Source: *Race of Prisoners Admitted to State and Federal Institutions, 1926–1986* (Bureau of Justice Statistics, 1991), and *Prisoners in 2001* (Bureau of Justice Statistics, 2002).

Significant changes occurred in Black male collegiate enrollment patterns between 1970 and 2000. One possible explanation for these changes is that contemporary Black males, especially those in urban areas, no longer recognize the socioeconomic and political value of education and/or it no longer seems attainable or desirable to them. Alternately, poor inner-city Black males may have become so commercialized in their thinking, as advanced via television and other media, that they presently prefer to engage in conspicuous consumption than in education. They would rather assume onerous credit burdens to purchase ephemeral, faddish items such as flashy clothes and fast cars than to finance their higher education. In other words, too many of today's Black male youth pursue validation through the management of image or outward appearance rather than substance, and they pursue their façades at whatever cost to self and community.

Compounding this, many inner-city Black males today lack living examples to help educate them about good and bad choices. They cannot identify with their historical forefathers who overcame economic, social, educational, and legal obstacles far more extreme than any currently encountered. As a result, those who lack father figures, or who have incarcerated fathers, turn to entertainment figures, especially rap artists, as role models. The all-too-common ghettoized music-video fantasy is too many of these young men's image of reality. As Wilson (1990) contends, this misguidance goes a long way in helping maintain both White economic and political dominance and Black subordination.

Conclusion

Without proper nurturing of young Black males by concerned, compassionate, and competent Black males, their emotional lives will continue to be informed by the images and lyrics presented in music/rap videos. To interrupt this pattern, Black males growing up in the inner city must be taught to identify with the historical struggles, errors, and triumphs of their forebears, and thus with themselves as the products of that past and examples of the future. Given a stronger sense of the contributions of and challenges facing independent-minded African American men who preceded them, they can better comprehend and appreciate their power as architects of their future and revisionists of their past.

The community of African American male scholars and activists must rise to the challenge of reaffirming manhood in young Black males. As a collective body, we must help our male youth meet and overcome successfully the life challenges they will face by providing them with positive examples of Black men in higher education, and by teaching them about the social and educational history of the Black experience in America. We must educate our urban males to this historical tactic by developing a comprehensive curriculum (K–12) that emphasizes and infuses the richness of African and African American culture and intellectual achievements. We must develop learning models that stress state competencies but require an in-depth study, which should begin at the kindergarten level using history to mentor, model, and map success for urban Black male students. We must insist upon African American history curricula during the beginning stages of these young men's academic foundation through high school as an important step. Given such materials, we can help thwart the learned psychological helplessness too many urban Black male youth develop due to exposure to years of institutionalized racist practices in education and better equip them to succeed.

References

Akbar, N. (1996). *Breaking the chains of psychological slavery*. Tallahassee, FL: Mind Productions.

Berlin, I. (1974). *Slaves without masters: The free negro in the antebellum South*. New York: The New Press.

Berry, M. F., & Blassingame, J. W. (1982). *Long memory: The Black experience in America*. New York: Oxford University Press.

Blassingame, J. W. (1972). *The slave community: Plantation life in the antebellum South*. New York: Oxford University Press.

Booker, C. (1996). *The state of Black America*. Retrieved July 15, 2004, from http://www.dc.peachnut.edu/~nreynold/Backup/stbm96htm

Boskin, J. (1986). *Sambo: The rise and demise of an American jester.* New York: Oxford University Press.
Bowles, S. (1976). *Schooling in capitalist America: Educational reform and the contradictions of economic life.* New York: Basic Books.
Carmichael, S., & Hamilton, C. (1967). *Black power: The politics of liberation in America.* New York: Random House.
Cullen, J. (1992). Divided houses. In C. Clinton & N. Silber (Eds.), *I's a man now: Gender and American men* (pp. 76–91). New York: Oxford University Press.
DuBois, W. E. B. (1935). *Black reconstruction in America 1860–1880.* New York: The Free Press.
———. (1969). *The souls of Black folk.* New York: Signet.
Elkins, S. M. (1968). *Slavery.* Chicago: The University of Chicago Press.
Foner, P. S. (Ed.). (1995). *The Black Panthers speak.* New York: Da Capo Press.
Franklin, J. H., & Moss, A. A. (1994). *From slavery to freedom: A history of African Americans* (7th ed.). New York: McGraw-Hill.
Hacker, A. (1992). *Two nations: Black and White, separate, hostile, unequal.* New York: Scribner.
Hine, D. C., Hine, W. C., & Harold, S. (2000). *The African American odyssey.* Englewood Cliffs, NJ: Prentice Hall.
Hughes, L. (1934). *The ways of White folks.* New York: Alfred Knopf.
Karenga, M. (1982). *Introduction to Black studies.* Inglewood, CA: Kawaida Publications.
King, M. L. (1967). *Where do we go from here: Chaos or community?* New York: Harper & Row.
Kunjufu, J. (1995). *Countering the conspiracy to destroy Black boys.* Chicago: African American Images.
———. (2001). *State of emergency: We must save African American males.* Chicago: African American Images.
Majors, R., & Billson, J. (1992). *Cool pose: The dilemmas of Black manhood in America.* New York: Touchstone.
McCartney, J. T. (1992). *Black power ideologies: An essay in African American political thought.* Philadelphia: Temple University Press.
Peterson, C., & Seligman, M. E. P. (1983). Learned helplessness and victimization. *Journal of Social Issues* 2, 103–16.
Phillips, U. B. (1966). *American Negro slavery: A survey of the supply, employment and control of Negro labor as determined by the plantation regime.* Baton Rouge: Louisiana State University Press. (Original work published 1918.)
Watkins, W. H. (2001). *The White architects of Black education: Ideology and power in America, 1865–1954.* New York: Teachers College Press.
Wilson, A. N. (1990). *Black on Black violence: The psychodynamics of Black self-annihilation in service of White domination.* New York: Afrikan World Infosystems.
Woodson, C. G. (1933). *The mis-education of the Negro.* Trenton, NJ: Africa World Press.

CHAPTER SIX

Racial Profiling

A Never-Ending Problem for America's Minorities

SHARON J. CHAMBERS

Introduction

The US Constitution guarantees all American citizens protective rights to life, liberty, and the pursuit of happiness. In the earliest days of the fledging nation, however, such privileges were not equally distributed to African Americans and other non-White minorities. It was not until the mid-twentieth century—when Blacks and other groups protested, rioted, challenged the establishment, fought, and died as participants in the civil rights movement—that these "inalienable" rights were rationed out to them.

Many American minorities have experienced firsthand the injustices and cruelties of racism and other forms of discrimination. They are well aware what lies beneath America's "dirty laundry." Their everyday living has helped them to distinguish American fact from American fiction and to see subtle injustices and inequalities for what they are. Of course, some minorities today believe that they have come a long way from those dismal days of second-class citizenship. Others, who have fought long and hard for justice and equality, view the rights and privileges that have been begrudgingly allotted to them as inadequate. They further believe those benefits are constantly under the threat of challenges, alterations, and elimination by the courts, by other mainstream sectors of American society, and by the insidious practice of racial profiling.

Racial profiling has a long and troubling track record in the United States. Long before the practice was labeled and defined, groups and cultures in America were predetermined to have certain attributes. For example, all Italian Americans were supposed to be associated with the Mafia; all Jewish Americans were viewed as cheap, money-grubbing swindlers; and all African Americans were believed to have strong tendencies to commit larceny and petty crimes (Kennedy, 1997). Racial profiling has served additionally as a dividing wedge, separating Blacks and other non-Whites from Whites in this country. African Americans in particular have encountered racial profiling in ways that affect their personal, professional, and business lives. Whether it occurs on the streets, highways, workplaces, or medical centers of this nation; or during the course of various transactions ranging from real estate, banking, marketing, and air, automobile and train transportation, the practice of racial profiling has plagued African Americans since the days of slavery. The terms *driving while Black, riding while Black, walking while Black, banking while Black, working while Black,* and *flying while Black,* are coined phrases that reflect how Blacks, in disproportionate numbers, are stopped, searched, singled out, interrogated, arrested, detained, scrutinized, watched, followed, assaulted, abused, and denied services by various sectors of American society that perpetuate injustice. Since the tragic events of September 11, 2001, Arab Americans have also experienced some of the same or similar forms of racial profiling that Blacks and other minorities have faced for years. As Sheridan (2004) reports, bias against Muslims is up 70% in the post-9/11 era.

In law-enforcement situations kindled by racial profiling, police officers have failed to read minority detainees their rights, applied excessive force, and been verbally abusive. Such actions, when they are not commensurate with the alleged crime committed, are violations of the US Constitution. They further perpetuate the breakdown of communication and the growth of mistrust between minority communities and police officials. In the face of recurrent patterns of police brutality, false arrests and imprisonments, police officials cannot expect such neighborhoods to freely welcome them with open arms and assist them with witness and fact-finding information.

The evidence about racial profiling comes in two varieties, anecdotal and statistical, but the values of both have been determined to be small and questionable because of the paucity of authentic research on either form. Harris (2002), for example, offers a story of how a Black man and his 12-year-old son were profiled by the Oklahoma Highway Patrol, not once, but twice. In both instances the victims were law-abiding citizens, and the patrol officer found no evidence of drugs or any crime having taken place. The father was handcuffed for trying to explain to the patrol officer he was violating his rights, as the patrol officer conducted a warrantless search and damaged the man's car. The victims' only recourse was to sue both the patrol officer and the state.

The limited amount of hard data available reveals that a significant number of Black motorists claim to have been routinely subjected to highway stops simply because of the color of their skin (MacDonald, 2003). After analyzing police traffic stops in Oakland, California, as well as data from a 2003 study conducted by The Rand Corporation, Johnson (2004) firmly concludes that racial profiling is worse than the police will admit. The Rand study found that 56% of the drivers stopped were Black compared to 14% of whom were White—a clear example of disparity in the criminal justice system. Equally disturbing is the finding that some police officers apparently have chosen to ignore their training, which obliges them to uphold the Constitution, and target minorities, an action that runs contrary to that document.

Statement of the Problem

The topic of this study became one of interest to this researcher for several reasons, two of which assumed the most prominence. First, racial profiling is a disturbing method that stems from stereotypical views and fears manifested from one generation to generation, and I wanted to get at the root cause of the practice. Second, the blatant unfairness of racial profiling was unsettling to me. That any human being could be pointed out and predetermined to have committed an unlawful act simply because of their race or cultural background is appalling, and such actions must be themselves the subject of scrutiny. Thus are my reasons for undertaking this examination. Further, this chapter will attempt to describe how racial profiling is unjust, harmful, and unconstitutional; and how it creates conflicts that divide communities in the United States and perpetuates mistrust of the criminal justice system by its citizens.

Research Questions

This research addresses the following questions:

1. What is racial profiling?
2. What are the causes of racial profiling?
3. Who is affected by racial profiling?
4. What harm does racial profiling cause?

5. Does racial profiling divide society?
6. Can it be avoided?
7. Is racial profiling a crime, and if so, what recourse does an individual have if he or she becomes a victim of it?

Assumptions

This research study is based on five assumptions:

1. Racial profiling is harmful to all.
2. Racial profiling is costly for the American judicial system.
3. Racial profiling breeds hostility among Whites and non-Whites.
4. Racial profiling creates distrust among Whites and non-Whites.
5. Racial profiling can ruin lives and cause deaths.

Limitations

This study is limited in the following ways:

1. The random selection of residents from Washington, D.C., Virginia, Maryland, Texas, and California jurisdictions.
2. The ages of the study sample, which were divided into the following categories: 19–25, 26–40, 41–65, and 66 years and older.
3. The sample population consisted of college and university students.

Critical Context

According to the laws in the United States, a person is innocent until proven guilty by a court of law. However, to some American minorities, the law reflects the unfair and inhuman treatment they received from those who are sworn to protect all citizens of our country—namely, police officers and agents of the American judicial system. In some instances, minority suspects' reports of threats, assaults, beatings, and abuse reveal that police officers' did indeed make premature predeterminations about their propensity to commit crimes based on their status as minorities. In short, absent any evidence of alleged wrongdoing, police officers placed too much attention on the color of their suspects' skin and/or the types of clothing they were wearing and subjected them to mistreatment before reading them their rights and giving them the opportunity to present their versions of what really happened, to obtain counsel, and to avoid forced self-incrimination. Tragically, some minority suspects will never get a chance to speak up for themselves or get a glimpse of justice in action because they died at the unruly hands of improperly trained officers. When reported by the media, news of such incidents can have an adverse effect on entire communities, resulting in rioting and protests. The impact can be surmountable and create lingering mistrust for the police and the court system.

Too often, the news coverage reveals that some minorities are tried twice at the time of the arrest and during the trial of an alleged suspect. This problem became quiet evident in the case of Rodney King, who was severely beaten by a group of White police officers at the scene of his arrest. What made this case unique is that the videotape evidence showed Mr. King lying on the ground, while police officers continued to use excessive force, by beating Mr. King senseless. The King incident brought excessive force to the forefront, ignited a riot in the neighboring community, and shook the conscience of American viewers, by showing them the ugly side of what happens when an arrest gets out of control. The citizens who participated in the riot caused vandalism, fires, severe property damage, and the increase police involvement that resulted in arrests.

The question is what rights do suspects have when police officers arrest them? Part of the answer would be the US Constitution and the other part would be consulting a criminal attorney to be helpful in the blanks. The US Constitution determines that a suspect has special rights under the Fourth and Fifth Amendments of the US Constitution. The Fourth Amendment involves protection from *unlawful search and seizure*. Several cases involving the Fourth Amendment and provide background information are *Terry v. Ohio*, 393 US 1 (1968); *Whren v. United States*, US (1968); *Schneckloth v. Bustamonte*, 412 US 218 (1973); and *Illinois v. Wardlow*, No. 98–1036 (2000). Under the Fifth Amendment, the Miranda rights stems from a landmark ruling issued by the US Supreme Court, from the *Miranda v. Arizona*[1] case. The Fifth Amendment rights includes *the right to remain silent, anything his rights are a person may say can will be used in a court of law, the individual has a right to an attorney*, and *if the person can't afford an attorney, one will be appointed to represent him or her*. The rights apply to all criminal cases. During the course of criminal proceedings, a case is generally processed following the arrest and up to the conclusion of trial and any appeals that may apply. The sets are as follows:

- Arrest
- Booking and bail
- Arraignment
- Plea bargains
- Preliminary hearing

- Pretrial motions
- Trial
- Sentencing
- Appeals

Racial profiling can occur in any of the above steps (Kalogeras, 2003). However, much debate continues among experts, criminologists, police officials, courts, White and non-White communities, about whether or not racial profiling is necessary, or problematic. Many civil rights activists and special interests groups have made some strong arguments against for racial profiling and have repeatedly demanded that the system be overhauled to remove impediments that have crippled the criminal justice system for years, because of reinforced racial disparities that have taken the place of fair justice for all.

The National Association for the Advancement of Color People (NAACP), Human Rights Watch, and the American Civil Liberties Union (ACLU) argues that racial profiling stems from racism and discrimination. These agencies lobby and fight for the individual rights and freedom afforded under the US Constitution and the applicable laws under the Civil Rights Act of 1964. When necessary, lawyers provide legal advice and representation when an individual's constitutional rights are violated or infringed upon. In some cases, these organizations have argued before the applicable appellant courts and the US Supreme Court.

According to information provided by the Justice Department, African Americans, Hispanics, and other minorities were on the federal death penalty more often than Whites were. An article printed in the October 24, 2003, issue of the *Washington Post* (Whitlock, 2003, p. B01) published reiterated a study citing disparity in Maryland drug incarcerations. The Maryland Legislative Black Caucus commissioned the study. The statistical data emphasized how Blacks are incarcerated 18 times more than Whites are. Between 1986 and 1999, more than 94% of the growths in drug prison admissions were African American prisoners.

The invisible divide still exist on America's soil and surfaces in the form of discrimination, racism, bias, and disparities that continue to separate the citizens of the United States because of stereotypical views, myths, and negative influences that have been perpetuated from generation to generation. If we were to scratch beneath the surface of racial profiling, we would find some of the contributing factors to be misguided, and stereotypical beliefs engrained in society that have found there way in the way police conducts arrest and how a suspect is treated throughout the criminal justice system process. Unfortunately, minorities of every economic level continue to fight an up hill battle in obtaining justice and their piece of the rock that is known to some as the United States as the "American Dream." It is important that regardless of race or cultural background, many minorities are hard workers, make an honest living, pay taxes, try to live and raise their children right, and want the same things in life that their White counterparts want out of life. Unfortunately, many minorities are continually being suspect and placed under a microscope because of their skin color, regardless of economic and educational background. The compelling historical evidence and documentation accumulated during and after the industrial revolution and civil rights era have proven what really happens to victims when brutal racial profiling tactics are used. Such tactics serve no purpose but to wreak harm on its intended victim.

The subject of racial profiling is experienced on a daily basis in the Black, Hispanic, and various other non-Anglo communities. It continues to stir mistrust between White and non-White communities, and strikes against the very fabric of our society, by dividing minority and White communities, while at the same time pit them against each other. The courts have many documented cases that provide information on the allegations of racial profiling and civil rights violations, stemming out of an excessive force complaint, false arrest, and imprisonment, as well as other forms of injustices.

Methodology and Research Design

Instrument

In this study, the researcher has created and developed a 10-item interview survey guide to make an attempt to measure perceptions and objectivity. While perceptions are also needed and welcomed, objectivity is necessary for this topic because of the social, political, and economic ramifications. To make sure that the interviewees have an accurate understanding as to what the interviewer is asking, clarifications may be provided.

Data collection

An in-depth review of the data collected has determined the study to be comprised of populations consisted of college and university students and other individuals from various racial, economic, educational, financial, and business backgrounds. Both sexes participated in the study. The age groups range from 19–25, 26–40, 41–65, and 66 and up. Due to limited administrative assistance and time constraints during the course of preparing this survey and collecting the data, the researcher circulated as many surveys as possible. A self-addressed, stamped envelope was given to the participants who were unable to complete the surveys immediately. Of the 50 completed surveys received by the researcher, 30 were completed and returned in person, 11 were completed by telephone, 8 were completed and returned by US mail, and 1 was completed and returned by e-mail.

The researcher embarked into several residential areas, a shopping mall area, and a neighborhood university in an attempt to interview individuals for completing a survey that consisted of 10 questions. Initially, the researcher conducted a dry run in order to assess the potential interests and responses from members in the southwest community. Five individuals, consisting of two Blacks and three Whites, declined to participate in the survey. The researcher noted the reluctance to participate in the survey and limited the locations where the data was collected. In addition to the physical location where the data was collected, the researcher used the telephone and an e-mail service as means of collecting data. The researcher conducted the 11 telephone interviews with participants who resided in Washington, D.C., Maryland, and California.

Data reduction

Once the data were gathered and compared, the items were tabulated manually. Afterward, the data were paired and analyzed, question by question.

Sample and pretest of analysis

While the sampling in this study is rather small and limited, it still remains to be an adequate indication of perceptions as well as objectivity concerning racial profiling of minorities in the United States. Of course, the researcher is not attempting in any way to say that perceptions can be measured; however, those human feelings are often "real" and are representative of members of a society. Therefore, the interview guide that is used in this study is only a clear format of questions that the researcher would like to have answered in conjunction with the research questions asked earlier in this work.

When the 50 study participants were asked if they had a friend or a relative who had experienced any form of racial profiling, 62% of the African American interviewees answered "yes," while 14% responded "no." The sample group included one member from African, Asian, Hispanic, Iranian, Native American, Latino, and Black African backgrounds, respectively. One member classified as "other" made up 2% of the sample and responded "no." One "unknown" member, representing another 2% of the sample, did not respond to the question. The number of White participants was three, which represented 6% of the sample. Of that 6%, there were 4% who responded "yes" and 2% who said "no."

According to the majority of responses, the interviewees felt that racial profiling was a crime against society. Forty-one of the respondents said "yes," including 35 Blacks and 3 Whites. The African, Asian, "other," and 1 Hispanic responded "yes," while the Latino and the Iranian said "no." The "unknown" participant declined to respond. The latter 3 participants who responded "no" or declined to answer probably did not have an accurate understanding of the question or were not in tune with the news reports and other forms of media available in the United States. In addition, 49 participants believed that racial profiling affected minorities negatively in the criminal justice system. The 3 Whites included in this study felt the same as the Blacks and are included in the 49. Only 1 participant, a Middle Easterner, disagreed. This is an indication that the majority of those interviewed perceived the criminal justice system in a dim light, which can also cause mistrust of law enforcers and those with legal authority. At the same time, 33 Blacks felt that racial profiling was avoidable and 14 answered "no." The 1 Hispanic, 1 Latino, 1 Iranian, 1 "other," and 2 Whites also agreed. However, 1 White respondent was undecided.

The participants had mixed opinions about whether or not the media perpetuated racial profiling through the types of programming shown on television, movies, cable television, and in the newspapers. Thirty-two members of the Black community felt strongly about media exposure and its influence; only 5 gave "no" responses. Two White participants agreed with the 32 Blacks and responded "yes," but the third White member was undecided. The 2 indigenous Africans, the 1 Asian, and the 1 Hispanic were against the idea that the media maybe problematic and marked their responses "no." The "unknown" interviewee agreed with the African and Asian participants and answered "no."

What was unusual about the responses to the question of skin color, religion, or national origin determining whether a person is a responsible US citizen, was that 47 responses were "no," and 2 Blacks and 1 Hispanic gave "yes" responses. The "unknown" participant gave no response to the question. The breakdown of the 47 "no" responses included 37 Blacks, 3 Whites, and 7 responses from the African, Native American, Asian, Iranian, Latino, and Hispanic members.

When asked about whether or not racial profiling breeds hostility between the police and minority communities, the responses were interesting. Blacks comprised 35 "yes," 2 "no," 1 no response to the question, and 1 no response to the question. The 3 Whites agreed and responded "yes." Seven (7) members, consisting of other participants, except for the "other," who responded "no." The unknown participant did not respond to the question. The Africans, Asian, and "other" agreed with the majority of the Black and White survey participants, responding "yes" to the question. The opinion of the Latino and Hispanic participants were split. This is an indication that the public may not be happy about the type of programming shown on television and that the public is getting better educated.

The issues of police officers' training and public outcry over the media may have influenced the responses given by the survey participants. Accordingly, Blacks strongly agreed, with a high response of 36 "yes," 2 undecided, and 1 "no." The 3 Whites also agreed, marking their surveys "yes." The African and Asian participants' responses of "yes" concurred with majority of the Blacks and all of the Whites. The Hispanic participant disagreed and marked his response "no."

It is interesting to see the numbers on whether the participants viewed racial profiling as a form of discrimination. Blacks returned 36 "yes," 1 "no," 1 undecided, and 1 no response to the question. The 3 White members agreed with Blacks, marking their survey forms "yes." The 1 Hispanic marked his response "no," and the African and Asian members agreed by marking their forms "yes." The fact that the Hispanic marked his form "no" may be indicative that he may not have been exposed to the news media. This individual may need more information, but the individual did not request any.

The events of September 11, 2001, are inescapable because of recurrent news coverage in print, television, and cable programming. A question about September 11th was included in the survey to gauge whether or not the public shows interest in post-September 11th scenarios and problems. On that question, Blacks comprised 22 "yes" responses, 10 "no" responses, 5 undecided responses, and 1 no response to the survey.

Integrative Conclusion

New understanding

During the research phrase of this project, the researcher was able to pinpoint resource information and recurrent instances of racial profiling to be a remote control away. Something as simple as television and cable repeatedly overemphasized negative imagines of minority men carrying guns, using drugs, and abusing women. The women are shown wearing provocative clothing and using foul language on drama, sitcoms, movies, and commercials, on a 24 hours basis. The media considered this entertainment! Anyone who turns on a television, cable, picks up a periodical, or listens to the music and news on the radio will get a daily dose of slanted reality among the propagandized stories and scenarios that reflect minorities in compromised or troubled situations.

Many parents, consumer activists, and specialists in the medical and mental health field have given television and other forms of media coverage a thumb down. They argue that too much unsupervised television and cable is unhealthy for children and adolescents, because they are vulnerable to learning and developing negative habits and attitudes from certain programs on television. According to articles written in the *Science Magazine*,[2] televisions have been linked to attention deficit hyperactive disorder known as ADHD that involves behavioral problems.

Racial profiling is used as a marketing tool, to market and target various products in minority neighborhoods that are not marketed in White neighborhoods. The researcher found that within 1-mile radius, there were 10 instances of advertisements of expensive tennis shoes, hip-hop fashions, party activities, fast cars, and movies. Further, very little information on education or educational programs were seen or available in stores, malls, and window displays. However, the reverse was seen in the downtown business district and suburbs of the District of Columbia and neighboring areas in Maryland and Virginia.

The researcher consulted a number of resources that include books, magazines, journals, articles, newspapers, and several television documentaries and relied upon questia.com, the world's largest online library, as a one of the primarily and secondary research tools. The search strategies used in the questia.com website was twofold. The first strategy was under the category of "racial" and "profiling" and "America," that yielded 376 books, 141 journal articles, 99 magazine articles, and 70 newspaper articles. The second strategy was under "racial profiling" and found to be in excess of 1,068 total results, that consists of 277 books, 202 journal articles, 208 magazines, 279 newspaper articles, and 2 encyclopedia articles. All of these resources show a true indication that current materials are available. However, the most notable sources used in this chapter are the following books: *Driving While Black; Race, Crime, and the Law; Profiles in Injustice; Crime and Punishment in America; Are Cops Racist?; Invisible Punishment: The Collateral Consequences of Mass Imprisonment;* and *The Many Costs of Racism*.

Recommendations

At the heart of racial profiling lie stereotypical views, misconceptions, misunderstanding, cultural adversary, racism, discrimination, bias, prejudices, injustice, disparities, and closed mindedness. All of which add more fuel to the fires that racial profiling has created. During the survey interviewing process, several questions were brought to the attention of the researcher. Several of the interviewees expressed concerned about how our society will not change, because racism and discrimination is a recurrent cycle that is engrained in the heart of man for hundreds of years. Several comments were mentioned about how stiffer laws will not change the attitudes of Whites, unless some minorities improve on the way they present themselves in public and in the way they conduct themselves by ridding the "thug mentality."

An article in the November 2003 issue of *Black Enterprise* magazine[3] stated that African Americans consumers are a powerful force in the US economy. As a minority population, they are a significant and major driving force in maintaining the economy. However, they still do not get the respect and treatment they deserve from White retailers, businesses, and vendors. The author of this article suggest that African Americans should not invest or spend money on goods and services, that do not respect the dignity and rights that African Americans and other minorities deserve. An article published in the *USA Today*[4] newspaper also focused on the spending habits of African Americans, who make up 12% of the US population, yet account for 30% of American's alcohol consumption. Additionally, the article pointed out about how Blacks and other minorities investing less than their White counterparts do.

The researcher notes that in the District of Columbia there is either a liquor store or convenient store in walking distant and on many corners and/or streets where minorities reside. This breeds alcoholism, crime, and an unsafe and unsanitary environment for minority children to live in. Unfortunately, there are minorities who have fallen prey to overly priced consumer goods, conveniences, and cheap liquors that do nothing but drain minorities' income, dignity, health, safety, and their ability to reenter into the work world and function in society. Surely, it is not enough for Whites to merely tolerate and piece meal respect to selected persons of color. The respect for minorities should be the same as Whites. Nevertheless, minorities must continue to fight for respect in an uncaring and underappreciated society.

Enough is enough; many minorities must learn to identify racial profiling for what it is and deal with it head on. They must stop patronizing businesses that conduct racial profiling, disrespect them, by treating them unprofessionally. Minorities are entitled to live, breath, and survive in the United States. They must demand respect from their White peers and other cultures that disrespect them and not be a continual doormat, to be walked over, on a daily basis. According to the book *Driving While Black* (Meeks, 2000, p. 105), "No person in the United States shall, on the ground of race, color, or national origin, be excluded from participation in, be denied the benefits of, or be subjected to discrimination under any program or activity receiving Federal financial assistance. This clause falls under Title VII of the Civil Rights Act of 1964. Thus, discrimination is illegal, but still operating in the United States of America.

Discrimination will never disappear as long as prejudice, hatred, bias, inequality, unfairness, because racism thrives in the hearts and minds of humankind. There are no absolute ways to alter the way a person thinks, decides, choose, and act on any impulse he or she desires, because he or she has *free will*. The laws that are suppose to protect all citizens of the United States look good on paper and serve an important purpose for society. However, the reality of everyday life, for some minorities affected by racial profiling, proves how much such laws mean to some individuals, businesses and institutions, who chose to ignore and trample on the rights and lives of others, and still get a good night sleep. It is important for all Americans learn to treat minorities, others who is less fortune, with respect regardless of their race, religion, culture, economic, financial appearance, or background. To target one race versus the other is discriminatory.

Many minorities strive to live decent lives, work hard, pay taxes, give back to their communities, and do the best they can to raise their children and take care of the family structure, despite their financial status. The negative things that an individual or small group of a specific race or culture does do not represent its entire population. Historically, there are many African Americans, Hispanics, and other minorities who have contributed to the growth, development and our country, the United States of America. Many minorities have the same hopes and dreams of getting their *piece of the rock*, known to many as "*the American Dream*." Unfortunately, too many minorities' dreams are delayed and crushed by the unfair and unequal opportunities that are rationed out to them, while their White counterparts receive an abundance of opportunities without lifting a finger.

Martin Luther King, Jr., Nelson Mandela, and a few other Black activists have led the way, with steadfast determination and diligence. Today, Martin Luther King, Jr. is gone, Nelson Mandela has his hands full in South Africa, and we do not have any real Black leaders in the United States who can fill their shoes or sincerely work toward fulfilling King's dream. According to Cornel West's book *Race Matters*, Black leadership is in crisis, because today's so-called leaderships are centered on high-profile men, who are self-absorbed, lacking moral leadership, and virtue. Blacks currently do not have the dedicated Black leaders who can step up to the plate and meet the challenge (West, 2001, p. 58). Therefore, it is up to Blacks, Hispanics, and other minorities, to do their best by gaining the essential knowledge, skills and education, and pass these positive qualities onto their children, because they are the future of our country. Now is the time for each one of us to take a detailed inventory of ourselves and take the necessary steps to improve our lives and help those we love, with an abundance of love, by creating and reinforcing positive educational and social elements in our communities.

Our country and the individual who hold the purse strings, of our country, needs a serious reality check, because globalization has arrived like a thief in the night and is here to stay. Blacks and Whites are no longer the primary races in the United States. According to an article in the *Newsweek Magazine* (Kantrowitz, 2004, p. 50), the face of America has changed. Many races and cultures from other countries are now citizens of the United States, have learned to live and thrive in our country by blending the East and West, and enriched their lives economy and financially. According to the Census Bureau, the population of the United States will change by the year 2025 and the White population will decrease by the continual increase of immigrants and culture that come to the United States on a daily basis.

It is essential that minorities pull their share of the weight by re-education and revitalizing positive images. More impact studies need to be conducted on race in criminal case, documenting the criminal charges, and the sentence imposed. Sensitivity, cultural, and diversity training should be given on a periodic basis in all government and private business sectors, to help reduce stereotypical views in society and bring clarity to the understanding to unusual cultural behavior and attitudes that are stigmatized, due to lack of awareness and knowledge.

Each parent should conduct an educational checkup and find ways to improve the quality time and attention with their young children. They must develop ways to refine, and promote a child's educational interests, social–psychological development, by eliminating destructive, degrading and negative conducts and attitudes from the family structure and replace them with humanity, love, understanding, patience, discipline, and random acts of kindness. Parents must tell children the reality of life and train them to handle critical decisions and problems in a constructive manner. The line of communication between parents and children must be bridged and tighten, because parents have no control on what goes on in society, but they do have control over how their children are to be raised and grow up to be educated, productive and responsible citizens and role models.

There is a sharp rise in juvenile committing serious crimes, occupying jail cells, and seats in courtrooms. According to an article by the *Washington Post*, the court system and the District of Columbia's Youth Services need to be fixed! They are incapable and unprepared to handle the increased juvenile cases (Chan, 2003, p. B01) and minors in criminal court, because of budgetary constraints, lack of workforce, and expertise needed (Labbe, 2004, p.

B3). Parents who have allowed television and cable television programs to babysit their children need to pull the plug, because these are time-wasting, unhealthy, anti-exercise pastimes that add little to the emotional, psychological, and physical development of children. A little compromising by parents can go a long way!

Timetable

This timetable has been created to give indications of tasks involved in this research. This study was carried out in a 10-week period.

Tasks	Weeks									
	1	2	3	4	5	6	7	8	9	10
Selecting topic	X									
Compiling data		X	X	X	X	X	X	X	X	
Interviews					X	X	X	X	X	
Drafts			X	X	X	X	X	X	X	
Completion of project										X

Appendix A: Racial Profiling Survey Results: Sex and Education of Participants

Educational background of participants	Race—Black/African American population	
Completed college	30	
Current college student	6	
Completed vocational/trade school	2	
Completed high school only	1	
Sex of participants		
Female population	25	Ages 37–69
Male population	7	Ages 25–63
Sex unknown	7	Ages 26–79
Total participants	39	

Appendix B: Interview Guide: Racial Profiling: A Never-Ending Problem Against Minorities

RACIAL PROFILING SURVEY

This survey is created in preparation of an academic report on racial profiling. It represents the views and perceptions of the public. Please answer all questions honestly and do not leave any question unanswered. If the participant does not have an opinion on a question presented, please mark the answer to the question as "undecided." Do not provide your name or residential information.

Demographics

- Your Age_____ Sex: Female_____ Male_____
- Race _____ Your Occupation _____
  (e.g., Student, Teacher, Professional, Police Officer, Medical Doctor, etc.)
- Your Education: (please check one) completed high school_____ completed college_____, took some college courses_____, or completed trade school_____, or other occupation_____.

	Questions	Yes	No	Undecided
1.	Have you, a friend or a relative of yours experienced any form of racial profiling?			
2.	Do you believe that racial profiling is a crime against society?			
3.	Do you believe that racial profiling negatively affects minorities in the criminal justice system? (i.e., police officers and the court system)			
4.	Do you believe racial profiling is avoidable? (e.g., driving while Black, walking while Black)			
5.	Do you feel that the media perpetuates racial profiling by the type of programming shown on television, movies, cable television, and in the newspapers?			
6.	Do you feel that a person's skin color, religion, or national origin should determine that they are a responsible US citizen?			
7.	Does racial profiling breed hostility between the police and minority communities?			

Survey continued on page 81

Questions	Yes	No	Undecided
8. Do police officers need more sensitivity training and diversity training in order to more effectively deal with the public?			
9. Do you believe racial profiling is a form of discrimination?			
10. Do you believe racial profiling has put a strain on the US economy, since the events of 9/11/2001?			

- Comment (optional)

Endnotes

1. *Miranda v. Arizona*, 384 US 436.
2. Johnson et al., "Television viewing and aggressive behavior during adolescence and adulthood," *Science*, May 29, 2002. p. 2468.
3. Williams, D., *Black Enterprise*, November 2003, p. 28.
4. Young, Y., *USA Today*, April 2, 2004, p. A09.

References

Harris, D. A. (2002). *Profiles in injustice*. New York: The New Press.
Kennedy, R. (1997). *Race, crime, and the law*. New York: Random House.
MacDonald, H. (2003). *Are cops racist?* New York: Ivan R. Dee.

Further Reading

Alpert, G. P. et al. (2002). How reasonable is the reasonable man? Police and excessive force. *Journal of Criminal Law and Criminology 85*, 481.
American Civil Liberties Union. (2004a, May). *Flawed enforcement*. Available from: www.aclu.org
American Civil Liberties Union. (2004b, February). *Sanctioned bias: Racial profiling since 9/11*. Available from: www.aclu.org
Berliner, M. (2003). *Diversity and multiculturalism: The new racism*. Irvine, CA: The Ayn Rand Institute.
Bork, R. H. (2003, July–August). Civil liberties after 9/11. *Commentary, 116*, 29–35.
Callahan, G. et al. (2001, August–September). *The roots of racial profiling*. Available from: http://reason.com/01081fe.gc.the.shtml
Carter, T. (2002, 14 January). Profiling is "flawed" tool to beat terror. *The Washington Times*. Available from: http://findarticles.com/plarticles/mi_go 1637/is_200201/ai-n6738660

Chan, S. (2003, 5 December). Violent crime arrests up for DC juveniles. *The Washington Post*, p. B1.

Chiagouris, L. et al. (1997). Where perception meets reality: The social construction of lifestyles. In L. R. Kahle & L. Chiagouris (Eds.), *Values, Lifestyles and Psychographics*. Mahwah, NJ: Lawrence Erlbaum Associates.

Davis, A. (2003). *Prosecution and race: The power and privilege of discretion*. Washington, DC: The Sentencing Project.

Davis, R. (2001). *Racial profiling: What does the data mean? A practitioner's guide to understanding data collection and analysis*. Alexandria, VA: National Organization of Black Law Enforcement Executives.

Ferguson, C. (2004). Black, White disparities abound, study says. *AOL News*. New York: The Associated Press.

Garner, B. (1979). *Black's law dictionary* (7th ed.). New York: West Group.

Garner, B. A. (1999). *Black's dictionary*. St. Paul, MN: West Group.

Harrison, G. (2002). From racial to religious profiling. *Free Inquiry* 22(3), 21.

Hughes, Z. (2004). Survival guidelines for supermoms. Available from: http://www.findarticles.com/plarticles/mi_m1077/is_5_59/ai-113681684

Johnson, C. (2004). *Profiling is worse than police will admit*. Available from: www.sfgate.com

Jones, R. (2002). Blacks just don't care: Unmasking popular stereotypes about concern for the environment among African-Americans. *International Journal of Public Administration*, 25(2), 221–251.

Kalogeras, S. (2003). *Annotated bibliography: Racial disparities in the criminal justice system*. Washington, DC: The Sentencing Project.

Kantrowitz, B. (2004, 22 March). America masala. *Newsweek*, p. 50

King, M. L., Jr. (1963). *I have a dream*. Available from: http://www.mecca.org/~crihts/dream.html

Knott, T. (1999, 2 December). DC cabbies deserve the right to choose their fares. *The Washington Times*. Available from: http://www.highbeam.com/doc/161--57901272.html

Labbe, T. (2004, 26 February). DC can fix youth services, official testifies. *The Washington Post*, p. B3.

LaFee, S. (2000). Profiling bad apples. *School Administrator* 57(2), 6.

Landau, T. (1996). When police investigate police: A view from complainants. *Canadian Journal of Criminology* 38, 291–316.

Leary, W. (2003). Eliminating racial profiling in school discipline. *School Administrator* 60(9), 41.

MacDonald, H. (2001, Spring). The myth of racial profiling. *City Journal*. New York: The Manhattan Institute.

Mansoor, S. (2002). I'm a Muslim, but I can still fly: Arabs and Asians complain of racial profiling, but the widely traveled Sarfaz Mansoor finds US airline security less onerous than he expected after the 11 September atrocities. *New Statesman Magazine* 131(4614), 32.

Marshall, T. (1999, 16 October). US concedes torture exists in justice system, but

contends punishment helps deter it. *The Washington Times*, p. A1.
Massaquoi, H. J. (1991, July). How to stop police brutality. *Ebony*, p. 46.
Matthew, C. (2001, 2 November). Traffic data raise profiling concerns. *Washington Times*, p. B1.
McEwen, T. (1996, April). *National data collection on police use of force*. Alexandria, VA: Institute of Law and Justice.
McLeod, L. J. (2003). The wages of sin: Glenn Loury's "The anatomy of racial inequality." *Social Theory and Practice Journal 29*(2), 226–237.
Meeks, K. (2000). *Driving while Black*. New York: Broadway Books.
O'Brien, P. (2004, 2 May). Redefining our basic rights. *The Washington Post*. Available from: http://www.highbeam.com/doc/1pz-168001.html
Ramirez, D. et al. (2003). Defining racial profiling in a post-September 11 world. *The American Criminal Law Review 40*(3), 1195–1233.
Random House. (2001). *Unabridged dictionary*. New York: Random House.
Reed, F. (2000, 2 February). Police "racial profiles" based on street instincts, not bias. *The Washington Times*, p. A4.
———. (2001, 12 February). Prince George's cop speaks out on police indifference. *The Washington Times*, p. A1.
Rocchio, V. F. (2000). *Reel racism: confronting Hollywood's construction of Afro-American culture*. Boulder, CO: Westview Press.
Schmitt, E. et al. (1999). *Characteristics of drivers stopped by police, 1999*. US Department of Justice. Washington, DC: BJS Statisticians.
Sheridan, M. B. (2004, 3 May). Bias against Muslims up 70%. *The Washington Post*, p. A-12.
Spencer, W. (2001, September). *Texas commission on law enforcement: intermediate arrest, search, and seizure, course number 2108*. Austin: Texas Commission on Law Enforcement.
Trende, S. P. (2002). Why modest proposals offer the best solution for combating racial profiling. *Duke Law Journal 50*(1), 331.
Washington, A. T. (1999, 2 April). For Black people, an everyday nightmare. *The Washington Times*, p. 2.
———. (2001, 5 May). To see racial profiling in action, just turn on the TV. *The Washington Times*, p. 2.
Whitlock, C. (2003, 24 October). Study cites race disparity in MD drug incarceration. *The Washington Post*, p. B1.
Williams, D. (2003, November). Hit discriminators where it hurts: African Americans must use their vast spending power to make change. *Black Enterprise*. Available from: http://blackenterprise.com/archiveopen.asp?source=archivetabl12003/H/1103-0z.htm
West, C. (2001). *Race matters*. New York: Vintage Books.
Young, Y. (2004, 1 April). Tough choices for tough times. *USA Today*. Available from: http://www.usatoday.com/news/opinion/editorials/2004-04-01-young-x.html

CHAPTER SEVEN

Equalizing Educational Opportunities for African American Students

The Evaluation and Evolution of Teacher Education

RENEE WHITE-CLARK, GRACE LAPPIN, AND ODESA WEATHERFORD-JACOBS

Abstract

At the 50th anniversary of *Brown v. Board of Education*, the educational opportunities of many African American students remain inferior because many teachers are academically and culturally unprepared. Training teachers for culturally diverse classrooms remains a major concern in teacher education and may be the single most important factor in achieving educational equity. Therefore, the evaluation of current and past practices of teacher preparation must shed light on the evolving process of teacher education reform. Educators must examine what we have done, what we are doing, and most importantly, what we must do to equalize educational opportunities for African American students.

Introduction

Fifty years after *Brown v. Board of Education*, we question the progress made toward educational equality for African American children. Some may contend that we as a nation have made significant progress toward equitable educational opportunities for all. Others believe that the educational opportunities of many African American students remain separate and unequal within the walls of America's culturally isolated "high needs" schools. Sadly, students from diverse backgrounds remain overrepresented in special education programs and have limited access to services for learners with gifts and talents. Clearly, significant numbers of culturally diverse children are being educated in schools with unequal resources and are receiving an inequitable education from cross-culturally—and often academically—ill-prepared teachers.

The *Brown* case was to mark the end of the physical segregation of students. In an attempt to equalize the education of African American children, the courts ordered the schools to desegregate, changing physical facilities and curricula. The assumption was that with exposure to the same facilities, teachers, and curricula these children would receive an equal education. Studies have found African American students were integrated with their White counterparts, attending schools with White teachers who were not trained to interact with cultural sensitivity nor to educate them from a multicultural perspective. Many multicultural advocates claim that for five decades a major educational factor has been overlooked and not sufficiently addressed: teacher preparation for America's culturally pluralistic classrooms.

Historical Perspective of African American Education (1619–1954)

Students of American education usually study the history and establishment of public schools from the perspective of the European American experience. However, upon reflection on the diverse participants in American public education, one must readily admit that the experience of European Americans, African Americans, and Native Americans is at once both separate and unequal. Educators know that experience and environment influence student attitudes, learning styles, and perceptions. The history of the social, cultural, and educational experiences of African Americans is different from the European American experience. Therefore, knowledge of African Americans' historical experiences related to education, and their efforts to participate in the social institution of public education, broadens the knowledge base of educators. This additional knowledge base provides educators with additional perspectives from which to approach teaching and learning in a pluralistic society.

Brown v. Board of Education is often the historical point at which discussion begins on the topic of seeking equal education for African Americans. However, a brief history of the conflicting sociological ideology in American public education is worthy of review. Educators who possess a multiperspective understanding of the history of American public education are more informed and perhaps better able to analyze issues and develop solutions to problems in American public education, especially in urban communities.

Courses in the foundations and history of American education usually begin by looking at life in America in the early seventeenth century. In colonial New England, education was used to promote and maintain the authority of government and religion. By using the tools of education (i.e., reading and writing), members of colonial communities would be able to read the Bible, obey the laws of God, and abide by the laws of the state. Also, New England Puritans viewed formal education as an effective tool for promoting the development of piety, instilling appropriate social behavior, and maintaining established social classes.

The town school and the Latin grammar schools were established in the 1600s. The locally controlled New England town school was attended by both boys and girls. The town school curriculum was a mixture of religion, reading, writing, and arithmetic. Class attendance depended on the needs of the family and the farm.

The sons of the upper class attended the Latin grammar school. The curriculum was designed to prepare students to attend college and focused on Latin authors such as Horace, Cicero, and Caesar. Greek authors, such as Isocrates and Homer, were studied by the more advanced students (Ornstein & Levine, 2003). In 1749, Benjamin Franklin published *Proposals Relating to the Education of Youth in Pennsylvania*. His proposal gives us insight into how deeply he valued education for youth. According to Franklin, the education of youth is the surest foundation of happiness for both family and nation. He believed that an increase in knowledge prevented mischievous consequences that resulted from ignorance. Further, Franklin encouraged the members of the community to unite to support youth, advance their usefulness, and help them to establish their business and family life. Franklin's proposal was among the first plans to provide a more utilitarian education than traditionally offered by the classical grammar schools. The academy movement spread very rapidly in the eighteenth and nineteenth centuries. Sometimes the academy was organized as a college, and other times it was high school. However, by the late nineteenth century, the academy was identified as any institution that provided secondary education. Benjamin Franklin's idea of education for the good of the youth of America was not extended to African American youth. However, the merit of his plan remains an important part of our American education history. This is also true of the monitorial school.

The monitorial school originated in England and was developed by Joseph Lancaster and Andrew Bell. In the United States, New York City established the first monitorial school in 1805. Monitorial schools allowed for the inexpensive education of large numbers of students by a single teacher aided by a cadre of better students. The monitorial school was not wildly successful, and by 1840 nearly all had closed. Although short lived, the monitorial system represented another step in the quest for better education for the American public (Pulliam, 1982; Johnson et al., 2005).

The African American Experience

In the early seventeenth century, Africans in America were classified as indentured servants. A large percentage of the European population was also classified as indentured servants. However, by the mid-seventeenth century, the colonial courts had begun to institute laws that contributed to separate and particularly different educational experiences for the African American and European American populations. To ensure a perpetual servant underclass, the colonies outlawed the education of African Americans (Wharton, 2002). Thus, less than 50 years after being brought to join immigrants in America, Africans and their descendants were denied formal education. However, Europeans in America continued their experiments in the development of programs and institutions for private and public education.

In 1837, Horace Mann became secretary of the Massachusetts State Board of Education and was the most active leader in the common school movement in the country (Pulliam, 1982). Briefly stated, there were three distinctive features to the common school movement: (1) to educate all children in a common school, (2) to use schools as an instrument of government policy, and (3) to create state agencies to control local schools. These three features are representative of the social and political organization of a school system. However, little or no serious consideration was given to the state or task of education for the African American population, free or enslaved, except by the African Americans themselves (Spring, 2000; Johnson et al., 2005). Even more distressing is that in states in which there had been at least segregated schools, laws were passed that outlawed education for African Americans. For example, in 1847 Missouri passed a law that forbade teaching African Americans to read and write.

Admittedly, from the early eighteenth century through the mid-nineteenth century and during the common school movement, some effort was made in the Northern states to educate African Americans. However, most Southern states declared education for African Americans illegal. In spite of social and legal barriers to their equitable participation in public education, African Americans courageously looked to the judicial system to solve issues of inequity in education more than 100 years before *Brown v. Board of Education*. For example, in 1849 attorney Charles Sumner represented a group of African American parents who petitioned the Massachusetts Supreme Court and sought to recover damages because their children were not allowed to enroll in any Boston school (except the Abiel Smith School for colored students). According to state law, it was unlawful to deny any student access to any public schools. However, in *Roberts v. The City of Boston* (1850), the court found that because special provisions (i.e., a school for colored children) had been made available, the plaintiffs' case was unfounded.

At the time of the Civil War (1861–1865), there were more than 4 million enslaved Africans. At the time of Emancipation (1865), at least 4 million Americans had been denied the opportunity to participate in the national endeavor for public education. Briefly stated, for nearly 250 years, an entire group of people in America had been denied experience and equity in education. In the mid-1860s, Congress established the Freedman's Bureau to create educational opportunities for the newly freed people. However, White resistance to African Americans potentially achieving the experience and realization of human rights, civil rights, and education was so extreme that by 1870 the education work of Freedman's Bureau had stopped. In contrast, for at least 250 years, generations of European Americans had experienced the social and cultural freedom to organize and participate in the social institution of education.

In 1870, the Freedman's Bureau was drawing to a close its activity in the education of African Americans. Although the country was moving toward developing the purpose and curriculum of the high school, the education experiences of African Americans continued to be a major challenge, and in 1899 the Supreme Court set the precedent for continued discrimination and inequity in education for African Americans.

In *Cummings v. School Board of Richmond County, Ga.* (1899), Supreme Court Justice John Marshall Harlan refused to grant relief to African Americans whose high school had been closed by county officials while the county's two high schools for White students remained open. Yet current education textbooks reflect the belief that high school was considered a necessary part of preparing citizens for work (Franklin, 2000; Spring, 2000). No mention is made of the fact that for the first half of the twentieth century, the majority of African American children who were able to attend school at all faced deplorable, inadequate, small, impoverished schools (Franklin, 2000). By the 1920s, the White majority population of students and parents had benefited from a more than 300-year experiment in improving American public education to meet their needs. Even so, in most of the Southern states during the 1929–1930 school year, more money was spent for school buses for White children than was spent for new schools for Black children (Franklin, 2000).

Between the 1920s and 1980s, and coinciding with the evolution of the junior high school (1920–1940) and the middle school (1960–1980), African Americans made major, and perhaps untold, efforts to achieve equity in education and civil rights. In 1954, the United States Supreme Court found in *Brown v. Board of Education* that separate was unequal. The truth is, *Brown* represents 335 years of inequity in American education. In other words, for at least 335 years, African American parents and their children did not, as a group of people, *experience* the knowledge Whites gained from having the freedom to participate in the activities of schooling, learning, and participating in society.

The *Brown* case was preceded by other cases that sought to address the issue of inequity in education in America. *Roberts v. The City of Boston* (1850) was cited earlier in this perspective on the history of American education. In April 1885, a bill was presented and passed by the Massachusetts legislature. This legislation provided that no distinction based on color, race, or religion should be made for any student applying for admission to any public school in the state of Massachusetts (African American Registry, 2004).

Fifty years after *Brown*, it is meaningful to recall that the move toward desegregation did not come easily. Reflection on what it took to arrive at where we are today is facilitated by examination of earlier Kansas education cases: for example, *Elijah Tinnon v. The Board of Education of Ottawa* (1881). In 1876, Elijah Tinnon and six other Kansas parents challenged the placement of their children in a separate room within the central school and questioned the qualifications of the teacher assigned to teach their children. Further, the parents demanded that their children be placed in the proper grades of the public school. The school board voted to place the African American students in graded classrooms. However, four years later, the school board opened a one-room school for Black children. Tinnon's demand that his son be returned to his original school was denied. In 1881, the Tinnon case was tried and found in favor of the plaintiff Elijah Tinnon (Brown Foundation for Educational Equity, Excellence and Research, 2000).

In *Knox v. The Board of Education of Independence* (1891), the Knox sisters, Bertha and Lily, passed one elementary school to reach the school they were assigned to. Their father, Jordon Knox, wanted his daughters to attend the school nearest their home. The case was decided in the Kansas Supreme Court. In its decision, the court cited the *Tinnon* case. The court found no authority for the second-class city of Independence to exclude Black children from schools designated for White children. Jordon Knox and four other parents (joint plaintiffs) won this case and were awarded court costs (Brown Foundation for Educational Equity, Excellence and Research, 2000).

Of course, Kansas, like other states, saw its share of disappointing cases. Consider *Reynolds v. The Board of Education of Topeka* (1903). In *Reynolds*, the Kansas Supreme Court held that first-class cities were allowed to operate separate elementary schools. Further, the Court held that the 14th Amendment of the US Constitution did not supercede Kansas' law (Brown Foundation for Educational Equity, Excellence and Research, 2000). In *Special Legislation for Kansas City, Kansas* (1905), the Kansas Legislature passed a special act permitting Kansas City to operate separate high schools. Student Mamie Richardson sued, but the Kansas Supreme Court upheld the constitutionality of the separation act (Brown Foundation for Educational Equity, Excellence and Research, 2000).

In *Cartwright v. The Board of Education of Coffeyville* (1906), the court's decision stated that the Board of Education had no power to exclude African American students from schools established for White children in the absence of a law that authorized such power in cities of the second class. This case seems to herald the eventual arrival of the findings in *Brown* (Brown Foundation for Educational Equity, Excellence and Research, 2000).

Knowledge of history is valuable to all stakeholders. This is especially true for educators. It is imperative that teacher education programs begin to require that preservice teachers know the history of the educational experiences of their diverse student populations, particularly in America. With this knowledge, teachers will have the foundation necessary to facilitate their endeavor to provide equity in education to all students.

Impacts on Teacher Education

> We must teach teachers how to teach to the average student. The needs of any student who is not average—special needs students, English as a second language students, and minority students—are to be met by specific courses on how to adapt or "compensate" the prototype curriculum to their needs. In other words these students are viewed as having deficits compared to "normal" students. (Wardle, 2003, p. 204)

In 1954, the *Brown* decision's ruling for desegregation was an attempt to equalize the educational opportunities for African American children. The courts ordered African American students to uproot from their neighborhood schools and attend schools with teachers who were, and still are, trained by Eurocentric and deficit-modeled teacher education programs. Many African American children were parted from the African American teachers who lived in their community, understood their cultural needs, and served as role models. Meanwhile, many African American teachers lost their teaching professions because the Black segregated schools were closed, and many of these teachers were not hired to teach in the integrated schools. The minority teacher pool was slim and has continued to decrease despite the increased enrollment of minority students. For example, in 1993–1994, Black, non-Hispanic teachers accounted for 9% of public school teachers, decreasing to 6% in 2002. Furthermore, more than 40% of schools across America have no teachers of color on staff (National Education Association, 2002).

Today, this academic concern continues to be compounded by the increase of African American students. The rapidly changing demographics of our country are being reflected in America's public schools. In 2002, 30% of the public school population was of minority descent. The steady increase of diverse students has been predicted to continue. By 2025, African American students will encompass 49% of the US public school population (US Census Bureau, 2000). This demographic trend will increase the probability of minority students completing their formal education without interacting with a teacher who represents their cultural or ethnic group. It also increases the likelihood of African American students being taught solely by middle-class White female teachers.

Despite these statistical changes, teachers are not receiving prerequisite training to meet the needs of African American children. To date, 50 years after *Brown*, research has substantiated that many teachers are still not receiving adequate training to teach this diverse student population, which reflects the increasingly diverse demographics of the country. Teacher education must be based on a multicultural perspective to ensure equal educational opportunities for all students, and teachers must be prepared to appropriately teach students who differ culturally from them.

Current Teacher Practices

Only a small fraction of my learning about diverse students was during teacher training. Most of it was obtained on a "trial-by-fire" basis. Many K–12 teachers may have the same sentiments and echo similar teacher education experiences. Others, too, are encountering "hands-on," "on the job," and "trial-and-error" teacher training. Due to the lack of multicultural training in teacher preparation programs, in-service teachers have resorted to less effective measures in an attempt to meet the needs of culturally diverse students. Often the instructional efforts to make learning more meaningful for diverse students consist of the teachers' minimal insertion of fragmented multicultural content by only discussing holidays, reading multicultural literature, and/or having international food fairs. Some teachers perceive themselves as multicultural proponents because they discuss Dr. Martin Luther King, Jr. during Black History Month. Many teachers are still at the initial contributions level of Banks' (2001) approaches to multicultural education. They equate multicultural education with food, holidays, and language (Mungai, 2002). Multicultural education is more complex and comprehensive than a partial coverage of multicultural content. It ensures educational equity and student empowerment.

The goal of teacher education programs should be to address Banks' highest approach to multicultural education and prepare competent teachers who can develop all students as proficient decision makers and social activists. To ensure educational equity, teachers must exceed their additive and superficial means of incorporating multicultural content and embrace the fullest possible implementation of multiculturalism.

Evaluation of Teacher Education

> Because our schools are getting more diverse, it is important that every teacher, no matter who they are or where they come from, have the skills and cultural competencies that are necessary to connect with these kids. (Eubanks, 2002, p. 5)

Despite the changing face of American schools, numbers of culturally diverse students are not receiving an optimal educational experience. Significant numbers of teachers have not acquired the skills, knowledge, or pedagogy to teach for diversity during their teacher preparation process. Teacher education has been found to insufficiently prepare teachers to teach in the nation's culturally pluralistic classrooms. A 1998 US study found that teachers were poorly prepared to teach in culturally diverse settings. The report states that, "increased classroom diversity has brought equity issues to the forefront of the educational agenda, but past studies have shown that many teachers were not trained to meet the needs of diverse student populations" (National Center for Educational Statistics, 1998, p. 2). The survey found that 17% of the teachers who taught limited English proficient or culturally diverse students were not prepared at all, 30% somewhat prepared, and 33% moderately prepared to meet these students' needs.

A significant proportion of in-service teachers have not received appropriate teacher preparation for cultural diversity nor have they had sufficient fieldwork in diverse settings. Research indicates that numerous in-service teachers do not have culturally diverse field experiences prior to teaching in diverse environments. Experts contend that teacher candidates must have consistent presence in diverse schools to increase their sensitivity and to understand the complexity of the educational issues of minority students (Goodlad, 1990; Meier, 1995). Preservice teachers should be afforded practicum opportunities in diverse school settings to link theory and practice through the actual implementation of culturally responsive teaching strategies.

Teacher preparation must underscore the fact that teaching students with backgrounds different from one's own is the norm rather than the exception for many teachers. Therefore, cross-cultural training is essential in any teacher education program. Research has found that cultural differences between teachers and students can impact the achievement of culturally diverse students. Teachers can, consciously or unconsciously, misread student behaviors, interactions, and abilities. Due to cultural differences in language, communication, and interaction styles, teachers can misinterpret students' aptitudes, intent, or abilities (Delpit, 1995). Teachers' personal beliefs, attitudes, and expectations can directly influence their behaviors, interactions, and teaching practices in culturally diverse classrooms.

Vavrus (2002) concurs that teachers' attitudes toward diversity can impact the effectiveness of their teaching. He suggests that teachers engage themselves in self-reflection exercises to better understand and embrace their role to infuse diversity issues in the classroom and throughout the curriculum. Teacher education programs should assume their proper role of adequately training teachers for the challenge of today's diverse classrooms.

Methodology

The purpose of the research study was to assess in-service elementary and high school teachers' perceptions of their teacher preparation to teach in a culturally diverse educational setting. The study was conducted in a Northeastern public school district serving approximately 2,209 prekindergarten to 12th-grade students. The culturally diverse composition of the student population is 83.8% African American, and 16.1% Hispanic. The district is categorized as "high needs" with a large proportion of "at-risk" students. Seventy percent of the school district's population is eligible for free or reduced lunch.

The 60% response rate yielded 24 prekindergarten to second grade and 13 ninth to 12th-grade teacher participants. The respondents consisted of 37 in-service teachers ranging in 1–31 years of teaching experience. Fifty-seven percent of the teachers had 1–10 years experience, 21% had 11–20 years, and 21% had more than 20 years experience in the classroom. The racial composition of the sample was 22 White and 12 Black, or African American, participants. Three participants identified themselves as "other."

The research paradigm for the study was predominately quantitative in nature, although qualitative data were acquired via open-ended questions. The research instrument was a survey consisting of three components: demographic information, Likert-type response items, and narrative response questions. The participants were asked to complete the survey at their school's monthly faculty meeting. The surveys were voluntarily and confidentially completed, and later submitted in sealed envelopes to the researcher. A comparative data analysis was promptly conducted.

Teachers' Perceptions of Teacher Preparation for Cultural Diversity

The study's findings confirmed prior research that many teacher education programs are not based on multicultural perspectives and are therefore not adequately preparing teachers for culturally diverse classrooms. A major portion of the teacher participants perceived their teacher training as culturally insufficient. It was found that 41% of the participants believed their teacher preparation for cultural diversity to be unsatisfactory. Eleven percent indicated no diversity training at all, and 30% were poorly prepared.

Diverse Fieldwork/Student Teaching Opportunities

Fieldwork and student teaching experiences are also crucial components to any teacher preparation program. Teacher candidates must have opportunities to link theory to practice. The study affirmed that many in-service teachers did not have practicum placements in diverse settings. Fifty-five percent had not been placed in a diverse setting, nor were such placements available. Forty-five percent of the respondents were placed in diverse classrooms. Only 12% of these participants were required to have a diverse fieldwork placement, whereas the remaining 33% volunteered.

It was noted that some participants defined diverse settings as including special education and socioeconomic status aspects. The length and intensity of the placements varied as well. For example, a participant indicated that her experience consisted of "1/2 semester in high needs school once a week." This statement amplifies the need for teacher education programs to incorporate systematic and structured diverse practicum placements for all teacher candidates.

Comparison of Teacher Experience and Their Perceptions

Findings indicate that current efforts of teacher education reform have attempted to address the diversification of the country's classrooms. The study's novice teachers expressed more satisfaction with their cultural diversity preparation than the veteran teachers.

Seventy-two percent of teachers with 1–10 years experience indicated satisfactory preparation compared to 49% of teachers with 11–20 years experience and 37% of teachers with 20+ years in the classroom. The more experienced teachers indicated the least satisfaction. Sixty-two percent of teachers with more than 20 years experience were dissatisfied with their teacher preparation for cultural diversity, whereas 28% of novice teachers felt inadequately prepared. According to the respondents, teacher education has improved over the years to better prepare teachers to meet the needs of all students. Although there has been progress, many deficits still remain.

Evolution of Teacher Education

At a deeper level, however, is the possibility that White teachers' disposition toward race may create internal obstacles to the implementation of both effective pedagogy and curriculum and a transformative response to inequitable policies (Chubbuck, 2004, p. 302). In this day and age, suburban and urban communities all over the United States consist of European Americans, African Americans, Asian Americans, Hispanic Americans, and Native Americans. Ours is a society composed of many cultural groups from a variety of backgrounds and traditions. Multiculturalism is a twentieth-century idea based on the historic principle of cultural pluralism. Although the term *multiculturalism* is a relatively new one, the philosophy is deeply imbedded in our history and our development into a country and world leader. Ignorance of the cultural habits and traditions of our students and neighbors allows members of our society to continue to promote prejudice and racism. As educators, we are concerned with providing instruction for all children in our classrooms and developing curricula that incorporate and celebrate diversity. Successfully employing practices of tolerance and implementing multicultural curricula will help prepare our students for their future role in the global society.

According to Campbell (2004), "teacher preparation programs and the present public school curricula generally reflect and promote the majority view of reality, reproducing ideological domination. Students need empowerment strategies to counteract the pervasive influence of disempowerment. These strategies should include goal clarification and establishing clear measures of progress" (p. 216). Teacher education programs must prepare competent, high-quality teachers who can develop all students as proficient and literate decision-makers. Therefore, teacher education must train teachers to implement culturally responsive pedagogy to ensure educational equity. Ladson-Billings (1994) argues that culturally relevant teaching is essential to the meaningful learning and empowerment of diverse students. Her case studies identified the following characteristics of effective teachers of African American students:

- possess high self-esteem and respect others;
- "see themselves as a part of the local community and see their work as contributing, or giving back to the community" (p. 38);
- "believe that all students can succeed, and organize their lessons based upon this belief" (p. 49);
- perceive their role as "digging knowledge out of the students" (p. 52) rather than disseminating new knowledge;
- create a "community of learners" (p. 69).

Culturally responsive teachers encourage students to think critically and to problem-solve societal injustices. Culturally responsive pedagogy also empowers students by teaching them to critically analyze educational content and examine their individual roles in a global society. Freire (1998) affirms that culturally responsive pedagogy can "establish an intimate connection between knowledge considered basic to any school curriculum and knowledge that is the fruit of the lived experience of these students as individuals" (p. 36).

As educators of all students, we must update our thinking by:

- Constructing a view of self with awareness of our culture and expectations of children.
- Considering the diverse backgrounds of the children in our settings and communities.
- Learning about the backgrounds of the children in our program or school.
- Using our knowledge of culture to talk with each student about values and practice.
- Building on what we have learned from each student.
- Infusing the literacy curriculum and classroom environment with a rich variety of materials from the cultures of our children and other cultures.

Teacher education programs have not included, but must now adopt, the philosophical ideology of multiculturalism that appreciates diversity and meets the needs of all students. A paradigm shift in teacher preparation is inevitable if schools and teachers are to embrace cultural diversity and differentiate instruction for all students.

Conclusion

Historically, Horace Mann developed public schools to educate the masses and assimilate young American citizens into the "melting pot" phenomenon. From a multicultural perspective, teacher education programs must now abandon the "color-blind" ideology and adopt a multiculturalism that appreciates cultural pluralism and perceives every student as unique. "Good teaching" should involve differentiated instruction that takes into account students' individualism, background knowledge, and prior experiences during the learning process. Effective classroom instruction should be personally and culturally relevant to all students for learning to be meaningful, and in turn, create critical, analytical, and empowered thinkers. Therefore, effective teachers must be appropriately prepared to infuse multicultural perspectives and implement culturally relevant pedagogy in our nation's schools.

Teacher education is ultimately responsible for training teachers who can meet the needs of all students. Institutions must evolve to better prepare teachers who embrace and wholeheartedly implement multiculturalism. Teacher education programs must model what teachers are expected to apply in the classroom, and these programs must reevaluate the current practice of only partially integrating multicultural content. Nieto (1996) asserts that multicultural education must not only permeate the curriculum, but also directly impact the interactions between teachers and students, and the conceptualization of teaching and learning.

As a teacher participant suggests, "[teachers] need to understand the lives of the culturally diverse population—family, language, customs, economic standing." The evolution of teacher education programs is essential to the development of highly qualified teachers who can effectively and confidently implement culturally responsive pedagogy and, as a result, equalize educational opportunities for all students, in particular African American children.

References

African American Registry (2004). *Roberts vs. City of Boston begins.* Minneapolis, MN: African American Registry. Available from: www.aaregistry.com

Banks, J. A. (2001). *Cultural diversity and education: Foundations, curriculum, and teaching.* Boston: Allyn & Bacon.

Brown Foundation for Educational Equity, Excellence and Research (2000). Brown

v. Board of Education *orientation handbook: Court cases in prelude to* Brown, *1849–1949*. Available from: http://brownvboard.org

Campbell, D. E. (2004). *Choosing democracy: a practical guide to multicultural education* (3rd ed). Upper Saddle River, NJ: Pearson-Merrill Prentice Hall.

Chubbuck, S. (2004). Whiteness enacted, Whiteness disrupted: The complexity of personal congruence. *American Educational Research Journal*, 41(2), 301–333.

Delpit, L. (1995). *Other people's children*. New York: The New Press.

Eubanks, S. (2002). Ask the experts. *Tomorrow's teachers: Help wanted—Minority teachers*. Washington, DC: National Education Association. Available from: www.nea.org

Franklin, J. H. (2000). From slavery to freedom: A history of African Americans (8th ed.). Boston: McGraw-Hill.

Freire, P. (1998). *Pedagogy of freedom: Ethics, democracy and civic courage*. South Hadley, MA: Bergin & Garvey.

Goodlad, J. I. (1990). *Teachers for our nation's schools*. San Francisco: Jossey-Bass.

Johnson, J. A., Musial, D., Hall, G. E., Gollick, D. M., & DuPuis, V. (2005). *Introduction to the foundations of American education* (13th ed.). Boston: Pearson, Allyn & Bacon.

Ladson-Billings, G. (1994). *The dreamkeepers: Successful teachers of African American children*. San Francisco: Jossey-Bass.

Meier, D. (1995). *The power of their ideas: Lessons for America from a small school in Harlem*. Boston: Beacon.

Mungai, A. (2002, Spring/Summer). Multicultural issues in the classroom: How prepared are our future teachers? *Taboo*, pp. 79–84.

National Center for Educational Statistics (1998). *Teacher quality: Report on the preparation and qualifications of public school teachers*. Washington, DC: Author.

National Education Association (2002). *Tomorrow's teachers: Help wanted—Minority teachers*. Washington, DC: National Education Association.

Nieto, S. (1996). *Affirming diversity: The sociopolitical context of multicultural education*. New York: Longman.

Ornstein, A. C., & Levine, D. U. (2003). *Foundations of education* (8th ed.). Boston: Houghton Mifflin.

Pulliam, J. H. (1982). *History of education in America* (3rd ed.). Columbus, OH: Charles E. Merrill.

Spring, J. H. (2000). *The American school: 1642–2000* (5th ed). New York: McGraw-Hill.

US Census Bureau (2000). *American FactFinder* (Tables and Charts). Available from: http://factfinder.census.gov/servlet/BasicFactsServlet

Vavrus, M. (2002). *Transforming the multicultural education of teachers*. New York: Teachers College Press.

Wardle, F. (2003). Introduction to early childhood education: A multidimensional approach to child-centered care and learning. In F. Wardle & M. I. Cruz Janzen (2004), *Meeting the needs of multiethnic and multiracial children in schools*. Boston: Pearson, Allyn & Bacon.

Wharton, M. L. (2002). *A peculiar institution: A primer on American slavery*. Available from: http://www.thenorthstarnetwork.com

Part Two

Student Performance and Assessment

CHAPTER EIGHT

The Brown *Decision and Its Impact on African Americans*

Examining Teacher Education, the Sociology of Education, and Agricultural Education

PATRICIA J. LARKE, ALVIN LARKE JR., AND EVANGELINE M. CASTLE

Abstract

In 2004, the *Brown v. Board of Education* decision has become woven inextricably into the legal and educational fabric. What was considered a momentous, nation-altering legal decision in 1954 had, indeed, been "a long time coming." Today, it still stands as the overarching legal protection—guarding the educational access and opportunity of millions of students nationwide—that so many have either lauded, supported, and relied on, or despised, challenged, and thwarted. For most scholars, consideration of the *Brown* decision, however imperfectly and painfully it has been implemented, is a necessarily critical nexus for addressing the status of contemporary education in the United States for African Americans. Not only has it influenced who is *in* the classroom (both teachers and students) and who *leads* the school (principals and other administrative staff), but also in many fields, it has definitely influenced *what* we study, *how* we study it, and *how* we teach it. Here we examine three educational areas: (1) teacher education, (2) the sociology of education, and (3) agricultural education—to discuss the impact of the *Brown* decision.

Introduction

In 2004, the *Brown v. Board of Education* decision has become woven inextricably into the legal and educational fabric. What was considered a momentous, nation-altering legal decision in 1954 had, indeed, been "a long time coming." Many would agree with the noted scholar, O. L. Davis, when he stated that in this golden anniversary year, most current educators were not alive at the time or were too young to recall how this benchmark decision, and its aftermath, shook and has shaped the social, educational, economic, and legal foundations of this country for decades (Davis, 2004). Today, it still stands as the overarching legal protection—guarding the educational access and opportunity of millions of students nationwide—that so many have either lauded, supported, and relied on, or despised, challenged, and thwarted. No matter the stance or the agenda, it stands as a definitive pre- and post-test to this country's fundamental principles, self-perceptions, and progress.

For most scholars, consideration of the *Brown* decision, however imperfectly and painfully it has been implemented, is a necessarily critical nexus for addressing the status of contemporary education in the United States. Not only has it influenced who is *in* the classroom (both teachers and students) and who *leads* the school (principals and other administrative staff), but also in many fields, it definitely has influenced curriculum and instruction. That is, *what* we study, *how* we study it, and *how* we teach it. Of necessity, no field was more affected than the field of education itself. By refuting the legitimacy and efficacy of the entire educational enterprise, *Brown* changed the canon, the contributors, and the participants in American education.

In one key area, the curriculum, the *Brown* decision has prompted significant changes at all educational levels, especially higher education. Since *Brown*, the core curriculum in higher education has included an increase both in the number of courses that focus on multicultural content and in the policies, programs, and practices designed to respond to the needs of a diverse student population. Admittedly, the number of college courses and their content vary by departments/colleges across universities.

Here we examine three educational areas: (1) teacher education, (2) the sociology of education, and (3) agricultural education, to discuss the impact of the *Brown* decision. Since the defendants in *Brown* were students who sought equal treatment in public school settings, and since the responsibility of teacher education is to prepare educators to work with students in public schools, it is natural to discuss the impact of the changes in the teacher education curriculum that resulted from the *Brown* decision. The sociology of education examines systemic policies, practices, and social justice issues such as institutionalized racism, classicism, and many of the complexities associated with differential educational participation and outcomes. Agriculture has played a historical role, and to some degree a current role, in developing and maintaining US wealth, which has been based in part on the exploitation of people of color and poor people, who traditionally have been excluded from meaningful educational participation. Since *Brown* sought to end the exploitation and educational exclusion of agricultural workers and to increase their representation among learned practitioners and scholars, an examination of its impact is particularly relevant. All of these topics directly relate to the original impetus for the *Brown* case.

Teacher Education

The *Brown* decision was fundamental to the mission of teacher education, which is to prepare educators to serve all students. It is ironic that the *Brown* case did not use employment settings, housing patterns, health-care services, and other public services to show discriminatory practices of "separate but equal," although all of these areas benefited from the decision. Instead, the case focused on public education, involving children and schools and how the delivery of educational services in public schools was unequal, from teacher salaries to pupil expenditures and from building maintenance to condition of and access to instructional materials.

Teacher education programs did not just take action voluntarily after the *Brown* ruling. Rather, it was educators at all levels—elementary to higher education—and concerned citizens, governmental agencies, and educational organizations that organized and provided support to ensure that education became more inclusive and responsive to the mandates of *Brown*. During the 1970s (almost 20 years after the Supreme Court's ruling), one impetus for change came from the American Association of Colleges for Teacher Education's (AACTE's) article, "No One Model American" (1973). This important work provided the theoretical and conceptual framework for multicultural education as the venue for change in teacher preparation. Additionally, this article shaped the diversity standards for the National Council for Teacher Accreditation (NCTA) and fostered the inclusion of multicultural education in teacher education programs and in programs of study for state licensure. Thus, these requirements have been instrumental in the development of the discipline and have increased the number of courses in multicultural education. In fact, multicultural education coursework is required in 45 of the 50 states among those seeking initial elementary and secondary licensure. Before *Brown*, multicultural education did not exist, although there were a few courses that dealt with ethnic groups and a very few "add-ons" to the school curriculum that dealt with the contributions of people of color. Although Carter G. Woodson, the father of Black History, developed some curriculum for African Americans, that information was not included in the school curriculum as outlined in basic instructional materials.

When we look at *Brown* 50 years later, we continue to see educational inequity, segregation, prejudice, racism, and unequal educational outcomes for African Americans. African Americans continue to be tracked in the lowest level classes; are treated differently by their teachers; are more likely than any other group to be labeled as in need of special education services; and have higher discipline, suspension, and expulsion rates from schools. Such treatment further supports the notion that *Brown* has not fulfilled its promise to African Americans in teacher education or in educational institutions.

While teacher education maybe given some accolades after *Brown* for implementing changes in the curriculum, it continues to fall short in increasing the number of African American teachers. One of the most catastrophic results of *Brown* was the loss and displacement of African American teachers. After 50 years, African American teachers only comprise of 8% of teachers, and it will take another 50 years for the percentage African American teachers to match the percentage of African American students. Teacher education institutions must be given a mandate to increase the number of African American teachers. Sadly, many African American students and others will go through their entire schooling without being taught by an African American teacher. That was not the intent of *Brown*. Therefore, *Brown* has left an "unfinished agenda" in teacher education.

The Sociology of Education

What surprised and angered many was *Brown*'s successful use of education to reform itself. For example, in unprecedented fashion, findings from the social sciences were central to the case. Among the arguments advanced by Thurgood Marshall and the National Association for the Advancement of Colored People (NAACP) legal team, clearly the most significant (and strongly challenged) pertained to the social and psychological harm committed to young African American children by the prevailing segregated "separate but equal" policies that had been supported by the Supreme Court's 1896 decision in *Plessy v. Ferguson*. *Brown*'s arguments that demonstrated the strong ties between educational opportunity and economic opportunity, while highlighting the built-in inequalities associated with a segregated educational system, established a measurable rationale for demanding and providing access and opportunities for greater participation in the nation's public schools. It is important to note that the benefits of *Brown* have extended not only to

African American students but to waves of many other new students, including growing numbers of women (especially Whites), Native Americans, immigrants from all over the world, and students with exceptionalities.

With the advent of *Brown* and its effective use of social science research, other analytical tools were applied, often prompting confusing and conflicting discussions and outcomes. As the 1950s gave way to the turbulent 1960s, "business as usual" no longer existed. For instance, as the "starts and stops" of implementing *Brown* occurred, the combined social fervor of the Civil Rights Movement, President Lyndon Johnson's War on Poverty, and the Vietnam War fed a need for greater understanding of a changing society and for greater inclusion of nontraditional participants in many aspects of national life.

For example, it was no coincidence that the field of sociology gave new theoretical and research emphasis to schooling, studying not only how (and why) various groups interact within its confines, but also how (and why) we fashion different institutional structures to achieve different societal and educational ends. (Thus, we differentiated between educational sociology and the sociology of education.) It was as if we saw schooling and all our related social institutions through a significantly expanded lens, one that prompted close systemic examination of both the old and the new. The field of sociology grew to reflect and systematically examine education and schooling across many socially relevant topics, such as the intersections of race, class, exceptionalities, and gender; inequality, racial and cultural identity, and marginality; the role of expectations and self-fulfilling prophecy; and dueling theoretical models (e.g., conflict versus structural functionalism). Courses were developed around "social problems" and "social values": diversity and urban education, symbolic interactionism and communication styles, social movements and legal issues. The content in psychology, demography, political science, and economics also expanded dramatically, as reflected by those who now studied, challenged, and enriched their knowledge base. During this exciting time, everything seemed subject to change. With new fervor, new questions were posed; new theoretical, statistical, and conceptual models were advanced; and new complexities were found.

From 1954 to the present, *Brown* has prompted us to ask many important questions from a sociological perspective, such as: How do our schools operate? Why do they operate as they do? Whom do they serve? To what end? How, and how soon, can we change them so that an increasingly diverse population benefits from their advantage? How much change is too much change? Staying true to the spirit of *Brown*, how can we develop and maintain a critical mass of African American students in college and graduate school, as we develop a cadre of young scholars in the field of sociology, to ensure continued examination of schooling in America from a racially and culturally relevant perspective—one that keeps the effective and appropriate education of African American children at its center? Today's representation suggests that maintaining relevant sociological course content is easier than increasing the number of African American scholars in sociology upon whom we can depend to ask critical questions, while advancing relevant and alternative theoretical frameworks and educational structures.

Agricultural Education

Although agricultural education is one of the oldest fields of study, it was one of the last fields to include courses regarding diversity. In fact, the Morrill Act of 1862 authorized and governed the establishment of land-grant colleges, and the Second Morrill Act of 1890 did the same for several institutions dedicated to the education of African Americans. While the original driving force for the land-grant system was the need to provide higher education for the majority of the US population, financial support for the teaching component of the land-grant mission has been largely relegated to states. The Second Morrill Act did not endow the 1890 institutions with the public land and other resources appropriated for the 1862 institutions, and the 1890 institutions were not compensated in subsequent legislation. Both Morrill Acts, 1862 and 1890, specifically covered general areas of agriculture. Later, the Smith-Hughes Act of 1914 provided funding for a curriculum by which secondary school students would be taught vocational agriculture. This was created for the advancement of production agriculture and was taught to farm boys.

Youth organizations soon developed and were named Future Farmers of America (FFA) for White males and New Farmers of America (NFA) for African American males. The curriculum was basically the same in course content, although the two groups studied separately. In 1965, the NFA and the FFA merged, and all students (males) participated in the same organization: the FFA. In 1969, women were permitted to study the curriculum and become members of the organization.

According to *Brown*, it is very important for us to include underrepresented groups in our classes and provide a curriculum to sensitize students to the life and the contributions that others have made to agriculture. However, in spite of the now widely known participation of many racial and ethnic groups, very few universities have courses within their colleges of agriculture that deal with the contributions of all groups to the field. Most students who enroll in an agriculture curriculum have little or no knowledge of contributions to the field—such as practical adaptations, patented inventions, and research-based knowledge—generated by anyone except European Americans.

A curriculum should allow students to gain an understanding of the racial and sociocultural heritage of American agriculture. Students should be given the opportunity to develop an appreciation for the contributions of many ethnic groups to American agriculture, should become acquainted with some of the literature in the area of American social diversity, and should be able to apply the academic principles of sound research and analysis as they develop their personal education about agriculture. In order for teachers to become sensitive to the educational needs of our students, we must understand the culture from which they come. Our teaching styles must address the learning styles of the students. We must become more inclusive as our classrooms become more diverse. Many teacher education programs devote some time in the teacher preparation curriculum to address diversity and sensitivity to underrepresented groups in the classroom. Yet there is not a well-defined course of study related to diversity that deals with teachers of agricultural science. It is clear, however, that since 1954 the curriculum has become more diverse in content.

Due to the dwindling participation of people of color in agriculture-related careers and the substantially increased percentage that this demographic population is expected to realize in the next decade, those charged with perpetuating the United States' leadership role in the area of agriculture and related fields should continue to find ways to enhance participation of this group (Jones, 1999). We must have an adequate number of culturally responsive workers in agriculture. We will not have this workforce if we continue to exclude significant numbers of the population from our teacher education programs and if we do not provide a curriculum that will educate this populace of its importance in the field of agriculture. Therefore, it is imperative that the ideals of *Brown* become more than rhetoric in agricultural education, a discipline that has such a long-standing history in American education.

Conclusion

Indeed, given the trade-offs and difficulties that we have encountered along the 50 years since *Brown*, many reluctantly ask, "Were we better off before?" Are the study of multicultural education and issues of diversity prompting us to fashion more effective schools for African American students and for the complicated demographic mix that characterizes many disenfranchised student populations within the United States? Indeed, is *Brown*, long considered by many as "the single most honored opinion in the Supreme Court's corpus," still relevant, or is it "fading to irrelevance" (Balkin, 2001)? Fifty years later, we face the hard question: Given the casualties and the costs, are African American children receiving a better education today, and do they have greater access and educational opportunity than they had in 1954? Has desegregation truly made a positive difference? Was it all worth it? Some of the answers we did not like; many of the questions we no longer ask.

Considering the setbacks and problems that now seem to dominate contemporary schooling for the majority of African American students, some might find it easy to disavow any long-standing benefits of a legal decision rendered 50 years ago. We are certainly in a different time and in a vastly different society. For most, however, it is difficult to view the *Brown* decision as anything other than an undeniably important milestone in the journey of African American survival and progress in this country. Clearly, it has provided equitable access and protected educational opportunity for many, though there are still too few who truly have benefited, especially when we examine the recent education, employment, and health-care statistics for African Americans. Admittedly, there is much work still to be done. Yet we must look with compassionate clarity to see *Brown* not as an aging boxer—once strong but now weakened by time, wear, and circumstance—but as an experienced relay runner, primed for ultimate success by the careful execution of good timing (in both receiving and passing the baton), with strength and dedication to the goal of crossing the finish line. Now, more than ever, we must be vigilant in recognizing and safeguarding a strong, hard-won legal foundation that continues to provide meaningful hope—that one day the belief that separate is equal will have no place in American society, especially for African Americans, other people of color, and poor people. Perhaps the goal will be achieved through teacher education, the sociology of education, and agricultural education working individually and collectively to fulfill the premise and promise of *Brown*.

References

American Association of Colleges for Teacher Education (1973). *No one model American*. Washington, DC: Author.

Balkin, J. M. (2001, November 9). Is the Brown decision fading to irrelevance? *The Chronicle of Higher Education*, p. B11.

Davis, O. L. (2004). Fifty years past . . . and still miles to go: curriculum development and the Brown v. Board decision. *Journal of Curriculum and Supervision 19*(2), 95–98.

Jones, W. (1999). *Factors influencing career choice of African American and Hispanic graduates of the College of Agriculture and Life Sciences at Texas A&M University*. Unpublished doctoral dissertation, Texas A&M University.

CHAPTER NINE

The LEAP for Accountability?

Ideology and Practice of Testing in a Louisiana Urban Elementary School

JIM HORN

Abstract

Louisiana educators at an urban K–5 school participated in a 2-year study to share their experiences related to the implementation of a state high-stakes testing program (LEAP 21) that is used to make promotion decisions in grades 4 and 8. Observations, document analysis, and interviews were used to study the development of attitudes, perceptions, and practices related to the use of and consequences emanating from this testing practice. It was found that the state test has far-reaching effects on teaching, curriculum, school climate, students, parents, and school administration. The *ideology of testing* as a positive reform idea and the *practice of testing* as a constant and tangible threat form the two poles of an experiential field that these educators encounter as figure and ground. The avoidance of failure and the threat of failure push these educators toward an ideological commitment to testing.

Introduction: New Millennialist Rhetoric or the Continuing Crusade?

Even with your parents' best example and your teachers' best efforts, in the end it is your work that determines how much and how well you learn. When you work to your full capacity, you can hope to attain the knowledge and skills that will enable you to create your future and control your destiny. If you do not, you will have your future thrust upon you by others. (A Nation at Risk, 1983)

In the early years of the new American Republic, the desire for universal education (at least universal for White males) represented the seeds of a new civic faith in the power of schooling to meld unceasing waves of immigrants with an emerging American ideology grounded in capitalism, Protestantism, and republicanism (Kaestle, 1983). As the inheritor of strong Calvinist traditions, Horace Mann, himself a lapsed Puritan, adopted a revivalist rhetoric based on individual initiative to sell his Crusade for Common Schools to all individuals and socioeconomic groups willing to listen, from the elite northeastern Brahmin seeking property insurance against the perceived threat of an uneducated immigrant rabble, to the Irish and Jewish immigrants of Boston and New York trying to leverage access through education to some semblance of prosperity and equality. The dream of universal schooling, it seemed, had something for everybody, and the faith in the power of education to deliver a better life would become the new secular American religion, even today remaining largely unchallenged if not entirely believed.

If the secular faith in education developed during the last century eventually lapsed into an implacable orthodoxy of practice, as some critics have contended, our most recent American socioeconomic initiatives restore a reformist vision that is no less sweeping, or grandiose perhaps, than the millennialist dreams of our Puritan forefathers or the Common School crusaders of the nineteenth century. Internationally, America is engaged in a struggle to maintain, far into the future, market supremacy in the global economy, a supremacy that will depend on continued increases in productivity that must be sustained with a shrinking supply of renewable resources. Still suffused with the moral and nationalistic fervor that marked earlier reform seasons, this new American mission provides the political rationale for the most recent educational reform crusade to establish world-class education standards for knowledge productivity and to establish accountability measures to make sure those standards are maintained.

This effort began in earnest in 1983, with the wide circulation of *A Nation at Risk*, a broadside against American public education that announced the condition of American schools constituted a form of "unilateral economic disarmament." Building on the sentiments and recommendations of that document, the Charlottesville Education Summit in 1989 laid out the road map for achieving high standards and educational accountability measures. From there, the movement has continued to pick up political steam, despite research studies (Airasian, 1988; Herman & Golan, 1993;

Mehrens, 1998; Amrein & Berliner, 2002a, 2002b), statements by testing authorities (Madaus, 1985; Bracey, 1998; Popham, 1999), and position statements by educational organizations (National Research Council, 1999; American Educational Research Association, 2000) that present good reasons for skepticism or caution regarding the use of standardized test scores as a suitable vehicle for making high-stakes decisions in schools. Despite calls, however, for more balanced multimethod accountability approaches, promoters of high-stakes standardized testing have won the day, partially it seems by offering an educational reform solution that appeals, as did Horace Mann's, to a wide variety of socioeconomic groups, while not challenging the organizational structure, or the underlying "grammar of schooling" (Tyack & Cuban, 1995, p. 9).

For proponents of high-stakes testing, there is the prospect of monetary rewards for recognizing excellence that will be accompanied by a well-deserved public denunciation of the slackers, whether students or educators. For other proponents more liberally affected, there is the prospect of financial help and other resources, if test success is not demonstrated in schools handicapped by poverty, isolation, and neglect. For educators and students of America's schools, there appears to be little choice offered in the matter as state and federal political elites of both left and right are conjoined in a mutual policy embrace that defies partisan convention.

The Voices of Educators on the Front Lines of High-Stakes Testing

Numerous research articles, books, news stories, and commentaries have appeared during the past decade regarding high-stakes testing in K–12 public education. Over the 2-year period of this research, for instance, over 200 news stories on high-stakes testing were obtained from a single Internet portal news clipping service. Only a small fraction of research literature, however, has dealt specifically with presenting and understanding the perspectives of frontline educators at sites of high-stakes testing. Several exceptions to the dearth of research aimed at presenting practitioner perspectives, however, are worth noting. Smith (1991) used observations and interviews to gather data over 15 months on the negative effects of testing on teachers. Gordon and Reese (1997) used surveys and in-depth interviews to collect data from Texas teachers on preparation for TAAS (Texas Assessment of Academic Skills), and the effects of TAAS on teaching and learning. A more recent study (Barksdale-Ladd & Thomas, 2000) combined individual interviews and focus groups in a phenomenological study to examine the perceptions of both teachers and parents regarding high-stakes testing. Even more recently, researchers (Hoffman et al., 2001) surveyed 200 Texas teachers and solicited their comments regarding the effects of TAAS. In this study, too, researchers found a preponderance of negative perceptions related to testing.

Purpose

The goal of this research project has been to present and to understand the perspectives of educators regarding the implementation and consequences of high-stakes testing at their own elementary school in an urban setting during the first 2 years of state testing in Louisiana. In much of the past and current testing discussions and debates, the voices of educators at testing sites have been conspicuously muted or even absent, particularly those voices from schools with large number of urban poor. Without a clear understanding of the ideas, beliefs, and actions of those who occupy that critical intersection of policy talk and policy action, or that juncture between the ideological and the pragmatic, our understanding of the implementation and consequences of high-stakes testing will remain, at best, partial. With the voices of educators from the testing site as an integral part of the research literature, we can hope to reach a more thorough understanding of the solution that testing offers, regardless of how appealing or how appalling we may view that solution or its appropriateness to the problem that high-stakes testing was supposed to address. If, as Gregory Bateson (1972, p. 271) has remarked, "sometimes . . . one does not know what the problems were till after they have been solved," then an examination of the "solving" that is going on now in Louisiana schools and across the United States may begin to help unmask some of the real problems that have been subsumed within or obfuscated by the rhetoric of reform.

Choosing the Site

As an assistant professor teaching graduate courses in educational foundations and curriculum at a small state university in the late 1990s, I was very much aware of Louisiana's efforts to catch the national wave of enthusiasm for high-stakes testing that was rolling toward the state, primarily it seemed from our rich neighbor to the west, whose TAAS had sucked the air from a number of other state reform initiatives coming online in the 1990s. Louisiana's own good work to revamp its K–12 curriculum is an example of such initiatives that were buried by the media attention given to Texas and other states whose reform directions took a more direct route to the bottom line—academic achievement as measured by test scores.

When Louisiana's Department of Education announced that it would be upping the ante in the high-stakes reform competition, many educators seriously began to question what would happen in schools if a standardized test became the sole criterion to determine the educational futures for fourth-, eighth-, and twelfth-grade students in Louisiana. My own students, many of them teachers working on master's degrees, were asking questions in my curriculum classes about the effects of this new test. Pessimistic predictions abounded as to what effect the new test would have on the relevance of the new State Curriculum Frameworks that occupied a central place in my own curriculum.

One student, a principal at an inner-city elementary school, was particularly eloquent and astute in voicing concerns about what might happen to her curriculum, her teachers, her students, her school, and her community. Since the following spring would bring the first testing session with high stakes, I suggested that we turn her questions into a research study that would begin in spring 2000. That would coincide, too, with the graduate research class that I offered, and such a study would give interested research students a chance to work on the initial phase of a study that eventually would find its way to publication.

Mrs. Roberts, the principal, would become an important asset to the study. Not only did she arrange meetings with her faculty at Alpha Elementary School to introduce the researchers—White academics or aspiring academics in an all-Black setting of practitioners—but Mrs. Roberts' office also provided a conduit through which signed consent forms, interview scheduling forms, and other documents were funneled. It was her close relationship with Alpha's faculty that enabled the confidentiality guaranteed to our individual human subjects; forms became translated into an element of trust that breathed spontaneity and candor into our observations and interviews.

In addition to her central role in establishing the researchers' access and credibility among the faculty at Alpha, Mrs. Roberts helped significantly in the verifiability process by reading sections of the research report and by providing feedback and clarification. She also asked faculty members to do the same, and their checking proved helpful, too, in insuring the veracity of our descriptions of their experiences.

The Setting: Alpha Elementary

Alpha Elementary is a K–5 Title One school located in the heart of a low-income residential area of a medium-sized city in Louisiana's northwest corner. The rumble of trains can be heard less than a mile to the east, and when the wind is from the west, there is the strong smell of the petroleum refinery whose torches cast an ominous glow over that part of the city at night. This is a neighborhood of high mobility and limited resources, with 84% of Alpha's children qualifying for free lunches. A significant share of Alpha's Adopt-a-School donations go to provide shoes, clothing, and school supplies for students who would otherwise go without. Ninety-eight percent of Alpha's 850 students are African American, the children of the working poor (though a growing number of parents have found better-paying jobs at the gambling casinos that line the river on the east side of town).

Just over half of Alpha's teachers are Black, and 53 of Alpha's 58 teachers are certified in the areas they teach. Turnover is low, a factor that can be attributed largely to the tenacity and leadership of the school principal, Mrs. Roberts, who is proud to point out that the five uncertified teachers are working toward full certification. Teachers find high levels of support from the school administration, and they point out that Mrs. Roberts usually finds a way to purchase the materials they request. Halls and classrooms are generally clean and orderly, even though some areas show serious signs of wear and tear. A new wing on the school has been built and another one is planned, partly from the need to house the burgeoning number of fourth and fifth graders that have resulted from the mandated retention policy that came with LEAP 21 (Louisiana Education Assessment Program for the 21st Century), the new statewide testing program for grades 4 and 8.

Louisiana: Taking the High-Stakes LEAP

> This test is now the deciding factor—it used to be a lot of things went into an education—there were social issues, there were a lot of different things—now it is just a test. It decides everything. (Assistant Principal, Alpha Elementary)

Accustomed to occupying a bottom slot in national comparisons of educational achievement, the State of Louisiana in March 2000 became recognized for its lead position among states on an education issue of national significance. In the "Quality Counts 2001" special report of *Education Week* (2001), Louisiana became the first state in the nation to use state test scores as the sole basis for the promotion of fourth- and eighth-grade students. Known as the LEAP 21, the criterion-referenced test was piloted statewide in 1999 to establish benchmarks. From those results, the Louisiana Department of Education mandated that, beginning in March 2000, all fourth and eighth graders must have passing scores on *both* the English Language Arts and Mathematics sections of the test to move to the fifth and ninth grades, respectively. Failing students are given a chance at summer school and another testing session at the end of the 4–5-week remediation. Those who fail the repeated examination are retained in the fourth or eighth grade, respectively.

Some weeks before the March 2000 test week, the state predicted that 20% of the Louisiana's students could fail to meet the minimum passing score of 37%, which the state designated as "approaching basic." The prediction proved on target for the 20% of students statewide who failed the English Language Arts in 2000, but the state underestimated the 28% who would fail the math part of the test. At Alpha Elementary, the urban Title One elementary school that was the site of this research project, state estimates would not come close. In the first year of high stakes, 52.5% (62 students) of fourth graders failed the English Language Arts section of LEAP, and 62% (73 students) failed Math 2. Only 30% of fourth graders would pass both parts during this first year of high stakes, meaning that 70% (75 students) would be retained in fourth grade.

Gathering Data

Over a period of 2 years beginning in March 2000, observations, interviews, and document analysis were used to generate data from administrators and faculty at Alpha Elementary School. Initially, researchers observed in fourth-grade classrooms before and during test week for the LEAP 21 in March 2000. Even though the test had been given the previous March to establish baseline data, the March 2000 examination was the first to carry high stakes for the students and the school. Prior to and during testing, researchers spent time in the classrooms speaking with students and teachers, and observing test preparation and testing procedures.

Two rounds of interviews were conducted with four fourth-grade teachers, their curriculum coordinator, and the assistant principal. Using the same semistructured protocol for all interviews, the first round was conducted at Alpha Elementary in March 2000, and the second round was conducted via telephone in September 2001. One special education teacher and the guidance counselor were interviewed once in September 2001, and Mrs. Roberts was interviewed three times in March 2000, September 2001, and March 2002. Interviews were intended to elicit attitudes, beliefs, and experiences regarding the purpose, use, and effects of high-stakes testing in the participants' school. Interviews were audiotaped and later transcribed.

Observation notes, school information notices, and transcriptions of audiotaped interviews were copied into *Hyperqual 3, Version 1.0*, a qualitative data analysis software tool (Padilla, 1999). This tool was helpful in the early phases of organizing and tagging data according to the initial categories that could be linked to words or phrases (in vivo codes) (Strauss & Corbin, 1998) that were used by the participants and the researchers during the observations and interviews. It also proved useful in searching the data within specific interview transcripts and across all transcripts.

Methodology

The understanding of data, the presentation of findings, and the subsequent interpretive discussion of the findings are framed by an evolving research model, *recursive enaction* (Horn, 1998, 2002). Recursive enaction is grounded in the search for a qualitative science of human experience (Varela, 1979; Goodwin, 1994) that is based on phenomenological description (Moustakas, 1990) and understanding through insight and interpretation (Lonergan, 1958; Gadamer, 1976) of experience as social phenomena (Glaser & Strauss, 1967; Blumer, 1969) in natural or nonexperimental settings (Lincoln & Guba, 1985). In short, the goal of this research approach is to locate, understand, and interpret the human patterning that sustains meaningful activity within social organizations. The process of understanding and presenting data follows a reflexive four-step process of immersion, insight, coherent patterns, and interpretation (Horn, 2002).

Findings

Getting Ready for LEAP 21
March 10, 2000

It is the Friday before LEAP (Louisiana Education Assessment Program) Week at Alpha Elementary in Delta Parish, Louisiana. For students, educators, and parents here and across Louisiana, it is the time that all have anticipated with varying degrees of anxiety since school began 7 months earlier with LEAP 21 as the primary focus for the school year. There is reason for anxiety among students, educators, and parents: This year is the first time that fourth graders at Alpha and throughout Louisiana must pass the State test to move on the fifth grade.

For the past couple of weeks, the local newspaper has featured articles explaining the new high-stakes test and bringing to the public's attention a number of community events aimed at helping parents and students in last-minute preparations for the big week. The local newspaper reports on March 4 that a local Baptist church hosted on the previous Saturday the "Lean on Jesus Test Rally," where 100 parents and children showed up for testing tips and to "build self-esteem." At Alpha Elementary, the K–5 school where two graduate students and I have been observing and interviewing teachers and administrators, a mood of guarded optimism mixes with anxiety and frustration. Not only will this year's test be the dominant indicator for the school's annual report card, but this year students who do not pass both the language and math sections of the test will be retained in fourth grade. The assistant principal reports that students are acting out more and that "teachers [are] edgier, writing up things they normally don't."

In all four of the fourth-grade classes at Alpha, LEAP review proceeds with the *Test Alert Booklet*, a recent publication the state has offered to schools to bone up on test-taking skills and to practice the math and reading skills that will be assessed by the LEAP test. In Mrs. T.'s class, she reminds her students, "on the LEAP, just do your best—that's all you can be asked to do." Near the end of her lesson, which has included work on choosing the correct mathematical operation to answer a question, she acknowledges that some of her students may be overwhelmed, but that "you know how important it [LEAP] is, your parents know how important it is, for you to take the test and pass the test."

Next door, Mrs. C., another fourth-grade teacher, is taking a break to relieve the tension of LEAP practice, and her students are working contentedly in pairs to construct miniature Mardi Gras floats from shoe boxes and colored paper. Mrs. C. worries that her students are too stressed to perform optimally on the 4-day test, and she says more than twice during a brief conversation, "I can't wait till this testing is over." Each time she sighs her demeanor shifts between nervous anxiety and weariness.

After this brief work break, Mrs. C.'s students put away their glue and construction paper and resume their practice of identifying mathematical operations from the clue words found in the sample math problems. At the end of the review, Mrs. C. says: "If you've paid attention all year, you'll do fine. You don't have to make 90%, just approaching basics. If you do that and your class work, you'll go to fifth grade. If not, you won't—it's against the law." As the children prepare to leave for lunch, she calls out, "Don't lose sleep, don't get sick. . . . I'll give you a treat for being here by eight o'clock every day next week." And once again, she points to next week's test schedule on the blackboard:

- Monday: Writing
- Tuesday: Language
- Wednesday: Math
- Thursday: Social studies
- Friday: Science

As the children stand to leave, she says, "If you're caught cheating, you'll get a zero and be in fourth grade next year—every girl and boy for himself, and God for us all."

March 15, 2000

At 8:30 on the following Wednesday morning of LEAP Week, the intercom pops and a female voice asks for an attendance report. Mrs. B. responds that all of her 30 fourth-graders are present for this third day of testing. She waits to see if there are further questions from the office before she pushes a button on a portable CD player. Relaxation music mixed with the twittering of birds fills the room. Mrs. B. instructs her students to stand and stretch. She leads them through several minutes of breathing and stretching, followed by a seated visualization exercise.

"Close your eyes and visualize the day ahead," she says, "and meditate on the math section." She instructs her students to think positively about their ability for completing this portion of the LEAP.

"Do you believe?" she asks her students.

"Yeah," they respond with eyes still closed but without much enthusiasm.

"Do you believe?" she repeats in a louder voice.

"Yes, Ma'am," comes a louder response, as a few students break into shy smiles. Test booklets with each child's name already recorded are passed around, and the students rigidly await the now-familiar instructions and warnings about cheating, causing disturbances, and the use of unauthorized materials. The math portion of the LEAP has begun.

The LEAP: Mechanics and Initial Consequences

> *A lot of our children can communicate with you verbally, and they can give you a response, but sometimes they freeze up when it comes to writing. So I am real afraid of what it's going to mean for our boys and girls as far as high numbers of retentions. (Fourth-Grade Teacher, Alpha Elementary)*

The scenarios just presented are based on observation notes recorded at Alpha Elementary School, but they could have occurred at any of the hundreds of elementary schools across Louisiana in the weeks prior to and during LEAP Week of March 2000. In 1998, Louisiana joined a growing number of states developing and implementing testing programs with high stakes for schools, teachers, and students. As stated in the *2000–2001 Annual Report*, LEAP 21 is a part of Louisiana's Reaching for Results, "an educational reform system designed to improve student achievement. The LEAP 21 tests are designed to ensure that grade 4 and grade 8 students have adequate knowledge and skills before moving on to the next grade" (p. 1).

When the ramifications of LEAP became known widely in the state, a significant number of parents made plans to enroll their children in private schools for their fourth- and eighth-grade years. As the assistant principal explained:

> ... everybody was losing students—what they were doing was dropping out in the third-grade, going to private school, and coming back as a fifth grader to avoid having to take that test. And the same thing, they would drop out in the seventh grade, go to private school in the eighth grade, and come back to public school in the ninth grade. And then the State Department came back and said everybody, no matter where they are going to school, has to take the test.

When initial observations and interviews were conducted at Alpha Elementary in early 2000, this K–5 inner-city school had an enrollment of 854 students with a high transfer rate, meaning approximately 200 students moved in or out of the school during the course of the school year. At the time of the first high-stakes LEAP examination in March 2000, the fourth grade at Alpha consisted of four regular education classes with 30–33 students in each, one special education self-contained class, and one inclusion special education teacher who works with the other teachers to meet the needs of the mainstreamed special education students in fourth grade.

Even though a new elementary school near Alpha drew away approximately 150 students in fall 2000, approximately 842 remained, only 12 students shy of the 854 students at Alpha the previous year. This was due significantly to more than 80 fourth graders who failed one or both of the high-stakes sections of the LEAP during the previous March. This bulge in fourth-grade enrollment necessitated the creation of two new sections of fourth grade, for a total of six sections averaging just over 30 students in each. The increasing number of fourth graders can be tracked by the rise in the number of tests given to fourth graders in 2000–2001, the second year of high stakes. In 2000, 118 students were tested, with 15 students exempted from the test. In March 2001, 174 students were tested, even though the number of exempted students more than doubled from 15 to 33.

In the second year of high stakes, 2000–2001, the percentage of students passing both parts of LEAP remained just under 50%, as compared to 30% passing both sections in 1999–2000. These results, on the face of it, were reason to celebrate, and celebrate the educators and students did. However, the impressive gains of 18 percentage points in overall passing percentages for regular education and 21 points for special education belie the fact that half of the students in a majority of the fourth-grade classes at Alpha had been there before, some more than once. The most recent scores from March 2002 have been even more sobering, with the percentage of students passing Language Arts and Math actually creeping downward slightly in comparison to the 2001 scores.

During the second round of interviews conducted soon after the summer retest numbers were issued in September 2001, the stress related to large numbers of repeating fourth graders began to show up in the remarks of the Alpha educators. Faced with 12 of her 25 students repeating fourth grade, one frustrated teacher put it this way just after school began:

> Fifty percent of the class has to repeat the fourth grade, and we are going to do the same thing over again. . . . They have already done the material once, so it is not particularly exciting or fun because you have already done it. . . . They start with resolve because they feel embarrassed, worried, because of the failure. . . . But they are doing the same thing over again. Nobody likes to repeat, to repeat, to repeat.

Another of the fourth-grade teachers noted that she had 31 students in September 2001, "and 12 of them have failed." This teacher reported that she knew two of her students to be in the fourth grade for the third time:

> Two of them I had two years ago. . . . Normally, you have a child and even if that child repeats, you wouldn't have them again because usually the next year they get it together and go on, but this was years ago and then I have the students again . . . and that is frustrating.

The assistant principal expressed concern about the likelihood of problems associated with the growing age disparity as students are repeatedly retained in fourth grade:

> I think there are some problems that are just coming to the surface—such as over-aged kids in a younger setting. . . . It has created some problems—some different kinds of problems that I don't think they thought through. . . . So you end up with a kid who is 14 in the fourth grade, and he is still sitting there, and everybody says, "I don't want my fourth-grade girl going to class with this 14-year-old boy."

These problems were confirmed in the final interview with Mrs. Roberts in 2002. One of the effects of retentions at Alpha is a growing discipline problem among students repeating fourth grade and among the new population bubble of former repeaters now being seen in the fifth grade.

Showing "Exemplary Growth" and Remaining "Academically Below Average"

While students are the ones most immediately affected by the high stakes related to LEAP 21, the test also carries consequences for teachers, administrators, and schools. Even though LEAP 21 is a criterion-referenced test, the state assigns to each school a norm-referenced School Performance Score

(SPS) based on a combination of test scores and attendance figures. Scores on the LEAP 21 test constitute 60% of a school's SPS. The Iowa Test of Basic Skills (ITBS), given in third and fifth grades, counts 30%. The remaining 10% is derived from attendance figures. Each year, the state requires that each school improve its overall score to reach a specified target that is determined in Baton Rouge. If attained, the targeted improvement keeps underperforming schools off the state's list of schools facing corrective actions, which may include allowance of student transfers out of the school, or closure for schools consistently failing to meet targets.

Following the initial test in 1999, the state assigned Alpha a 2-year growth target of 12.5 points, a gain that would move their SPS from 33.1 to 45.6. In 2000, the first year of high stakes, Alpha's SPS improved only slightly to 34.7, while the state average increased from 69.4 to 77.3. Needless to say, there was widespread concern at Alpha as to what might happen if the gains remained as flat in subsequent years. In 2001, however, Alpha's SPS Index shot up 18 points, thus ending the 2-year cycle with a 20-point gain.

There is an irony that accompanies these gains for which the school was recognized by the state in 2001 as showing "Exemplary Academic Growth." For even though Alpha's SPS shot up by 20 points in 2 years to 53.7, the state-average SPS also moved up by 8 points, from 69.4 to 77.3, thus making Alpha's climb from the "Academically Below State Average" category even more of a challenge. If the state average continues to move upward as it did again in 2002, this time by almost 5 points to 82.1, Alpha's chances of moving out of the "below-average" category appear daunting, given the fact that in 2002 Alpha's SPS actually moved down by 1.6 points to 52.1. Given these facts, it appears unlikely that below-average scoring schools such as Alpha can escape their inferior status assigned on the basis of the state's SPS. Regarding this phenomenon, the assistant principal commented wryly:

> . . . we're probably judging one school against another more than we should be because of the scores in the paper. . . . It's not match play . . . it should be how you are performing against the course, and we're turning it into match play, head-to-head competition, and that is not good.

Mrs. Roberts noted that the increasing distance to the next rung on the performance ladder had been a subject of discussion among principals, some of whom expressed anger and dismay. Her focus, however, came back to her school:

> It concerns me as to how people interpret that data and how they look at our school, but with me being right there in the classrooms on a regular basis, I see constant progress. I am not concerned. I know that the teachers are working

hard, and they are working smarter. And I see that teachers are changing in attitudes. And when you see something like that, you can't help but be positive about what is going on. My teachers did not focus on the data—we celebrated like we had brought home the gold and the silver in the Olympics. I can't push them anymore—I can't ask for more than what I am getting right now.

The LEAP: Perceived Purposes

> I remember saying, give me motivated kids and I will be a better teacher—maybe we can use this to motivate kids. (Assistant Principal, Alpha Elementary)

A number of the questions put to the Alpha educators were intended to elicit their thoughts and feelings regarding the purposes of the LEAP 21. Early in the interview protocol, participants were asked what they considered the purposes of the LEAP 21, and later in the interviews they were asked to discuss the intended consequences and the unintended results. In analyzing the results, it became clear that these educators perceive the test as positively intended. Most Alpha educators see the LEAP as an attempt to end social promotion, to hold educators responsible for teaching the prescribed curriculum, and to increase student learning. All participants supported the goal of higher academic achievement for students and the elimination of social promotion, and they identified LEAP as instrumental in enforcing these goals. While expressing hope, if not certainty, about the overall purposes of LEAP, one fourth-grade teacher answered, "I hope that the purpose is trying to help the young boys and girls because in the past we have had just social promotion, just passing on."

While the participants saw the connection between LEAP and these purposes, they saw teacher and student accountability as the primary reasons for the LEAP. One educator put her response in terms that addressed the state's low rankings in national comparisons:

> To me, it is to monitor and make sure we are teaching what we should be teaching and that our boys and girls are mastering those skills—because they have been down on Louisiana in terms of education, in terms of our students ranking last. We ranked last in terms of student performance, we ranked last in terms of teacher salary, so look at it as a means of monitoring what is going on in the classroom.

Another participant spoke of how the responsibility of educators to make decisions regarding student promotion had been preempted by the use of this new singular determinant called LEAP 21:

> I feel like for 100 years or more educators decided who deserved to be promoted and who didn't, and we kind of messed that up. So now the public, through the

politicians, has taken that away from us, and now they are deciding. I don't know if that is right or wrong.

The question related to purposes for LEAP brought responses that indicated a belief that the state's purpose was to show that the teachers had taught and that the children had learned. There was a consensus among these educators that LEAP was intended as "a tool to use to say you actually taught the material, and the children retained the material that we asked you to teach." With further questioning during the interviews related to consequences, both intended and unintended, the respondents began to elaborate perspectives that would indicate a complex relationship between purposes and outcomes.

The LEAP and School Climate

> You know everything is so focused on this one thing . . . it has kind of taken the joy out of teaching and learning. (Special Education Teacher, Alpha Elementary)

Since the inception of LEAP, Alpha educators describe the climate at their school as focused, serious, and stressful. Recess time has given way to a direct instruction program in reading that runs school-wide every morning from 8:30 to 9:45. Assemblies that are not motivational sessions for LEAP are rare. Field trips prior to the March testing each year are just as uncommon, and the attention has diminished for school observances such as Black History Month. Emphasis on diagnostic testing has moved down to second grade, and in the 2002–2003 school year, all first graders will be tested for the first time. Testing is the order of the day, and there is no school program that has remained unaffected. As one educator explained:

> We've got to teach to those standards and not a lot of the fluff. We've got to stop having assemblies, taking these kids out of class and doing things that are fun to do—Christmas program, Black History Month. And all of that is important to a person's overall education, but this is important now—it is the LEAP that is important. The other stuff you'd better pick up through church or recreational groups or whatever. High stakes means we're going to have to change everything.

The pressures associated with testing have had unforeseen effects on faculty relations at the school, particularly among fourth-grade teachers. These teachers, their curriculum coordinator, and the administration have grown closer both personally and professionally as they work as a team to improve LEAP scores. Although each of these teachers experienced an increase in stress as a result of LEAP, they all noted an increase in sharing of ideas related to teaching tactics and strategies, both successful and unsuccessful:

> After 3:00 we [fourth-grade teachers] are in the hall yelling and hollering among ourselves, and we communicate on the phone, or we sit in the library and say, "Well, I did this, but nothing happened, but when I went back and retaught this, something happened."

Another teacher also noted closer relations with other fourth-grade teachers:

> We gave a lot of grade-level meetings . . . and we are constantly back and forth on a daily basis finding out, "How is this student doing in your class" . . . we are having to do a lot more team preparation.

The curriculum coordinator responded this way when asked about relations among faculty:

> For my fourth-grade teachers, it has brought us much closer together. There are things I have done for my fourth-grade teachers this year that I have not done for the other teachers because I am aware of how stressed they are. . . . We have done a lot of fun things together in terms of going out, away from the school, and just hanging out, just trying to relax.

The LEAP and the Curriculum

> I still believe in a well-rounded person and extracurricular activities, be it athletics or band. I think those are important, but they're not important anymore. There's only one thing: To be an educated person in the state of Louisiana, you'd better pass the LEAP. (Fourth-Grade Teacher, Alpha Elementary)

It is not uncommon for educational reform efforts to set in motion unintended and counterproductive consequences that have a neutralizing effect on the measured successes of intended outcomes. This phenomenon seems to be at work at Alpha, and it is manifested in the remarks of the educator participants regarding the curriculum changes that have come about since LEAP began. Educators at Alpha are intensely focused on helping more students to pass the LEAP, and that focus has brought about significant changes in the content that is presented, how that content is taught, and how the learning of that content is evaluated. Though primarily impacting the fourth-grade curriculum, there is a strong perception that the school program in K–3 should work actively to offer a curriculum consistent with and supportive of the basic goal of improving LEAP scores. The gravity arising from this centripetal pressure can be appreciated through one educator's observation:

> . . . the LEAP test is fourth-grade level [but it] is not a test for fourth graders—it is a test of first, second, third, and fourth graders . . . right now the ones feeling the pressure to pass the test are fourth graders, but really the pressure to learn the material—you've got to learn it all the way along. . . . This test is now

the deciding factor. It used to be a lot of things went into an education—there were social issues, there were a lot of different things—now it is just a test. It decides everything.

During the 2000–2001 school year, the fourth-grade curriculum for Delta Parish was revised to reflect the math, English, science, and social studies skills that are assessed by LEAP 21. These standards and benchmarks, along with a renewed emphasis on test-taking strategies, form the core for lessons presented to fourth graders at Alpha from August to March in each year. The process of selecting and sequencing the skills that are tested and, therefore, taught during the school year begins early when Mrs. Roberts meets with her coordinators. Most teachers admitted that "the curriculum is much more test-directed than before because of the pressure." Another said, "We're getting information all the time about which particular parts of the curriculum to zoom in on."

Interviews with Alpha educators yielded remarks that show that the LEAP has had a powerful funneling effect that continues to pull content, instruction, assessment, and other school activities into an ever-tightening spiral. When asked if the curriculum had changed since the introduction of LEAP, Mrs. Roberts summed up most responses when she said, "We're a lot more focused, and we're teaching to the test." All participants indicated that the primary focus of the fourth grade was to teach the skills that are tested with the LEAP. Teachers were quick to point out that LEAP was the primary determinant in which of the state curriculum standards and benchmarks are addressed and evaluated during the school year, even though other goals could be addressed "after March":

> We're doing a lot of our testing in the classroom on the format of the LEAP. . . . If we know it is a skill that weighs heavily on the LEAP test, instead of teaching in April we make sure that the children are exposed to those skills a little sooner. It dictates when we teach certain things because we teach skills other than just those on the LEAP, but we make sure that are children are exposed to those skills on the LEAP prior to March.

In a study on the effects of high-stakes testing (Gordon & Reese, 1997), researchers found that high-stakes testing may become the primary learning objective rather than the tool to measure the attainment of learning objectives. What became clear from our conversations with Alpha educators over time is that the scale used to measure negative or positive effects of curricular decisions has become a scale derived from the measured or predicted effect on student test scores. In effect, the multiple criteria that educators often use to judge the veracity of curricular decisions has been reduced to a single criterion: Is this curricular decision likely to raise or lower student scores? As Mrs. Roberts explained, the LEAP has essentially replaced the parish curriculum guide, and it has become the primary tool used in choosing the State Content Standards and Benchmarks. One teacher at Alpha saw the change in terms of offering more challenging content:

> Students are being exposed to information that is much more challenging and interesting, and it's making them thinkers—causing them to sit down and analyze, which is something that they have to be able to do in terms of being prepared for the future.

When asked if the LEAP has narrowed or widened the curriculum, Mrs. Roberts responded that she thought the LEAP "has narrowed the curriculum, but I do not think that is the bad thing." She went on to elaborate that she, as a former classroom teacher, had also offered a rather narrow curriculum, but one chosen for its practical import related to life skills and not because it was intellectually exciting or academically demanding:

> I was guilty of not focusing in on some areas because I thought, "They are not going to need that," you know, "They are not going to need this algebra and this is higher stuff." That was an injustice because when a child left, I didn't know where the child might go, and my focus was narrow. I didn't give the children some of the tools they needed that they could have built on when they got to high school—and I don't know what they might have turned out to be if I had touched on some of these areas.

When discussing the issue of teaching to the test, Mrs. Roberts indicated that some teachers see their creativity threatened by the strong emphasis on teaching only the skills, concepts, and facts that may appear on the LEAP. She offered little consolation:

> We have got to understand that we didn't accept this job and come to work so we can be creative. . . . if only we had been hired for these wonderful, creative, fantastic . . . ideas, then we would have gone into being an artist, a sculptor, that type of thing. . . . I equate it to getting on a train and trying to get the Dallas and I want the train to stop so I can go over here and look at these daisies. . . . and that is the way that I tried to explain it to my teachers. . . . previously we had a tendency to do that—we had a destination and half the time we didn't get there because we felt the need to go into these other things. Now you don't have a choice—you've got to get the Dallas by March.

The LEAP and Teaching

> ... children can know information, but if it is not presented to them in the same way that it is presented on the test, then that doesn't work. (Fourth-Grade Teacher, Alpha Elementary)

All the participants noted the unerring focus on the LEAP, and they all indicated that the test has affected what and how they teach, as well as how they assess students. Educators saw the LEAP as providing a new focus for instruction, and their response to this new focus varied. One teacher saw the new focus as an implicit, if not explicit approval, to teach the test: "LEAP gives us a direction. Now we're going to have to teach the test. And before, that was always like cheating, for a teacher to say, 'teach the test.' But now, why not? What else is there to learn?" Another teacher, less liberated by the prospect of teaching to the test, remarked that "it's more focused on the test. . . . Before, I could do a lot of things that were student generated. . . . I don't have that leeway to do it as much. I will be able to do some after the test, but since August it's been totally this test, this test." These educators' reactions ranged from a grudging acceptance to determined resignation, and the following reaction shows, perhaps, a wistful and more detailed recollection of teaching prior to LEAP:

> I really feel like there are so many things socially that I could share with the children from my experience, social experiences that I believe these children miss, that they don't get from television or home. They don't understand the holidays sometimes, you know the way we understand the holidays, and stories, and little pieces of experiences that I used to do but I don't do anymore with the kids.

The LEAP has certainly affected teaching, and it has affected the teachers as significantly. The major effect that teachers noted was an increase in stress levels arising from inward and outward pressure to obtain results, but teachers also noted stress that arises from the frustration that comes the adoption of an unyielding scope and sequence that leaves little latitude for dealing with the many students who are not on the fourth-grade level, where their instruction is focused:

> It has made me hyper, stressful—very stressful, that is, if you care and you have some concern. . . . I have these children two or three levels behind. I can't teach them second or third grade level. I have to introduce or I have to present to all

of them fourth-grade material. I don't go back to second or third and pull that, even though I know that they are there. I have to do what my curriculum guide says for fourth grade.

Direct Instruction and "Learning Your Lines"

In an effort to increase reading comprehension, which is seen by Alpha's teachers as a key to greater gains in all four areas of LEAP, the school purchased the reading component of Direct Instruction from Science Research Associates in fall 2000. *Direct instruction* is a scripted drill-and-practice teaching technique pioneered by Siegfried Engelmann in the 1960s as a remedial instructional strategy. Initially intended for K–3 reading and math, direct instruction has expanded to include components, too, for science, writing, spelling, and social studies. Both the assistant principal and principal attended a summer institute devoted to explaining the benefits of direct instruction and how the program works. The assistant principal explained the benefits of the program for teachers this way:

> . . . it took a lot of the planning time away from the teacher—the teachers didn't have to do any planning for reading. I told them to swap off—instead of planning, you have to practice so that you don't walk in there cold—you can't just read it to them. It's like a bad actor in a good movie—you're given a script, but how you deliver that script is what makes a difference . . . in direct instruction, we were in there from 8:30 to 9:45. . . . It was pretty intense.

Though highly unpopular when first introduced, fourth-grade teachers now appear resigned to this new strategy if it can be linked to increases in test scores. Following the 26% increase in the passing rate for Language Arts in 2001, all the teachers and administrators attributed gains to the new focus on reading that came with direct instruction. For the 20-point gain in their SPS, the state gave Alpha $24,000 in "award money." Mrs. Roberts reports that they will use that money to purchase the direct instruction component for math, so that all fourth graders in the 2002–2003 school year will receive direct instruction in math. The assistant principal enthused:

> . . . I love it. I have always hated canned programs . . . but this program works. I had teachers who hated it last year—thought they were going to be a bunch of robots reading a script. By the time we got to January, they're dragging me into their room and showing me what kind of success they were having.

Even with the success, the acceptance of direct instruction was also accompanied by a sense of loss that was expressed by this teacher when she said:

> . . . it's a much more serious attitude here . . . than what we had before, so you know there's a joy in succeeding somewhat, but there's also that loss of individ-

ual ways that teachers have when they present materials and information, and you kind of lose some of yourself because you are in this really structured program.

The LEAP and School Administration

Mrs. Roberts pointed out that the price of accountability through testing is being paid in the loss of teachers (both competent and incompetent), as well as the loss of prospective teachers whose career choices are negatively affected by the perceived pressures and possible consequences associated with LEAP. Mrs. Roberts reported that she and other principals in the parish were having difficulty filling fourth-grade positions "because of the stress level" associated with the LEAP 21. Some principals had fourth-grade teachers who were requesting transfers to the lower grades in order to reduce stress, and most of the inquiries from applicants were for grades other than fourth. Mrs. Roberts felt herself fortunate to keep her fourth-grade teachers, a fact she attributed to their determination "that they were going to bring up scores or just keel over." She went on to point out, however, that, "We're losing a lot of good people in education," a fact that compounds the permanent shortage of certified teachers in poor, urban schools:

> We have got a shortage in education like I have never seen before, and I have seen a lot of people who would make a good teacher and I see now because we're so focused on test scores that we're throwing people off the train—we're not even bothering to fool with them—if you're not cutting it, then you're out of here . . . you're going to get them out of there, or they are going to leave on their own. And I am seeing that we're not taking the time to nurture and work with and produce good educators because time is always of the essence. And we're throwing away a lot of good teachers.

Mrs. Roberts noted that the LEAP has affected every facet of her work, including personnel decisions related to hiring and reassignments, curriculum planning, budgeting for and purchasing materials, planning assemblies, staff development, and communications with parents:

> I use those scores when I'm purchasing materials, manipulatives, purchasing programs for the computer. When I'm inviting people into the school to work with the teachers and . . . children . . . I go back and look at my test scores to see if this is going to help me. When I'm looking at interviewing . . . I talk about test scores and "If you have test scores that were low in this area, what would you do?" . . . We look at test scores of individual teachers—if I'm looking at test scores on an individual teacher, and I am seeing those scores fall down year after

year after year, then it's a school problem, it's a teacher problem, and I need to move that teacher out of that area. . . . We keep those scores focused constantly every time we talk with teachers.

Perhaps the most significant administrative change that the principal could attribute to LEAP was the change in management style to a more actively engaged approach:

> It's making a bunch of people get up off their butts, me included . . . and raising a whole bunch of people's level of concern. . . . It is making teachers teach, administrators get out of the office, put the paperwork aside—lord knows we're taking it home and staying up to one or two in the morning to get done—but it is making us get into those classrooms to see what is going on. It is making us give more direction to the vision of the school and making us have a mission. It is making us have a hard look at what we did in the past, and focus—[laughs] and it is killing us in the process.

Mrs. Roberts noted that the LEAP has affected her relationships with teachers both positively and negatively. On the positive side, she saw her role as shifting from school manager to instructional leader, and this has brought her closer both professionally and personally to her faculty:

> I'm finding that in the past, I was more of a manager. . . . With the high-stakes testing, you make yourself get in the classrooms more, so I found out a lot more about my teachers, their abilities, their skills. That came hand-in-hand with finding out more about your teachers at a personal level. . . . I think right now we're hand-in-hand, we're all working together, and that came along from them feeling comfortable about coming to share things with me on a personal level about what was going on with their lives and things that might affect their job. . . . It forced us to be more comfortable, to share, to have a one-on-one relationship now because we have so much at stake.

At the same time that Mrs. Roberts noted more involvement with the instructional process and more personalized knowledge about her teachers, she also pointed out that time constraints imposed on her by the LEAP had decreased her capacity to assist or nurture teachers, as she became aware through her new hands-on approach that they needed such assistance from her:

> [I] have always looked at my role as an administrator—if you're not where you are supposed to be [as a teacher], it is my job to get you there—it is my job to sit down with you and to work with you, provide services for you and classroom demonstrations for you and the lesson plans, but you don't have time for that.

The LEAP and Parents

> We've done about everything we can do. I'm very prayed up. (Parent quoted in local newspaper two weeks before the 2000 LEAP)

Alpha educators have taken a number of measures to inform parents about LEAP and to involve parents in the preparation of their students for the tests. All of the participants agreed that the academic gains demanded by LEAP require a strong commitment by parents to help their children attain higher test scores. Teachers emphasized an open-door policy for parental visits, and they made regular contact through letters, phone calls from school, and even some home visits. One teacher noted that parents were invited to call her on weekends and to visit the classroom at any time. Multiple yearly contacts with parents or multiple attempts at contact with parents are the norm at Alpha among fourth-grade teachers.

All participants agreed that LEAP "has brought about an increase in our parent concern." This increase in concern, however, has not always translated to increased involvement by parents:

> We still have a multitude of workshops that parents have been invited to come to, and we have had sharing sessions. I have things organized with the bus to bring them over here, but I have not seen those numbers increase. The only time that we had a large number of parents who came was [when] we sent out [letters] home saying we were going to share some information about fourth-grade testing—[part of message being] if you do not come, your child will fail the fourth-grade test. You get to bribing and always thinking creatively and hope that it does not come back on you—just to get parents to come [laughs]. We had wall-to-wall parents, but we were trying to share information with them that they could take home, so they could use this packet.

As in many other poor, urban schools, the parents of these children are often the least capable of providing the support needed for their children to improve academically. Both principals and teachers pointed out that, despite ongoing efforts to maintain contact with parents, the majority of parents did not become engaged in actively helping their children, even when parents expressed concern and worry about their child's need for improvement. This is attributable, in part, to the fact that these parents' own educational attainments often reflect an inadequacy that many of the children of this school came to inherit. One teacher remembered: "When we had our parent meeting, the parents found they were unable to comprehend the state practice test that was given out at the meeting. Some of the activities had to be worked out step by step so that they had a better idea of what their children were facing and [would be] better able to help their children."

Another of the educators made the following observations related to parental awareness and a sense of desperation and confusion arising from an increased awareness that is not matched by an increased confidence in being able to help their children:

> They are helpless. They cannot teach their children. In this low socioeconomic area, they can't help them. The parents cry . . . they come and say, "Where can I get a tutor? Where can I get a program?" I see them more aware, but they are confused too. . . . I also see them as totally frustrated, confused, and admitting, "I didn't do well in school, but I didn't have to take this test." And they say that a lot. So I see the parents as extremely frustrated.

The LEAP and Students

> We have some children who come and want to learn, but they are just not able to do it, so they don't pass the test. And they are staying after school, but they are still not getting to the point where they can pass that test. We are seeing improvement in those students but not enough to pass the LEAP. (Mrs. Roberts, Principal, Alpha Elementary)

One teacher noted that LEAP 21, combined with the predominantly weak or nonexistent home support system, contributed to a widespread fear of failure among her students. Faced with a large number of students receiving minimal encouragement or coaching outside of school, one of the fourth-grade teachers resorts to the recounting of morality tales as a method to counter that fear:

> I have been telling them there's no need to be afraid. Just because you don't have anybody at home that cares, you as an individual person, you should be caring. Because you are that age now where you ought to be telling yourself, "I want to be somebody—I want to do something with my life." . . . I use . . . a story that was read where a little boy had parents, but they didn't care about what he did. And he just went on, and there were a lot of people on the outside of the school that helped him, and he graduated with honors. He went on to college, and he was a doctor. So . . . you can be anything that you want to be, but it's left up to you as that individual.

Even though Alpha educators were often positive and sometimes ambivalent regarding LEAP, they were unanimous in their belief that the LEAP should not constitute the sole criterion for determining promotion and retention of their students:

> [We] have a concern about determining whether a child passes or fails over

> something they do over a five-day span. . . . I think we need to use the test to see where we are lacking with this child and develop a program for this child or these children to address those concerns or skills and put him in an enriching type situation, but just to say they're going to be in fourth grade and stay there until they pass the test is not a good thing.

Another teacher expressed her concern this way:

> I don't like . . . some of the things I see when our students don't pass it, especially when you have children who do really well during the school year, and you know it's not a situation where the teacher is just giving students grades . . . and then they don't pass that test and you have to hold them back. That's kind of hard to deal with—it's kind of hard to say to the child that everything you did during the school year doesn't matter, doesn't count.

Stress in a Ziplock Bag

> I knew there was going to be some stress on the students, but I didn't see the extent of it where children before testing are just getting physically ill and throwing up and this kind of thing and children crying and not wanting to come to school. (Mrs. Roberts, Principal, Alpha Elementary)

All the educators noted increased stress levels in their students that they attribute to the high-stakes nature of a test that is the unrelenting focus of their school day. The fact that a year's worth work can be wiped out on a single test creates distress among students at test time:

> . . . you have a child that has done well all year long, and they think that the week of the test, if they blow it here, they have blown it for the entire school year. I think we need to look at some other things in terms of promotion to fifth grade, rather than basing it on whether or not you passed [the LEAP] in language arts or math—that's very stressful for the child.

Teachers shared a number of harrowing stories related to their students' reactions to testing. One teacher recalled the previous year when one of her students became ill and threw up on a test. The soiled test had to be sealed in a plastic bag and turned in for test security purposes. Another student developed a nosebleed that was so severe that she had to be taken to the hospital. A second teacher told us about one of her students who simply bubbled in her test before the directions were completely explained. The test was turned in, but the student had to retake that section of the test on a make up day. During observations during the March 2000 Test Week, one student was observed crying during the LEAP. The teacher attempted to comfort her with encouraging words and hugs. Later, the teacher informed us that the child was just overwhelmed with all the stress of the test.

Although the stress at test time is almost palpable, for some students the more significant distress comes in waiting for the results or after the results are provided. Here is a gripping example offered by the curriculum coordinator of one student's pain of waiting:

> Well, just this week, it was very difficult . . . I have a student—this is his fourth year in fourth grade—and we received our LEAP results for summer school yesterday. So he has been asking me every day . . ."Did I pass, did I pass?" And I was reluctant to tell him, so I asked the teacher, "Do you want to tell him?" and she said "no." So we had to pull him out—while he was waiting for me to tell him the results, you can hear his heart pounding.

Another teacher recalled how another student dealt with the news of failure, this time a special education student with spina bifida whose failure quickly turned to shame:

> . . . he hid under the bed last time—I mean this is a child who can't walk—he scooted out of his chair, he was embarrassed, he was upset. He crawled under the bed when he found out he didn't pass last time—he was afraid to see his mom when she got home. So it is really an esteem knocker.

Discussion

Problems and Winners: Promise and Losers

The debate swirling around the issue of high-stakes standardized testing shows signs of becoming increasingly polarized (if that is possible), with the two opposing camps fortifying positions familiar to the traditionalist and the progressivist armies that have waged the curriculum and policy wars for the past 100 years in American education. And as talk gives way to policy battles fought mainly through an American press bent toward the sensational, much of the debate is replaced by the exchange of propaganda salvos intent upon causing damage to the other side. The experiences, then, of Alpha educators to the test talk and the test practice of LEAP 21 are not likely to satisfy either proponents or opponents of high-stakes standardized testing; for these teachers' remarks have consistently expressed both the hopes and fears, the celebrations and concerns, and the joys and the anguish of professional educators intent upon doing the best they can for their students given the orders of the day, which they had no voice in issuing. This is articulated so poignantly in a remark by a special education teacher:

> To me, it is heartbreaking to see. . . . It is really, really hard for everyone involved to go through this, the preparation, the judgment, the consequences—so many

lives have been—it is so serious now. And it is one test, one time, fourth and eighth grades—you lose your childhood, and yes, maybe it helped us focus on doing things better. . . . but I don't think this one test was the answer. . . . I still have a teacher thing, still hopeful, and still looking for more changes to make things better for everyone involved, especially for my . . . kids.

High-stakes testing proponents, whose research and commentary inevitably finds evidence to support high standards and high stakes as a way to ensure that we "leave no child behind," may be dismayed, if undeterred, that so many children at Alpha Elementary are being left behind. In 2000, 70% of fourth graders (75 students) were left behind, and in 2001 almost 50% (82 students) were retained in fourth grade. *(At the time of this writing, retention figures for 2001–2002 were not yet available.)* These same proponents of testing who rail about bad teaching may be flummoxed by the fact that Alpha and other area schools are finding it difficult to recruit fourth-grade teachers, either good or bad, to teach the burgeoning fourth-grade classes. At Alpha, for example, it was necessary to transfer a fifth-grade teacher and to call back to active duty one of their retired teachers. These same proponents who summon parents toward more responsibility and involvement may be taken aback that some parents have chosen to send their children out of state to live with relatives during the fourth grade in order to escape the LEAP; or perhaps they may be bewildered that a significant portion of the parents who came to school to get their LEAP coaching materials could not answer the sample LEAP questions. Further, proponents who see high stakes as a way to motivate individual responsibility among students may become uneasy, or even queasy, when told of anxious fourth graders crying uncontrollably, having nosebleeds, or throwing up on their test booklets (that must be resealed and returned to the state for security purposes). These proponents may feel a twinge of regret or empathy, even, when they hear of the boy whose heart could be heard beating from across the teacher's desk as he waited to find out that he would be in the fourth grade for a fourth time. Or will these proponents of high-stakes testing be temporarily quieted when told of that boy with spina bifida who failed the LEAP for the second time and who, in shame, managed to crawl from his wheelchair and hide under the bed rather than face his disappointed mother.

On the other hand, opponents of LEAP 21 and other forms of high-stakes testing may find ammunition or at least register some grim consolation in the disturbing findings just cited. However, opponents of testing will be less sanguine when they hear teachers argue in support of LEAP that, "Students are being exposed to information that is much more challenging, interesting, and . . . making them thinkers." Opponents of high stakes, too, may be dismayed when Alpha educators speak of LEAP "making teachers teach and administrators get out of the office and into the classrooms." Opponents of testing may be disappointed to hear teachers claim that with LEAP, "You can see exactly what the child's deficits are and their strengths. . . . You can use those things for building blocks and . . . remediation." And what are opponents of LEAP to make of this math teacher turned principal who recognizes for the first time that her prior teaching had been patronizing and intended to placate children whom she had determined would need only survival skills rather than algebra, thus keeping them from the requirements that would at least make the consideration of college a possibility?

The story contained in the thoughts, feelings, and experiences of these Alpha educators is far too complex to satisfy the requirements of ideological polarities that attract ardent supporters or ardent detractors of testing. The experiential field of Alpha Elementary includes the entire spectrum of seemingly dichotomous testing consequences that, unlike the arguments of ideologues, cannot be separated out into neat columns to be added up into sums of virtues or vices, depending on the ideological pole to which one may become magnetized. The experiential field of these educators contains the strong ideological components that result from such large-scale state commitments as LEAP; and it contains, too, the behavioral, or sensory, components that arise from these educators' direct observations and participation in events that follow from this ideological commitment as it moves from concept to practice to consequences. For these teachers, coordinators, counselors, and administrators, the ideological commitment and the participatory events, though often at odds, form a unitary experiential field within which they are embedded. This does not mean, however, that these educators are unable to distinguish between these two aspects of their experience, as their remarks indicate a clarity that exposes the strong divergences that do exist between concepts of testing and consequences of testing in their school.

When the ideology of high-stakes testing is not aligned with the observed outcomes, which is often the case, these educators are exposed to two sides of an experiential field that most often forms a dichotomy of figure and ground (Varela, 1979, pp. 271–278), of the explicit and the implicit. We can see this in the distinctions that the educators made in regard to the confrontation of the ideological commitment and the practical effects of testing as instituted in their school. As these educators see state testing raising standards and expectations, they are very much aware that testing increases pressure, stress, and failure. With increased accountability comes widespread retention. As curriculum and assessments become focused and clear, we see the narrowing of subjects, school activities, and the constriction of assessment strategies. As high stakes provide a strong impetus to improve or remove ineffective teachers, so, too, do they push out some competent teachers and discourage new applicants where they are most needed. Just as instruction becomes more rigorous and focused, there is loss of the spontaneity, creativity, and professional judgment. Just as teachers see academic gains among some of their students, they see more failure and a loss of joy in coming to school and learning.

As Alpha's school performance initially showed "exemplary academic growth" and brought financial awards, Alpha remains "academically below average" and finds the next rung of the performance ladder even farther away as state average scores move upward and gains go flat. While the school administrators are more engaged in the instructional program in active ways, there is less time to focus on the individual growth needs of teachers that their increased involvement has helped them to identify. Even though increased parental outreach has increasingly brought parents into the school, more parents are grasping, sometimes with desperation, for ways to help their children. And while the high-stakes testing at Alpha has provided an impetus to work "harder, faster, and longer," these educators face increasing levels of exhaustion and the potential for burnout. In the end, these educators present themselves as determined, persistent, and hopeful, at the same time that they exhibit signs of serious stress, anxiety, and continuing worry about their students' prospects. How can this be so?

At Alpha Elementary, the ramifications of failure, ranging from student retention to public renunciation to school closure, are severe enough to create a relentless pressure to do, within legal bounds, whatever is necessary to raise the test scores. The words and deeds of these educators make that point clear. Having had this mandate forced upon them with these potential and real consequences intact, it should come as no surprise which aspects of their experiential field these educators choose to make figural: If they are to minimize the negative consequences of testing, they must surely focus on the ideological promise. It is against this dark background of failure that the brighter promises of testing are placed front and center, thus transforming the terrible prospect of tangible failure into an attraction to the ideology of testing and all that it demands. To survive in this setting requires nothing less than—and the data gathered at Alpha clearly shows—a shift over time to the direction of the "positive" and away from the "negative." After numerous conversations and three interviews over 2 years, one of the last points Mrs. Roberts made was this:

> We had to improve our test scores—we didn't want people coming in and taking over our school. The bottom line was we were going to have to improve our test scores, and the children, our children, were going to be the beneficiaries of

> the hard work that would have to be done. So I don't even want to hear that—even at faculty meetings, my last thing is, "Does anybody have any announcements, anything positive to say? Anything negative, keep it to yourself." Because it doesn't help. If you've got to do it, just do it.

The implications of this shift remain unknown, as does the degree of its persistence. If it seriously diminishes the failure that these teachers want most to avoid for their students, themselves, and the school, then their choice will have served the purpose for which it was chosen. On the other hand, if the attention and commitment given to testing do not produce the sought-after results, then one must wonder how these educators may come to view those students, and themselves, whose failure embodies that reality they have attempted most diligently to extinguish.

Measurable Results With Immeasurable Meaning?

> As long as learning is connected with earning, as long as certain jobs can only be reached through exams, so long must we take the examination system seriously. If another ladder to employment were contrived, much so-called education would disappear, and no one would be a penny the stupider. (E. M. Forster, 1927)

As the source of accountability pressures moves beyond Louisiana and other individual states to the federal level, the stakes, indeed, become elevated as cash-strapped states face tough decisions about how to meet the mandates set out in the *No Child Left Behind Act*. With seven other states already joining Louisiana in linking grade promotion in the lower grades to high-stakes tests (Amrein & Berliner, 2002a, 2002b), it is likely that this trend will increase, particularly, it seems, in those states with large minority populations. For instance, Amrein and Berliner report that "none of the ten states with the lowest populations of African-Americans have implemented high-stakes tests, whereas all of the ten states with the highest populations of African-Americans have done so" (p. 12). Similarly, my own analysis has yielded these findings related to the use of high-school exit examinations. Of the 20 states with the highest percentages of African Americans, 16 have high school exit examinations. Of the 20 states with the highest percentages of Whites, one has high school exit examinations. Of the 20 states lowest in White population, only two do not have exit examinations.

Whether or not these facts will be read as simple coincidence, bitter irony, or the most virulent form of covert racism, our response will depend in part on a focus that is subject to moving between the ideological promise of testing and the effects of testing on students, educators, and parents. In the meantime, at Alpha Elementary more than 4 in 10 of the fourth graders who took the last big test are now repeating fourth grade.

It would appear to this researcher that the politically energized and research-starved juggernaut of high-stakes testing presents an unparalleled opportunity and need for further study by educationalists, sociologists, psychologists, anthropologists, and historians. It is time to begin a coordination of the long-term study—statistical, observational, interview, and otherwise—of the individual, community, and societal effects for those who benefit and those who suffer from what has become a national reform obsession. However, it may prove an unfortunate irony that the longitudinal, in-depth, cross-disciplinary, and multimethod research needed to understand the individual and societal dimensions unfolding from this reform movement may, in the near future, fall short of the evidentiary demands placed upon research by those at the top of this policy food chain who seek to limit federal funding of research to experimental or quasi-experimental methods. This new demand for research based on a "medical model" (Davis, 2002) would most likely preclude the research presented here or even that which is here proposed. There is a further irony, of course, in that the unwavering policies emanating from federal decisions regarding educational accountability, school instruction and curriculum, and research practices, do not, themselves, adhere to the conventions of science, neither the normal conventions nor the more constricted ones that are intended to be placed on researchers attempting to understand and report on the educational benefits and the harrowing human costs of such policies in action.

References

Airasian, P. W. (1988). Measurement driven instruction: A closer look. *Educational Measurement: Issues and Practice* 7(4), 6–11.

American Educational Research Association (2000). *AERA position statement concerning high-stakes testing in preK–12 education.* Retrieved July 11, 2002, from http://www.aera.net/about/policy/stakes.htm

Amrein, A. L., & Berliner, D. C. (2002a). *The impact of high-stakes tests on student academic performance: An analysis of NAEP results in states with high-stakes tests and ACT, SAT, and AP Test results in states with high school graduation exams.* Tempe, AZ: Educational Policy Studies Laboratory (EPSL), Arizona State University. Retrieved January 3, 2003, from http://edpolicylab.org

———. (2002b). *An analysis of unintended and negative consequences of high-stakes testing.* Tempe, AZ: Educational Policy Studies Laboratory (EPSL), Arizona State University. Retrieved January 3, 2003, from http://edpolicylab.org

Barksdale-Ladd, M. A., & Thomas, K. F. (2000). What's at stake in high-stakes testing: Teachers and parents speak out. *Journal of Teacher Education* 51(5), 384–397.

Bateson, G. (1972). *Steps to an ecology of mind.* New York: Ballantine Books.
Blumer, H. (1969). *Symbolic interactionism.* Englewood Cliffs, NJ: Prentice-Hall.
Bracey, G. W. (1998). High stakes testing comes a cropper? *Phi Delta Kappan 79*(8), 630.
Davis Jr., O. L. (2002). New policies and new directions: Be aware of the footprints! Notice the nightmares. *Journal of Curriculum and Supervision 18*(2), 103–109.
Education Week (2001). A direct challenge. *Education Week 18*(27), 41–43.
Forster, E. M. (1927). *Aspects of the novel.* New York: Harcourt.
Gadamer, H. (1976). *Philosophical hermeneutics.* Berkeley: University of California Press.
Glaser, B., & Strauss, A. (1967). *The discovery of grounded theory.* Chicago: Aldine.
Goodwin, B. (1994) *How the leopard changed its spots: The evolution of complexity.* New York: Charles Scribner's Sons.
Gordon, S. P., & Reese, M. (1997). High-stakes testing: Worth the price? *Journal of School Leadership 7*, 345–368.
Herman, J. L., & Golan, S. (1993). The effects of standardized testing on teaching and schools. *Educational Measurement: Issues and Practice 12*(4), 20–25.
Hoffman, J. V., Assaf, L. C., & Paris, S. G. (2001). High-stakes testing in reading: Today in Texas, tomorrow? *The Reading Teacher 54*(5), 482–492.
Horn, J. K. (1998, January). *Recursive enaction: an evolving methodology.* Paper presented at 1998 International Qualitative Research in Education conference, Athens, GA.
———. (2002). *Recursive enaction and the search for a science of qualities.* Unpublished manuscript.
Kaestle, K. (1983). *Pillars of the republic: Common schools and American society, 1780–1860.* New York: Hill & Wang.
Lincoln, Y., & Guba, E. (1985). *Naturalistic inquiry.* Beverly Hills, CA: Sage.
Lonergan, B. (1958). *Insight: A study of human understanding.* New York: Philosophical Library.
Louisiana Department of Education (2000). *Reaching for results: LEAP 21.* Baton Rouge: Louisiana Department of Education.
Madaus, G. F. (1985). Test scores as administrative mechanisms in educational policy. *Phi Delta Kappan 66*(9), 611–617.
Mehrens, W. A. (1998). Consequences of assessment: What is the evidence? *Education Policy Analysis Archives 6*(13), 1–30.
Moustakas, C. (1990). *Heuristic research: Design, methodology, and application.* Newbury Park, CA: Sage.
National Commission on Excellence in Education (1983). *A nation at risk: The imperative for educational reform.* Washington, DC: Government Printing Office. Retrieved July 15, 2002, from http://www.ed.gov/pubs/NatAtRisk/risk.html
National Research Council (1999). *Testing, teaching, and learning: A guide for states and school districts.* Washington, DC: National Academy Press.
Padilla, R. (1999). *HyperQual 3, Version 1.0* [Computer program]. Chandler, AZ: HyperQual.

Popham, W. J. (1999). Why standardized tests don't measure educational quality. *Educational Leadership 56*(6), 204–208.

Smith, M. L. (1991). Put to the test: The effects of external testing on teachers. *Educational Researcher 20*, 8–11.

Strauss, A., & Corbin, J. (1998). *Basics of qualitative research* (2nd ed.). Thousand Oaks, CA: Sage.

Tyack, D., & Cuban, L. (1995). *Tinkering toward utopia: A century of public school reform.* Cambridge, MA: Harvard University Press.

Varela, F. (1979). *Principles of biological autonomy.* New York: North Holland.

CHAPTER TEN

The Use of Jigsawing in Second Language Acquisition Among Third- and Fourth-Grade Hispanic Migrant Students in Kansas

RUDOLPH BUSTOS

Abstract

The purpose of this study was to determine whether the Jigsawing cooperative-group technique would facilitate second language acquisition (SLA) among third- and fourth-grade migrant Hispanic students in Kansas. A mixed-methods research with triangulation was conducted with 15 students in the Newcomer Program at two Kansas schools. Although standardized test results proved insignificant, criterion-referenced test differences (t-test) between experimental and control groups were significant at the 0.05 level ($p = 0.03$, df = 4). Observations noted purposeful, cooperative behavior among treatment participants. Their responses to open-ended questions correlated with active participation. Triangulation confirmed observations to be consistent with quantitative results. Although the sample size was small, results indicated that Jigsawing is a valuable tool in SLA with Hispanic migrants. The results support further research.

Introduction

Current findings from the National Center for Education Statistics indicate that the average scale score in reading for US fourth graders basically remained the same from 1992 to 2002 (*Nation's Report Card: Reading Results for Grades 4, 8, and 12*, 2002). The findings revealed that Caucasian children, nevertheless, outperform African American and Hispanic children in reading (*Special Analysis 2003: Reading: Young Children's Achievement and Classroom Experiences*, 2004). The national reading composite grades (4, 8, and 12) for Kansas showed a scale score of "222 from 1995 to 2002" (pp. 3–8). For about 10 years, fourth-grade reading achievement has been on a plateau with no apparent changes in performance. The implications to second language acquisition (SLA) are many.

Grade 4 is a pivotal point in SLA. Transitioning begins as early as grade 3 and usually at grade 4. The majority of the United States, including Kansas, utilizes bilingual education. The primary proponents of Spanish to English transitioning are Thomas and Collier. Thomas and Collier (1997) note that the quality of SLA is contingent upon the primary language (L1) usage for instruction. "The more L1 academic work provided, the higher their achievement in the long term" (p. 56). The authors support the use of L1 across the curriculum for a half-day from kindergarten to first grade, "gradually increasing English instruction until L1 is phased out of the curriculum by Grade 4" (p. 57).

There are few studies that compare alternative approaches to instruction in Spanish or English for Hispanic migrant and nonmigrant children, and fewer studies that have "examined alternative methods of facilitating transition from Spanish to English reading, whenever that transition takes place. Studies of . . . such methods specifically designed for Latino or English language learners are [few]" (Fashola et al., 1997, p. 44). The areas of reading and educational achievement could best be explored through a research methodology combining a sociocultural approach with SLA.

Purpose of the Study

1. To understand the relationship of the socially contextual process of the Jigsawing technique to SLA.
2. To understand the relationship of Jigsawing to Hispanic migrant third- and fourth-grade children learning English in a newcomer group (transitional program for Hispanic newcomers).
3. To provide an interdependent forum as a means to give and to receive feedback regarding utterances in English and to correct utterances in order to be understood.
4. To determine if there exists a positive correlation between Jigsawing and SLA.

Study Conducted Against a Backdrop of Inequality

Teaching non-English-speaking children of color in Kansas was an established practice before Kansas became a state in 1861. The first free public school was established in the Native American territory of Kansas by the Wyandot Nation in 1844 (Smith, 1973). "John McIntyre Armstrong [an attorney] was the teacher . . . authorized by the Wyandot Council . . . White children were admitted free" (pp. 71–75). Cutler (1997) noted Kansas territory laws on educating children of color. Section 71 of Chapter 8 of the laws of 1858 declares: "All school districts established under the authority of this act shall be free and without charge for tuition to all children between the age of 5 and 21 years, and no sectarian instruction shall be allowed therein" (Cutler, 1997, *The Era of Peace, Part 19*, para. 3).

The Hispanic population began to grow significantly in Kansas around 1900, from 71 in that year to 8,429 individuals in 1910 (Avila, 1999), because of the prospect of laying track for the Atchison, Topeka, and Santa Fe Railway. The largest "migration of Hispanics came during the Mexican Revolution of 1910 to 1921 when Mexico was at war with itself" (Chavez, 1997, p. 1). Migrant farm work necessitated the cyclical removal of Hispanic children from their studies. Due to these disruptions, "most Mexican American children never progressed beyond middle school" (Chavez, 1997, p. 4). There were no educational mechanisms in place to accommodate these children. "Frank Rodriguez from Garden City, Kansas became the first Mexican American man to graduate from high school in 1950" (p. 6), 4 years before the *Brown v. Board of Education* decision.

Today, the Kansas teaching staff is heavily skewed in favor of Caucasian teachers (95.7% versus 1.4% Hispanic) (Fultz, 2004). This translates into a lack of role modeling for Hispanics, which manifests itself in a lack of success. "The graduation rate for Hispanics is '59.5 percent' " (Miller, 2003, pp. 45–46). In the contiguous state of Colorado—for comparison—about 7% of teachers are Hispanic, with a 65.5% Hispanic graduation rate (*Colorado Department of Education Fall 2002: Teacher Count by Race/Ethnicity*, 2002).

Kansas is one of the top 10 migrant states with a high percentage of limited English proficiency (LEP) students at 27.5%, compared to California's 28.2% (Kindler, 1995). Additionally, Kansas has the third highest dropout rate in the United States for Hispanics, and their dropout rates nationwide have remained between 30% and 35% for 25 years (*Crisis in Education: Soaring Hispanic Drop-Out Rates*, 2003), while the "Kansas immigrant population is the third fastest growing in the nation" (Stuart, 2003). Only 4.6% of Hispanics drop out in Colorado (*Colorado Education Facts*, 2002).

Research Questions

The research questions guiding this study are as follows:

1. To what extent does a sociocultural approach to Jigsawing affect SLA among third- and fourth-grade Hispanic migrant students in a Kansas newcomers group?
2. Can Jigsawing serve to facilitate:
   (a) *Peer feedback*: Do students call attention to each other's language errors? Cultural differences?
   (b) *Modification of input*: Do students let one another know whenever they do not understand, and help one another understand?
   (c) *Output*: Do students modify output to make it comprehensible?
   (d) *Awareness of grammatical features*: Are students following language rules?
   (e) *Awareness of cultural features*: Is the frame of reference meaningful to students?

Nature of the Study

The study used a mixed-methods approach in which quantitative research is primary, and qualitative research becomes secondary. Sociocultural and educational theory perspectives served as research guides. The study also featured control and experimental groups: pretesting, treatment interventions, and posttesting techniques. Feedback from personal student interviews and observations, as well as teacher interviews and observations, were combined to offer a holistic perspective. Social interactions of Hispanic migrant and nonmigrant students *within* Jigsaw groups and *among* the groups were observed. The qualitative data serve to triangulate results and offer a solution to SLA within a sociocultural learning environment.

The Theoretical Bases for the Study

Stephen Krashen, a linguist from the University of Southern California, developed a theory of SLA that forms the basis of much research in language. The theory consists of five major hypotheses:

1. *The Acquisition Learning Hypothesis*: There are two independent learning systems: (a) acquired learning, done subconsciously, and (b) formal learning of grammar, done consciously in the mezzosystem of the school.
2. *The Monitor Hypothesis*: The interplay between acquisition (utterance

initiator) and learning (editor), leading to refinement in language.
3. *The Natural Order Hypothesis*: The acquisition of grammatical structures follows a predictable sequence independent of learners' characteristics.
4. *The Input Hypothesis*: The focus is on acquisition and not learning. Progress occurs when the student receives second language input beyond his or her stage of linguistic competence.
5. *The Affective Filter Hypothesis*: The affective filter includes anxiety, motivation, and self-confidence. Increased anxiety, low motivation, and low self-confidence impede acquisition, while low anxiety, high motivation, and high self-confidence facilitate SLA (Krashen, 1987).

Jim Cummins (1989), an SLA researcher, put forth his *linguistic interdependence* hypotheses: "To the extent that instruction in Lx [minority language] is effective in promoting proficiency in Lx transfer of this proficiency to Ly [majority language] will occur provided there is adequate exposure to Ly (either in school or environment) and adequate motivation to learn Ly" (p. 22). Cummins reports that in many bilingual programs, children educated in a minority language develop skills in the majority language, which he asserts supports his linguistic interdependence hypothesis.

Cummins notes two types of communication, depending on the context in which it occurs:

1. *Context-embedded communication*: Meaning is supported by a wide range of cues such as objects, gestures, and vocal inflections. Examples are a conversation between friends talking about a commonly shared topic, and storytelling activities that include visual props.
2. *Context-reduced communication*: This type provides fewer communicative clues to support understanding. An example of this type of communication would be listening to a lecture on an unfamiliar topic. Most of what happens in the classroom is context-reduced, since the teacher is trying to convey information or teach new skills to the students (Cummins, 1981, pp. 3–49).

In 2002, C. E. Renner wrote *Serving Linguistically and Culturally Diverse Students in Kansas Schools: A Handbook for Implementing the Kansas State Bilingual Education Act*. He suggests grouping an equal portion of language minority students with language majority students, with instruction provided in both languages. "Native English speakers and speakers of another language have the opportunity to acquire proficiency in a second language while continuing to develop their native language skills. Students serve as native-speaker role models for their peers" (pp. 23–24). Renner's concept builds on peer influences and verbal interactions as facilitative processes to SLA.

Phonological and Other Linguistic Processes

An effect of transfer from "Spanish to English exists for phonemic segmentation skills for all Spanish-speaking students and for letter identification and word reading skills for Spanish-speaking students initially instructed in Spanish" (pp. 14–15). Phonemic segmentation refers to the ability to deal explicitly and segmentally with sound units smaller than the syllable (Stanovich, 1993–1994). Stanovich noted that "phonological awareness appears to play a casual role in reading acquisition" (p. 291).

Lev Vygotsky's *social cognitive development* theory proposes that social interaction profoundly influences cognitive development. Central to Vygotsky's theory is his belief that biological and cultural developments do not occur alone. A child's cultural development occurs socially and individually. It occurs "first, between people (interpsychological) through a dialectical process, and then inside the child (intrapsychological). This applies equally to voluntary attention, to logical memory, and to forming concepts. All the higher functions originate as actual relationships between individuals" (Vygotsky, 1978, p. 57). Complementing Vygotsky's theory and reinforcing social learning concepts are Bandura and Bruner.

Bandura, a social learning theorist, hypothesized that reciprocal interactions continuously occurring among behavioral, cognitive, and environmental factors determine behavior (Bandura, 1977). A child internalizes "tools" of intellectual adaptation to help him or her negotiate his or her culture of origin as well as the dominant culture.

Vygotsky's sociocultural theory of learning emphasizes that human intelligence originates in our society and culture (mezzosystems), and the potential for cognitive development he calls the *zone of proximal development* (ZPD): "The distance between what an individual can accomplish independently and what he/she can accomplish with the help of someone who is more competent" (Vygotsky, 1978, p. 86). Educators serve as facilitators and modelers, to challenge students toward new learning. Peer interaction and modeling are important ways to facilitate individual cognitive growth. Educators' use of scaffolding increases during ZPD and decreases as learners and groups internalize the "tools" for solutions.

Jerome Bruner's *constructivist* theory is based on the study of cognition. Learning is an active process in which learners construct new ideas or concepts based on their current and past knowledge. Learners construct knowledge and meaning individually and during interaction with others. The instructor's task is to present materials based on learners' current state of understanding and organize lessons in a spiral manner so the student builds upon prior knowledge (Bruner, 1963). Like Vygotsky's theory on cultural development, learning occurs at two levels. Primarily, "Learning is a social activity: Our learning is intimately associated with our connection with other human beings, our teachers, our peers, our family as well as casual acquaintances" (Hein, 1991, p. 4).

The influence of Vygotsky's theory can be seen in Krashen's approach. Social interactions are prevalent in both their works. "Krashen's *input hypothesis* resembles Vygotsky's concept of *zone of proximal development*" (Schütz, 2002, para. 12). According to the input hypothesis, progress occurs when the student receives second language input beyond his or her stage of linguistic competence; in Vygotsky's ZPD, new learning challenges the student above his or her competency level. The linguistic and social cognitive theories are complementary and serve as a foundation for this study.

Relevant Research Guiding the Study

Cooperative Learning

Cooperative learning refers to students working together to achieve a common goal. Aside from the usual learning goals, it includes the goal of establishing a collaborative helping relationship among participants (McCulloch, 1985). Lampe et al. (1996) studied the effects of cooperative learning and the interaction of gender on social studies and self-esteem of Hispanic fourth graders in America. The three researchers addressed the following questions:

1. Is there a difference in the social studies achievement self-esteem of fourth-grade students according to the treatments of cooperative learning or traditional instruction and according to gender across treatment groups?
2. Is there a difference in the social studies achievement of fourth-grade students according to the treatments of cooperative learning or traditional instruction and according to gender across treatment groups? (p. 187)

The 12-week study included 105 Hispanic students in eight fourth-grade social studies classrooms in two elementary schools. Twenty-five boys and 26 girls received instruction based on cooperative learning; and 24 boys and 30 girls received traditional, teacher-directed instruction. Results from this quantitative study revealed a positive difference between the cooperative and traditional groups, and both genders performed equally. Due to the small sample size, the measure of self-esteem was inconclusive. In the cooperative groups, extensive interaction "was apparent through the variety of exchanges—summarizing, explaining, clarifying, encouraging, probing, extending, and questioning. Intensive interaction was exhibited by the on-task behavior, the high level of motivation, and the 'eye-to-eye' communication posturing as the students interacted in cooperative-learning groups" (p. 191).

A meta-analysis of 99 studies of cooperative learning in US elementary and secondary schools that involved durations of at least 4 weeks compared achievement gains in cooperative learning and control groups. Of 64 studies of cooperative learning methods that provided group rewards based on the sum of group members' individual learning, 50 (78%) found significantly positive effects on achievement, and none found negative effects (Slavin, 1995, p. 30).

Gumperez et al. (1999) researched collaborative practices in bilingual classrooms among third- and fourth-grade students who were left to themselves. In this 3-year study, data were collected qualitatively (ethnography) in the form of video recordings. The researchers concentrated on "in-depth conversational and interactional sociolinguistic analysis of selected excerpts that illustrate key learning and teaching issues that arise in cooperative learning situations in monolingual and bilingual classrooms" (p. 4). The outcomes reveal that third- and fourth-grade children rely on communicative practices that are significantly different from adult talk, practices teachers may not readily comprehend:

1. Students shift their communication style from informal peer-group conversational forms to more formal styles of schooled discourse in negotiating solutions to particular tasks.
2. The children relied on shifts in intonation or tone of voice, stress, volume, and tempo to convey information that adults tend to convey through words.
3. Bilingual students' code switching [from one language to another] functions in ways that are equivalent to the above strategies and thus constitutes a communication resource for learning in bilingual cooperative groups. (p. 20)

Jigsawing

Jigsawing is a specific form of cooperative activity that requires interdependency, cooperation, and negotiations for meaning to complete a task. Dr. Aronson from the University of California at Santa Cruz invented the Jigsaw concept in Austin, Texas, in 1971 as an attempt to quell racial tension among newly desegregated public school students (Aronson, 2000). Caucasian, African American, and Hispanic students found themselves in a competitive classroom environment, which further increased tension. Aronson and staff focused on a fifth-grade class that was learning about the life of Eleanor Roosevelt. "We divided the students into small groups, diversified for race, ethnicity and gender, making each student responsible for a specific part of Roosevelt's biography" (para. 5). Aronson saw positive differences in a few weeks. The Jigsaw students (compared to traditional classroom students) expressed less prejudice and were more self-confident. They showed "greater academic improvement; poorer students in the Jigsaw classroom scored significantly higher on objective exams than comparable students in traditional classes, while the good students continued to do as well as the good students" (para. 10).

Glasser (1986), a noted psychiatrist and a proponent of quality education, advocates learning by teaching:

> Students retain knowledge in the following way: 10% of what they read, 20% of what they hear, 30% of what they see, 50% of what they see and hear, 70% of what they discuss with others, 80% of what they experience personally, and 95% of what they teach someone else. (p. 63)

Jigsawing incorporates Glasser's perspective. Combining the experiential learning approach with Hispanics' cultural preference for cooperative learning and Glasser's observation will serve to raise the retention rate, motivation, and English skill levels of Hispanic migrant children.

In a typical Jigsaw method, students study material on one of five topics distributed among the group members. They meet in "expert groups" to share information on their topics with members of other teams, who had the same topic, and then take turns presenting their topics to their own team. Johnson and Johnson (1987) note eight steps to ensure cooperative and individualistic thinking:

1. Describe the skill needed from the students.
2. Provide explanation of the skill from an expert.
3. Set up practice situations.
4. Ensure that each student receives feedback both from fellow students and the teacher on how well the skill is being performed.
5. Encourage perseverance in practicing the skill.
6. Set up situations in which the skill can be used successfully.
7. Integrate the skill and use it often.
8. Set up classroom norms to support the use of the skill.

Ghaith (2003), American University of Beirut, researched effects of the "Learning Together" cooperative learning model in improving English as a Foreign Language (EFL), reading achievement, academic self-esteem, and feelings of school alienation. Participants were 56 Arabic speaking, Lebanese high school learners of EFL. This was a quantitative study with control and experimental groups with pretests and posttests. "Student Team Learning includes the Jigsaw method. . . . The Jigsaw method has five major components: reading, expert group discussion, team report, testing, and team recognition" (p. 453). Although the findings did not support any significant difference between control and experimental groups in the areas of self-esteem and school alienation, the "results revealed a statistically significant difference in favor of the experimental group on the variable of EFL reading achievement" (p. 460).

Demographic Data in Kansas

The Southwest Kansas Area Cooperative District 613 is one of the largest geographical cooperatives in the state, covering 10,000 square miles. It encompasses 16 school districts (representing 18 towns), 25 elementary schools, 2 middle schools, and 16 high schools. The student population in the district is over 10,000. Of those students, 4388 are Hispanic children, or 44% of the school population (*K–12 School Reports*, 2003).

The population studied is located in Dodge City, Kansas (Ford County), a major town in the southwest area of the state with a large Hispanic population. The population in 2000 was 25,176, of which 10,793 were Hispanic (42.9%), and 12,974 were Caucasian (51.5%) (*Dodge City, Kansas Population and Demographics Resources*, 2004). The school year 2002–2003 dropout rate total for Dodge City was 18. Of that total, 3 were Caucasian (17%), and 13 were Hispanic (72%) (*K–12 School Reports*, 2003).

In 1999, a lawsuit was filed on behalf of students, parents, and administrators in the Dodge City school district alleging that the state's school finance system was constitutionally flawed. The plaintiffs alleged that the state was not putting enough money into the system and that the money was not distributed fairly. The plaintiffs argued that the districts having the highest number of hard-to-educate students, those with LEP, were not equally funded. The outcome will have a bearing on minority education. At the time of this writing, however, the case had not been decided (*Eric & Ryan Montoy et al. v. State of Kansas 99-C-1738: Decision and Order Remedy*, 2004).

Participants for this study were drawn from The Dodge City Migrant Education Program (MEP) for English as a Second Language (ESL), which serves more than 2,000 students who are at risk of failure because of their mobility, and consequently may miss essential services. "Migrant workers and their families represent many ethnic groups and are the focus of special federal and state programs because they are affected by repeated moves, poverty, health needs, social isolation, language barriers, and school disruption" (Davis, 2003, para. 1). Removal of barriers to school enrollment and attendance allows children of migrant families entitlement to equal access and opportunities for a normal education.

The major part of Dodge City MEP is the Newcomer Program (serving grades 2 through 4), which lasts for a minimum of 8 weeks. In this transitional program, newly arrived Hispanic children from Mexico and other parts of the United States are given grade-level content (second to sixth grade) in Spanish. They are also taught "survival" English (Vinton, 2004). A review of the *Newcomer Handbook,* under "Suggestive Strategies for Instruction," notes an absence of cooperative learning as a strategy. The five strategies listed are "thematic approaches," "total physical response," "graphic organizers," "bilingual approaches," "and stress-free approaches" (Vinton, n.d., pp. 7–8). The program is located in two elementary schools where approximately 73% of the student bodies are Hispanic and 83% are approved for free and reduced-price meals.

Research Design

This was a mixed-methods approach in which quantitative research was primary, and qualitative research was secondary. Sociocultural, educational, and linguistic theory perspectives served as research guides. This study used control and experimental groups: pretesting, treatment interventions, and posttesting techniques. The qualitative data served to triangulate results:

I. Quantitative section
   1. Demographic data from student records
   2. Pretests
   3. Criterion-referenced tests
   4. Posttests
II. Qualitative section
   1. Observations
   2. Open-ended questions
III. Triangulation

Demographic variables for each student were recorded, whether the student was:

1. *Migrant or nonmigrant*: Would there be a significant difference in performance between a migrant Hispanic child and a nonmigrant Hispanic child?
2. *Male or female*: Could gender be an influential variable?
3. *The primary language spoken at home (Spanish, English, or mixed)*: Would a Hispanic child from a monolingual (Spanish-speaking) household perform differently than a child from a bilingual household?

Each classroom teacher had a Hispanic paraprofessional teacher and used a bilingual approach in conducting daily lesson plans. Both paraprofessionals conversed in Spanish with the students and would sometimes assist them by paraphrasing or elucidating what their teachers were requesting of them.

Fifteen Hispanic third- and fourth-grade children participated with parental approval. All except three were from migrant families, and all spoke Spanish at home. For the quantitative portion of the study, 5 students were randomly assigned to control groups, and 10 were assigned to experimental groups in order to assure an adequate number of students per experimental subgroup.

All students received a pretest to establish a baseline for comparisons. The standardized test was Form K of the Iowa Test of Basic Skills (ITBS), Vocabulary and Usage and Expression. As an adjunctive measure, "IDEA Proficiency Test I-Oral English" (IPT) scores were obtained from students' folders to compare with pretest ITBS scores. "The IPT Tests were created for and normed on a population that represented a broad diversity of ELL [English Language Learner] students in terms of ethnic background, socio-economic status, and language ability. . . . It assesses for cognitive academic language proficiency" (*How the IPT Tests Help Decision-Makers Address the Assessment Standards for ELLs*, 2002, pp. 1–4). The IPT also tested for reading and writing; however, the results from the oral section are used. The IPT I-Oral, in comparison with ITBS Vocabulary and Usage and Expression, also measures language proficiency.

Publishers of the IPT correlated the test with the national standards of "Teaching English to Speakers of Other Languages" (TESOL), and the results supported its use with ELLs (*Correlation Between TESOL Standards and IPT Tests*, 2002). R. Vinton, ESL Migrant Director, noted that newly arrived Hispanic children are eligible for the Newcomer Program, if their IPT scores indicate a grade equivalency (GE) of three or below (R. Vinton, personal communication, April 12, 2004).

Data Analysis

To rule out pre-research variability between participants in the experimental and control groups, a paired-samples correlation t-test was used, comparing the means of IPT scores gathered from students' folders. If variability between groups was significant, then errors would be introduced in statistical analyses, producing meaningless results. There were no significant differences between experimental and control groups at the 0.05 level, $p = 0.29$. Therefore, the group compositions remained, and the research continued.

A pretest was given to all the participants to establish a baseline for measurement: Form K, Vocabulary and Usage and Expression of ITBS. As an added measure of strengthening the finding that no variability existed between the experimental and control groups prior to treatment, a paired-samples correlation t-test was done with mean vocabulary scores of the ITBS. There were no significant differences between experimental and control groups at the 0.05 level, $p = 0.50$.

In order to examine a relationship between the IPT GE scores and the pretest GE scores of the ITBS, a Pearson correlation test was used. The correlation between the IPT scores and the scores from the ITBS pretest vocabulary was significant at the 0.01 level (Pearson correlation 0.698). This strongly suggests that a student's outcome on both tests would be similar, supporting a strong relationship between the two tests. Likewise, a Pearson test between the IPT GE scores and the ITBS pretest usage and expression GE scores revealed a significant correlation at the 0.01 level (Pearson correlation 0.767), suggesting a similarly strong relationship. Together, these data support an inter-test relationship.

In the experimental groups at School C, two students were assigned to Group A, and two were assigned to Group B. One student from each group studied the history of popcorn (*palomitas de maíz*); the other students studied the uses of popcorn. Each student was supplied with daily handouts of either history or uses. A list of vocabulary words was handed out to the "history" students, which was different from that given to the "uses" students. Students had 15 minutes to study in their home group. Afterward, all students responsible for learning history gathered in their expert group, and those studying uses gathered in their expert group, for 15 minutes to go over their materials and interact. The students then rejoined their home groups for another 15 minutes to teach popcorn history and their vocabulary list to those students responsible for popcorn uses. Next, the roles were reversed. Total time expended for this activity was 45 minutes. In the experimental groups at School S, three students were assigned to Group A and three to Group B. The same procedure was used as in School C.

For the control participants at School C, two students were assigned as control. Each student was given daily handouts of both history and uses, with both vocabulary lists. They were told to study the materials and to ask questions when necessary. No further instructions were offered. At School S, three students were assigned as control with the same procedure as in School C.

After 3 weeks, a criterion-referenced test was given to experimental and control participants. This test measured for knowledge of popcorn history, uses, and vocabulary words from both lists. Seventeen test items consisted of fill-in-the-blanks, multiple choice, and writing definitions (one-word synonyms accepted).

A paired-samples correlation t-test was conducted on the test results from both experimental and control groups. The results were significant at the 0.05 level ($p = 0.03$, df = 4). The experimental groups (with treatment) scored significantly higher than the control groups.

At week 6, a posttest (Form L, Vocabulary and Usage and Expression of ITBS) was given to the 15 participating students. An analysis of covariance (ANCOVA) was used to tabulate the results, comparing pre- and posttest vocabulary results, and pre- and posttest usage and expression. There were no significant differences found between control and experimental group performance. There were no significant differences across independent control variables such as gender, migrant or nonmigrant status, and age. Given that there were only 6 weeks separating the pre- and posttests, the ITBS could not capture any relative degrees of significance in that short span of time.

As an added measurement, the χ^2 was run on gender and migrant status. A nonparametric was chosen because the measurements were categorical and the sample size was small. There were no significant differences on gender. There were an equal number of males and females. However, there was a significant difference with migrant status at the 0.05 level. $\chi^2 (1, N = 15) = 5.40$, $p = 0.02$ (see Table 10.1). This significance may be attributed to the fact the IPT average GE for the nonmigrants was 3.5, while the IPT average GE for the migrants was 1.5. Also, the nonmigrants were randomly assigned to the treatment group. Their average grade on the criterion-referenced test was 62, while that of the migrants was 42. The results suggest a possible relationship between achievement and migrant status, favoring nonmigrants. Nonmigrants experience consistency of environment and, consequently, consistency of schooling.

Table 10.1 x^2 Analysis on Gender and Migrant Status

	Gender	*Status*
x^2	1.67	5.40
P	0.07	0.02*
Df	1	1

*Significant values at 0.05 level of confidence.

For the qualitative portion of the study, the qualitative approach used was participant observer. Participation consisted of the following:

1. Answering questions about procedures, handouts, and English pronunciations.
2. Walking around the classroom and monitor for any unacceptable school behavior (e.g., peer aggression, leaving the room without permission).
3. Administering tests.
4. Asking for feedback from members of the treatment groups.

Observations consisted of watching and listening for the following:

1. Intergroup interactions.
2. Intragroup interactions.
3. Control participants' interactions.
4. Body language.
5. Paralinguistic utterances.
6. Voice levels.

Some of the boys in the treatment groups resisted being paired with girls. Whenever a boy sat with a girl, another boy would loudly remark, "*¡Ha-ha. Tu se está sentando con una muchacha!*" (Ha-ha. You are sitting with a girl!). The boys would say on several occasions: "*No deseo trabajar con ella*" (I don't want to work with her). Then they would add: "*¿Podemos trabajamos juntos?*" (Can we work together?), as they sat together at a table. The boys cooperated with reluctance manifested by groans as they looked at the ceiling with their hands on their foreheads.

After the first week, two boys assigned to control decided to sit together and study. The next day, a third control boy joined them. Their activity ranged from studying handouts to singing "The Popcorn Song" in unison. "*Escuche nosotros cantan*" (Listen to us sing), they would say. Despite the control boys singing in loud voices, the treatment groups were focusing on tasks. The control girls opted to remain working alone.

"*No entiendo*" (I don't understand) was a common defensive expression when students were given new handouts. Often, an explanation in a combination of Spanish and English placated the students, and they would focus on their tasks. On average, all the students were physically animate during the tasks, moving from group to group, inquiring what the other groups were doing. When an activity peaked their interest or whenever they did not understand a task, their voice levels increased. One quiet child (assigned as control) who arrived recently from Guatemala spoke no English. Whenever he was asked what certain words meant, he would answer indiscriminately, "Popcorn." He worked alone.

Students in both control and experimental groups would often raise their hands, asking how certain words were pronounced (e.g., *pericarp, embryo, archaeologist,* and simpler English words). Experimental students were noted to either correct another's pronunciation of a word or slide a finger slowly over a word while sounding out a few syllables at a time (phonemic segmentation). Occasionally, students would giggle when certain attempts at correct pronunciation failed.

In the remaining weeks after a routine was established, the students worked diligently on studying the history and uses of popcorn. The control students continued to sit together and either worked off-task (e.g., reading a library book) or settled on the assigned task. The treatment group members took turns being the *profesor* (teacher) and the *estudiantes* (students). The girls were not as animate as the boys and remained at their assigned groups.

After the posttest (ITBS), each participant from the experimental groups was asked a series of eight open-ended questions regarding how he or she felt about the group experience. Their verbal responses were tape recorded. The recordings were transcribed for examination. The tape recording was further transcribed by an impartial medical transcriptionist. Responses from both transcriptions were coded to numerical ratings (1 = negative; 2 = neutral; and 3 = positive).

A Reliability Scale (Alpha), intraclass correlation coefficient (ICC) was used. The interrater reliability was 0.99 at the 95% confidence interval ($N = 10$). There was a pattern of key words noted in all responses. The major responses were "fine," "fun," and "good." On question three (Is there anything you did not like about it?), the major response was "nothing." Two students responded negatively: "You had to read all of it." On question five (How did you feel teaching other students in your group?), a girl responded, "That I have an ability to teach." Others responded with one-word answers such as "good." On the final question (How would you explain to a new student what this group work was all about?), two students gave relatively lengthy responses: "We were partners and then we trade, and then we taught each other," "Explain and read the papers." When asked how they did on the different tests, the majority thought that they did well.

Triangulation efforts began with a Spearman bivariate correlation that was performed on the numerically coded responses of the eight open-ended questions and the experimental group's posttest ITBS, usage and expression. There was no significance at 0.05 level (r_s =–0.167). However, when the Spearman was performed with the open-ended questions and the vocabulary section of the posttest ITBS, the correlation was significant at the 0.05 level (r_s =–0.784). There is a negative correlation between the two.

The following is a possible explanation of the significance: Responses to the open-ended questions were primarily positive, while performances on the ITBS vocabulary section were primarily below grade level (only two had scores at or above grade level). The standardized test results depicted the children's low academic levels relative to vocabulary words. Their responses to the questions about the cooperative group technique depicted their receptiveness to the novel learning experience. Moreover, the open-ended questions were experientially based, while the ITBS questions were not. Had the ITBS scores been positive, the Jigsawing technique responses would have been mediocre at best. The logic is that when learning is occurring at or above grade level, the introduction of Jigsawing would be superfluous. However, that was not the reality with Hispanic students at either School C or School S.

The results of the criterion-referenced test revealed a positive relationship between high scores and assignment to the experimental group. This strongly suggests the cooperative group technique of Jigsawing has a facilitative effect on learning in both Schools C and S. Moreover, responses to the eight open-ended questions were primarily positive, indicating a generally positive experience with the group technique.

Conclusion

This study was conducted against a backdrop of inequality, in a school district involved in litigation over inequality of school funding. The sociocultural approach of Jigsawing facilitates SLA among migrant and nonmigrant Hispanic children in third and fourth grade. The performance of the students in the treatment groups was statistically significant on the criterion-referenced test when compared to those assigned to control. This is especially important since certain vocabulary words (e.g., *kernels* and *garland*) would have been challenging to any student in elementary school. Additionally, the handouts were in English and written primarily for English-speaking third and fourth graders.

A significant observation occurred when the control participants decided to sit together. Also significant is the experimental students' positive responses to the eight open-ended questions and the observation of purposeful interaction within their groups. The significant difference (0.05 level) in performance discovered by χ^2 between migrants and nonmigrants clearly supports the use of a facilitative group technique.

A caveat to the study is the small number of Hispanic students studied (15 students) in the Newcomer Program at the two elementary schools in Kansas. Also, the pre- and posttests of the ITBS were done at intervals too close to bear out any significant findings. The findings, therefore, should be accepted with caution, and as having significance to the Newcomer Program, but should not be generalized to other schools.

The Jigsawing technique allowed students to focus on one aspect of popcorn (either history or uses) and become the expert on that particular facet. Consequently, students taught their peers about that facet of popcorn. It is in the act of teaching that the "teacher" retains new knowledge, as expounded by Glasser (1986). There was much sharing of information within groups. Cooperation ensued since the test would be on both aspects of popcorn (i.e., its history and uses).

Jigsawing is compatible with the Hispanic learning experience, in which a cooperative (collectivist) environment is the norm. One particular observation noted an older girl helping a second-grade girl with her reading assignment. Another observation revealed that some control members formed their own group, in which they stayed for the remainder of the study. Hispanic children are often comfortable with polychromic behavior (e.g., talking at once, being animate while learning, talking loud). This behavior was evident during frequent observations. Not only was the topic of popcorn interesting for the children, but it was also culturally relevant. Students who read the history of popcorn discovered that it was first used in Mexico—which enticed them to delve into the topic.

Jigsawing served to facilitate peer feedback relative to the pronunciation of words, which led to modification of input. Observations supported students correcting each other, which led to modification of output. There was difficulty experienced with awareness of grammatical features, but generally language rules were followed. Popcorn had cultural relevance for Hispanic students. Students' use of language as a cognitive tool in repairing grammar forms indicates how they use language to co-construct the language they need to express the meaning they want and to co-construct knowledge about language (Swain & Lapkin, 1998).

As the research utilizing the Jigsawing technique for SLA with third- and fourth-grade Hispanic migrant children is scarce, there should be a continuing effort to further explore this area. This study has led to significant findings supporting Jigsawing as a viable tool in SLA, especially for children newly arrived in Kansas from Mexico and other South and Central American areas. Further research into Jigsawing and Hispanic migrant children should include a longitudinal study to track language ability of Hispanic migrant students after integration from newcomer groups into standard elementary classrooms.

References

Aronson, E. (2000). *Jigsaw classroom: history of the jigsaw*. Retrieved December 1, 2003, from http://jigsaw.org/history.htm

Avila, H. J. (1999). Mexican American immigration in Kansas (from "The history of Mexican American migration in Southwestern Kansas"). *The Brown Quarterly 3*, 1–6.

Bandura, A. (1977). *Social learning theory*. Englewood Cliffs, NJ: Prentice-Hall.

Bruner, J. (1963). *The process of education*. Cambridge, MA: Harvard University Press.

Chavez, G. (1997). *Ethnic communities: Hispanic heritage* [Transcript.] Topeka, KS: KTWU, Channel 11.

Colorado Department of Education fall 2002: Teacher count by race/ethnicity (2002). Retrieved July 27, 2004, from http://www.cde.state.co.us/cdereval/download/pdf/2002Staff/20022003TchDistEth.pdf

Colorado education facts (2002). Retrieved July 27, 2004, from http://www.cde.state.co.us/cdereval/download/pdf/EDFacts/2002EdFactSheet.pdf

Correlation between TESOL Standards and IPT Tests (2002). Brea, CA: Ballard & Tighe.

Crisis in education: Soaring Hispanic drop-out rates (2003). Retrieved October 30, 2003, from http://hispaniccreo.org/about/crisis.html

Cummins, J. (1981). The role of primary language development in promoting educational success for language minority students. *Schooling and language minority students: A theoretical framework* (pp. 3–49). Los Angeles: California State University, Evaluation, Dissemination, and Assessment Center.

———. (1989). Language and literacy acquisition in bilingual contexts. *Journal of Multilingual and Multicultural Development 19*, 17–31.

Cutler, W. G. (1997). Era of peace. In B. Bunce & R. Whitenight Transcribers (Eds.), *History of the state of Kansas*. Chicago: A. T. Andreas (Original Work Published 1883). Retrieved February 5, 2004, from http://www.kancoll.org/books/cutler/eraop/era-of-peace-p19.html#SCHOOLS_OF_KANSAS

Davis, G. (2003). *Dodge City migrant education program: ESL*. Retrieved January 4,

2004, from http://www.usd443.org/migrant/mep.htm

Dodge City, Kansas population and demographics resources (2004). Retrieved January 4, 2004, from http://dodgecity.areaconnect.com/statistics.htm

Eric & Ryan Montoy et al. v. State of Kansas 99-C-1738: Decision and Order Remedy. District Court of Shawnee County, Kansas 2004.

Fashola, O. S., Slavin, R. E., Calderón, M., & Durán, R. (1997). Effective programs for Latino students in elementary and middle schools. In *Hispanic drop-out project* (pp. 1–45). Santa Barbara: University of California at Santa Barbara.

Fultz, B. (2004). *Licensed personnel report: State profile 2003–2004.* Topeka: Kansas State Department of Education, Teacher Education and Licensure.

Ghaith, G. (2003). Effects of the learning together model of cooperative learning on English as a foreign language reading achievement, academic self-esteem, and feelings of school alienation. *Bilingual Research Journal 27*(3), 451–474.

Glasser, W. (1986). *Control therapy in the classroom.* San Francisco: Harper and Row.

Gumperez, J., Cook-Gumperez, J., & Szymanski, M. (1999). *Collaborative practices in bilingual cooperative learning classrooms* (No. 7). Santa Cruz, CA: Center for Research on Education, Diversity and Excellence.

Hein, G. E. (1991, October 15–22). *The museum and the needs of people: Constructivist learning theory.* Paper presented at the CECA (International Committee of Museum Educators) conference, Jerusalem, Israel.

How the IPT Tests help decision-makers address the assessment standards for ELLs. (2002). Brea, CA: Ballard & Tighe.

Johnson, D. W., & Johnson, R. T. (1987). *Learning together and alone: Cooperative, competitive and individualistic learning.* Englewood Cliffs, NJ: Prentice-Hall.

K–12 school reports (2003). Retrieved January 4, 2004, from http://www.ksbe.state.ks.us/Welcome.html

Kindler, A. (1995). *Education of migrant children in the United States.* Retrieved July 29, 2003, from http://www.ncela.gwu.edu/ncbepubs/directions/08.htm

Krashen, S. D. (1987). *Principles and practice in second language acquisition.* London: Prentice-Hall International.

Lampe, J. R., Rooze, G. E., & Tallent-Runnels, M. (1996). Effects of cooperative learning among Hispanic students in elementary social studies. *The Journal of Educational Research 89*, 187–191.

McCulloch, J. (1985). Lickona's curriculum for cooperation. *Ethics in Education 4*, 12–15.

Miller, J. (2003). *Kansas consolidated state application accountability workbook for state grants under Title IX, Part C, Section 9302 of the Elementary and Secondary Education Act (P.L. 107–110).* Topeka: Kansas State Department of Education.

Nation's report card: Reading results for grades 4, 8, and 12 (2002). Washington, DC: National Center for Education Statistics, US Department of Education.

Renner, C. E. (2002). *Serving linguistically and culturally diverse students in Kansas schools: A handbook for implementing the Kansas State Bilingual Education Act.* Topeka: Kansas State Department of Education.

Schütz, R. (2002). *English made in Brazil: Vygotsky and second language acquisition.*

Retrieved November 6, 2003, from http://www.sk.com.br/sk-vygot.html
Slavin, R. E. (1995). *Research on cooperative learning and achievement: What we know, what we need to know.* Washington, DC: Center for Research on the Education of Students Placed At Risk.
Smith, R. E. (1973). *The Wyandot Indians, 1843–1876.* Stillwater: Oklahoma State University.
Special analysis 2003: Reading—Young children's achievement and classroom experiences (2004). Retrieved January 28, 2004, from http://nces.ed.gov/programs/coe/2003/analysis/sa04.asp
Stanovich, K. E. (1993–1994). Romance and reality. *The Reading Teacher 47*(4), 280–291.
Stuart, M. (2003). *State and federal resources for English language learners in Kansas.* Paper presented at the Hispanic Education conference, Topeka, KS.
Swain, M., & Lapkin, S. (1998). Interaction and second language learning: Two adolescent French immersion students working together. *Modern Language Journal 82,* 320–337.
Thomas, W. P., & Collier, V. P. (1997). *School effectiveness for language minority students.* Washington, DC: National Clearinghouse for Bilingual Education.
Vinton, R. (2004). *Dodge City migrant education program.* Retrieved March 27, 2004, from http://www.usd443.ruraltel.net/index.asp?DocumentID=359
———. (n.d.). *Newcomer handbook: ESL/migrant program.* Dodge City, KS: Unified School District 443.
Vygotsky, L. S. (1978). *Mind in society: The development of higher psychological processes.* Cambridge, MA: Harvard University Press.

CHAPTER ELEVEN

Achieving Success

Voices of Successful African American Mathematics Students

ANGILINE POWELL AND ROBERT Q. BERRY III

Abstract

Since the landmark *Brown v. Board of Education* decision, it is easy for many to assume that schooling opportunities for all students are equitable. Prior to the decision, there were gross inequities between the education of African Americans and European Americans. Unfortunately, there continue to be major inequities in resources, quality of instruction, and outcomes. These inequities have adversely affected all academic areas but have been particularly problematic in mathematics. While research emphasizes the gap in mathematics achievement between African Americans and European Americans, little research is focused on successful mathematics students. This study examines the mathematics education of successful African American middle school and college students from their perspectives, finding five common themes: (a) caring ethic, (b) peer interactions, (c) positive perceptions and persistence in mathematics, (d) tracking, and (e) familial support.

Introduction

There has been an ongoing concern about the shortage of students pursuing expertise in the disciplines of mathematics, science, technology, and engineering (Herzig, 2004). The mathematics community has been concerned with the preparation of all students in mathematics, specifically students of color and second language learners (Rousseau & Tate, 2003; Herzig, 2004). Many mathematics educators and mathematicians are concerned about the near absence of underrepresented students in upper-level mathematics courses and mathematics doctoral programs (Rousseau & Tate, 2002; Chan, 2003). Due to the underrepresentation of students of color in mathematics, it is important to consider the experiences of students who have achieved success. This chapter is a compilation of two separate studies about successful African American mathematics students. One study captures the stories of eight male middle school students, and the other captures the stories of six college students (four males and two females). The stories of successful African American students are powerful in that they provide perspectives rarely discussed in the educational discourse.

Historically, African American students have experienced little success on mathematics achievement assessments, with few gaining access to upper-level mathematics courses during their secondary school years (Anick et al., 1981; Burton, 1984; Jones et al., 1984; Strutchens & Silver, 2000). Access to upper-level mathematics and the mathematics achievement of African American students has caused great concern for mathematics researchers and educators. Despite these concerns, very little research addresses the causes of this phenomenon; even less examines why some African American students achieve at a high levels in mathematics despite many obstacles.

Academically successful African American students experience common factors: strong parental influence, caring adults, high teacher expectations, exposure to challenging curricula, participation in special academic programs in mathematics and science, participation in extracurricular activities, coping strategies, advocacy, positive messages about identity, and a history of membership in high-ability groups (Lee, 1996; Hebert, 1998; Hrabowski et al., 1998; McGlamery & Mitchell, 2000; Powell, 2000; Fordham, 2001). Hrabowski et al. (1998) examined the stories of mathematically successful African American male college students and reported that parental advocacy, proper educational placement, positive peer influence, and exposure to quality mathematical and scientific materials were contributing factors to the success of these high-achieving students. Students in the Hrabowski et al. (1998) study participated in summer programs that focused on mathematics and science. In their secondary school years, students reported that teachers and peers motivated them academically.

African American students who experience success academically can provide the basis for examining the challenges confronting other African American students. For many of these students, success is often achieved despite challenges facing them. Many African American students are successful with mathematics; however, their success stories often go undocumented. In order for more African American students to succeed in mathematics, it is critical to examine perceptions and experiences of students who are accomplished.

Methodology

Participant interviews, surveys, mathematical autobiographies, and classroom observations were utilized in both studies for data collection. The middle school study also included parental interviews, teacher interviews, and reviews of students' academic records. The study on successful African American male middle school students included eight students: four students who participated in a precollege program that focused on mathematics and science, and four who did not participate in the precollege program. A precollege program was the context of this study because it contained additional learning opportunities, advocacy, caring adults, and a support system. The participants in the middle school study were matched based on course enrollment. That is, a non-precollege student and a precollege student were in the same school and same class. All the students were either seventh or eighth graders enrolled in Algebra One. At the time of this study, enrollment in Algebra One in middle school meant that these students were on an advanced track in mathematics. The parents and teachers of each student participated in the study. The parents completed a consent form, and the students completed an assent form after their parents gave consent for participation.

The selection of participants in the college study was based on a criterion sampling. All the participants were African Americans students who had completed Calculus I, II, and III courses in college. These courses were chosen because they are prerequisites for continuing in upper-level mathematics courses. The context of this study was a Southern state-supported university. Two female participants completed the study: Christa, a 22-year-old senior mathematics education major, and Emily, a 22-year-old senior majoring in computer science engineering. Four male participants completed the study: Lou, a 21-year-old computer science major; Jim, a 29-year-old mechanical engineering major; Byron, a 25-year-old statistical mathematics major; and Jarrell, a 23-year-old statistical mathematics major. These students were enrolled in courses on numerical analysis, differential equations, and the theory of probability at the time of this study.

Findings

This chapter brings together two research studies focusing on two distinct populations of African American students. Although the populations are distinct, interestingly, the findings within both studies bear a striking resemblance. This is significant when we consider success in mathematics as a pipeline that is difficult to enter in later stages. The information reported in this section reveals the similar findings between both studies. There were five common aspects between both studies: (a) caring ethic, (b) peer interactions, (c) perception and persistence within mathematics, (d) tracking, and (e) families.

Caring Ethic

When looking at the results of both studies, the notion of a caring ethic overlaps across the experiences of the middle school and college students. *Caring* refers not merely to an affective connection between teachers and students, but also to the demonstration of high expectations, positive classroom interactions, and a belief that African American students are capable of performing well in the mathematics classroom. The college students wanted their teachers to care about whether or not they succeeded in mathematics. These students identified teacher availability, clear explanations, and the ability to answer and ask questions as indications of a caring ethic. The middle school students described caring in terms of the ways their teachers helped them when help was needed, held them accountable for their work by calling parents, and made them feel comfortable within the classroom environment. When asked, "How does a mathematics teacher show that he/she cares about you?" One middle school student, Bilal, recognized the positive interactions he had with his mathematics teacher and how these positively influenced his mathematical achievement:

> One teacher that really stands out is Ms. Williams. Unlike other teachers, Ms. Williams always stayed on me about getting my work done. If I didn't apply [myself] or didn't do [my work], she would tell me that I could do better. She demanded nothing but my best. She really cared about me.

The college students' perceptions of caring were based on their relationships with their professors, specifically the ability to explicitly explain mathematics content, as described in Jarrell's response:

> If you got stuck at a certain point, he'd tell you what you needed to do to get through that point, or if you really weren't understanding, he would, like, do a little bit of it just far enough where you could catch on and do the rest yourself.

Peer Interactions

Peer interactions were significant to both the middle school and college participants. Both groups of students contended that they used peers to clarify their mathematics understanding, to study in mathematics, and for support beyond the mathematics classroom. This type of interaction is consistent with research that identifies African American cultural style and learning preferences as communal and relational. The communal aspect is one of nine interrelated but distinct dimensions Boykin (1986) identifies as a part of the African American cultural experience. *Communalism* refers to the awareness that social bonds are important and to inclinations toward people. Consequently, many African Americans have a relational learning preference characterized by freedom of movement, variation, creativity, divergent thinking, inductive reasoning, and focus on people (Shade, 1997).

The college students' peer interactions were seen as they actively sought help from other students and in the ways they assisted fellow students. At this level, study groups were indicative of this peer interaction. Jim's description of his study group provides an example. He felt that he learned a lot from the study groups that he formed, even though some members talked too much. He expressed the value of the interaction with his peers by stating: "I realize that if can help somebody else, then I already done [*sic*] helped myself a whole lot, you know."

Similarly, the middle school students sought peer interactions. They, too, sought help from peers and assisted fellow students. However, these interactions were competitive in nature because they were motivated to do better than or as well as their peers. Interestingly, they felt a sense of responsibility to their peers; yet at the same time, they wanted to outperform their peers in mathematics. Jabari, one of the middle school participants, described how he and his best friend do homework together: "We race to see who finishes first, then we talk to see if we got the same answer."

Perception and Persistence

Tucker (1999) asserted that for African American students to be successful in school, they must adopt high levels of self-motivation, posses perceived self-control, and engage in successful behaviors. In both studies, the middle school and college students were motivated to succeed in mathematics, expressed strong beliefs in their mathematical ability, and developed a perception that success in mathematics was dependent on their actions. This was evident in the ways the participants set high expectations for themselves, displayed positive attitudes about their mathematical ability, and were motivated to be among the "smart" students. Five of the six college students expressed that they "loved" mathematics. These students were resilient, persistent, and goal-oriented: They wanted to complete their college degrees. In order to realize this goal, they had to complete advanced mathematics courses, persisting even when they experienced disappointing grades and poor teaching. While it would be easy to say that we need to encourage persistence in African American students in order for them to attain educational goals, persistence does not exist in a vacuum. Why were these participants able to persevere?

All of the middle school students were motivated to succeed in mathematics and establish goals for success. Seven of the eight middle school students indicated that mathematics was their favorite subject. They were cognizant of their successes and were aware of the requirements necessary to maintain them. Andre stated, "Good math students are focused, do their work, and want to make A's all the time. . . . I am a good math student." Bilal explained, "I gotta excel in everything I do. Be the best that I can be . . . being the best means doing your work, asking questions, and being involved in class." These students perceived themselves as having control over their academic success. They knew that, in order to maintain their good standing in mathematics, they needed to ask questions, do homework, and attend tutorial sessions when necessary.

Tracking

Tracking is a widely used practice that groups students who appear to be similar in their needs, potential, and academic performance to be taught together but separately from other students (Donaldson, 1996; Oakes & Lipton, 1996). Tracking is, in part, responsible for lower assessments in mathematics among students of color, particularly African American students (Mickelson, 2001). All the participants in both studies experienced tracking. For the college students, four of the six were in an advanced or academic track in high school, in which they took upper-level mathematics courses. The fifth student, Jarrell, said that he was not in the advanced track in high school and took what he described as general or basic courses. And the sixth student, Jim, was initially placed in special education classes and negotiated with his parents and teachers until he was placed into the vocational track.

All of the middle school students were in the advanced mathematics track; this was a prerequisite for participation in the study. In fact, for these students, being placed in an advanced track was a motivation to succeed. Being placed among the perceived "smart kids" served as a motivating factor to achieve. As Cordell explained, "The smart kids make me work harder."

Another student, Clayton, commented, "I like being with the smart kids because that means I am one of the smartest . . . since I answer all of the questions in math, that means I am the smartest of the smart kids."

Family

The role that families play in the lives of successful African American students is significant because family members provide the necessary support system to ensure success. The families of the students in this study placed the highest value on education and academic success. The students' bonds to the family members were sometimes academic, sometimes emotional, and sometimes financial, but the bonds appeared strong. Harris (1995) suggests that peers are the most powerful influence on students' lives. However, these studies recognize that even though peers are influential, they do not replace families or their support. The college students looked to their families as well as their peers for emotional support. This support helped them persist in their academic endeavors. In addition to the emotional support, the participants' families frequently provided financial support, enabling them to stay in school. Jim's mother and father were of a low socioeconomic status. The financial help from his family came from older sisters and brothers who were already working in their respective fields.

Unlike the college students, the middle school students lived with their families directly impacting their day-to-day lives. Parents stressed the importance of getting an education and doing well in school; they adopted the roles of protectors, supporters, and advocates. Parents indicated that doing well in school was not optional. Clayton's mother described her expectation:

> Well, I just expect for him to just do well in math and in school. At the times when he gets a low grade on a test, I ask him why and what happened. But he knows not to bring too many low grades around here.

Parents fulfilled the role as protectors by describing how they safeguarded their sons. These parents were not fearful for their sons' safety; rather, they were concerned about low expectations for African American males and wanted to protect them from this danger. School presence was important to the parents. They believed that their involvement reflected their high expectations for their sons. Bilal's father described his involvement at his son's school as a way of making sure that African American males received equitable treatment. He stated: "That school knows me. . . . I am up there all the time." These parents were activists early in their sons' schooling. Hrabowski et al. (1998) found that other successful African American males were successful when their parents advocated for proper class placement.

Conclusion

The two complementary studies presented in this chapter distinguish themselves from most other studies because they focused on characteristics of successful African American mathematics students. The research was conducted independently. One study concentrated on African American male middle school students, and the other study examined male and female African American college students. Five themes related to success in mathematics emerged across both studies: (a) caring ethic (b) peer interactions (c) positive perceptions and persistence in mathematics (d) tracking, and (e) family support. These themes are found individually in the literature on African Americans (Berry, 2003; Fordham, 2001; Powell, 2000). By combining the findings of two separate studies, a clearer picture of successful African American mathematics students emerges.

The studies spawn more questions: Why did these five themes emerge? Are they consistent across socioeconomic levels and regions of the country? Do they apply to other content areas? How can we foster persistence? More research is needed on factors that positively influence African American success in academic settings.

References

Anick, C. M., Carpenter, T. P., & Smith, C. (1981). Minorities and mathematics: Results from the National Assessment of Educational Progress. *Mathematics Teacher 74*, 560–566.

Berry, R. Q. III. (2003). *Voices of African American male students: A portrait of successful middle school mathematics students.* Unpublished doctoral dissertation, University of North Carolina at Chapel Hill, Chapel Hill, NC.

Boykin, A. W. (1986). The triple quandary and the school of Afro-American children. In U. Neisser (Ed.), *The school achievement of minority children: New perspectives* (pp. 57–91). Hillsdale, NJ: Lawrence Erlbaum Associates.

Burton, L. (1984). Mathematical thinking: The struggle for meaning. *Journal for Research in Mathematics Education 15*(1), 35–49.

Chan, T. F. (2003). The mathematics doctorate: A time for change? *Notices of the American Mathematical Society 50*, 896–902.

Donaldson, K. (1996). *Through students' eyes: Combating racism in United States schools.* Westport, CT: Praeger.

Fordham, S. (2001). Why can't Sonya (and Kwame) fail math? In W. Watkins, J. H. Lewis, & V. Chou (Eds.), *Race and education: the roles of history and society in educating African American students* (pp. 140–158). Needleham, MA: Allyn & Bacon.

Harris, J. R. (1995). Where is the child's environment? A group socialization theory of development. *Psychological Review 102*, 458–489.

Hebert, T. P. (1998). Gifted Black males in an urban high school: Factors that influence achievement and underachievement. *Journal for the Education of the Gifted 21*(4), 385–414.

Herzig, A. (2004). Becoming mathematicians: Women and students of color choosing and leaving doctoral mathematics. *Review of Educational Research 74*(2), 171–214.

Hrabowski, F. A., Maton, K. I., & Greif, G. L. (1998). *Beating the odds: Raising academically successful African American males.* New York: Oxford University Press.

Jones, L. V., Burton, N. W., & Davenport, E. C. (1984). Monitoring the mathematics achievement of Black students. *Journal for Research in Mathematics Education 15*, 154–164.

Lee, C. C. (1996). Successful African American male youth: A psychosocial profile. *Journal of African American Men 1*(3), 63–71.

McGlamery, S., & Mitchell, C. T. T. (2000). Recruitment and retention of African American males in high school mathematics. *Journal of African American Men 4*(4), 73–87.

Mickelson, R. A. (2001). Subverting Swann: First- and second-generation segregation in the Charlotte-Mecklenburg Schools. *American Educational Research Journal 38*(2), 215–252.

Oakes, J., & Lipton, M. (1996). Developing alternatives to tracking and grading. In L. I. Rendon, & R. O. Hope (Eds.), *Educating a new majority: Transforming America's educational system for diversity*, 168–200. San Francisco: Jossey-Bass.

Powell, A. (2000). *Reflections on exemplary mathematics teachers by two African American students.* Paper presented at the American Educational Research Association, New Orleans, LA.

Rosseau, C,. & Tate, W. F. (2003). No time like the present: Reflecting on equity in school mathematics. *Theory into Practice 42*(3), 210–216.

Shade, B. J. (1997). African-American cognitive patterns: A review of the research. In B. J. Shade (Ed.), *Culture, style and the educative process: making schools work for racially diverse students* (pp. 70–91). Springfield, IL: Charles C. Thomas.

Strutchens, M. E., & Silver, E. A. (2000). NAEP findings regarding race/ethnicity: Students' performance, school experiences, and attitudes and beliefs. In E. A. Silver & P. A. Kenney (Eds.), *Results from the Seventh Mathematics Assessment of the National Assessment of Educational Progress* (pp. 45–72). Reston, VA: NCTM.

Tucker, C. M. (1999). *African American children: A self-empowerment approach to modifying behavior problems and preventing academic failure.* Needham Heights, MA: Allyn & Bacon.

CHAPTER TWELVE

Reasons African American Men Persist to Degree Completion in Institutions of Higher Education

JOHN P. HAMILTON

Abstract

The purpose of this study was to examine the experiences of African American men who persisted to baccalaureate degree completion in 4-year colleges and universities. A further purpose of this study was to identify any noncognitive variables that had a significant impact on these African American men. This study used qualitative research to discover the reasons African American men persist to degree completion at institutions of higher learning. The research design used for this study was descriptive. The population selected for this study was African American men who graduated from 4-year universities in Southern California with an undergraduate degree in May/June 2004. In this study, 12 African American men revealed the noncognitive variables (availability of a strong support person, academic adjustment, attachment to college, personal emotional adjustment, and social adjustment) that were instrumental in assisting them toward degree completion. These young men also made recommendations to help other African American men to succeed in college.

Introduction

Malcolm X (1970) once compared education to a passport. He stated that, "Education is our passport to the future, for tomorrow belongs to those who prepare for it today" (p. 43). The metaphor implies that education allows a person to travel beyond his or her own environment and perceptions. Indeed, education can increase one's knowledge on a wide range of specific topics, and it offers a variety of worldview lenses that can open one's mind to personal and social improvement. In addition, education can provide employment opportunities and improve one's economic status:

> Education and work are the levers to uplift a people. Work alone will not do it unless inspired by the right ideals and guided by intelligence. Education must not simply teach work—it must teach Life. The Talented Tenth of [African Americans] must be made leaders of thought and missionaries of culture. (DuBois, 1903, p. 75)

DuBois' (1903) statement on education depicts the challenge of educational institutions to produce leaders, more specifically African American leaders who will become the "Talented Tenth." "W. E. B. DuBois envisioned that the 10% of Black Americans who acquired the skills and/or education that enabled [Black Americans] to succeed in the larger society would eventually 'come home' and use [Black American] tools and talents to build a bridge between the Black 'haves' and the Black 'have-nots' " (Thomas, 2000, p. 1). The "Talented Tenth" concept for African Americans promotes the idea that education can be readily transformed into freedom and equality. However, this concept of education as a panacea seems almost unattainable when one examines the education history of African Americans.

African Americans have not always been afforded equal access to education in America. The disparate initial education experiences of African Americans have been difficult to surmount, despite a rich cultural history of being the first to write, study the stars, and provide unsolvable equations that yielded architectural wonders (Welsing, 1990; Williams, 1992; Van Sertima, 2003). In America, African Americans were forbidden to read and write during slavery. After the Civil War, only 10% of the adult African American population had basic education (Patton, 1981). African Americans continued to be subjected to unequal schools, even after the *Brown v. Board of Education* decision required otherwise. According to Oliver (1989), "The American educational system has played a major role in perpetuating negative images of [African Americans] by portraying them as descendants of savages and people who have failed to make significant contributions to America or world civilization" (p. 18).

Today, African Americans still lag in education. Moreover, the education of African American males has become its own major issue with regard to their disproportionate representation in special education programs, high rates of suspension and expulsion, and high dropout rates. Patton (1981) is critical when describing the state of African American males in education. He believes:

> Several devices are widely used to relegate [African American men] to low status positions in the educational system. Norm-referenced tests, other assessment devices, and labeling/tracking tactics. . . . In spite of the negative impact of the educational system on the collective [African American man], he has survived. (p. 200)

African American men continue to endure, although there have been statistical studies that cast their experience in a negative light. Due to alarming statistics related to homelessness, violence, homicide, suicide, incarceration, and dropping out of school, African American men are often called an "endangered species."

An endangered species is "a class of individuals having common attributes and designated by a common name [that is] in danger or peril of probable harm or loss. This description applies in a metaphorical sense, to the current status of young [African American men] in contemporary American society" (Gibbs, 1988, p. 1). This definition describes the state of African American males, not only in society, but also in the American education system, especially colleges and universities.

Studies have shown racial and gender disparities in education with regard to African American males (Woodson, 1993; Jones & Jackson, 2003). Some of these studies uncovered "tremendous racial disparities in levels of educational performance, educational attainment, college enrollment, and college graduation rates between Blacks and Whites" (Jones & Jackson, 2003, p. 72). These studies paint a grim picture of what African American males lack.

For example, the Center for the Study of Social Policy (1995) conducted a national study focusing on students age 10–19 who were two or more grades behind in school (Table 12.1).

These data provided evidence that African American males lagged behind African American females and Whites from elementary school to their first year of college. A closer evaluation of the study revealed that African American male percentages increased in each age group, widening the education attainment gap between African American males as it relates to African American females, White males, and White females.

Table 12.1 Percentage of Students Two or More Grades Behind in School by Race and Gender

	Black		White	
Age	Male	Female	Male	Female
10–13	10.3	5.9	4.2	3.0
14–15	13.1	8.9	6.9	3.7
16–17	16.0	7.9	7.2	3.9
18–19	16.5	7.9	5.5	3.9

Academia is overwhelmed with studies that indicate the plight or absence of African American men in higher education (Gibbs, 1988; Morgan, 1996; Wilson, 2000). Many African American men are not persisting to degree completion in 4-year institutions. African American men face various simultaneous risk factors that may prohibit them from continuing and completing their education. These risk factors are "delayed enrollment, part-time enrollment status, self-dependent for college financing, having children or other dependents, being a single parent, lacking a high school diploma, and being employed full-time while attending college" (Wei & Horn, 2002, p. 25). Additional studies by J. Levin and M. Levin (1991), Parker (1998), and McNairy (1996) suggest lack of financial aid, leadership, support, mentors, and campus involvement as factors that often prohibit minority students (especially African American men) from succeeding in college.

In higher education, African American males have not reached the academic success of Whites, other ethnic groups, and their African American female counterparts. National Center for Education Statistics (1997) notes that among African American students, African American men face more obstacles than African American women entering college and, even when enrolled, have a long history of earning fewer degrees at all levels than African American women.

According to Harvey (2002), college participation rate among African American females has increased by 4 percentage points, to 43.9%, while the rate for African American males has declined by 5 percentage points, to 33.8%. The participation and graduation rates of African American men are deteriorating at a disproportional rate when compared to their African American female counterparts, Whites, and other ethnic groups (Harris, 1996; Morgan, 1996; Harper & Wolley, 2002).

Kunjufu (2001) believes that African American male students are in a crisis. He postulates that this crisis is related but not limited to the lack of African American male role models, absence of support systems, and low self-esteem among African American male students. He also believes that with certain added factors (strong family background, less negative peer pressure, higher teacher expectations), African American males can excel.

Problem Statement

More needs to be known about the successes of African Americans in education, especially African American males. Majors and Billson (1992) argue that many African American males are successful; however, not enough of these success stories are studied. Academic success can be measured by a variety of factors: grades, class rank, and degree completion. However, using noncognitive variables as a predictor of students' academic success provides an overall interpretation of students' success factors.

Schwartz and Washington (2002) view noncognitive variables as being influential in predicting academic success. Noncognitive variables tend to measure a student's success in forms other than grade point average (GPA), Student Assessment Test (SAT) or American College Admissions Test (ACT) scores, and high school rank (all of which are considered cognitive variables). Three noncognitive variables—academic self-concept, integration to a campus, and commitment to gaining education—are listed by Schwartz and Washington as influential factors for predicting academic success in general.

Schwartz and Washington (2002) identified several other noncognitive variables as predictors of academic performance *for college students*. These variables are not only good indicators for academic performance, but are also indicators of what factors assist students in persisting to degree completion. Notable among these noncognitive variables are:

- Availability of a strong support person
- Academic adjustment
- Attachment to college
- Personal emotional adjustment
- Social adjustment

These variables also serve as predictors of the success of African American men. The problem is that literature and research have failed to include the experiences of successful African American men to couple with the qualitatively derived predictors. What lived experiences lead African American male students to persist in higher education and develop the skills to earn a college degree?

Little research identifies the reasons African American men persist and graduate from college. Moreover, the current research fails to thoroughly ask questions of those African American male students who successfully graduate from college. What lived experiences enable African American men to succeed? How do these successful African American men defeat the odds that much research indicates are overwhelmingly against them?

Purpose Statement

The purpose of this study was to examine the experiences of African American men who persisted to baccalaureate degree completion in 4-year colleges and universities. A further purpose of this study was to identify noncognitive variables that have had a significant impact on these African American men.

Research Questions

The following questions guided the study:

1. What campus services contribute to the persistence of African American men to degree completion?
2. What experiences are dominant factors in degree completion?
3. What challenges are key to degree completion?
4. What role did the university play in facilitating degree completion?
5. What noncognitive variables have a significant impact on African American men graduating from college?
6. What role (if any) did elementary school, middle school, or high school play in the persistence of African American men to attain baccalaureate degrees?

Significance of the Study

Numerous studies have demonstrated the negative and often bleak chances for African American men to succeed. "The African American male has even been described as an 'endangered species,' and the successful African American male is viewed as something of an anomaly" (Wilson, 2000, p. 176). The lack of evidence to indicate that African American men succeed in college makes the case that more research needs to be developed to give the academic community data about the factors that contribute to the success of African American men in college (i.e., their attainment of college degrees).

In addition, studies of African Americans in higher education, such as those by Roach (2001), continue to demonstrate the widening gap in the degree completion of African American males compared to that of African American females. "Black women are scoring big gains in education, particularly at the college level; the progress for Black men has either stagnated or increased slightly from year to year over the past decade" (p. 19). Providing research that places the successes of African American men in college under a microscope will offer colleges and universities strategies to meet the challenges facing a diverse campus and society. Moreover, a blueprint of success can be developed for other college-bound African American male students. The use of this blueprint will not only facilitate greater success on college campuses, but African American males will also have the opportunity to be more successful in their families, communities, employment, and society, where statistics for them are not favorable.

Overview of African Americans and African American males

In the first part of this study, the researcher provided an overview of what African Americans, especially African American men, have encountered in American society. African American men and women have made some tremendous gains from a historical perspective. However, both groups tend to be featured prominently in an abundance of literature that supports negative perceptions.

Why is this so for African Americans, or more specifically, African American men? In general, African American men have been overrepresented in literature that espouses a "deficit" perspective. This deficit perspective focuses on the group's weaknesses and societal barriers. For this reason, scholars who have used a deficit perspective have guided the majority of literature and studies to examine the negative aspects of African American men's experiences, rather than the successes. Categories such as homelessness, violence, homicide, suicide, incarceration, and dropping out of school tend to flood the literature. Representation of African American men in research that provides anecdotes of success and perseverance are scarce.

In the field of educational research, "Very little work . . . has focused on the role of gender in the higher education experience of Black students and specially how gender informs the experiences of African American males on campus" (Davis, 1999, p. 136). When studies do address gender-specific experiences in education, often women's participation and outcomes are analyzed. Rarely are the experiences of males considered. Davis argues that gender has played a vital role in the social and academic experiences of African American males. However, many of these experiences are not documented.

Historical Overview of African Americans in Education

Kunjufu (2001) states that the omission of African and African American achievements and others has affected the psyche of African American students, because they are unable to establish their culture's contributions to society. African American students are unable to use these omitted cultural contributions as a catalyst to learn. The distorted curriculum creates a dynamic that suppresses African American students' school performance, retention, and persistence from elementary to college completion.

When discussing the education of African Americans with emphasis on African American males, Kunjufu (2001) identified African American males as being in a state of emergency. This emergency stems from the negative statistics that have categorized African American males, stereotyping them from conception to adulthood. He argues that these statistics, stereotypes, and expectations of society, especially from teachers, contribute to African American males' dismal plight.

In higher education, African American students have been critically evaluated for some time. Steele (1999) believes this preoccupation and fascination with African American students and their education is more than a matter of drawing upon statistics about college students. Steele suggests that evaluating the failures or successes of African American students dictates whether America has been successful in integrating African Americans into the educational system since the Civil Rights Act. "Nonetheless, throughout the 1990s the national college-dropout rate for African-Americans has been 20 to 25 percent higher than that for whites. Among those who finish college, the grade-point average of black students is two thirds of a grade below that of whites" (p. 45).

In addition, studies of African Americans in higher education, such as those by Roach (2001), continue to demonstrate the widening gap between the degree completion of African American males compared to that of African American women. "Black women are scoring big gains in education, particularly at the college level; the progress for Black men has either stagnated or increased slightly from year to year over the past decade" (p. 19). The *Journal of Blacks in Higher Education*'s spring 2003 issue provided recent statistics that African American women have earned 58% of bachelor's degrees awarded to African Americans in the United States. African American women also earned 63% of master's degrees and 66% of doctoral degrees awarded to African Americans.

Roach (2001) questions: Where are the African American men on campus? African American men are visible when being discussed in the athletic arena. African American men are also mentioned when they are not performing well academically. But where are the African American men who are doing well and will graduate from a 4-year institution? Limited literature has attempted to answer this question by offering quantitative and qualitative studies about successful African American students and what African Americans need to be successful on college campuses.

African American Men in Higher Education

Due to the overwhelming amount of literature that permeates academia and pop culture concerning African American males, there is some literature that defends African American males, especially in higher education. Some studies reveal that successful African American males in higher education (those who persist to degree completion) are not an anomaly (Harris & Duhon, 1999). Moreover, African American male students have shared their experiences to uncover their struggles toward degree completion. Davis's (1999) study reveals some illuminating findings about the challenges facing African American male students. He discovered, "They struggle to become socially integrated in a community of peers who are supportive but often confining; they struggle to overcome academic hurdles created by inadequate precollege preparation; and they struggle against hostile schooling environments that marginalize their presence on campus" (p. 135). The African American males in this study overcame these challenges and emerged with lessons learned about life, character, persistence, and survival—and a college degree.

Harris (1996) agrees that African American males face many problems. He further declares that African American males must reframe the issues affecting them in colleges and universities. According to Harris, reframing the issues consists of moving from a "deficient 'blame-the-victim' model" to one of success (p. 92). In order for African American men to reframe higher education issues that are overtly and covertly tainted with racism, they must have the opportunity to view themselves as successful. Harris (1996) has been involved in an ongoing study that examines successful African American men in higher education. Three ideas have emerged from his study of successful African American men:

> Those males who defined themselves as successful could clearly articulate a personal concept of success. The frame from which these young men viewed their lives was clearly not the frame of an endangered species. It was a frame of success. Secondly, those young men who defined themselves as successful were especially adept at networking. Finally, the successful respondents in this research project all had a keen sense of balance. (p. 92)

This study is one of very few that seek to provide colleges and universities a model for success. African American men *are* successful in college. That is, they are able to overcome challenges and persist to degree completion.

Many scholars challenge the plight of African American males in college (Wilson, 2000; Hall & Rowan, 2001). They believe that the successes of African American male students are more than an anomaly. Hall and Rowan (2001) contend that, despite the barriers African American males face, they are succeeding in higher education. More importantly, the Hall and Rowan study of African American males suggests that institutions of higher education are failing this group.

According to Hall and Rowan (2001), institutions of higher education are not providing an environment conducive to the learning of African American males. These institutions are not culturally relevant, which creates a hostile environment. Universities also lag in addressing the human needs of African American males. Furthermore, Hall and Rowan argue that to remedy higher education institutions' culturally irrelevant environments and lack of personal development of African American males, policies need to be designed or redesigned to accommodate them. Not only should policies be designed or redesigned, but African American males must also be a part of the decision-making process in order to implement these policies in a democratic manner. "Any strategies and programs that flow from policies that accommodate African-American males will gain momentum from the democratic process" (p. 13).

Noncognitive Variables

Traditionally, students' success, retention, and persistence have been measured by evaluating variables related to students' academic achievement or performance as predictors of graduation. These types of variables are commonly known as *cognitive variables.* Cognitive variables include students' grades, GPA, SAT and ACT scores, and class rank (Schwartz & Washington, 2002). "However, there is considerable controversy about the utility of standardized test scores. It appears that standardized scores may be predictive for minority students but only when used with other cognitive measures such as high school grades and rank" (p. 358). Due to this controversy, the need to broaden the scope of measurement from a traditional to a nontraditional approach is becoming a reality (Sedlacek, 2004).

Nontraditional approaches use *noncognitive variables* to examine students as more than statistics. Influential in predicting academic success, noncognitive variables are those that tend to measure students' success in forms other than GPA, SAT and ACT scores, or high school rank (cognitive variables). Schwartz and Washington (2002) have recognized the following three noncognitive variables as being influential in predicting academic success: academic self-concept, integration to a campus, and commitment to gaining education.

In their research, Schwartz and Washington (2002) also identified specific noncognitive variables as predictors of academic performance for college students. These variables are not only good indicators for academic performance, but also indicators of what factors assist students in persistence to degree completion. More importantly, "Noncognitive variables have been successful in improving predictions about both academic performance and retention of African American students" (p. 358). Notable among the noncognitive variables identified by Schwartz and Washington are:

- Availability of a strong support person
- Academic adjustment
- Attachment to college
- Personal emotional adjustment
- Social adjustment

These variables are also predictors of success for African American men in general.

Sedlacek (2004) defined noncognitive variables as those that are unpredictable but represent the lived experiences of nontraditional students. These variables are predictive in assessing students' motivations and perceptions. Cognitive variables, on the other hand, are used to understand students from a quantitative perspective. This understanding is achieved through standardized-test results and grades.

Sedlacek (2004) identifies eight variables that are useful in assessment of students of color, especially African Americans. These eight variables—positive self-concept, realistic self-appraisal, successfully handling the system (racism), preference for long-term goals, availability of a strong support person, leadership experience, community involvement, knowledge acquired in a field—provide a unique guide when analyzed as factors for retention and persistence.

Whether these noncognitive variables provide any type of motivation, assist with adjustment, or improve students' perceptions is determined using various forms of measurement. Sedlacek (2004) used questionnaires, short-answer questions, portfolios, essays, and application reviews. "Noncognitive variables have been found effective in predicting student success in higher education and employed by many institutions in their admissions and retention programs" (p. 67).

Additionally, Sedlacek (2004) presents a case study in which St. John Fisher College implemented a NonCognitive Questionnaire (NCQ) to use as a predictor to measure students' success at the college. It was also used to determine which students would participate in a special educational development program. Counselors individually evaluated the students with high NCQ scores. According to the needs assessed from the scores, counselors provided assistance in tutoring, study skills, and campus adjustment, as well as financial and general support. "Results of the studies at St. John Fisher showed that the number of students of color increased, and that students in the special program did particularly well in school" (p. 73). When some or all of these noncognitive variables are examined in reference to African Americans, especially African American male students, these variables become crucial to understanding the retention and persistence of African American males in higher education.

Methodology: Qualitative Research

This study used qualitative research to discover the reasons African American men persist to degree completion at institutions of higher learning. "Qualitative research . . . is a broad approach to the study of social phenomena; its various genres are naturalistic and interpretive, and they draw on multiple methods of inquiry" (Marshall & Rossman, 1999, p. 2). Qualitative research provided the researcher an opportunity to explore the social interactions of African American men from various college campuses. The ability to draw upon these social interactions made the lived experiences of the participants available to help connect and develop themes surrounding the research questions. Rossman and Rallis (1998) identify four characteristics of qualitative research and researchers. Qualitative research is (1) naturalistic, (2) interpretive, (3) emergent and evolving, and (4) draws on multiple methods that respect the humanity of the participants. Gay and Airasian (2003) characterize qualitative research as being "exceptionally suited for exploration, for beginning to understand a group or phenomenon" (p. 163).

The research design used for this study was descriptive. A descriptive study determines and reports the way things are through collection of data and answers to questions that concern the current subject of the study (Gay & Airasian, 2003). Isaac and Michael (1995) state, "The purpose of descriptive research is to describe systematically the facts and characteristics of a given population or area of interest, factually and accurately" (p. 50). Descriptive research does not aim to prove or disprove hypotheses or make predictions.

Descriptive research often uses surveys, questionnaires, and/or interviews to obtain the data needed. Isaac and Michael (1995) outline four circumstances in which surveys, questionnaires, and interviews should be used:

1. To collect detailed, factual information that describes existing phenomena.
2. To identify problems or justify current conditions and practices.
3. To make comparisons and evaluations.
4. To determine what others are doing with similar problems or situations and benefit from their experience in making future plans and decisions. (p. 50)

Surveys or questionnaires are used to gauge the perceptions of a group toward a specific phenomenon. In the qualitative research design of this study, interviews allowed theories, themes, and assumptions to emerge from the data.

Aligned with the qualitative approach is *grounded theory*. "Grounded theory aims at deriving theory from the analysis of multiple stages of data collection and interpretation" (Gay & Airasian, 2003, p. 17). Grounded theory tends to involve inductive rather than deductive reasoning to ascertain theories. The method of obtaining data for this study was through grounded theory. Strauss and Corbin (1998) emphasize that grounded theory in qualitative research "can refer to research about persons' lives, stories, behavior, but also about organizational function, social movements, or interactional relationships" (p. 17). In other words, the purpose of grounded theory in descriptive research is to build theory related to complex social phenomena and allow for theory development in an area where research is sparse.

The population selected for this study was African American men who graduated in May/June 2004 from 4-year universities in Southern California with an undergraduate degree. Due to the large number of colleges and universities in Southern California, the researcher elected to focus the study on African American men who graduated from two universities in the California State University (CSU) system; one university in the University of California (UC) system; and one small, private Jesuit University.

The California State University system is composed of 23 campuses throughout California. Student enrollment for the entire CSU system was 409,000 as of fall 2003. CSU employs approximately 44,000 faculty and staff. The CSU system operates on a semester calendar, with the exception of one campus that operates on a quarterly calendar. The CSU system awards more than half of the bachelor's degrees and a third of the master's degrees granted in California.

The University of California system was chartered in 1868, and there are 10 campuses within this system. Student enrollment for the entire UC system was 201,000 students as of fall 2003, and the UC system employs approximately 160,000 faculty and staff. The UC system operates on a quarterly calendar. It has a $14 billion budget, which includes 10 campuses, five medical and teaching hospitals, three law schools, and a statewide Division of Agriculture and Natural Resources.

Founded in 1911, the private Jesuit University is the largest Catholic university in Southern California. Total student undergraduate enrollment for the university is over 5,000 and there are 3,000 graduate and law school students. Jesuit University employs approximately 1,148 faculty and staff. The university operates on a semester calendar, and its budget is $150 million. The Jesuit University includes four colleges (Liberal Arts, College of Business Administration, College of Communication and Fine Arts, and College of Science and Engineering), as well as the School of Education, School of Film and Television, Graduate Division, Extensions, and Law School.

The sample of African American males for these schools was as follows:

1. The two universities in the CSU system had a combined total undergraduate enrollment of 36,354; African American undergraduate enrollment of 4,005; and African American male enrollment of 1.165.
2. The one university in the University of California system had a total undergraduate enrollment of 25,715; African American enrollment of 895; and African American male enrollment of 332.
3. The private Jesuit University had a total undergraduate enrollment of 5,456; African American undergraduate enrollment of 368; and African American male enrollment of 112.

Purposive sampling was used to identify and determine the experiences of 12 African American men who persisted to baccalaureate degree completion at the universities listed above. "In purposive sampling . . . the researcher selects a sample based on his experience and knowledge of the group to be sampled" (Gay & Airasian, 2003, p. 115). Participants were also selected based on the researcher's ability to choose individuals who would be informative and who had some experience related to the research topic.

Two forms of instrumentation were used in this study: the NCQ (Sedlacek, 2004) and interviews. The NCQ was developed by Tracey and Sedlacek (1987). The NCQ contains 36 items and measures eight noncognitive variables. These variables are: (1) positive self-concept, (2) realistic self-appraisal, (3) demonstrated community service, (4) knowledge acquired in a field, (5) successful leadership experience, (6) long-range goals, (7) ability to understand and cope with racism, and (8) availability of a strong support person/system. Tracey and Sedlacek found this "specific set of noncognitive [variables] related to grade point average and persistence, especially for minority students" (p. 3).

Findings

Since the researcher used two instruments to determine the reasons African American males persist to degree completion in higher education, he separated his findings for each. Findings for the NCQ and interviews were as follows:

Noncognitive Questionnaire

1. The participants strongly agreed that they possessed positive self-concept or confidence.
2. The participants strongly agreed that they gave themselves realistic self-appraisal.
3. The participants agreed that they understood and dealt with racism.
4. The participants were neutral when determining long-range goals.
5. The participants strongly agreed upon the availability of a strong support person.
6. The participants agreed that they had a successful leadership experience.
7. The participants were neutral in relation to demonstrated community service.
8. The participants were neutral in the knowledge acquired in a field.

Interviews

Findings from the interviews with the 12 African American male college students focused on their lived experiences as related to the question of why some African American men persist to baccalaureate degree completion in 4-year colleges and universities. In addition, the interviews identified noncognitive variables that had a significant impact on the African American men in the study. The participants in the study were asked seven questions:

1. What campus services contributed to your persistence as an African American male?
2. What experiences were dominant factors for you to complete your degree?
3. What challenges do you believe provided a key role to completing

your degree?
4. What role did you believe the university facilitated to assist you with completing your degree?
5. What noncognitive variables (availability of a strong support person, academic adjustment, attachment to college, personal emotional adjustment, and social adjustment) do you believe had a significant impact on your graduating from college?
6. What role (if any) did elementary, middle school, or high school play in your persistence to attain your baccalaureate degree?
7. What do you believe will assist other African American males to succeed and graduate from college?

The following is a summary of the responses from the participants. The 12 participants agreed that the campus services that contributed to their persistence in college were the ethnic and minority programs and organizations on campus. Challenges ranged from racism and absence of other African American males, to lack of departmental support within their major. However, these challenges also became motivators for the participants. The participants concluded that family, precollege programs, and self-actualization were dominant factors.

All of the noncognitive variable categories (availability of a strong support person, academic adjustment, attachment to college, personal emotional adjustment, and social adjustment) had some kind of impact on the participants' college experience. The participants' responses focused on family, ethnic organizations, leadership roles in organizations, friends, accessibility to faculty during office hours, and mentors. All of the participants believed that either elementary, middle school, or high school played a role in their decision to obtain a college degree. Last, 100% of the participants responded that setting goals, being focused, and having a strong support system would assist other African American males with graduating from college.

Conclusion

As an African American male, I am overwhelmed by the findings of this study. As I interviewed these young men, I wished that I had been as focused and determined as they were when I was an undergraduate. Although I was involved in organizations (as a member and leader), I did not see the value at the time. My support system consisted of my family (my mother), an African American Greek Lettered Fraternity (Alpha Phi Alpha Fraternity, Inc.), and relationships with other students, faculty, and staff. I believe that I failed with setting long-term goals. My goal was degree completion. These young men see further than degree completion. They see their entire lives, including the ultimate transition of becoming a man and being productive in society.

Throughout my academic tenure, my focus has been African American males. It has always been my passion to assist other African American males with identifying resources and to allow myself to be a resource. I hope this study will help open the minds of student affairs professionals, as well as academic affairs professionals who have the power to create resources for African American men to succeed in and graduate from college.

However, it should be stressed that African American males must take on the challenge of reframing the issues in higher education to identify their own needs. African American males must organize in support groups to enhance their education experience and academic success. African American males must also learn that higher education is a 4- to 5-year boot camp. In academic boot camp, things are learned both inside and outside of the classroom. African American males in college should learn to be better critical thinkers, to be proactive instead of reactive, to be leaders, to increase their ability to network, and to become facilitators and builders of relationships and scholarship within their respective major fields.

References

Center for the Study of Social Policy (1995). *Keeping pace with change: Black males and social policy.* Washington, DC: Author.

Davis, L. E. (Ed.). (1999). *Working with African American males: A guide to practice.* Thousand Oaks, CA: Sage.

DuBois, W. E. B. (1903). The talented tenth. *The Negro problem: A collection of articles by African Americans.* New York: James Pott.

Gay, L. R., & Airasian, P. (2003). *Educational research: Competencies for analysis and application* (7th ed.). Upper Saddle River, NJ: Pearson Education.

Gibbs, J. (1988). *Young, Black, and male in America: An endangered species.* Dover, MA: Auburn House.

Hall, R. E., & Rowan, G. T. (2001). African American males in higher education: A descriptive/qualitative analysis. *Journal of African American Men 5*(3), 3–13.

Harper, S., & Wolley, M. A. (2002, May). Becoming an "involving college" for African American undergraduate men: Strategies for increasing African American male participation in campus activities. *The Bulletin,* 16–24.

Harris, W. G. (1996). African-American males in higher education: Reframing the issue. *Black Issues in Higher Education 13,* 92.

Harris, W. G., & Duhon, G. M. (1999). *The African American male perspective of barriers to success.* Lewiston, NY: Edwin Mellen Press.

Harvey, W. B. (2002). *Minorities in higher education 2001–2002: Nineteenth annual status report.* Washington, DC: American Council on Education.

Isaac, S., & Michael, W. B. (1995). *Handbook in research and evaluation.* San Diego, CA: EdITS.

Jones, N. A., & Jackson, J. A. (2003). The demographic profile of African Americans, 1970–71 to 2000–01. *The Black Collegian 31*(3), 72.

Kunjufu, J. (2001). *State of emergency: We must save African American males.* Chicago: African American Images.

Levin, J., & Levin, M. (1991). A critical examination of academic retention programs for at-risk minority college students. *Journal of College Student Development 32*, 323–333.

Majors, R., & Billson, J. M. (1992). *Cool pose: The dilemmas of Black manhood in America.* New York: Maxwell Macmillan International.

Marshall, C., & Rossman, G. B. (1999). *Designing qualitatitve research* (3rd ed.) Thousand Oaks, CA: Sage.

McNairy, F. G. (1996). The challenge for higher education: Retaining students of color. *New Directions for Student Services 74*, 3–14.

Morgan, J. (1996). Reaching out to young Black men. *Black Issues in Higher Education 13*, 16–19.

National Center for Education Statistics (1997). *Digest of education statistics, 1997.* Washington, DC: US Department of Education.

Oliver, W. (1989). Black males and social problems: Prevention through Afrocentric socialization. *Journal of Black Studies 20*, 15–39.

Parker, C. E. (1998). Cultivate academic persistence—now! *Black Issues in Higher Education* 14, 104.

Patton, J. (1981). The Black man's struggle for education. In L. Gary (Ed.), *Black men* (pp. 199–214). Beverly Hills, CA: Sage.

Roach, R. (2001). Where are the Black men on campus? *Black Issues in Higher Education 18*(6), 18–24.

Rossman, G. B., & Rallis, S. F. (1998). *Learning in the field.* Thousand Oaks, CA: Sage.

Schwartz, R. A., & Washington, C. M. (2002). Predicting academic performance and retention among African American freshmen. *NASPA Journal 39*, 354–359.

Sedlacek, W. E. (2004). *Beyond the big test: Noncongnitive assessment in higher education.* San Francisco: Jossay-Bass.

Steele, C. M. (1999, August). Thin ice: "Stereotype threat" and Black college students. *The Atlantic Monthly, 284*(2), 50–54.

Strauss, A., & Corbin, J. (1998). *Basics of qualitative research: Techniques and procedures for developing grounded theory* (2nd ed.). Newbury Park, CA: Sage.

Thomas, L. X. (2000). A plea to the talented tenth. *Cultural expressions.* Retrieved March 17, 2004, from http://www.cultural-expressions.com/thesis/pleatotenth.htm

Tracey, T. J., & Sedlacek, W. E. (1987). Prediction of college graduation using noncognitive variables by race. *Measurement and Evaluation in Counseling and Development, 19,* 177–84.

Van Sertima, I. (2003). *They came before Columbus.* New York: Random House.

Wei, C. C., & Horn, L. (2002). *Persistence and attainment of beginning students with Pell Grants.* Washington, DC: US Department of Education, National Center for Education Statistics.

Welsing, F. C. (1990). *The Isis papers: The keys to the colors*. Chicago: Third World Press.

Williams, C. (1992). *The destruction of Black civilization: Great issues of race from 4500 BC to 2000 AD*. Chicago: Third World Press.

Wilson, M. (2000, October). Reversing the plight of African American male college students. *Black Issues in Higher Education 17*, 176.

Woodson, C. G. (1993). *The mis-education of the Negro*. Chicago: African American Images.

X, Malcolm (1970). *By any means necessary*. New York: Pathfinder Press.

CHAPTER THIRTEEN

Moving Beyond National Standards and Assessment

BOYCE C. WILLIAMS

Introduction

In the world of educational reform, teacher capacity is critical, and debates over how to build teacher capacity are quite common, appropriate, and very much needed. There are times, however, when rival viewpoints emerge that are nonproductive, and sometimes debilitating. This is particularly the case when false dichotomies leave educators with "either/or" options, when embracing "both/and" perspectives would have a greater yield. A widely discussed and insidious example of this phenomenon is the *either* excellence *or* equity debate. This chapter argues that this "either/or" option needs to be reconstructed to allow for the coexistence of both excellence and equity. In more subtle ways, this "either/or" option is being challenged by the National Council for Accreditation of Teacher Education's (NCATE's) continuum of teacher preparation and development, increases in the use of performance-based assessment in teacher education, and the inclusion of diversity in accrediting standards. All are part of the quality control mechanisms for improving the capacity of teachers, increasing the diversity of the teaching force, and raising the academic achievement levels of K–12 students.

This chapter discusses quality and diversity in teacher education and professional development. The first section describes the NCATE's three-phase educational continuum, which encourages continuous engagement by teachers in the teaching and learning process. The second section focuses on performance-based assessment, suggesting that NCATE's evolving quality-assurance measures for performance-based assessment reflect new possibilities for bridging the gaps between indirect assessment and authentic assessment, teaching and testing, and ultimately between the "tested" and "taught" curriculum. The last section describes NCATE's existing diversity standards and discusses the impossibility of achieving excellence without equity, or equity without excellence. Throughout this chapter, special attention is given to implications for African American institutions, preservice and in-service teachers, teacher educators, and students.

Continuum of Preparation and Development

In many fields, accreditation provides a measure of quality control with regard to appropriate levels of expert knowledge and performance needed for effective participation in the profession. In the teaching profession, the NCATE plays a central role in establishing quality assurance measures. Interest in how teachers develop and change over time has gained new importance with increased focus on teacher quality. Indeed, NCATE's view of how to build teacher capacity is reflected in its philosophy of preparation and development as a continuum.

NCATE describes teacher preparation as a three-phase continuum: Phase I, preservice preparation; Phase II, extended clinical preparation and assessment; and Phase III, continuing professional development. Phase I focuses on the NCATE/State quality assurance measures in teacher preparation. These measures cover recruitment, entry, preservice programs, state subject matter and teaching knowledge assessments, and graduation. The teacher's role as learner does not end with Phase I. Instead, teachers are expected to be career-long learners, as reflected in Phases II and III of the continuum.

Phase II extends the continuum through state licensing agencies that monitor further development of entry-level teachers. This development includes intern programs such as clinical practice, mentoring, clinical studies, and professional development schools (PDSs). State licensure assessment, which focuses on the application of research-based knowledge, skills, and dispositions, are also emphasized in this phase of the continuum. Phase III extends the learning continuum to experienced teachers and includes a focus on professional development, license renewal, national board assessment, and advanced certification.

Across the continuum, different parties are responsible for assessment. For example, Phase I uses multiple assessments developed and scored by schools and colleges of education; Phase II relies heavily on state internship assessments; and Phase III utilizes the assessments of state and national agencies and associations. Given the different, but related, demands and responsibilities of quality assurance agencies, the success of the three-phase continuum is largely dependent on collaboration. Without collaboration, each of the various stakeholders would likely operate as separate entities, and the possibilities for bringing order to the enhancement of teacher capacity and improved education would suffer. Many of these diverse stakeholders are using partnerships as a means of realizing the benefits of a continuum for improving teacher capacity.

One initiative that recognizes the importance of a continuum to sustaining teacher capacity is the National Partnership for Excellence and Accountability in Teaching (NPEAT). In this initiative, NCATE is engaged in a collaboration with the National Board for Professional Teaching Standards (NBPTS) for graduate programs. NPEAT hopes to address problems that could impede the development of systemic change. Its mission is to:

> . . . energize and enable those who teach and influence teaching to use knowledge based on research and the wisdom of practice to ensure that teachers have the capabilities, motivation, and opportunity to help all students, especially those placed at risk, achieve challenging academic standards. (NPEAT brochure)

Effective partnerships between institutions of higher education and K–12 schools are required, if the three-phase continuum is to be successful. A successful model of collaboration is the conceptualization and development of PDSs. Similarly, NCATE, the Interstate New Teacher Assessment and Support Consortium (INTASC), and the NBPTS have aligned their standards through collaboration efforts. As a result, teacher preparation, licensure, and advanced certification have standards that embrace excellence and equity. The value of this continuum of professional preparation and development is threefold: (1) it calls attention to the need for continuity in the cycle of teachers as learners; (2) it pushes professional educators toward serious collaborative initiatives in all parts of the system; and (3) it forces us to confront the challenge of moving from *either/or* to *both/and* options.

The continuum of professional preparation and development provides a structural framework for moving away from "either/or" debates. On the one hand, it has been argued that teacher education programs should control both preprofessional preparation and in-service development. On the other hand, some argue that teacher education programs should be limited to preprofessional preparation, while school districts focus on in-service development. Some of the factors that have fueled this "either/or" debate are the absence of trust, the assumption that teacher education programs prefer to focus more on theory than practice, and the view that schools are unable to provide leadership in the design and implementation of professional in-service programs. Conflicting viewpoints are exacerbated by competition for control of resources allocated for professional development. Again "either/or" is limiting, while "both/and" is expansive. Rightfully, both institutions of higher learning and K–12 schools should operate as coequals, since each needs additional resources to respond to the demands for more comprehensive preservice and in-service programs. Collaboration serves as an important mechanism for making more explicit the need to look for "both/and" options as a means of realizing the goals of increased teacher capacity.

Special concerns must be taken into account when considering the continuum of teacher preparation and professional development at historically and predominantly Black colleges and universities (HBCUs). At many of these institutions, collaboration has been difficult at each phase of the continuum. First, collaborative initiatives in each phase of the continuum demand resources that are generally not readily available to HBCUs. Second, assessments in each phase threaten to exclude an already dwindling pool of minority teachers. Third, collaboration with majority institutions has often left HBCUs with fewer real benefits from partnerships than their peers. At first glance, the continuum would appear to work against HBCUs. Quite fortunately, though, there is now an initiative, the HBCU Technical Support Network (HBCU-TSN), that helps HBCUs share in the benefits of the continuum and do so largely through developing strategic plans for collaboratives (SPCs).

Viewing the continuum of teacher preparation and professional development as reflective of the "both/and" possibilities, the HBCU-TSN has initiated a model for supporting quality improvements. The model consists of four major components: (1) assessing, (2) educating, (3) coaching, and (4) collaborating. To make the continuum work for, rather than against, HBCUs, this TSN has redefined collaboration so that barriers are reduced. Accordingly, the HBCU-TSN's explanation of collaboration sets the tone for HBCUs to realize the potential benefits of collaboration.

Collaboration is a much used and abused word. Unexamined, it suggests that whatever tasks are to be done can be done equally well by all participants. Here, the author's concept of collaboration implies neither an unthinking acceptance of the view that all partners in an activity are equally fit to do all things, nor an elitist view that one group has wisdom and experience superior to the other. This chapter posits an idea yet to be realized: collaboration that capitalizes on the research and experience of the best professors in the academy and on the expertise and experience of the best teachers in the schools, recognizing that valuable attributes reside in both places (Williams, 1997, p. 191).

In keeping with this philosophy, the HBCU-TSN's major collaboration goal is to situate HBCUs for interdependent work that encourages self-sufficiency while discouraging the perception that their unique circumstances call for unique solutions or that their benefits are derived largely from working dependently. The technical support program uses collaboration as a critical component that ultimately enhances the other three components of the model. HBCU-TSN's guiding principles for developing SPCs (see Williams, 1997, pp. 92–93) are outlined below:

1. SPCs must complement the strategic goals of the institution and the teacher education unit.
2. SPCs must allow for the involvement of key partners in the development and implementation of the strategic plan.
3. SPCs must provide for participants in collaborative efforts to be trained in effective strategies for engaging in collaboration.
4. SPCs must give consideration to collaboratives both within the institution, and between the institution and external groups.
5. SPCs will actively seek ways and means of integrating related functions across units.

SPCs include mechanisms for strengthening communication about the teacher education program and fostering collaboration between teacher education units and development offices for joint resource development activities. Minimally, such a plan should include mechanisms for ensuring that the acquisition of external funds supports the goals and conceptual framework of the teacher education unit.

Further, SPCs should allow for the development of professional networks between teacher educators and teachers. The evolving work on PDSs has begun to bridge the gap between the knowledge acquired in teacher education programs and the application of that knowledge to performance in the classroom. Reminiscent of the laboratory schools that were at one time an integral part of teacher education in HBCUs, the PDSs are particularly attractive as a means of restoring a tradition that worked well.

In extending collaboration to the coaching component of the HBCU-TSN, SPCs should allow for productive engagement. All participants must enter the coaching relationship with clearly identified needs and expectations about what each will give and receive from the collaboration. The work of the HBCU-TSN suggests that one way to address concerns related to the continuum is by strategically planning to address potential harmful effects by developing collaboratives that maximize existing resources and generate new ones. HBCUs should also find ways to work interdependently with others toward shaping the types of partnerships that will be mutually beneficial to all partners.

The HBCU-TSN model demonstrates that the negative perceptions associated with the continuum of teacher preparation and professional development can be turned into "both/and" possibilities that work to support the desires of HBCUs. This will improve the quality of teacher education programs, assist in meeting the related quality assurance measures of accreditation agents, as well as address issues of diversity in the nation's teaching force.

Performance-Based Assessment

In the new millennium, an emphasis on the performance of teacher candidates, not just curriculum and evidence that certain courses and subjects are included in education programs, is expected to bring teacher education in line with the larger movement to set higher standards for both teachers and students. A combination of performance-based evaluative measures, including candidate work samples and other outcome measures, on-site examining teams, and state licensing examinations, will be used to judge the quality of a program under review. States are introducing new measures in teacher licensing to improve the effectiveness of teacher performance. New requirements in licensing will encourage close examination of teacher candidates' content knowledge, professional knowledge, and demonstration of classroom skills and dispositions. In keeping with this trend, NCATE is moving toward a performance-based system of accreditation.

Elliott (1997) considers how performance-based assessment may be adapted to accreditation as part of a quality assurance process. He presents potential elements that need to be considered in assessing program quality that would depend less on evaluation of courses offered and more on evaluation of actual performance of candidates and institutions. In particular, Elliott states that:

> First, the performance-based standards would describe not programs and experiences that should be offered to candidates, but the knowledge, skills, and dispositions that the candidates should acquire. . . .

> Second, the performance-based standards would also describe some expectations of institutions where their actions can make a major contribution to the performance of the candidates. . . .

> Third, the information used to evaluate whether the . . . program meets the standards would be radically different from current practice. . . . The intent would be to make information available that would demonstrate that . . . candidates have mastered the subject content appropriate for teaching and the ability to teach. (1997, pp. 41–42)

Elliott further notes that evidence of performance might include portfolios with journals, reflections, results of performance assessments taken during the college experience, grades, evaluations by practicum faculty and cooperating teachers, success on state licensure examinations, and on-the-job evaluations.

According to Elliott (1997), performance-based assessment will translate into institution standards in two ways: (1) by refocusing documentation of program effectiveness on information that will demonstrate that the institution is using multiple assessment indicators and (2) by operating in ways that increase the likelihood that its graduates will be able to perform effectively in the classroom.

The field is just beginning to use performance assessment as a tool for improving teaching and teacher preparation. This new tool is changing the structure of teacher preparation and state regulations relating to teacher preparation. At the core of divisiveness over performance-based assessment are two "either/or" options: (1) use either indirect assessment or authentic assessment; and (2) accept either an assessment-driven curriculum or curriculum-driven assessment. Part of the solution is to be found in understanding the interdependent relationship between the "taught" and "tested" curriculum. This chapter proposes modeling effective practices in both teaching and assessment as an approach to change that embraces the notion of "both/and" options in the move toward performance-based assessment.

The authentic assessment movement has a rich theoretic history. The language/language arts discipline was among the first to emphasize the need for authentic assessment. Calling attention to the need for direct assessments of language performance, language and language arts professionals provided a theoretical backdrop and evidence of the types of materials that include authentic data on language performance (i.e., real writing in natural writing settings). In part because of this movement, more attention has been given to the need for assessment data to be collected over time, rather than using data from a single performance on a given test. Typical of the kind of data that would be generated from authentic assessments are student journals, portfolios of writing, and real writing samples as opposed to only multiple-choice items on an examination.

Constructivist pedagogy also provides a theoretical basis for authentic learning and assessment. In constructivist pedagogy, emphasis is placed on authentic learning experiences, authentic materials, and authentic assessment, all integrated into the delivery of the curriculum across disciplines. Constructivist approaches emphasize the learner as meaning maker, actively engaged in inquiry and discovery of meaning, rather than passively receiving meaning made by the teacher or others. Perkins and Blythe (1994) delineate a four-part framework for use in a constructivist way. Their framework included using generative topics, developing understanding goals, planning understanding performances, and conducting ongoing assessment. Ongoing assessment in constructivist classrooms emphasizes students' need for regular feedback and opportunities for reflection on their progress in learning.

Brooks and Brooks (1993, p. 17) offer eight characteristics of constructivist classrooms. These include:

1. Curriculum is presented with emphasis on big concepts.
2. Student questions are highly valued.
3. Curricular activities rely heavily on primary sources of data and manipulative materials.
4. Students are viewed as thinkers with emerging theories about the world.
5. Teachers behave in an interactive manner, mediating the environment for students.
6. Teachers seek students' points of view to base future lessons on their conceptions.
7. Assessment is interwoven with teaching and occurs through student exhibits and portfolios.
8. Students work primarily in groups.

In these descriptions of constructivist pedagogy are elements that parallel views about how to make performance-based assessment work. Specifically, one way to make performance-based assessment work to improve the capacity of teachers is by establishing linkages between content and pedagogy. Edwards (1997), for example, recommends that:

> If content and pedagogy are to be valued by prospective teachers, a college faculty needs to create quality learning experiences that merge content and pedagogy for its teacher candidates. This implies restructuring the teacher education program so that faculty who teach traditional content courses and pedagogy courses form working partnerships. (p. 44)

As educational reform moves increasingly toward performance-based assessment, more of the elements of constructivist pedagogy must become part of discussions on bridging the gap between *content* and *pedagogy*.

Arguing that performance-based assessment will have little impact unless it is part of a coherent process of teacher development, Diez and Hass (1997) support the notion of linkages. Their work brings to the forefront the need for alignment between what some have called the "tested" and "taught" curriculum. What is taught and what is tested are often disparate. Diez and Hass (1997, p. 23) stress six basic elements they believe are necessary for performance-based learning that can bridge the divide between the tested and taught curriculum:

1. Expected learning outcomes or abilities.
2. Explicit criteria for performance.
3. Expert judgment.
4. Productive feedback.
5. Self-assessment.
6. Assessment as a process that involves multiple performances.

In the area of performance-based assessment, it is important to move from the issues of either indirect or authentic assessment to situationally appropriate ways of assessing. It is becoming immensely clear that the tested and taught curriculum will need to be aligned, allowing for both teaching what is tested and testing what is taught. Furthermore, as reform initiatives move toward an emphasis on authentic content, learning experiences, and materials, the notion of authentic assessment must find its place or there will be a continued mismatch between what is tested and what is taught. This mismatch can be blended through the engagement of teacher educators in pedagogical practices that model both authentic teaching and authentic assessment strategies, demonstrating not only the what, but also the how of teaching and assessment.

It is well accepted in the research community that teachers teach the way they were taught instead of the way they were taught to teach. Embedded in this notion is the suggestion that teachers draw upon their experiences as learners instead of their knowledge of pedagogy, an "either/or" option. The "both/and" option, however, calls for teachers to draw upon both their experiences as learners as well as the knowledge acquired and constructed in teacher education programs. Such modeling of effective constructivist practices in teaching invites teacher educators to practice what they preach.

Modeling is an approach to delivery that has been offered to provide greater continuity with the apprenticeship model of teaching in homes, particularly homes of nonmainstream groups. To the extent that performance-based assessment encourages the use of the "practice what you preach" axiom and that modeling serves as a means to translate this axiom into pedagogical practices, it appears that performance-based assessment could work for the preparation and development of African American preservice and in-service teachers.

While the benefits of performance-based assessment may seem clear, the potential for bias in performance-based assessments is a growing concern. It is reasonable to take action in the early stages of performance-based assessment to prevent bias in the ways that those who evaluate performance observe and rate the performance of African American teachers. In fact, there is a growing body of information that describes effective practices of African American teachers (Ladson-Billings, 1990) and suggests that the pedagogical practices of African American teachers and teacher educators are informed partially by their cultural experiences. The implication is that attention must be given to including effective practices of teachers from different ethnic backgrounds in developing performance-based assessment instruments, so that those assessing performance can know what they are observing and adequately assess its effectiveness. Clearly, more research is needed to better interpret culturally responsive pedagogy. Until that information is available, it is reasonable to expect developers of performance-based assessment instruments to take into consideration the findings of available research. Modeling effective teaching and assessment practices provides at least one means of steadying the course toward performance-based assessment.

Diversity

The ethnic and racial composition of American schools has changed considerably over the last few decades. While racial and ethnic minority students will soon comprise more than 40% of the nation's elementary and secondary school student population, the teaching force is becoming more homogeneous. With the nation's attention keenly focused on improving preschool through grade 12 student performance, the need to examine and enhance teacher preparation and performance is critical. For racial and ethnic minority students, the problem is compounded as the call for greater teacher preparation and teaching for diversity escalates.

Educating students in the twenty-first century demands not only teachers who can teach, but also those who will be responsive to the needs of students of color and who reflect the cultural, racial, and ethnic diversity of their classrooms. Currently, the average American public school teacher emerges from a monolithic teaching force that is overwhelmingly White and female. While the nation's urban schools need more teachers, they also need better teachers.

NCATE's existing diversity standards convey the basic messages that all children deserve a quality educational experience and that all students should be taught by qualified, culturally aware, and competent teachers. NCATE maintains that prospective teachers must be prepared to cope with the challenges of a multicultural classroom and to be conversant about its perspectives. Both diversifying the nation's teaching force and improving the quality of learning are integral parts of improving the quality of education. Wise et al. (1997) also urged that working successfully with students of different backgrounds requires a respect for the differences students bring. NCATE recognizes that in order to foster a teaching environment that is responsive to the needs and talents of diverse learners, the profession must be engaged in and committed to teaching all students.

Thus, NCATE promotes racial and ethnic diversity as a value within education and has ultimately made it a part of the accreditation process. For example, the existing NCATE standards encourage the recruitment of a diverse student and teacher educator population, as well as admission and retention of students of diverse backgrounds. These areas are often associated with equity issues. The standards also address diversity across the curriculum and within the instructional and field experience components of teacher education programs. These latter areas are most often discussed in relation to excellence. Too often, educators operate as though they must choose *either* equity *or* excellence.

Surely, both excellence and equity are needed, and one should not and cannot work without the other. There remains confusion about the dependent relationship between excellence and equity. As Postman (1996, p. 80) explains:

> Diversity does not mean the disintegration of standards, is not an argument against standards, does not lead to a chaotic, irresponsible relativism. It is an argument for the growth and malleability of standards, a growth that takes place across time and space and that is given form by differences of gender, religion, and all categories of humanity.

In other words, there is a thin line between "pride and prejudice." Progress toward the *both* equity *and* excellence option is impeded as the education community takes pride in excellence, while maintaining prejudices against equity. There is an urgent need to move toward more "both/and" options with serious consideration given to teacher research. This research, also referred to as *action research*, shows promise for involving teachers in the types of changes needed to translate principles and guidelines of diversity into pedagogical action.

Principles of effective practice can be found in the growing body of literature on integrating multicultural and international perspectives into the curriculum. Some of the topics that need to be considered are: (1) teachers' attitudes and beliefs about students of different backgrounds (Scott & Smitherman, 1985; Winfield, 1986; Scott, 1998); (2) content and materials used (Banks, 1993; Ladson-Billings, 1994); (3) instructional approaches that ensure equitable pedagogy; (4) educational settings that are heterogeneous and diverse; and (5) limited access to information about diverse groups, particularly in teacher education programs.

In the area of instruction in multicultural settings, Morterella (1990, p. 312) suggests that effective teacher education programs should incorporate the following experiences: (1) learning how and where to obtain objective, accurate information about other cultural groups; (2) identifying and examining positive accounts of other cultural groups or individuals; (3) learning tolerance for diversity through experimentation in the school and classroom with alternative customs and practices; (4) encountering, where possible, firsthand positive experiences with different cultural groups; (5) developing empathic behavior . . . through role playing and simulations; and (6) practicing using "perspective glasses," that is, looking at an event, historical period, or issue through the perspective of another cultural group.

While it is helpful to have these guidelines, the missing link is in the application of the guidelines. Getting the guidelines and principles into an application mode requires teachers' experience-based inquiry. Postman (1996, p. 71) highlights the problem in an analogy between assumptions about schooling and punctuation marks. He points out that educators tend to operate on the assumption that all children enter school as question marks and leave as periods. Stressing the need for new stories on schooling in diverse societies, Postman views the story of America as an experiment, a perpetual and fascinating question mark. Here, Postman is advocating for the spirit of inquiry. It is the author's contention that in dealing with diversity in the classroom more effectively, educators need to reverse attempts to make periods when they should be making question marks. Through teacher research, educators can begin the process of making question marks, as well as set up a framework for improving the pedagogical content knowledge of teachers. Shulman's (1987, p. 8) explanation of pedagogical content puts the challenge before us in a provocative way:

> Pedagogical content knowledge is the category most likely to distinguish the understanding of the content specialist from that of the pedagogue. . . . But the key to distinguishing the knowledge base of teaching lies at the intersection of content and pedagogy, in the capacity of a teacher to transform the content

knowledge he or she possesses into forms that are pedagogically powerful and yet adaptive to the variations in ability and background presented by the students.

For this discussion, the key phrase is "adaptive to the variations in ability and background presented by the students." To adapt to the diverse needs of students, teachers need a broad repertoire of strategies to draw upon during the act of teaching, not just a neat little set of activities that are planned and implemented in a controlled way. Changing the face of diversity in the classroom depends on spontaneous decision making in response to the various needs of the students as these needs are manifested in virtually all aspects of the teaching and learning process.

Another area of concern is broadening teachers' repertoire of strategies in ways that change practices. Herein lies the call for more teacher research with a focus on teachers' reflections on practices in diverse settings. With teacher research comes a continuum of reflectivity. Zeichner (1993) postulates three levels of reflectivity: (1) technical rationality, (2) practical action, and (3) critical reflection:

> Technical rationality refers to "delivering" the curriculum in much the way it is presented in the official documents of the school. Practical action involves teacher selection from among alternatives that are available in light of the projected practical outcomes of each. "At this level every action is seen as linked to particular value commitments, and the actor considers the worth of competing educational ends." (Zeichner, 1993, p. 24)

Kindsvatter et al. (1996) add that "critical reflection transcends practical action by asking questions in the ethical and moral dimension, involving concerns for justice, equity, and concrete fulfillment, and whether current arrangements serve important human needs and satisfy important human purposes" (pp. 364–365).

It is the second and third levels of reflectivity, practical action, and critical reflection that lead us directly to teacher research. Teachers have looked suspiciously at any mention of their involvement in research. Too often, they have been the subjects of other people's research. As subjects of their own research, their interest in being involved in research changes. Moreover, the value of teacher research as a means of making discoveries about pedagogy has gone far in encouraging teacher involvement in teacher research. When broadly conceived as critical reflection, teacher research becomes more palatable, partially because of its linkage with the kinds of decisions teachers must make moment by moment in the classroom. This point becomes clear when considering some of the descriptions of teacher research, also called action research. Kemmis and McTaggart (1982, p. 5) see action research as providing "a way of thinking systematically about what happens in the school or classroom, implementing action where improvements are thought to be possible, and monitoring and evaluating the effects of the action with a view to continuing the improvement" McCutcheon and Jung (1990, p. 148). describe action research as "systemic inquiry that is collective, collaborative, self-reflective, critical, and undertaken by the participants of the inquiry."

The International Reading Association (IRA, 1989) articulated a number of benefits of teacher research. These benefits are thought to be directly related to everyday classroom practices and include the following: (1) it helps solve classroom problems; (2) it empowers teachers to make decisions in their classrooms; (3) it identifies effective teaching and learning methods; (4) it verifies what methods work; (5) it promotes ownership of effective practices; and (6) it provides a connection between instructional methods and results. Beyond the classroom, the IRA's list gives the following: teacher research promotes reflective teaching, encourages effective change, revitalizes teachers, widens the range of teachers' professional skills, helps teachers apply research findings to their own classrooms, and enables teachers to become change agents. Due to the quality of attention given to teaching in teacher research, this route seems the most promising for transforming well-conceived diversity principles and guidelines into classroom practices.

In the above discussion of performance-based assessment, it was suggested that African American teachers could relate to the "practice what you preach" axiom, which emphasizes the need for teacher educators to model effective practices in both teaching and assessment. The other side of that axiom is "preach what you practice." Teacher research offers the mechanism for more formalized, explicit descriptions of effective teaching strategies used by teachers of color. The value of this work is potentially great (Ladson-Billings, 1990). It would, as suggested above, add to the body of work needed to incorporate the effective practices of teachers of diverse backgrounds into performance-based assessment measures. Second, it would enrich the existing knowledge base on multicultural education. Most importantly, teacher research offers a way to enable teachers to increase their effectiveness in teaching diverse students. This research should be based not only on the theories and experiences of others, but also on the integration of those theories with teachers' own wisdom of practice. This type of practical wisdom is made more explicit through the type of reflection that teacher research is best suited to address.

Conclusion

This chapter has suggested several opportunities for changing the limiting "either/or" options in educational reform to "both/and" possibilities for substantive changes in teacher education. Attention is shifting (1) from control by either in-service preparation or preservice development; (2) from either indirect assessment or authentic assessment; and (3) from either controlling excellence through exclusion of diversity or equity through exclusion of excellence.

Educational reform is moving toward solutions that allow "both/and" options. These solutions include: (1) a continuum of teacher preparation and development through partnerships; (2) the interdependent nature of the "taught" and "tested" curriculum through modeling effective practices; (3) the dependent relationship between excellence and equity through engagement in teacher research.

The continuum of professional preparation and development allows for a three-phase process of activities that provide continuity and coherence to the teacher as a career-long learner. The problems of control of in-service training by either K–12 schools or teacher education programs can be partially resolved through partnerships where each operates as a coequal. Predominantly African American institutions may find resolve in the evolving work of the HBCU-TSN network that establishes a framework that will allow partnerships with majority institutions to be mutually beneficial to all entities of the partnership.

Performance-based assessment represents an area that is driving educational reform. This chapter discussed some of the ways that accrediting bodies are responding to this shift. Understanding the interdependent relationship between the tested and taught curriculum will help to open the way for the use of situationally appropriate assessment measures that include both indirect and authentic assessments of knowledge and performance. Teacher educators modeling effective practices in both teaching and assessment is one mechanism for resolving the tensions between indirect and authentic assessment. Further, the modeling of effective practices supports an already popular axiom in the African American community: "Practice what you preach."

The final section of this chapter treated diversity, pointing to existing NCATE standards that encourage *both* equity *and* excellence. The problem of *either* excellence *or* equity is resolved in the expression of the dependent relationship between the two. The mandate to improve the quality of education requires the coexistence and complementarity of both excellence and equity. As a mechanism for offering more "both/and" options, the author suggested the increasing use of teacher research as a mode of inquiry that allows reflection on and explicit articulation of teachers' wisdom of practice. Implications for African American teachers and teacher educators are that their involvement in teacher research is quite critical to achieving unbiased performance-based instruments, to contributing to the knowledge base in the area of multicultural education, and to empowering all teachers to become more effective in their work with diverse populations.

In every phase of educational reform, educators have debated different sides of the issues, sometimes offering "either/or" options when "both/and" possibilities would have a greater yield. And educators will continue the debates, create new stories, and engage in the ongoing experiment with schooling in a pluralistic society. As Postman (1996) points out, "The only thing we have to fear is that someone will insist on putting in an exclamation point when we are not yet finished" (p. 73).

It is essential to keep asking questions while moving toward improved education for all.

References

Banks, J. (1993). Multicultural education for young children: Racial and ethnic attitudes and their modification. In B. Spodek (Ed.), *Handbook of research on the education of young children*. New York: Macmillan.

Brooks, J., & Brooks, M. (1993). *The case for constructivist classrooms*. Alexandria, VA: Association for Supervision and Curriculum Development.

Diez, M., & Hass, J. (1997). No more piecemeal reform: Using performance-based approaches to rethink teacher education. *Action in Teacher Education XIX*(2), 17–25.

Edwards, N. (1997). Integrating content and pedagogy: A cultural journey. *Action in Teacher Education XIX*(2), 44–54.

Elliott, E. (1997). Performance: A new look at program quality evaluation in accreditation. *Action in Teacher Education XIX*(2), 38–54.

International Reading Association (1989). Classroom action research: The teacher as researcher. *Journal of Reading 33*(3), 216–218.

Kemmis, S., & McTaggart, R. (1982). *The action research planner*. Geelong, Australia: Deakin University Press.

Kindsvatter, R., Wilen, W., & Ishler, M. (1996). *Dynamics of effective teaching*. White Plains, NY: Longman Publishers.

Ladson-Billings, G. (1990). Like lightning in a bottle: Attempting to capture the pedagogical excellence of successful teachers of Black students. *Qualitative Studies in Education 3*(4), 335–344.

———. (1994). What we can learn from multicultural education research. *Educational Leadership* April, 22–26.

McCutcheon, G., & Jung, B. (1990). Alternative perspectives on action research. *Theory into Practice 29*(3), 144–151.

Morterella, P. (1990). *Teaching and social studies in middle and secondary schools*. New York: Macmillan.

Perkins, D., & Blythe, T. (1994). Putting understanding up front. *Educational Leadership* 51(5), 4–7.

Postman, N. (1996). *The end of education: Redefining the value of school.* New York: Vintage Books.

Scott, J. (1998). The serious side of ebonics humor. *Journal of English Linguistics* 26(2), 137–155.

Scott, J., & Smitherman, G. (1985). Language attitudes and self-fulfilling prophecies in the elementary school. In S. Greenbaum (Ed.), *The English language today.* Elmsford, NY: Pergamon Press.

Shulman, L. (1987). Knowledge and teaching: Foundation of the new reform. *Harvard Educational Review 57*, 1–22.

Williams, B. (1997). Challenges and opportunities for collaboration in teacher education programs. *Action in Teacher Education XIX*(2), 89–96.

Winfield, L. (1986). Teacher beliefs toward at-risk students in inner-urban schools. *The Urban Review 18*, 253–267.

Wise, A., Leibbrand, J., & Williams, B. (1997). *Action in Teacher Education XIX*(2), 1–6.

Zeichner, K. (1993). *Educating teachers for cultural diversity.* East Lansing, MI: National Center for Research on Teacher Learning.

Part Three

Legal Issues and Black Colleges

CHAPTER FOURTEEN

Blacks Still Not Equal Even After the Civil Rights Act of 1964

OTIS D. ALEXANDER

Introduction

From the first 23 Africans who arrived in Jamestown, Virginia, in 1619, the African experience has been integral part of the American experience and has left its stamp on the country's institutions. The human relationship between the White economists (plantation owners/slave traders) and the Black population was and still remains imbalanced and rocky. After all, the White power structure never accepted Africans as human beings. (Otherwise, it would not have been so easy for Whites to enslave them.) This not only demonstrated the ideology of White supremacy, but also represented a progressive economic system that lasted approximately 400 years.

African Americans had always been denied rights by White plantation owners, even that of marriage to another slave. Their destiny was in the hands of others (Fishel & Quarles, 1967, p. 113). Free Blacks poured most of their energy, both emotional and spiritual, into the church, mainly the Baptist and Methodist denominations (p. 135). There were no other ways that Blacks could fight the power of the gun, the number of White plantation owners, and the vicious racism that came along with dismantling the economic system of slavery that had brought great wealth to the White establishment.

Four hundred years after slavery, African Americans continued to experience inequality, even after promises after promises. Therefore, laws protecting Blacks were necessary for their further growth and development, and that of the country; New World Africans would no longer be an economic base.

Of course, because of White racists' refusal to accept the newly free Black population, several federal civil rights laws were enacted during the Reconstruction period. The Thirteenth Amendment abolished slavery in 1865. However, the terrorism continued. In 1868, the Fourteenth Amendment affirmed citizenship for African Americans under the Constitution. Two years later, in 1870, the Fifteenth Amendment provided that the right to vote could not be denied to US citizens on the basis of "race, color, or previous condition of servitude."

The 1960s were a critical period for the Civil Rights Movement. It was the zenith of protest, radicalism, freedom train rides, marches, and demonstrations (Alexander, 2003, p. 518). Also, this was the period in which President John F. Kennedy was assassinated, causing many African American civil rights leaders to later split over the best strategies to use to address the federal government's refusal to enforce existing civil rights laws. All of this led to the Civil Rights Act of 1964.

Even though the Civil Rights Act of 1964 was needed to address discrimination against African Americans, it was only a temporary relief of the tension between Whites and African Americans, giving the former time to regroup for future discrimination. The passing of the act was probably expedited to stop protests and stall the legal system, while identifying a subtle manner of fairly sharing "the pursuit of happiness" with Blacks in the United States. The act has not been fully monitored and pushed to its limits. Therefore, the primary purpose of this chapter is to investigate the quality of equality for African Americans after the Civil Rights Act of 1964.

The Civil Rights Act

There is an abundance of information available online about the Civil Rights Act of 1964 as well as *Brown v. Board of Education*. However, Leslie H. Fishel Jr. and Benjamin Quarles' (1967) *The Negro American: A Documentary History* serves the purpose of being the primary source for the angle in which this writer has chosen to explore the topic. Another outstanding source is Gabriel Burns Stepto's *The African-American Years: Chronologies of American History and Experience*. This book clearly outlines that the beginning of the twentieth century was very harsh in the history of African Americans and that because of Jim Crow in the South and the lack of financial opportunities in the North, African Americans were placed in a difficult position: They were caught in a vise of poverty and illiteracy (Stepto, 2003, p. 245).

While laws do not demonstrate everything about a people's behavior, they do tell us what kinds of behavior a given society values—what it permits and even encourages (p. 246). Of course, during the 1960s, civil rights leaders had an accurate understanding of this, as did President John F. Kennedy. In his "Message to Congress" on February 28, 1963, President Kennedy stated that,

> the Negro baby born in America today . . . has about one half as much chance of completing high school as a white baby born in the same place . . . , one third as much chance of completing college, one third as much chance of becoming a professional man; twice as much chance of becoming unemployed . . . , a life expectancy which is seven years less, and prospects of earning only half as much. (Fishel, 1967, p. 514)

This statement was an indication that White leaders in the United States knew that it was unjust, cruel, vicious, and un-American that the nation allowed African Americans to be treated as second-class citizens. President Kennedy went on to say,

> The right to vote is the most powerful and precious right in the world. This is a right that should not be denied on the grounds of race or color. Also, this is one of the greatest stepping stones to achieving other rights of citizenship. . . . it is not merely because of the Cold War, and not merely because of the economic waste of discrimination, that we are committed to achieving true equality of opportunity. The basic reason is because it is right. (p. 514)

Kennedy's appeal to conscience still did not forestall denial of James Meredith's entry to the University of Mississippi in 1961–1962, despite a US Supreme Court ruling in his favor (Lindsey, 1994, p. 122). It also did not deter Governor George C. Wallace of Alabama from personally blocking the entrance of the University of Alabama's auditorium to keep the young Miss Vivian Malone Jones and the young Mr. James A. Hood from enrolling. Again, it was President Kennedy who ordered the Alabama National Guard to remove the governor so that these two students could register the same as the White university students (Hebel, 2004, p. A24). In 1963, when Robert Kennedy was the US Attorney General, he noted that outside of Africa, "the only places on earth known not to provide free public education are Communist China, North Vietnam, Sarawak, Singapore, British Honduras—and Prince Edward County, Virginia" (Nussbaum & John-Hall, 2004, p. A8). He also talked to civil rights marchers in the nation's capitol and decried discrimination in hiring. However, he did not endorse the idea of affirmative action (Lindsey, 1994, p. 121).

The Civil Rights Act of 1964 assisted in dismantling a system that violated human rights. It is divided into 11 titles, which covered: voting, where the standards were different for African American and White voting applicants; public accommodations, including the use of public restrooms, hotels, restaurants; public facilities, to allow African Americans to use the public swimming pools, sit in the parks without harm, and attend events in publicly owned arenas; public schools, to obtain financial and technical assistance regardless of race; extension of the Civil Rights Commission; federal aid without discrimination in federally funded programs; protection against employment discrimination on the part of employers or unions; a system that provides and compiles voting statistics by race in certain areas of the country that have been designated by the Civil Rights Commission; courts, to prevent lower courts from returning a civil rights case to state or local court; conciliatory services for the purpose of mediating racial discrimination at the local level; and "miscellaneous," which is misleading, to provide that the Civil Rights Act would not be affected by the invalidation of any section of it.

Methodology

The instrument used in this chapter was an interview guide with 20 items (Appendix). It was primarily designed to obtain perceptions about the Civil Rights Act of 1964 from high school students, university students, college professors, as well as the unemployed and ex-offenders. Also, through the cooperation of the Dean of Faculty and Academic Affairs at Southeastern University in the District of Columbia, the interview questionnaire was administered in selected classes within the institution. In addition, all questions and concerns were clarified, as the interviewer was always available. The participants were encouraged to answer all questions as honestly as possible, even though a few of the answers were based on perceptions.

The population of the participants used in this study consisted of 100 members in the Washington, D.C., metropolitan area. The participants included African Americans, Whites, students, and professionals. The data were collected from an interview questionnaire eliciting participants' responses regarding their observations, needs, desires, personal experiences, and study of the topic. The interview was comprised of 20 questions that were answered by all of the participants. It gathered perceptual data on the Civil Rights Act of 1964 and related information. It was administered on the campus of Southeastern University, University of the District of Columbia,

Howard University, and on the streets in front of the District of Columbia Superior Court.

In response to the research questions that were stated earlier in this chapter, the study focuses on examining the effectiveness, gains, losses, and direction of the Civil Rights Act of 1964. This study dealt primarily with perceptions and made every attempt to measure objectivity. Therefore, it is believed that the study provides an assessment of area professionals, university students, ex-offenders, Whites, and African Americans who have been affected by the Civil Rights Act of 1964, whether in a positive or a negative manner.

Data Collection

Using an interview guide, 100 professionals, undergraduates, graduate students, and ex-offenders participated in this study. While the sampling was very small, it provided a clear indication of perceptions about the Civil Rights Act of 1964.

When asked if the Civil Rights Act of 1964 was understood, all of the 100 interviewees responded in the affirmative. At the same time, 83 of the 100 participants believed that African Americans benefited from the Civil Rights Act of 1964. Seventeen participants did not feel the same.

It was interesting to note that all of those interviewed said non-US citizens benefited from the Civil Rights Act, even those 17 who did not think African Americans benefited. This could have been because they felt that all other groups outside of those in mainstream America were riding the coattails of African Americans.

As far as being terrorized by White racists, all of the participants in this study felt that the Civil Rights Act of 1964 did not stop intimidation. They all believed that the racial terrorism is now more subtle and operating at a higher level of sophistication. It is no longer executed by burning a church or throwing a homemade bomb through the window of a segregated school, or lynching. It is done through economics—or the lack of economic and other opportunities. Therefore, all of the 100 interviewees agreed that the act was necessary for achieving equality for African Americans in the United States. However, they all also felt that in spite of the act, White racists continue to be defiant because lawmakers have not really enforced it at all levels. They believed that the higher courts were just passing the buck to the lower ones. As a result of this belief, none of the 100 interviewed—White, African American, or international—had any faith in the act or the judiciary system of the United States with regard to equality. This is an indication that they had observed the system, been victimized, or know of people who have been victimized.

All of the 100 participants attested to the fact that the standard of living changed for the better for African Americans, even though they continue to have economic problems. Also, it was unanimously stated that more African Americans attended and graduated from predominantly Black colleges and universities throughout the country prior to 1954. All of the 100 interviewed said that the Civil Rights Act of 1964 was the best thing that happened for African Americans, especially after the turbulent years leading up to the act. The Civil Rights Act of 1964 served as a guard dog against the overt injustices toward African Americans. Participants agreed that the act did create a little bit of peace in a country that was on the verge of continuous civil disobedience from state to state, city to city, and even territory to territory.

Seventy-five of the 100 interviewed felt that African Americans had regressed and become passive since the passing of the Civil Rights Act of 1964. The remaining 25 disagreed. The majority of Blacks were probably fearful of losing the equity they thought they had gained and did not see a reason to continue the struggle for total equality. Also, it was shocking that all of the 100 interviewed did believe that the United States would accept African Americans being equal to Whites. At the same time, the participants did not think African Americans were inferior to Whites. However, they did feel that Whites thought of themselves as being superior to African Americans.

The interviewees agreed that a given law cannot make one treat others fairly. They had an accurate understanding of human behavior and knew that people's mind-sets had to be changed. The culture of racism would have to be reprogrammed over an extended period with watchful eyes, warm hearts, and sincerity. All participants indicated that African Americans should continue to hold protest marches until the civil rights acts are truly upheld.

Conclusion

The writer would be remiss to deny some of the noticeable gains from the Civil Rights Act of 1964, which were numerous. African Americans were able to get into prestigious colleges, universities, fraternities, and sororities to which they had never before been afforded access. In addition, federal and private educational and intellectual partnership grants became available. The act also assisted many African American educators in their intellectual and financial progress. A greater number of qualified teachers were in high-risk, economically depressed urban Black areas. African Americans gained in the educational equality movement by dispelling the myths about things that they could not achieve. They proved that they were capable of excelling academically, scientifically, artistically, and otherwise. They were able to discuss and demand equity. Accountability was in place. Formerly "second-class citizens," African Americans benefited later, during the 1970s and 1980s, because the opportunities associated with the Civil Rights Act of 1964 were still in place.

However, African Americans were still not equal because the qualities needed for peace, acceptance, and equality come out of the human consciousness. There is not any law in place, nor will there ever be, that can force human acceptance. This is evident with *Brown v. Board of Education* even after civil rights legislation passed. *Plessy v. Ferguson* (1896) said that separate was equal. This was primarily because the White community was afraid of having Blacks and Whites in the same room. *Plessy* held that as long as educational opportunities, supplies, and facilities were equal, being separate was acceptable. But when equality did not happen, African American leaders moved on to *Brown v. Board of Education* (1954), which said that separate was *not* equal because a little African American girl had to travel across town to attend a Black school. She could not attend the all-White school that was closer to her. But when she obtained the right to go to the White school, the Whites moved and the demographics changed—and African Americans were still stuck with an all-Black school and a separate and unequal education.

Since the Civil Rights Act of 1964, there have been those who refused to comply. To be sure, George Wallace, governor of Alabama, personally blocked the entry of African Americans into the University of Alabama in 1967 (Lindsey, 1994, p. 124). In recent years, mainstream society has been beating on Affirmative Action. A large number of African Americans who have not been able get jobs, qualified or not. In addition, there are qualified African Americans who have not gained entrance into top universities because of the *Regents of the University of California v. Bakke* (1978) case. There are numerous White students who get into Yale, Harvard, Princeton, and Cornell based on "family legacy." Meanwhile, African American students are still underrepresented in doctoral degree programs; African American faculty members and administrators are in short supply at plenty of predominantly White institutions; and historically Black colleges and universities are still attempting to perk up their reputations after decades of neglect by their home states (Hebel, 2004, p. A24).

Historically, African Americans had difficulties excelling on par with the Whites in the United States, unlike other African peoples coming into the country. Whites had a missionary complex for helping "Third World" people, especially those who were going back to help their people. But, for example, if Yale could allow indigenous Africans into the university, then the same should have been extended to African Americans. After a while, Blacks from other countries began to experience the same problems as African Americans because they did not return to their native lands. They, too, began competing with Whites for jobs, education, housing, and the like.

In a workshop conducted by Lorraine Monroe, the educator-lecturer read a report in which projections were being made from a reading test of African American males in the fourth grade. The fourth graders' poor performance on the test gave the researchers indicators that a 2005 prison could be built.

In the end, the Civil Rights Act of 1964 was just another exercise for African Americans in their struggle to obtain basic civil rights. It is part of an ongoing struggle that has spanned several centuries—from mutinies by Africans during the Atlantic crossing, to the insurrections organized by slaves in the New World, to the civil rights marches and demonstrations of the twentieth century (Lindsey, 1994, p. 35). It was not until both its violence and nonviolence that the federal government began to consider stronger enforcements (Low & Clift, 1981, p. 257).

Challenges to the gains of the past are ongoing. This is evident in the range of inequality issues that are still being dealt with 40 years after the Civil Rights Act of 1964. There will always be attempts to deny rights and to revive old battles fought by the civil rights movement (Stepto, 2003, p. 251). The struggle for civil rights will go on forever, unless there is a concerted effort to change the nature of those who oppose equality.

Appendix: Interview Guide

Blacks Not Equal: Even After the Civil Rights Act of 1964

Interviewee_____ Interviewer_____ Date_____ Time_____

Type (Please check only one):
    Professional_____Undergraduate_____Graduate Student____Ex-Offender____

Directions: Please answer each question as honestly as possible. If you need clarification, please feel free to ask interviewer.

    1. Do you understand the Civil Rights Act of 1964?
        Yes____ No____

    2. Have African Americans benefited from the Civil Rights Act of 1964?
        Yes____ No____

3. Have non-United States citizens benefited from the Civil Rights Act of 1964?
   Yes____ No____

4. Has the Civil Rights Act of 1964 stopped terrorism of White racists against African Americans?
   Yes____ No____

5. Was the Civil Rights Act of 1964 necessary for equality of African Americans in the United States?
   Yes____ No____

6. Have White racists continued to be defiant of the Civil Rights Act of 1964?
   Yes____ No____

7. Are lawmakers enforcing the Civil Rights Act of 1964?
   Yes____ No____

8. Does the African American community have faith in the Civil Rights Act of 1964?
   Yes____ No____

9. Do African Americans have faith in the judiciary system when it comes to equality?
   Yes____ No____

10. Did the Civil Rights Act of 1964 change the living standards of African Americans?
    Yes____ No____

11. Due to the Civil Rights Act of 1964, did more African Americans graduate from predominantly White colleges and universities?
    Yes____ No____

12. The Civil Rights Act of 1964 was the best thing that happened for African Americans?
    Yes____ No____

13. The Civil Rights Act of 1964 created peace for the United States?
    Yes____ No____

14. African Americans regressed after the Civil Rights Act of 1964?
    Yes____ No____

15. African Americans became passive after the Civil Rights Act of 1964?
    Yes____ No____

16. Will the United States ever accept the African Americans as being equal to Whites?
    Yes____ No____

17. Do African Americans feel inferior to Whites?
    Yes____ No____

18. Do Whites feel superior to African Americans?
    Yes____ No____

19. Can a law make you treat others fairly?
    Yes____ No____

20. Should African Americans continue to hold protest marches until the civil rights acts are truly upheld?
    Yes____ No____

References

Alexander, O. D. (2003). Roy Wilkins. *Scribner encyclopedia of American lives: The 1960s.* New York: Gale.

Fishel Jr., L., & Quarles, B. (1967). *The Negro American: A documentary history.* New York: William Morrow.

Hebel, S. (2004, May 14). Segregation's legacy still troubles campuses. *The Chronicle of Higher Education 50*(36), p. A24.

Lindsey, H. O. (1994). *A history of Black America.* Greenwich, CT: Chartwell.

Low, W. A., & Clift, V. A. (1981). *Encyclopedia of Black America.* New York: McGraw-Hill.

Nussbaum, P., & John-Hall, A. (2004, May 12). Fight for school equality still leaves scars for many. *The Philadelphia Inquirer*, 175th Year, No. 347.

Stepto, G. B. (2003). *The African-American years: Chronologies of American history and experience.* New York: Charles Scribner's Sons/Gale.

Further Reading

Ahmed, A. An-Na'Im (1992). *Human rights in cross-cultural perspectives: A quest for consensus.* Philadelphia: University of Pennsylvania Press.

Alexander, O. D., & Alexander Sr., J. G. (2001). *Berkley: The other side of town as told by the griots.* Christiansted, VI: The Odaque Group.

Appiah, K. A., & Gates Jr., H. L. (1999). *Africana: The encyclopedia of Africa and African American experience.* New York: Basic Civitas Books.

Barksdale, R., & Kinamon, K. (1972). *Black writers of America: A comprehensive anthropology.* New York: Macmillan.

Belz, H. (1997). *Abraham Lincoln, constitutionalism, and equal rights during the Civil War Era.* New York: Fordham University Press.

Chafe, W. H. (1981). *Civilities and civil rights: Greensboro, North Carolina, and the Black struggle for freedom.* London: Oxford University Press.

Commager, H. S. (1973). *Documents of American history.* Englewood Cliffs, NJ: Prentice Hall.

Contemporary Black biography: Profiles from the international Black community (Vol. IV) (1993). Detroit, MI: Gale Research.

Davis, M. W. (1982). *Contributions of Black women to America* (Vol. I). Columbia, SC: Kenday Press.

Estell, K. (1994). *African America: Celebrating 400 years of achievement.* Detroit, MI: Visible Ink.

Friedland, M. B. (1998). *Lift up your voice like a trumpet: White clergy and the civil rights and antiwar movements, 1954–1973.* Chapel Hill: University of North Carolina Press.

Hine, D. C. (1993). *Black women in America: An historical encyclopedia.* Brooklyn: Carlson Publishing.

Hughes, L. et al. (1995). *A pictorial history of African Americans: From 1619 to the present.* New York: Crown.

Keyes, A. J., & Blakely, G. (2002). *Great African-Americans.* Lincolnwood, IL: Publications International.

King, R. H. (1992). *Civil rights and the idea of freedom.* London: Oxford University Press.

Lindsey, H. O. (1994). *A history of Black America.* Greenwich, CT: Chartwell Books.

Logan, R., & Winston, M. (1982). *Dictionary of American Negro biography.* New York: W. W. Norton.

Lowery, C. D., & Marszalek, J. F. (1992). *Encyclopedia of African-American civil rights: From emancipation to the present.* New York: Greenwood Press.

Olson, S. (2002). *Mapping human history: Genes, race, and our common origins.* Boston: Houghton Mifflin.

Page, T. N. (1897). *Social life in old Virginia before the war.* New York: Charles Scribner's Sons.

Ralph Jr., J. R. (1993). *Northern protest: Martin Luther King Jr., Chicago, and the civil rights movement.* Cambridge, MA: Harvard University Press.

Roach, H. (1992). *Black American music: Past and present.* Malabar, FL: Krieger.

Robeson, S. (1981). *The whole world in his hand.* Secaucus, NJ: Citadel Press.

Rodriquez, D. B., & Weingast, B. R. (2003). *The positive political theory of legislative history: New perspectives on the 1964 Civil Rights Act and its interpretation* (Vol. 151). Philadelphia: University of Pennsylvania Law Review.

Smith, J. C., & Giovanni, N. (1988). *Images of Blacks in American culture: A reference guide to information sources.* New York: Greenwood Press.

Southern, E. (1982). *Biographical dictionary of Afro-American and African musicians.* Westport, CT: Greenwood Press.

Spring, J. (1998). *Education and the rise of the global economy.* Mahwah, NJ: Lawrence Erlbaum Associates.

Thernstrom, A. (1998, Spring). Black progress: How far we've come and how far we have to go. *Brookings Review 16*, 12–16.

Wasby, S. L. et al. (1977). *Desegregation from Brown to Alexander: An exploration of Supreme Court strategies.* Carbondale: Southern Illinois University Press.

Williams, J. B. (1997). *Discrimination in public higher education: Interpreting federal civil rights enforcement, 1964–1996.* New York: Praeger Paperback.

Wirt, F. M. (1997). *We ain't what we was: Civil rights in the new South.* Durham, NC: Duke University Press.

CHAPTER FIFTEEN

Curriculum Violence

The New Civil Rights Issue—How Efforts at Standardization Impact the Academic Achievement of African Americans

ERHABOR IGHODARO

Introduction

Since the recent release of the Florida Comprehensive Assessment Test (FCAT) results, there has been constant debate as to its implications, especially as it impacts the lives of school children, performance of school districts, and to a greater extent the status of race relations in this country. Why race relations? Many complain that this test ascribes more significance than the mere assessment of students' and school districts' performance. A leading organizer of a planned protest in Tallahassee, Dr. Frederica S. Wilson, a former Miami-Dade County school principal, board member, and current state senator, remarked, "I think it's not culturally sensitive to the children who are ethnic minorities. I think the vocabulary that's on the test—our children have no correlation with that vocabulary." This assertion, especially in light of an age-old debate over "intelligence," assessment, and measurement, undergirds the subject of this chapter.

Curriculum violence is defined as the deliberate manipulation of academic programming to ignore and compromise the intellectual and psychological well-being of the subject of direct instruction. As a student of conflict analysis and resolution, I use the term *violence* to connote the destructive and injurious element of this educational programming. Educators have inadequately assessed or perhaps neglected the psychological and cognitive toll of inappropriate educational models on children. While our society complains about the proliferation of violent acts and school shootings throughout the educational landscape, most seldom consider the devastating effect of irrelevant curricula that breed the type of alienation that masks itself as truancy, school dropouts, and failure. Renowned Cuban educator José Martí is reported to have said, "In order not to punish adults, we must educate children." This chapter on curriculum violence addresses not only our inability to educate children, but also the inappropriateness of academic programming that invalidates students' social–cultural experiences.

Many proponents of standardization would take exception to the author's invoking the taboo of "cultural relevance." Critics of culturally centered pedagogy would argue the "impracticability" of our educational system responding to the multiplicity of cultures in our increasingly diverse society. Yet, this is the challenge before our society. And it is a matter of will, rather than ability. Are we willing, despite the complexities of American cultural reality, to reform our educational system to serve its non-White, non-English-speaking student population?

The dubious record of standardization, at least as it relates to the education of minorities, has been quite documented. Although this chapter is not designed as one more indictment on the standardization movement, this body of knowledge illuminates the conceptualization of curriculum violence.

Last year, over 40,000 third graders, mostly minorities, and disproportionately African Americans, failed the FCAT, Florida's statewide standardized examination. Anyone who doesn't subscribe to a belief in Black social and intellectual inferiority—as in the flawed analysis furnished by Herrnstein and Murray in *The Bell Curve*, which makes outlandish statistical claims as to the intellectual ineptness of Blacks and other minority groups—ought to be as disturbed as anyone to see any particular group of people labeled as failures.

This chapter sets forth the concept of curriculum violence by elaborating on a theory of mind development propounded by Robert Ingram. In a sermon from the book of Romans (chapter 12, verse 2), Ingram asserts that present-day disciples of the gospel must liberate themselves from the doctrine and dogma of "religiosity." In his opinion, the process of indoctrination follows five specific stages: *formation, deformation, conformation, reformation,* and *transformation.*

The following analysis of curriculum violence in light of Ingram's theory of mind development relies on three fundamental assumptions. The first is that all human beings are created equal. And that even in cases of "abnormalities," it is primarily due to the standards of our "normality" that we make such attributions. Second, English, like all other languages that preceded it, is a social construct, and it is possible to use any other language as a standard or frame of reference. And third, a primary goal of any educational enterprise is for the subject to "know thyself," that is, to make sense of a present that is intricately entwined with past and future.

Formation

In expounding on the theory of mind development, the author drew on Apostle Paul's admonition in his letter to the Romans: "And be not conformed to this world, but be ye transformed by the renewing of your mind." This text seems profoundly relevant in analyzing the concept of curriculum violence, because all that we think we know is determined by that which has been socially constructed for us. To date, there have been different theories put forth to describe the basis of human knowledge. Most of these theories can be put into two broad categories: regressivism and progressivism.

Regressivists are those theorists who espouse the general notion that human intelligence is determined by nature. This category includes those who believe in biological determinism and the idea of variety in the human species. The progressivists on the other hand, are those who espouse the "nurture" rather than "nature" argument for human intelligence development. This category includes those who believe that human intelligence is the product of social culturalization.

Although there are different schools of thought that have evolved from these two perspectives, they are all progenies of the age-old "nature versus nurture" debate. This conceptual phase of the theory is very important, primarily because dominant cultures have historically manipulated, in sophisticated ways, the "nature over nurture" argument in a manner that maintains and perpetuates their culture (power).

According to the theory of curriculum violence, the FCAT is a present-day manifestation of a historical pattern of cultural dominance. The minority culture is ever at the mercy of the dominant culture. Intelligence, in the mind of the regressive, is framed and disguised as some "objective" human quality, instead of the accumulated understanding of a particular group or people. Even the *American Heritage Dictionary* defines intelligence as "the capacity to acquire and apply knowledge." This definition properly qualifies the negotiated, rather than innate, nature of intelligence. But, what *knowledge*? And how does this relate to culture? The same dictionary defines culture as "the behavior patterns, arts, beliefs, institutions, and other products of human work and thought." There is a pattern of thought and behavior, by virtue of socialization rather than biology, that distinguishes minorities from dominant groups. The fact that the dominant culture, by virtue of its privilege and desire to maintain that privilege, invalidates the minority group's "intelligence" by using its privileged understanding (culture) as the standard for measuring others, constitutes the basis and beginning of curriculum violence.

Deformation

The aforementioned dialectical relationship of privileged and underprivileged, so far as thought and behavior are concerned, necessarily leads to a state of *affirmation* for the privileged and *deformation* for the underprivileged. Since this chapter's focal point is the process of curriculum violence, it examines the process of deformation for the underprivileged group. Due to the thought patterns and behaviors of the privileged group being affirmed as the standard in the schoolhouse, the underprivileged group is placed at the perpetual mercy of copying the understanding of the dominant group. Children born into a minority culture, whose sense of cultural self-awareness is not protected, have their psyches flooded with sub- or superstandard understanding of the relationship between the minority and dominant cultures. In these situations, parents who are supposed to be models for their children are replaced with external elements because even the parents are disconnected from a historical memory of their ancestry and culture. Indeed, as one African proverb contends, "The destruction of a nation begins in their homes."

In a heterogeneous society such as the United States, these destructive external elements permeate every facet of children's lives from the home (house), to the schoolhouse, to the church house. In every facet of children's lives, images of "perfection," are represented and controlled by the dominant culture. In the schoolhouse, models of correct thought and behavior are ascribed to the dominant group. For African American students in particular, the unfortunate omission and misrepresentation of the African intellectual (cultural) heritage creates a perpetual gap between what was, what is, and what is possible. At the core of the stage of deformation, lies the atrocity of the institution of slavery. The infamous 1619 arrival of Africans in Jamestown, Virginia, becomes a significant landmark in understanding deformation: a condition that has created a state of psychological arrest for the descendants of Africa, whose self-image is haunted and stunted by a near past. No thought is given to the history of Africa that predates 1619—the history that records Africa as the cradle of humanity and Africans as builders of classical civilizations.

The unwillingness and inability of the institution of slavery to provide meaningful education for descendants of Africa is a travesty and horror that our society has inadequately addressed. From the early years of slavery until today, there has not been any evidence that America has provided an educational system designed to benefit the children of former slaves. At the time of slavery, Africans were not given any kind of education, except the kind of training that would keep them perpetually in bondage. In his letter to the slave owners in America, Willie Lynch, a slaveholder from the West Indies, wrote " . . . the Black slave after receiving this indoctrination shall carry on and will become self-refueling and self-generating for hundreds of years, maybe thousands." What kind of indoctrination was Mr. Lynch talking about? He asserted,

> . . . you must use the female slave vs. the male, and the male vs. the female. You must also have your white servants and overseers distrust all Blacks, but it is necessary that your slaves trust and depend on us. They must love, respect and trust only us. Gentlemen, these kits are your keys to *control*.

The significance of this indignant acculturation today is profound in light of the fact that it was not until 1995, less than a decade ago, that the state of Florida passed legislation that allows the "infusion" of African and African American content into the school curriculum. It is mind-boggling and a travesty that after over a century of public education, the state has only recently begun talking about "infusing" content relevant to a significant student population. As an example of the kind of mental arrest this mal-pedagogy perpetuates, a young Black male once told the author, "I don't want to look like no African." This student's unfortunate revelation brings to bear the error in our educational framework, at least so far as the FCAT is concerned. The author calls it the ERR (exposure, relevance, and reinforcement) model, because it encapsulates the place where we *err* in the education of African Americans.

This theory of curriculum violence is based fundamentally on my belief that the crisis we face in our educational system, so far as curricular content is concerned, is one based on culture conflict. Every major civilization, be it African, Asian, or European, has undergone and is experiencing, in varying degrees, vestiges of "cultural wars." The American "civilization" is by no means an exception, and the African living in America, the "African American," is by default the scapegoat of this particular cultural revolution. That said, African American students can compete in a fashion comparable with their European American counterparts, if they are *exposed* to the thought and behavior (culture) patterns that constitute the standard of measure, which by default is also Eurocentric. That is, if our intent is to make "European" the "African." The problem with this assertion, at least for African Americans, is the invalidation of their own cultural perspective. The issue of *relevance* represents the basis of this chapter. The notion that children drop out of school because they find curricula irrelevant and meaningless to their lives has been quite documented. The issue of *reinforcement*, then, becomes even more significant in that, even if children are exposed to information that they find culturally relevant, there has to be a system of reward, validation, and feedback that keeps students motivated to excel academically.

It is a miscarriage of justice for us to continually remind children of their nonexistence in history and to expect them to excel academically. Africans living in America have always been called to meet the challenges of a manipulative and unjust system. Even right after the abolition of slavery and passage of the Thirteenth Amendment in this country, African Americans were subjected to all kinds of schemes to deny their citizenship rights. Of notoriety was the literacy test, even though they were denied any formal education, which precluded them from exercising their citizenship rights. The FCAT is another in a litany of attempts to invalidate and relegate the advancement of a group of people under the guise of "standardization," "competence," and "intelligence."

Conformation

The most prolific proponent of how conformation takes place within the context of curriculum violence is Dr. Carter G. Woodson. In his book, *The Mis-education of the Negro*, Woodson asserts, "If you control a man's thinking you do not have to tell him to go back door or go yonder. If there is no back door he would carve one out for his special benefit. His *education* makes it necessary." What about the education of Africans living in America made it necessary for them to conform to this abusive state of mind? Woodson further asserts,

> In history, of course, the Negro had no place in this *curriculum*. He was pictured as a human being of lower order, unable to subject passion to reason, and therefore useful only when made the hewer of wood and the drawer of water for others. No thought was given to the history of Africa except so far as it has been a field of exploitation for the Caucasian. You might study the history as it was offered in our system from elementary school throughout the university, and you will never hear Africa mentioned except in the negative. You would never thereby learn that Africans first domesticated the sheep, goat, and cow, developed the idea of trial by jury, produced the first stringed instruments, and gave the world its greatest boon in the discovery of iron.

Woodson, himself a Harvard University graduate with a Ph.D. but no understanding of the African origins of history, literature, and chemistry, would have been, by virtue of his definition, "miseducated." This assertion puts in context the implications of the debacle over the FCAT. It invites us to ask the question: What is the purpose of education? What is the purpose of any test, and standardized tests in particular? Is it sufficient that an African American knows how to count 1–2–3 and can speak the Queen's English, yet does not know anything about his family, cannot relate to people in the African American community, and does not have an understanding of the African influence on our numbers and language systems?

Woodson underscores what others like African Jamaican Marcus Garvey have referred to as "mental slavery." In his 1923 book, *The Philosophies and Opinions of Marcus Garvey*, Garvey, a leading proponent of African identity formation, puts forth the admonition that individuals concerned with group empowerment and nation building must "know thyself" and that it is through this historical memory that the group gains strength and solidarity. From Woodson's analysis of the state of education afforded Blacks in the 1930s, it is understood that the curricula then, as today, is intrinsically entrenched in a European worldview. At this crossroads in history, there are children who are nonconformists who have been labeled "failures" because they reject an alien system that has failed to validate their "beingness." A world of conformists labels as truant, delinquent, criminals, failures, dumb, and abnormal those it fails to understand. It is hoped that those who have managed to navigate the terrain of conformity will garner the courage to help liberate and affirm the genius of those bold enough to defy the system and its contradictions.

Reformation

The noted African scholar, historian, professor, and human rights advocate, John Henrik Clarke once said, "you cannot consciously oppress a consciously historical people." The hallmark of the reformation phase is to begin introducing in the subject what other scholars have referred to as "emancipatory knowledge." This type of information is not the kind that only engenders insight on the contradictions in the system, but the type of knowledge that is also strong enough to liberate the subject from "mental slavery." It is information that is not only new, but also emanates from an emic, empowering, meaningful, insightful, and critical perspective. The main thrust of the reformation phase is the availability of a juxtaposed alternative view to the Eurocentric conformist ideology. Scholars have made clear distinctions between Eurocentric and Afrocentric worldviews.

There is an African adage that "until lions have their own historians, the tales of the hunt will always glorify the hunter." The purpose of a reformist scholar is to "give voice" to the lion and allow the subjects the opportunity to write their own history. The following is an inscription taken from a sixth-dynasty (2300–2150 B.C., Kemet) ancient Egyptian tomb inscription that illuminates some of the untold histories of classical African civilizations:

> I have come from my town,
> I have descended from my home
> I have done justice for its King,
> I have satisfied him with what he loves,
> I spoke truly, I did right,
> I spoke fairly, I respected fairly,
> I seized the right moment,
> So as to stand well with people.
> I judged between two so as to contend them,
> I rescued the weak from one stronger than he
> As much as was in my power,
> I gave bread to the hungry, clothes to the naked,
> I brought the boatless to land.
> I buried him who had no son,
> I made a boat for him who lacked one.
> I respected my father, I pleased my mother,
> I raised their children.
> So says he whose nickname is Seshi.

The quoted inscription speaks volumes as to the literary, moral, and political thought of ancient Africans, and it could help rebut the notion that Africans have contributed nothing of significance to civilization. To reformists, the absurdity of such an assertion would be challenged by the statements of ancient African scholars and even classical Greek scholars who referred to the Africans as their teachers and the fathers of mathematics, chemistry, medicine, astronomy, and the other hard sciences. The noted Egyptian statesman Imhotep, scientist, mathematician, and architect of the Step Pyramid, has been heralded by African and European scholars alike as the "real" father of medicine. Recently, Gabriel Oyibo, a world-renowned mathematician, astrophysicist, professor, and 2003 nominee for the Nobel Prize in physics, underscored the African intellectual heritage at a lecture in Miami, Florida, where he asserted that the word *chemistry* was derived from ancient Kemetic (African) peoples.

The importance of this type of historical memory in the development of students' sense of self, affiliation with a rich intellectual heritage cannot be overemphasized. This process of reframing history is necessary for the psychological well-being of a people. It is not only important that African Americans know about their present civilization, but also they must constantly remind themselves and others of how they as a people have influenced civilization. From the classical ancient civilizations to our contemporary scientific and artistic inventions, the ubiquity of the African presence is profoundly undeniable.

Transformation

The last phase of the theory of mind development leads us to the realization of the goal of human enterprise. The hallmark of this phase of mind development is the realization that we as human beings live an interdependent and interrelated existence. Dr. Martin Luther King Jr., who personifies all that is possible for a transformed mind, wrote the following in his 1963 *Letter from Birmingham Jail:* "We are caught in an inescapable network of mutuality, tied in a single garment of destiny. Whatever affects one directly, affects all indirectly."

In spite of the evolution and history of cultural wars, we have been called to hold on to the vehicle of a transformed mind: love. The only way for a person to endure and transcend the politics and divisions of a troubled world is through love: the kind of love that undergirds the African belief that "it takes a whole village to raise one child." Only this type of love can bring about a true and lasting societal change, eliminating the boundaries that separate people. People are called to love others as they love themselves, and only through the love of self can one truly begin to understand how to love others. With love, minds can be transformed and all vestiges of "curriculum violence" can be eliminated to truly bring about a change in our educational system that allows the public to invest in every child as they would their own.

With hate and prejudice in their hearts, teachers neglect and maliciously instruct those they categorize as "unfit," and the powerful design curricula in a manner that authenticates their own hegemony. But for individuals, "intellectuals," and a society transformed with the consciousness of collective edification, there is a higher calling to develop "nonviolent" curricula: inclusive program designs that affirm, recognize, and enhance the intellectual and psychological well-being of subjects of direct instruction.

CHAPTER SIXTEEN

The Use of Corporal Punishment on Minorities in the Public Schools

CYNTHIA NORTHINGTON

Corporal punishment is the oldest and most controversial form of school discipline. The legal definition of corporal punishment designates it as any sort of punishment "of or inflicted on the body" (Black, 1990, p. 306). In schools, the term is used to describe the application of physical pain (via paddles, painful body postures, excessive exercise drills, or the prevention of urine or stool elimination) as a method of changing student behavior (US Department of Education, 2001; Greydanus et al., 2003). In 22 of the United States, it can be legally administered to public school children. The frequency of this practice has decreased overall in the past decade. Yet, it has long been known that minority students remain disproportionately on the receiving end of this form of discipline in US public schools (Doyle, 1989). The rationale for this practice often implies that a different standard of discipline is necessary for children who are minorities.

This practice remains legal (under various circumstances) in the following states: Alabama, Arizona, Arkansas, Colorado, Florida, Georgia, Idaho, Indiana, Kansas, Kentucky, Louisiana, Mississippi, Missouri, New Mexico, North Carolina, Ohio, Oklahoma, Pennsylvania, South Carolina, Tennessee, Texas, and Wyoming. From 1980 to 1989, 14 states voted to ban this practice outright. In the 1990s (1990–1999), 10 states finalized their ban on this practice (American Academy of Pediatrics, 2000). In 2003, the state of Delaware was the first state in the new millennium to ban corporal punishment.

Unlike convicted criminals and prison inmates, school children are not protected by the Eighth Amendment of the US Constitution, which prohibits the use of cruel and unusual punishment. This lack of protection stems from the *Ingraham v. Wright Case* (1977) in which the US Supreme Court held that the Eight Amendment's "cruel and unusual punishment" mandate did not apply to the corporal punishment of children in public schools. Furthermore, it has been ruled that the "due process" clause (which would entitle a student to the right to be heard in their own defense) of the Fourteenth Amendment "does not require notice and hearing prior to the imposition of corporal punishment" because "imposing this burden would significantly intrude into the area of educational responsibility" (Data Research Inc., 1991, p. 113).

In 2001, the Bush administration supported a provision in the No Child Left Behind Act to protect teachers from liability for harm caused to students under various circumstances. It specifies that a teacher is not liable for an act (physical or otherwise) as long as they are certified and adhering to the rules. According to the Teacher Liability Protection statement, a teacher will not be liable for harm caused to a student or for the choice of inaction on behalf of the school, if the teacher was acting within the scope of the teacher's employment, did not break any laws, and was properly licensed and authorized by the proper authorities to administer the punishment (US Department of Education, 2001). It would appear that legal protection for teachers and the lack of it for students are equally indisputable.

To date, the most recent statistics available state that in the year 2000, a total of 342,038 students were paddled in US public schools. It should be noted that this is the lowest number in history. This is in part due to the states and individual school districts that have abolished this practice. Out of that number, however, 132,065 of those students paddled were African American. That is roughly 39% of the students paddled for that year (US Department of Education, Office of Civil Rights, 2001; Starr, 2002).

According to the National Research Council Institute of Medicine (2004), African American students are twice as likely as White students to be recipients of corporal punishment. The most recent statistical information indicates that African Americans represent 17% of the student population of the United States. While comprising 63% of the school population, White students receive 55% of the reported corporal punishments (via paddling). For example, in Mobile County, Alabama, in 2000, the school system was 49.5% African American. Yet, 70% of the 781 reported spankings were administered to African Americans, and of that, 83% were boys (Catalanello, 2001).

In a political climate that demands accountability in education, classroom management practices that yield quantifiable results are lauded as the standard for best practices. By utilizing corporal punishment, it is argued that teachers and school authorities are acting *in loco parentis* (from the Latin: in place of parents) in the educational environment. They are, therefore, acting as the parent would if the parent were present (Conte, 2000). Advocates state that children who are on the receiving end of corporal punishment are better behaved and more respectful of authority. As a result, advocates contend, these students are more proficient at controlling their own behavior and possess better self-discipline (Society of Adolescent Medicine, 2003).

For example, high school students surveyed in Calhoun, Georgia, which is 60% African American, stated that when corporal punishment is administered at their request (rather than formal detention), they feel less apt to repeat the behavior. The students who opted for paddling in this study were also less likely to have in-school suspension for repeating those same behaviors. These students reported that the memory of the corporal punishment deterred them from future infractions of school rules (Yancy, 2001). It has also been argued that in light of the school shooting incidents, "noncorporal forms of discipline" are ineffective in promoting self-discipline and moral clarity in students (Society of Adolescent Medicine, 2003, p. 387). The US Department of Education (2000) therefore asserts that severe punishment may be an effective way to reduce serious behavioral offenses (including drug offenses) in public and private schools.

When public schools were first established in the United States, corporal punishment was a common and accepted form of discipline. The majority of the students participating in public school education were White and Christian. It appears, however, that our discipline practices still reflect the influence only of the culture that established them two centuries ago. History has shown that oversights like this can have dangerous societal outcomes (Northington, 1993, 2000; Andero, 2002). Harvard professor Dr. Alvin Poussaint asserts that the disproportionate use of corporal punishment on African American children is due to the enduring societal perception of them as aggressive or out of control. This is particularly the case with African American males. This implies that the practice of corporal punishment will not cease without alteration of societal beliefs (Catalanello, 2001).

The civil rights struggle of the 1960s embraced nonviolent solutions to unfair and unjust laws in the United States. Corporal punishment is the antithesis of the nonviolent behavioral ideal encouraged in schools across the

United States. The codes of conduct in most public schools teach effective communication as a means of voicing complaints. Conflict resolution and peer mediation are also encouraged in order to empower students to resolve disputes. One would be hard pressed to locate a unit of curriculum that encourages students to inflict pain (via hitting) on their peers. Nevertheless, corporal punishment is modeled for students by teachers and administrators across the country in response to various behavioral infractions. Corporal punishment is even used to penalize students who resort to violence against their peers. The practice of penalizing students via corporal punishment for fighting with their peers on school grounds seems illogical and hypocritical. Yet, such incidents continue to be mediated in court.

If, as Albert Bandura (1973) proposes, all behavior is learned via reinforcement and modeling, what have the students in this example learned from their role models? It has been suggested that the practice of corporal punishment in schools teaches children to use violence in order to achieve their own social goals. Children learn that violence is sanctioned under certain circumstances. The modeling and acceptance of physically and psychologically aggressive behavior for students is tantamount to teacher-sanctioned violence. It is sanctioned due to teachers' lack of awareness of its impact and unwillingness to choose prosocial alternatives to physical discipline. If, as Alvin Poussaint proposes, society perceives African American students as potentially more aggressive than others, then it is argued that the sanctioning of violence as a solution to behavior problems creates a self-fulfilling prophecy.

References

American Academy of Pediatrics (2000). Corporal punishment in schools (RE9754). *Pediatrics 106*(2), 343–346.

Andero, A. A. (2002). Issues of corporal punishment: Re-examined. *Journal of Instructional Psychology, 29,* 90–96.

Bandura, A. (1973). *Aggression: A social learning analysis.* Englewood Cliffs, NJ: Prentice-Hall.

Black, H. C. (1990). *Black's law dictionary* (6th ed.). St. Paul, MN: West.

Catalanello, R. (2001). Boys, Blacks paddled the most. *Mobile Register, Alabama* 19 July, p.1.

Conte, A. E. (2000). In loco parentis: Alive and well. *Education 121,* 195–200.

Data Research, Inc. (1991). *US Supreme Court education cases* (2nd ed.). Rosemount, MN: Data Research, Inc.

Doyle, W. (1989). Classroom management techniques. In O. C. Moles (Ed.), *Strategies to reduce student misbehavior* (pp. 11–31). Washington, DC: Office of Educational Research and Improvement.

Greydanus, D. E., Pratt, H. D., Spates, C. R., Blake-Dreher, A. E., Greydanus-Gearhart, M. A., & Patel, D. R. (2003). Corporal punishment in schools: Position paper of the Society for Adolescent Medicine. *Journal of Adolescent Health 32*, 385–393.

National Research Council Institute of Medicine (2004). *Engaging schools*. Washington, DC: National Academies Press.

Northington, C. (1993). A brief analysis of the societal tendency to preserve its thought style. *Critical Issues: The Journal of GSO-SEHNAP, NYU 1*(1), 47–54.

———. (2000). The color of dirt. *Multicultural Perspectives 2*(3), 32–33.

Society of Adolescent Medicine (2003). Corporal punishment in schools. *Journal of Adolescent Health 32*, 385–393.

Starr, L. (2002). Corporal punishment: Teaching violence through violence. *Education World*. Available online at http://www.educationworld.com

US Census Bureau (2000a). *State and county QuickFacts*. Available online at http://www.census.gov

——— (2000b). *Census 2000 redistricting data (Public Law 94–171) Summary File*, Matrices PL1, PL2, PL3, and PL4.

US Department of Education (2001). *Paul D. Coverdell Teacher Protection Act of 2001. No Child Left Behind Act of 2001, Subpart 5—Teacher Liability Program*. Available online at http://www.ed.gov

US Department of Education, Office of Civil Rights (2000). *Elementary and secondary school civil rights compliance report*. Washington, DC: US Government Printing Office.

——— (2001). *2000 Elementary and secondary school civil rights compliance report individual school report: ED102*. Washington, DC: US Government Printing Office.

Yancy, T. (2001). Voluntary corporal punishment reduces suspension rates. *Secondary English*. Available online at http://www.secondaryenglish.com

CHAPTER SEVENTEEN

Historically Black Colleges and Universities

An Opportunity for Leadership in the Twenty-First Century

Louis A. Castenell Jr.

Overview

Tomorrow's colleges and universities will be dramatically different from today's institutions. Current marketplace forces, serving as the catalysts for fundamental changes, are reshaping the focus and delivery of higher education (Keith, 1998). The shift in demographics, the need to firmly establish and retain our place in the global economy, and the growing emphasis on quality of life issues in local communities demand a major transformation of the education infrastructure required to support the future economic and social requirements of our nation. Already, we are experiencing rapid changes in the traditional teaching, research, and service frameworks. Teaching is increasingly linked to the use of technology and developing strategies for a more diverse population. The mere passage of time in a teaching position as a sufficient basis for tenure and promotion is being challenged in institutions at all levels, and new requirements are being imposed. There is tremendous pressure in the research community to focus on applied research to advance instructional innovations and to advance new findings in a world thirsty for knowledge. Service is no longer an academic altruism limited to participation on campus committees. Today, service defines the value of the college or university. Increasingly, higher education institutions are measured by public expectations for involvement in an international community. Institutions are also called to be responsive to economic, social, and political mandates facing our nation. Service is rapidly becoming an obligation to participate in advancing the quality of life for local communities and to successfully compete in the global marketplace.

Policymakers have not been reticent in voicing their belief that our academies are not responsive to the needs of students, society at large, or the changing economy. One cannot listen to a presidential speech or the rhetoric of policymakers without hearing two themes: Universities must be more responsive to immediate demands generated by the need for economic growth and development and, to that end, must support PK–12 (prekindergarten through grade 12) education reform in the preparation of the future teaching force. These twin messages have significant implications for the current role of institutions of higher education, particularly colleges of education that produce the teachers who deliver PK–12 education. Yet, as America demands a new role and new pedagogies to support education reform, there is less money to support the universe of American academic institutions and their transformation. The dynamic force created by the convergence of these factors not only sets a context for discussing the future role of higher education institutions in the global positioning of America, but more particularly, it also offers the opportunity to recast the relationship between majority and minority institutions as a strategy in responding to the PK–12 education reform challenge.

The Logic of a Partnership Between Majority and Minority Institutions

Historically Black colleges and universities (HBCUs) have produced one-third of the African American teaching force across this nation (Mollison, 2002a, 2002b). Moreover, research has confirmed the importance of a diverse teaching force in delivering quality education and closing the long-standing achievement gap between White and minority students (Miller & Stayon, 1999; Olson, 2000; Mollison, 2002a, 2002b). In addition, if one reflects on the cadre of African American leadership across every societal sector, the contributions of HBCUs to the economic health and well-being of the nation are undeniable. The reality is that the vast majority of African American leaders graduated from minority institutions, and they play a vital role in serving on state boards in local, state, and national governments; as CEOs of private sector corporations and nonprofit organizations; and as advisers at the highest leadership levels, from US presidential cabinets to corporate boardrooms. Given these contributions from HBCUs, it is clear that any education reform strategy is only strengthened by an appreciation of and support for the role HBCUs can and must play in responding to twenty-first century marketplace demands. This kind of thinking, however, is in itself transformational. It represents a major paradigm shift from a deficit model in which HBCUs are viewed not for their assets, but from the vantage point of their perceived deficits. Clearly, the crossroads at which America finds itself offers the opportunity for, and in fact may demand, a new relationship between majority and minority institutions of higher education to meet the call to be more responsive to marketplace demands. The question is whether the larger education community is prepared to pierce the historical insularity of majority and minority institutions to fashion a new partnership that is committed to mutual support and leverage the assets of both partners in the interest of the economic well-being of the nation, to meet the need for competitive positioning in the global marketplace.

Higher Education at the Crossroads

It is not accidental that the provocative report *A Nation At Risk* (National Commission on Excellence in Education, 1983) was released during the advent of globalization. The 2001 report, *Investing in Teaching*, by the National Alliance of Business (NAB), calls for a new workforce. This is indicative of the national mindset that has spawned the PK–12 education reform movement. As framed by NAB and echoed in every chamber of the business sector, a new generation of workers with the associated skills necessary to compete in the global marketplace is critical. Accordingly, the PK–12 and higher education institutions are being influenced to rethink how they do business, with a greater emphasis on accountability for the quality of education in the nation's schools. As Slaughter and Leslie (1997) argue, the participation of universities in the marketplace has begun to undercut the traditional faculty–administration relationship, thus opening the door for change. Most recently, the push for education reform is being driven strategically through the call for bottom-line accountability. However, as the need for funding institutional changes to support better preparation of students to meet new accountability standards has grown, funds for higher education initiatives have begun to shrink. As a result, faculty at institutions of higher education are increasingly having to compete for external dollars that are tied to "market" interests, to support the paradigm shift. While this new call for accountability is equally applied to all higher education institutions, the impact on HBCUs will be greater. Historically, funds for HBCUs (especially from the public sector) have been limited to missions that often reflected the larger system of racial subordination (Anderson, 2001). This is life threatening in an environment whereby the contributions of HBCUs are a significant part of the national dialogue to produce more leaders for the international marketplace. This chapter focuses on the need and opportunity for new partnerships with HBCUs and the benefit to be gained from the more equitable positioning of HBCUs.

An Examination of the Marketplace Forces That Create the Opportunity to Forge a New Partnership

Institutions of higher education are facing the challenge of answering the call to be responsive to political and economic influence of the American marketplace (Martinez, 2002). In the South especially, the parallel existence of majority White institutions and historically Black ones is an ill fit for the call. A case study by Martinez (2002) of a Western state's oversight system of higher education institutions demonstrates the statewide impact of multiple levels of marketplace factors on state institutions. The levels of marketplace factors have been identified by Richardson et al. (1999): policy environment, state variables, and tax revenue. How the higher education community ultimately elects to address the impact of these multiple levels of factors, promises to shape the delivery of education for many years to come.

At the first level of marketplace factors, the " . . . policy environment includes characteristics of the state and state government that are a product of history and current events" (Martinez, 2002, p. 351). Thus, one can argue that in the South the core values of equality, economic growth, and world leadership are at stake. These are the values that the education reform movement seeks to protect and promote. Policies that ignore the tempest of the past will fail. All parties must be in agreement for institutional realignment. An appreciation of this one level is critical to understand the challenges we face as a nation in successfully transforming the delivery of education.

To appreciate the impact of policy environment on the ability of higher institutions in the South to rise to the challenge, it is important to appreciate the history of the relationship of majority and minority higher education institutions in the South. Between 1870 and 1890, nine Black federal land-grant colleges were established in the South. By 1915, the number had increased to 16 (Anderson, 1988). Based on an analysis of their curricula, only one school taught at the collegiate level. By contrast, according to Anderson, private liberal arts colleges supported by the private philanthropy of North and South progressive leaders taught collegiate classes. Not surprisingly, only 25% of Blacks attended public HBCUs as late as 1927 (p. 238). The Southern education movement was advanced by large corporate philanthropic foundations, Northern White benevolent societies and, most importantly, religious organizations. The sense of mission shared by these groups clashed sharply with the regard Southern states had for African Americans. Any examination of the Southern policy environment, then, must appreciate the influence of Southern history and its impact on the current struggle of majority institutions and HBCUs to become less insular and more inclusive as they seek to play a significant role in positioning America to be more competitive in the global marketplace. The Southern historical context cannot be ignored. It is the 800-pound gorilla on the kitchen table as institutions of higher education in the South struggle to respond to the twenty-first century economic and political demands of the marketplace.

Simultaneously, the second level of marketplace factors, state variables, must also be examined to appreciate the demographic, geographic, economic, and sociopolitical trends that are shaping the efforts to reform education in America (Martinez, 2002, p. 351). It also helps to understand the potential partnership opportunity the convergence of these forces presents for majority and minority institutions. The United States is becoming increasingly diverse. Hodgkinson (2002) reports that shifts reflected in the 2000 Census changed forever how we must think of Americans. It is anticipated that 61% of the population growth in the next 20 years will be Latinos and Asians, about 40% Latinos and 20% Asians. According to many demographers, the US population could be so diverse by 2050 that no race or ethnic group would be a majority (Olson, 2000). The demographic makeup of today's school children reflects the demographic makeup of the immediate future. California does not have a single majority group. By 2010, Latinos are projected to account for 43% of the US population; Asians and Pacific Islanders will increase in population by 64% in the next 20 years; and African Americans (12%) and Native Americans (1%) will remain stable. This trend has caused policymakers and corporate leaders to charge PK–12 schools and universities with closing the achievement gap between minority groups and Whites to assure the continued economic health of the nation. In the South, however, the history of race relations and the ongoing cultural chasms that are the historical aftermath make institutional change difficult to initiate, manage, or institutionalize. Mandates by state higher education oversight systems that fail to recognize and address this issue in the effort to implement education reform are doomed to repeat the mistakes of the past. Successful partnerships involve power sharing across institutional lines (Carroll et al., 2001). Today's relationships for many minority–majority institutional partnerships seem to be premised on a deficit model that fails to acknowledge and build equity upon the assets of all parties, thereby forfeiting the opportunity to be responsive to marketplace demands.

At the third level of marketplace factors—tax revenues—the states find themselves facing a shortage of funds. The current economic recession, exacerbated by the need to respond financially to the tragedy of September 11, 2001, has widespread consequences for the reform movement as states find that the priority for a short pool of funds has been diverted. States are experiencing funding shortfalls, the effects of which are not likely to be short lived. State agencies are having to absorb budget reductions at the very time that there is a need for budget expansion. Given the historical context of relationships between majority institutions and HBCUs, the shortage of financial resources portends the likelihood for failure of institutions on both sides of the racial divide. This is particularly true for HBCUs, which do not share the same financial reserves or have the privilege of the better-appointed infrastructures found in majority institutions. It is also likely that the real and perceived discrimination in equitable funding of institutions of higher education will continue.

The challenge for Southern institutions of higher education and for state oversight systems is to appreciate the impact of the historical context on the present marketplace. Instead, educators are called to create in its wake the opportunity to correct past injustices rather than submitting to a continuation of the dysfunctional system of the past. A strategy must be crafted for realizing the future that the education reform movement seeks to create. The current marketplace forces provide a rare opportunity for the South to become a national leader in the delivery of education reform. To do so, however, will require that majority and minority institutions that are currently parallel consciously fashion a new relationship. This relationship is anchored in the equality of the partners, which facilitates the leveraging of their respective assets to achieve a common goal. That goal is the delivery of quality education that supports the economic growth and development of all sectors of the American society. This necessary agenda requires a redefinition of the relationship between HBCUs and majority institutions in the South. At the heart of the renegotiation, there must be the genuine acknowledgment of the host of challenges faced respectively by *both* majority and minority institutions. They must also embrace a new partnership that bridges the cultural divide in order to close the achievement gap that can no longer be afforded in a global economy.

The Benefits of Forging a New Partnership to Meet the Needs of the Twenty-First Century

The successful renegotiation of the relationship between minority and majority institutions must begin with an understanding of the mutual benefits that such a partnership offers. State oversight systems of higher education, which are the gatekeepers of the status quo, must take stock of HBCU's assets—for example, their human capital, exemplary experiences with addressing the teaching needs of nontraditional students, and credible inroads to communities where majority institutions do not hold market share. Moreover, they must acknowledge that HBCUs offer a climate that supports the unique needs of African American students in a way that majority institutions are ill-equipped to do. Simultaneously, HBCUs must acknowledge their shortcomings and focus more on closing the achievement gap. Whether the gap is real or not, all graduates should be prepared to successfully compete on standard measures of excellence—in particular standardized tests for admission to professional and graduate schools.

Recent research points out that a remarkable 40% of all African American college graduates graduated from HBCUs (Garibaldi, 1991; Mollison, 2002a, 2002b). Concomitantly, majority institutions struggle with retention and graduation of African Americans. Although most have some percentage of minority students, graduation rates remain low (Carter & Wilson, 1997). A cursory review of the literature reveals disparities that are troubling. For example, majority institutions have a 71% dropout rate for African Americans, compared to 55% of Whites, and a 20% gap in graduation rates. Setting aside for a moment the judgmental discussion that is almost always the focus of responses to this scenario, the facts alone should validate the wisdom of creating equitable partnerships between HBCUs and majority institutions. Such partnerships would serve the best interest of all stakeholders and effectively address the mandates that higher education institutions be more responsive to shaping and supporting a healthy economy.

In reality, all institutions of higher education are facing similar challenges with respect to the diversity agenda. Consider the following:

1. Nationwide, only 8% of the full-time faculty members at higher education institutions are minorities. African Americans account for 5% of the 8%. Fifty percent of this number work at HBCUs. The proportion of African American faculty at majority institutions is 2.3%, virtually the same as it was 20 years ago (Wilson, 2002).
2. Corporate universities and the for profit educational services industry can be expected to begin to cut into the traditional markets for higher education. "It is estimated that more than $4 billion will be invested in educational companies this year [2000]" (Von Holzen, 2000, p. 57). This funding drain for public and nonprofit-based institutions of higher education will dramatically impact academic freedom as well as access to an affordable, quality education for the average citizen.

3. Public perception has shifted. The public generally views colleges and universities as out of touch with reality. A growing number of politically influential groups see research universities as having eluded the beneficial effects of market-driven efficiency (Francis & Hampton, 1999). As resources for higher education institutions shrink, it will be mandatory for research universities to collaborate among themselves.
4. Educating and graduating the African American students who choose to matriculate at professional and graduate schools at majority institutions must become a priority. Davidson and Foster-Johnson (2001) point out " . . . with the scarcity of mentors in graduate school who are knowledgeable about culturally appropriate ways of guiding women and people of color, these students are likely at greater risk."
5. The poor curriculum alignment between higher education institutions and PK–12 institutions will become a more complicated crisis, as the demographics of elementary and secondary schools change faster than expected. If a diverse teaching force is critical to the success of a diverse student body, how will majority institutions handle this influx of minority students in the next few years in the absence of a minority teaching force?

Miller and Stayon (1999) sum it up best: "Structures in higher education continue to support isolation, independence, and competition among faculty. The culture of higher education appears to be perceived by many faculty as risk aversive" (pp. 300–301). Research, however, has proven that institutions that promote a supportive culture for change are more successful. The change process shapes culture (i.e., vision or mission is modified as a result). Institutions need to reflect on the opportunity that change presents to reshape the culture (Kezar & Eckel, 2002) and to be responsive to a new role of education institutions in shaping the economy.

Challenges

A report issued in 1990 by the Southern Regional Educational Board states that one of the major challenges for public White institutions (PWIs) is the perceptions of African American students on their campuses. In their survey, African American students reported feelings of alienation and noted the lack of knowledge White students had about them (Abraham, 1990). More recent studies confirm the persistence of this problem (De Sousa & Kuh, 1996; Antonio, 2002). As climate plays a major role in whether people stay or leave, it is in the best interest of PWIs to collaborate with HBCUs in shaping a leadership class prepared for today's and tomorrow's needs.

A second challenge is having HBCUs forge a leadership niche in the twenty-first century. Historically, HBCUs were overtly oppressed by a "separate but equal" public policy. Public HBCUs were purposely underfunded to appease social pressures to integrate. Private HBCUs were often directed by boards that forced acculturating African Americans to participate in society at large (Anderson, 2001). Today, minorities have become 29% of those entering college. According to John Garland, president of Central State University and chair of the American Council on Education's Commission on Minorities in Higher Education, minority institutions hire more minorities and do a better job of helping them advance academically (Mollison, 2002a, 2002b).

US Secretary of Education, Rodney Paige, encouraged HBCUs leaders to do a better job of educating teachers to educate disadvantaged children (Mollison, 2002a, 2002b). Minority institutions educate one-third of minority students in higher education and supply about half the minority teachers in the nation's public schools. This issue of teacher quality is a concern shared by all. Through partnerships, statewide institutions can collaborate as equal partners, unlike past relationships. Given their phenomenal success, HBCUs ought to share experiences and mentoring support with PWIs. In turn, PWIs can share technologies, research, and facilitators to prepare the next generation of teachers to benefit all children. In addition, faculty at both types of institutions can benefit from mentoring, role modeling, and governance (Antonio, 2002).

The good news is that over the past decade, the number of African American and Latino undergraduates increased by 32% and 98%, respectively (Nettles & Perna, 1997). Though impressive, these numbers pale when considered as a subset of the universe of graduates. A partnership that draws on the complementary assets of the minority and majority institutions of higher education could significantly impact the gap.

Forging the New Partnership

There is no model for the new partnership being proposed herein. Certainly, there have been partnerships in the past, and lessons learned from them should provide a framework for discussions. A summative exploration of how school, community, and university partnerships have fared was reported by Carroll et al. (2001). They affirmed earlier research by Osguthorpe et al. (1996) that successful partnerships involve four components:

1. Curriculum for preparing students for a teaching career.
2. *Professional development* opportunities for teachers and faculty to enhance their skills.

3. *Curriculum development* that seeks to improve student performance.
4. *Research* that promotes continuous renewal for all parties.

There are, however, certain premises that must be honored at the negotiating table to assure that this partnership attempt will be different from failed or short-lived efforts of the past. As a starting point, both parties must be expected to be equal partners. Southern state oversight systems must design and align their critical components, such as organizational structures, resource allocations, and infrastructural support systems, to the current political climate. Anticipated demographic changes and the prudent use of scarce resources will be extremely necessary for the goal of supporting equity across parallel institutions. Key stakeholders must be encouraged to speak frankly about the past treatment of HBCUs as a causal factor in the current achievement gaps—not as an excuse, but as a context for intentionally fashioning an equitable partnership committed to closing the achievement gap and increasing the graduation rates of African Americans. Moreover, without an acknowledgment of the systemic pattern of oppression by past administrations, HBCUs cannot be expected to trust the rhetoric of policymakers—an essential ingredient to assure the integrity of the negotiations. Perhaps Bertman (2000) said it best, "Like personal memory, cultural memory is subjective and in the eye of the beholder. What one group sees and cherishes, another fails to recognize; what is important to some is meaningless to others" (pp. 105–106).

The current sociopolitical climate offers a rare opportunity for developing a constructive framework for the honest discussions that must take place to create a healthy interdependence between minority and majority institutions, beginning with the historic systemic differential funding of state universities. HBCUs cannot be expected to compete if history continues to cast its shadow over attempts to design a different future.

Rather than being viewed as deficient institutions that offer little or no value in the reform conversation, HBCUs must be viewed genuinely as resources in reforming the delivery of education and crafting a new role for higher educational institutions in the care of the economy. The shift in perspective from a deficit model to an asset model is absolutely essential. Without this shift, the renegotiation of relationships required to support the kind of inclusive education reform demanded in the face of the changing marketplace realities is doomed to failure.

There is an opportunity to build on the rich history of HBCUs in successfully educating African American students. The ability of HBCUs and majority institutions to escape the traps set by the historical headlock on defining the identity of and relationship between minority and majority institutions will heavily influence, if not define, the probability of the long-term success of the education reform effort. And yet, our willingness to face head-on the unpleasant tensions born out of our historical relationships, and to move beyond knee-jerk reactions and responses engendered by that history, is a challenge that is rarely addressed in reform strategies.

Opportunities to team teach, to share research projects, and to extend collaborative services to all citizens through strategic alliances extend the possibility of an equitable, asset-based, working partnership between minority and majority institutions. A variety of teaching strategies mastered by HBCU faculty and employed in the HBCU environment can help reduce the high dropout rate of minorities in majority institutions. Multiple ways to assess talent will become increasingly necessary as demographics change. Genuine partnerships between minority and majority institutions hold the promise of collaboratively tackling policy issues such as criteria for admission based on scientific and experiential learning. These kinds of joint efforts will benefit both minority and majority institutions and will produce the results the market increasingly demands and the public expects from higher education institutions. If the US can conduct business across the globe, there is no reason why its institutions of higher education cannot become exceptionally creative in advancing cross-campus partnerships at both minority and majority institutions as a strategy for increasing the number of minority graduates in professional and graduate schools and improving the quality of education.

Concomitantly, state systems should encourage presidents of these institutions to collaborate and simultaneously fashion support systems that will assist them in the transformation. A recent report by the American Council on Education (1999) supports the idea of presidents leading the nation's campuses in a major improvement in the quality of education provided to teachers and school leaders. A review of the literature confirms the centrality of a willing president, the presence of collaborative processes, and the provision of rewards as essential to successful change (Kezar & Eckel, 2002). Too often, the attention of university and college presidents is entirely spent on reluctant faculty, indifferent students, vocal alumni, and high-maintenance donors, and they do not dedicate themselves to leading institutional change. Yet, global competition, increasing diversity, economic pressure, and the infusion of technology signal an inescapable moment of transformation for contemporary colleges and universities (Austensen, 1997). One of the ways to leverage resources is to take advantage of this transformational moment and to address these challenges to help and support each other.

In confronting the challenges of the present and looking to invent a different reality for the future, Southern higher education institutions have a rare opportunity to lead the nation. Despite a conflicted past, the current sociopolitical climate, shifting demographics of minorities, and the potential to become an economic engine for America demand that the South not passively allow its history to define its relationships nor benignly neglect the opportunity for transformation because the parties are hopelessly locked in a dance driven by that history. Without forging a new model of partnership, the field of higher education risks repeating the sins of the past. By being slow to act, placing tradition before excellence, and excluding HBCUs from the "first table," educators virtually assure compromising a promising moment to meet the challenges of educating a population for the social, economic, and political challenges of the twenty-first century.

References

Abraham, A. (1990). *Racial issues on campus: How students view them*. Atlanta, GA: Southern Regional Education Board.

American Council on Education. (1999). *To touch the future: Transforming the way teachers are taught*. Washington, DC: American Council on Education.

Anderson, J. D. (1988). *The education of Blacks in the South, 1860–1935*. Chapel Hill: University of North Carolina Press.

———. (2001). Separate and unequal, 1950–1980, education. In S. Mondale & S. B. Patton (Eds.), *School: The story of American public education*. Boston, MA: Beacon Press.

Antonio, A. L. (2002). Faculty of color reconsidered: Reassessing contributors to scholarship. *The Journal of Higher Education 73*(5), 582–602.

Austensen, R. A. (1997). Faculty relations and professional development: Best practices for the chief academic officer. In J. Martin, J. E. Samels, & Associates (Eds.), *First among equals: The role of the chief academic officer*. Baltimore, MD: Johns Hopkins University Press.

Bertman, S. (2000). *Cultural amnesia: America's future and the crisis of memory*. Westport, CT: Praeger.

Carroll, G., LaPoint, V., & Tyler, K. (2001). Co-construction: A facilitator for school reform in school, community and university partnerships. *Journal of Negro Education 70*, 38–58.

Carter, D. J., & Wilson, R. (1997). *Minorities in higher education, 1996–1997 15 annual status report*. Washington, DC: Office of Minorities in High Education of the American Council on Education.

Davidson, M., & Foster-Johnson, L. (2001). Mentoring in the preparation of graduate researchers of color. *Review of Educational Research 71*, 549–574.

De Sousa, D. J., & Kuh, G. D. (1996). Does institutional racial composition make a difference in what Black students gain from college? *Journal of College Student Development 37*, 257–267.

Francis, J. G., & Hampton, M. C. (1999). The adaptive research university and the drive to market. *The Journal of Higher Education 70*, 625–641.

Garibaldi, A. M. (1991). Blacks in colleges. In C. V. Willis, A. M. Garibaldi, & W. L. Reed (Eds.), *The education of African-Americans*. New York: Auburn House.

Hodgkinson, H. (2002). Demographics and teacher education. *Journal of Teacher Education 53*, 102–105.

Keith, K. (1998). The responsive university in the twenty-first century. In W. G. Tierney (Ed.), *The responsive university: Restructuring for high performance*. Baltimore, MD: Johns Hopkins University Press.

Kezar, A., & Eckel, P. S. (2002). The effect of institutional culture on change strategies in higher education. *The Journal of Higher Education 73*, 435–460.

Martinez, M. C. (2002). Understanding state higher education systems. *The Journal of Higher Education 73*, 349–374.

Miller, S. P., & Stayon, V. (1999). Higher education culture—A fit or misfit with reform in teacher education. *Journal of Teacher Education 50*, 290–302.

Mollison, A. (2002a). Minority teacher training stressed: Challenges made to Black colleges. *The Atlanta Journal-Constitution* September 17, A-3.

———. (2002b). Rates of minorities in college. *The Atlanta Journal-Constitution* September 23, A-3.

National Alliance of Business. (2001). *Investing in teaching*. Washington, DC: National Alliance of Business.

National Commission on Excellence in Education. (1983). *A nation at risk: The imperative for educational reform*. Washington, DC: Author.

Nettles, M. T., & Perna, L. W. (1997). *The African-American education data book: Higher and adult education* (Vol. 1). Fairfax, VA: Frederick D. Patterson Research Institute.

Olson, L. (2000, September 27). Minority groups to emerge as a majority in US schools. *Education Week*, 17–20.

Osguthorpe, R. T., Harris, R. C., Harris, M. F., & Black, S. (1996). *Partner schools: Centers for educational renewals*. San Francisco: Jossey-Bass.

Richardson, R. C., Reeves-Bracco, K., Callan, P. M., & Finney, J. E. (1999). *Designing: State higher education systems for a new century*. Phoenix, AZ: American Council on Education/Oryx Press.

Slaughter, S., & Leslie, L. (1997). *Academic capitalism: Policies and the entrepreneurial universities*. Baltimore, MD: Johns Hopkins University Press.

Von Holzen, R. (2000). A look at the future of higher education. *Syllabus* November, 56–65.

Wilson, R. (2002). Stacking the deck for minority candidates. *The Chronicle of Higher Education 68*, A10–A12.

CHAPTER EIGHTEEN

Vyuo vya Weusi (Black Colleges)

Their Future, Use, and Survival in a White Country

BARUTI I. KATEMBO

Abstract

A college, in general, is supposed to produce a critical mass of thinkers, intellectuals, and technologists who are useful to the economic and technological development of the nation in which the college resides. If *Vyuo vya Weusi*, which means "Colleges of Blackness" in Kiswahili, are assumed to be catalysts of Black advancement and living repositories of African thought, intellect, and culture, then what is their current use and value in the advancement of the United States, a predominantly White nation? In this work, Vyuo vya Weusi is used as a synonym for historically Black colleges and universities (HBCUs), or simply Black colleges. This chapter will examine this question and will analyze the limitations, challenges, strengths, and viable niches of these institutions in the context of their existence in a White (and sometimes hostile) society. It will also examine these schools' current resource potential, both human and material, in relationship to the development of viable strategies and initiatives that will facilitate their optimum service to global needs and markets, particularly in Africa and its diaspora for long-term gain.

Introduction: The Peculiar Position of HBCUs

Vyuo vya Weusi (pronounced *vee-yoo-oh vee-yah way-oo-see*), is a Kiswahili phrase that means "Colleges of Blackness." This concept implies that within such institutions the curricula encourage the research and study of Africa, its people, history, culture, and global contributions. On the surface, historically Black colleges and universities (HBCUs) are regarded conceptually as *Vyuo vya Watu Weusi* (literally "Colleges of Black People" in Kiswahili), meaning those institutions that historically serve Blacks as the primary matriculating population, without any regard to the kind of curricular slant offered. A demographically Black school, having a curriculum steeped in the traditions, views, and values of Europe, would be ineffective in preparing Africans to build themselves as a people. In the modern sense, HBCUs should strive to embody the philosophical thrust implied by the Kiswahili name in that they should produce Black intellectuals who can integrate and combine technology, economics, and African sociocultural connectedness.

In this work, HBCUs have been denoted in a cultural context (i.e., Vyuo vya Weusi) to identify them in relationship to their African sociocultural roots. Located in the United States and its Virgin Islands territory, these institutions operate and function within the context of a larger, White physical and geopolitical environment. A college, in general, is supposed to produce a critical mass of thinkers, intellectuals, and technologists who are useful in and to the development of the economy and technical base in the nation in which the college resides. Today's Black colleges should exist and function as living repositories of African thought, intellect, and culture; they should supply the African diaspora with the training and intellectual resources needed to administrate and advance modern African societies. They must also be engaged in promoting strategies, research, and practical initiatives that minimize Black internalization of American, European, or White stereotypical perceptions of Africa (for example, that it is a land of childhood, primitivism, and cultural backwardness), a widely held view published in many books by noted German philosopher Georg W. F. Hegel (1731–1830) during the eighteenth and nineteenth centuries (Carr, 2001).

Historically, Black colleges in the United States, generally born within 10–20 years after the Civil War, were created mainly by legislation, White philanthropists, and to some extent, Black organizations such as the African Methodist Episcopal Church (AMEC), for the purpose of educating Blacks to maintain their own affairs within a larger, White society that enforced harsh social, political, and economic restrictions upon Blacks as a matter of law, custom, and practice; in other words, these colleges produced the academic talent base for a quasi Black nation whose boundaries were and are within a White one (The Texas State Historical Association, 2002). The academic focus of these colleges could be grouped into either of two historical categories: (1) preaching and teaching and (2) farming and mechanical arts.

The purpose of these colleges during legal segregation was clear. However, their function is now seen by many, both Black and White, as unclear or outdated, as evidenced by the fact that HBCUs today only enroll 16% of the Black population matriculating at 4-year colleges and universities. Three historically Black colleges—Bluefield State College (West Virginia), West Virginia State College, and Lincoln University (Missouri)—now have majority-White student body populations of 91%, 87%, and 67%, respectively. Nationally, White enrollment at Black colleges has climbed about 30% in the past two decades, that is, since the 1980s. The usual reasons cited for the demographic shift in Black college enrollment are: (1) economic lure of White students based on research indicating that attending HBCUs costs half as much as attending White universities; (2) aggressive recruitment tactics and strategies by White colleges to enroll Black athletes to maintain competitive sports programs; (3) aggressive recruitment tactics and strategies by White colleges to enroll Black students to satisfy affirmative action mandates; and (4) the opinion of many Blacks, influenced mainly by media and allegiance to the concept of integration, that HBCUs are inferior to White universities in terms of prestige, academic preparation, degree quality, and being a conduit to corporate America. The decline in Black enrollment at HBCUs, along with other trends and factors, has caused these colleges to recruit multiracially as a medium of financial compensation (Blitzer, 2000; Katembo, 2001, p. 40; Donaldson, 2003).

Although Black colleges educate only a small proportion of the number of Blacks matriculating in college today, a significant proportion of Black professionals have earned their degrees, particularly undergraduate ones, from Black institutions. Though more had been established during the post-Civil War era, only 106 HBCUs survive today. They are defined by the White House Initiative on HBCUs as "Those institutions of postsecondary education that were originally founded or whose antecedents were originally founded for the purpose of providing education opportunities for individuals of the Negro or colored race, and which continue to have as one of the primary purposes the provision of postsecondary opportunities for Black Americans." The 106 HBCUs are located in 20 states, the District of Columbia, and the US Virgin Islands, with 49% of them public and the other 51% private (Roscoe, 2001). They are responsible for producing the majority of college-trained, professional Black talent currently working in mainstream, corporate America. This fact should be touted and promoted nationally by Black educational and political leadership organizations as a cornerstone point in encouraging the majority of college-bound Black students to attend HBCUs. The effects would be the to bolster the economic coffers (i.e., reserves, endowments, assets) and academic offerings of these institutions collectively to a level far beyond their current capacities.

Corporate America's Need for Black Colleges May Shrink

Colleges are supposed to produce products, namely skilled workers who supply the nation's professional workforce. In the industrial sense, no buyers for a product translates into a shutdown of the manufacturing operation. Allegorically speaking, recent student graduates are the product; businesses are the buyers (consumers); and the college is the manufacturer. If a college cannot market its students, it, like any other business, will fold. Corporate America is the largest market to which Black colleges direct their graduates in exchange for reciprocal corporate rewards and gifts—for example, new campus buildings, money, college-industry research partnerships, and the like. Many of the top-ranking employers of Black students, including technology companies, have taken a noticeable beating in terms of layoffs and falling stock prices since 2001. The economic slump continues to impact the attractiveness of these companies as employers, causing students to look to other market sectors when deciding what companies to join (Miller, 2002, p. 22).

In the near future, the demand for Black professionals in the workforce may shrink significantly for a variety of reasons, including corporate downsizing, the passing of anti-affirmative action legislation, and well-educated immigrants. As the economy slumps and job competition becomes fierce, particularly in professional employment sectors, cries from Whites will grow louder and more hostile for political action to be taken to abolish all affirmative action initiatives designed to increase the number of Blacks in white-collar jobs. As an unwritten rule, Whites, especially professionals, are uncomfortable with having to compete with Blacks for jobs (Katembo, 2001, pp. 17–18). Soon, all race-based affirmative action policies in the employment arena may be totally dismantled for the following reasons: (1) Neither corporate America nor the US government is dependent on Black technical and administrative skills in comparison to available White talent; (2) White and non-Black immigrants can easily supplant Blacks in the workplace without decreasing productivity or work quality; and (3) the political leverage of Whites to eliminate programs perceived to be "unfair" or anti-White. In this scenario, Black colleges will face diminishing opportunities to market their students into the mainstream American job scene. Corporations will not continue to give money to Black colleges if there is no critical need for their graduates in terms of their performance being at a level above that of their counterparts, White job entrants. Revenue, reinvestments, and other resources from these White donor entities are and will be proportionate to the perceived need that corporate America sees in Black college graduates' ability to help the corporation make money over and above the productivity level of White hires.

Like it or not, White people do not really need Blacks to run the technical infrastructure of America; in essence, Blacks simply serve as surplus labor within the professional and technological circles of White society. That said, how will Black colleges be affected by downturns in the Black hiring rates of White-owned firms? HBCUs' dependence on the mainstream American market as the major outlet to which to supply employment talent can only place them on shaky economic ground. Racism, downsizing, supply and demand, and a tricky economy are four major factors that influence the Black presence in corporate America. The number of Blacks sought after by corporate America is a barometer for measuring HBCUs' value as suppliers of Black talent. Black colleges serve as the largest resource pool for American corporations to find significant numbers of Black professionals in their most critical areas: finance, technology, management, and research. As the demand for Black professional talent wanes, so do HBCUs' financial supplements and infrastructure reinvestment monies from corporate America.

In the United States, Blacks do not outnumber Whites in technical and managerial expertise and credentials. For practical purposes also, their productivity level is on par with, not superior to, that of Whites. In sports, Blacks are primarily recruited as labor (i.e., athletes) but not as coaches, team administrators, sportscasters, or other professional nonathlete jobs in the sports industry. Corporate America tends to choose Whites over equally qualified Blacks because these entities run and controlled by Whites don't lose economically by hiring their own. Besides, the phasing out of carrot-bait federal funds, affirmative action, and other legislated race-parity schemes (all of which were designed to force companies to implement fair hiring mandates) will severely lessen incentives to hire Blacks. Perhaps a few Blacks whose skill, talent, and productivity level is 10 times greater than that of White counterparts may be absorbed or hired by corporate America without the need for legislated hiring mandates as a coercive. However, new strategies will have to be designed to optimize the marketability of graduates of Black colleges.

Beyond the American Market: Benefits and Advantages

Blacks must begin to look abroad (i.e., outside the United States) for viable employment, economic opportunities, and entrepreneurship, instead of settling for economic crumbs from the American infrastructure. In November

2002, the National Association for the Advancement of Colored People (NAACP), under the leadership and direction of its president and CEO, Kweisi Mfume, reached an agreement with the Cuban government to buy food products from US Black farmers, accessing that country's $1.5 billion import agriculture market. The NAACP's role in this agribusiness initiative is to work with the Black farmers to coordinate their capacity to get their goods to market; these goods would include items such as rice, chicken quarters, flour, and other grocery products (Muhammad, 2002c). Various HBCUs, especially those with strong programs and research facilities in agribusiness and technology, can support the NAACP's efforts by forming consultant teams comprised of professors and researchers who have expertise in the design and implementation of agriproduct delivery and distribution methods.

In order for Black colleges to make global initiatives a practical reality, in terms of applied research and job placement of graduates, concerted efforts will have to be made to provide basic training and knowledge about the demographic and socioeconomic structure of the world's nations, particularly those that have been targeted for research ventures. The areas of targeted countries that need to be explored and concentrated upon as vehicles to facilitate collaborations and partnerships are: major languages, cultural nuances, history, and current events. Language is of utmost importance because it is the basis of culture and is the major conduit through which relationships are established. Particularly with regard to HBCU–Africa links, Kiswahili courses should be mandatory at all HBCUs because the language serves as a gateway and practical medium by which US Blacks can reconnect with their brothers and sisters in Africa at the cultural and linguistic level. Spoken by more than 120 million people, Kiswahili is the most widely spoken indigenous African language, by both population and geography. However, the east, central, and southeast regions of Africa are the most concentrated Kiswahili regions. Given that many African languages are structurally related to Kiswahili with regard to vocabulary and syntax, the study of this language by faculty, researchers, and students at HBCUs will increase basic communication with Africans and provide a better understanding of African societies from a sociocultural perspective. There are other advantages to setting up Kiswahili programs: They increase marketability of students seeking to be hired by companies doing business in Africa or establishing branches there (increased student marketability translates into leverage and incentives for corporate and philanthropic financial investments in Black colleges); and they strengthen HBCU student exchange programs with Africa (Katembo, 2001, pp. 46–47).

In addition, Black colleges can export skilled advisers, teachers, and workers with specifically requested expertise in an assortment of areas (such as technology, engineering, agriculture, management, and economics) to many developing nations, particularly African ones, in exchange for mineral/mining rights (e.g., diamonds, gold, tantalum) and investment opportunities (e.g., energy, telecommunications, real estate, sugar) as adequate financial compensation and revenue. African nations, though contemporarily Black-led politically, are usually run by Europeans, Jews, Arabs, or Asians in their economic and technology sectors. Three of Africa's most noted former White colonies—Zimbabwe, South Africa, and Kenya—are current examples of this predicament, with the latter two having small but influential populations of Asians, the descendents of East Indian migrant laborers forcibly imported by European capitalists 200 years ago. In South Africa and Zimbabwe, the Whites are largely descendants of Dutch and British colonists and settlers who arrived in Southern Africa at least 300 years ago (Muhammad, 2002). HBCUs could supply Africa with a sufficient cadre of researchers, teachers, technicians, and even a small workforce contingency (to some extent) to make Black reliance on White skill obsolete. Some possibilities include: (1) Black replacements for the current exodus of White medical doctors from South Africa and (2) Black replacements for the approximately 3000 White farmers in Zimbabwe—a country with less than 1% European population—who grow, raise, and cultivate most of the country's food products (including meat, poultry, fruits, and vegetables) on 9,154 White-owned farms covering more than 40 million acres (Horner, 2002; Muhammad, 2002).

Conclusion

Black colleges must increase and strengthen research partnerships, academic collaborations, and student exchange programs with each other and with companies, universities, and nations abroad, particularly those in Africa and the Caribbean. These joint ventures are useful in generating revenue by tapping into global markets and are also critical initiatives in developing powerful think tanks and institutes to address and solve the political, economic, and environmental concerns of Africa, the Caribbean, and the global community (Katembo, 2001, p. 41).

References

Blitzer, W. (2000). *Enrollment of White students on rise at historically Black colleges.* Retrieved December 18, 2002, from www.cnn.com/2000/US/05/18/black.colleges

Carr, G. (2001). *African and African-American studies curriculum framework essay*

Addendum. Retrieved December 12, 2002, from www.citycom/web/heruseye/Textfiles/AAACurriculumEssay.html

Donaldson, S. (2003, January). Top 50 colleges and universities for African Americans. *Black Enterprise*, 76–83.

Horner, B. (2002). *Young doctors plan to bolt en masse*. Retrieved January 8, 2003, from www.allafrica.com/stories/200212080223.html

Katembo, I. (2001). Elephants in a bamboo cage. *The Black condition, the American psyche, and the next step forward*. Raleigh, NC: Mkuyu Books.

Miller, R. (2002, October). Diversity gives employers a competitive edge. *The Black Collegian*, 19–22.

Muhammad, J. (Ed.) (2002a, December 17). Should African languages be used in African schools? *The Final Call*, 14.

———. (Ed.) (2002b). *UK official: pay Zimbabwe for land reform*. Retrieved January 2, 2003, from www.finalcall.com/artman/publish/article_138.shtml

———. (2002c). *Journalists see Zimbabwe's land crisis up close*. Retrieved January 2, 2003, from www.finalcall.com/artman/publish/article_116.shtml

Muhammad, N. (2002, November 26). NAACP inks farm deal with Cuba. *The Final Call 3*, 30.

Roscoe, W. (2001). *What is a historically Black college or university?* Retrieved December 18, 2002, from www.thehighschoolgraduate.com/editorial/UShbcu.htm

The Texas State Historical Association (2002). *The handbook of Texas online: Black colleges*. Retrieved December 18, 2002, from www.tsha.utexas.edu/handbook/online/articles/view/BB/khb1.html

Part Four
School and Community

CHAPTER NINETEEN

Community Uplift Theory for Positive Change of African Americans in Urban Schools

FLOYD D. BEACHUM, FESTUS OBIAKOR,
AND CARLOS R. MCCRAY

Abstract

Education in urban settings and inner-city areas remains a difficult and motivating task. Federal and state mandates are compounded with social issues, placing increased stress on educators and educational leaders working in these settings. Community Uplift Theory (CUT) is presented as a means for educational leaders to unite urban schools in philosophy and practice. This theory focuses on individual and collective responsibility within a framework of critique, justice, and caring. This chapter explains the benefits of using CUT to initiate possible changes for African Americans in urban schools.

Introduction

The task of educating urban students continues to be a daunting task. Increased federal and state mandates, legal and fiscal quandaries, and sociopolitical conflicts have tended to complicate the already difficult job of educating urban learners. Educational leaders have the responsibility of setting the tone, developing the culture, and creating the environment for learning to take place (Sergiovanni, 1992; Owens, 2001; Cunningham &

Cordeiro, 2003). Many of the problems these leaders face are linked to the problems found in urban African American communities. The issue of community has always been at the heart of the African American experience. From Africa through antebellum slavery and beyond, there has been an effort to maintain a strong sense of community (West, 1994).

The history of African Americans is one characterized by pain, love, turmoil, and triumph: in historical terms, African Americans have experienced kidnapping and slavery in America, years of second-class citizenship (segregation), struggles for civil rights, and continued quests for social justice. "In America, there have been deliberate efforts to block African Americans from overcoming the legacy of slavery and creating a self-sustaining, self-sufficient, self-determining community" (Rogers, 2000, p. 127). In this new century, many African Americans and their communities continue to face challenges across the United States, especially within inner-city areas. As Dyson (1997) points out, many African American communities are plagued by high unemployment, high crime, failing schools, and an overall loss of hope (Dyson, 1997). However, as West (1994) notes, "for as long as hope remains and meaning is preserved, the possibility of overcoming oppression stays alive" (p. 23).

The Urban Context: Old Versus New Framework

The relationship between African Americans and "urbanness" should not come as a surprise. In America, many African Americans gravitated toward urbanized cities and settled in communities to work in factories and perhaps escape the dark shadows of racism. As the factories relocated, so did the American Dream for the people in these communities. As West (1994) succinctly puts it:

> The exodus of stable industrial jobs from urban centers to cheaper labor markets here and abroad, housing policies that have created "chocolate cities and vanilla suburbs," white fear of black crime . . . all have helped erode the tax base of American cities just as the federal government has cut its support and programs. The result is unemployment, hunger, homelessness, and sickness for millions. (p. 9)

Urban schools are often a microcosm of the economic, political, social malaise in urban communities. In these schools, there is an even greater need for positive change because students in central cities and metropolitan areas are confronted with numerous issues that place them at greater risk. Urban schools tend to be located in urban environments, reflective of and responsive to the greater society, hierarchical by nature, and complicated by issues of class and race or ethnicity. In addition, these schools deal continuously with negative characterizations of city students, lack of funding and support, and mounting bureaucracies (Alston, 2002). A general disdain for city schools provides the rationale for the underfunding, marginalization, and collective criticism of urban schools (Ayers, 1994). In order to combat overwhelming odds and skillfully avoid "circular hopelessness" (Sanders, 1999), new and innovative paradigms and theories are needed (Alston, 2002). One such theoretical framework is the Community Uplift Theory (CUT).

CUT is a comprehensive philosophy for the effective change to a more Afrocentric value system. This theory combines aspects of normative ethics and the seven principles of Nguzo Saba (Karenga, 1989). Within this framework, there are two fields of thought: the individual and the group (Starratt, 1991). With regard to the individual, the Afrocentric values of *self-determination, purpose,* and *creativity* are stressed; and with regard to the group, *unity, collective work and responsibility,* and *cooperative economics* are fostered. The final principle, *faith,* permeates both fields. The result is a synergy that does not fall prey to the philosophical fallacy of dichotomous thought; rather there is the utility of collaboration in a genuine effort to build community. In effect, this model fuses the positions of liberal structuralists and conservative behaviorists (West, 1994) into a philosophy that acknowledges structural inequities while also emphasizing the responsibility of the individual. This chapter presents CUT as a way to redirect, refocus, and reform urban schools to enhance individual pursuits and collective efforts of African Americans.

CUT and Multidimensional Ethics

The theoretical framework of CUT has some foundational relationships with multidimensional ethics as postulated by Starratt (1991). Based on Starratt's model, the ethics of critique, justice, and caring are interconnected. "None of these ethics by itself offer a fully adequate framework for ethical judgments; together however, each ethic complements the others in a developmental context of practice" (Starratt, 1991, p. 186). Similarly, CUT integrates Afrocentric values into a comprehensive philosophy. As a result of logic or common sense, multidimensional ethics (critique, justice, and caring) provide a framework for CUT.

The Ethic of Critique

The ethic of critique is based on critical theory. Its aim is to deconstruct established attitudes, values, and actions that foster inequity. Starratt (1991) explains that:

> Whether considering social relationships, social customs, laws, social institutions grounded in structural power relationships, or language itself, thinkers must ask questions such as the following: "Who benefits from these arrangements?" "Which group dominates this social arrangement?" "Who defines the way things are structured here?" "Who defines what is valued and disvalued in this situation?" (p. 189)

The ethic of critique has important personal implications as well as organizational implications. With regard to the school organization, it forces educational leaders to question structural inequities and move beyond a status quo mentality. At the same time, the ethic of critique implores the individual to question personal motives, beliefs, and values.

The Ethic of Justice

In reference to the ethic of justice, educational leaders must ask the question: How shall we govern ourselves? The answer is found in the appropriate balance between two schools of thought: the individual and the community. The first school of thought places primary value on the individual. According to Starratt (1991), "Individuals are driven by their passions and interests especially by fear of harm and desire for comfort" (p. 192). The individual is the source of moral judgment according to this nonconsequential assertion. This position coincides with the concept of equal respect. The principle of equal respect involves three subsidiary principles: (a) people must be treated as ends rather than means; (b) people must be regarded as free and rational moral agents; and (3) as moral agents, people must have equal value (Strike et al., 1998).

The second school of thought highlights society as the primary source of human reality. "Participation in the life of the community teaches individuals how to think about their own behavior in terms of the larger common good of the community" (Starratt, 1991, p. 193). This school of thought is further supported by the concept of benefit maximization. According to Strike et al. (1998), "The principle of benefit maximization holds that, whenever we are faced with a choice, the best and most just decision is the one that results in the most good or the greatest benefit for the most people" (p. 16). This consequentialist theory is motivated by the maximization of societal benefit.

The Ethic of Caring

Starratt (1991) completed his ethical framework with the ethic of caring. Here, the primary question should be: What do our relationships ask of us? "Such an ethic does not demand relationships of intimacy; rather it postulates a level of caring that honors the dignity of each person and desires to see that person enjoy a fully human life" (Starratt, 1991, p. 195). Caring is both the process and the product. Starratt (1991) concluded that:

> It [caring] recognizes that it is in the relationship that the specifically human is grounded; isolated individuals functioning only for themselves are but half persons. One becomes whole when one is in relationship with another and with many others. (p. 195)

Infusing CUT in Urban Schools

Within the frameworks of critique, justice, and caring are the seven Afrocentric principles, namely self-determination, purpose, creativity, unity, collective work, cooperative economics, and faith (Table 20.1). Infusing CUT in urban schools provides a guide for using these seven principles to create positive change in the educational experiences of African Americans.

Table 20.1 Theoretical Underpinnings of CUT

Critique	Justice	Caring
Purpose	*Individual* Self-determination Creativity *Collective* Unity Collective work and responsibility Cooperative economics	Faith

Purpose

The idea of *purpose* fits well with the ethic of critique. Under this idea, the educational leader must determine his or her purpose as exhibited by vision and mission. The leader of a school has a unique position in which he or she must set the tone, shape the culture, and work to achieve several objectives (Decker, 1997; Alston, 2002; Cunningham & Cordeiro, 2003). Bryant and Jones (1993) argue that:

> They [educational leaders] are visionary and future-oriented. They not only possess images of the high potential to be reached by teachers and students in their school, but they operate in ways that assure the constant feedback that both motivates and measures organizational change and educational renewal. (p. 14)

Moreover, a leader must foster an environment in which students are able to explore multiple options and discover their purpose. Purpose must be the key concept in the development of a healthy self-identity in African American students. Urban schools must become places where the ideas, aspirations, and direction of African American children and youth (i.e., adolescents) intersect and sometimes collide. As Tatum (1997) points out:

> The adolescent capability for self-reflection (and resulting self-consciousness) allows one to ask, "Who am I now?" "Who was I before?" "Who will I become?" The answers to these questions will influence others about who one's romantic partners will be, what type of work one will do, where one will live, and what belief system one will embrace. Choices made in adolescence ripple throughout the lifespan. (p. 20)

In a practical sense, school leaders must cater to the unique needs of African Americans in urban schools by (a) responding to their multiple learning styles through diverse curricula, (b) exploring nontraditional career options and programs, and (c) exposing students to as many educational and experiential opportunities as possible.

Individual Growth

To initiate individual growth, there must be self-determination and creativity. Self-determination refers to the empowerment of individuals to define themselves, think for themselves, and determine their own reality (Obiakor et al., 2002). Many schools operate like factories where students are told what to do and when to do it. Today's urban schools tend to foster indoctrination as opposed to self-determination (Kohn, 1997). The role of the "self" cannot be downplayed in the educational process (Obiakor et al., 2002).

Creativity refers to a person's ability to bring an idea or concept into being, that is, from abstraction to fruition. In many urban schools, talents of African Americans go unnoticed, underutilized, or undercultivated. Curricula must be broad and inclusive enough to reach students on intellectual, cognitive, and social levels (Tatum, 1997; Cunningham & Cordeiro, 2003). In addition, innovative and insightful teacher- and student-initiated programs are needed. Kunjufu (2002) notes that, "You can observe Master Teachers after school, tutoring students and creating after-school clubs for chess, investment practice, computer skills, rap, rites of passage, newspaper reading, martial arts, and whatever other activities the students are interested in" (p. 74). Creativity is a crucial aspect of individual development in urban schools.

On the whole, curricular insight is key in the development of African American students' self-determination and creativity in urban schools. Ackerman (2003) challenges general educators and school leaders to maximize students' learning potential and creativity. In other words, they must:

1. Promote "active learning" that mentally activates students' capabilities.
2. Build strong disciplinary pillars that exist within a set of knowledge-integration structures.
3. Recognize the value and limitations of both "depth" and "coverage" in knowledge dissemination and acquisition.
4. Focus on collaborative, culturally sensitive activities that value each student.
5. Evaluate students on their progress in achieving personal excellence.

Collective Growth

Collective growth involves unity, which implies becoming a unit, existing in harmony, and mobilizing and organizing for action. Lack of unity has been noted as one of the major barriers to African American progress, upward mobility, and economic growth (Dumas & Mills, 1999; Rogers, 2000; Vance, 2001; Asante, 2003). Unity within and among schools is emerging as a way to assist and build school communities (Sergiovanni, 1992; Alston, 2002). Under the second school of thought within the ethic of justice is the idea of the community. CUT incorporates concepts embedded in collective works and cooperative actions, and energies of the comprehensive support model (Obiakor et al., 2002).

Collective works in urban schools happen on two levels: *within* schools and *among* schools. Within schools, collective work emphasizes sharing school-wide duties, collaborative lesson planning (Bryant & Jones, 1993; Obiakor, 2001), increased teacher and student leadership opportunities, and shared decision-making (Obiakor et al., 2002). Collective works among schools could involve African American high school students working with elementary schools, computer teachers hosting workshops for other teachers, or groups of culturally diverse teachers from different grade levels getting together to set goals or discuss problems.

Funding urban schools must become a collective responsibility. Fiscal issues are a major concern in African American education and in urban schools in particular. "Fiscal stewardship is of the utmost importance and is a responsibility that no administrator should take lightly. The funds an administrator allocates each day are public funds, and there is an inherent expectation that they will be accounted for properly" (Cunningham & Cordeiro, 2003, p. 324). In today's educational climate, where state budgets are already under numerous constraints, urban schools find themselves in an even more perplexing financial situation. Alston (2002) notes that, "considerations of equity in school funding are embedded in the history related to the financing of public education. Urban schools since their inception have been plagued with inadequate and misappropriated funding" (p. 24). An inequitable funding situation is a problem for public education in general and a harsh reality for many urban schools (Sergiovanni et al., 1999; Weiner, 1999).

In reference to CUT, cooperative responsibility would indicate cooperation among urban schools with regard to finances. In this cooperative spirit, urban schools must collaborate to determine financial strategy by writing grants and seeking partnerships. Collaboration on financial issues has the ability to positively influence academic outcomes of African Americans in urban schools.

Faith

Faith is a common denominator throughout the CUT theoretical construct. In this instance, faith relates to educational leaders' faith in themselves, constituents, subordinates, and the organization. Bolman and Deal (2001) confirm that "over the centuries, people have found meaning in work, family, community, and shared faith" (p. 4). In the CUT model, faith coincides with the ethic of caring. "Caring includes modeling, dialogue, practice, and confirmation. Modeling for educators means demonstrating to students that we care, rather than just saying it" (Noddings, 1992, p. 17).

Faith involves trusting others, empowerment, confidence, and vision. It is manifested in schools that have open and honest communication, reflective practice, and belief in the school's personnel, students, and mission (Cunningham & Cordeiro, 2003).

> Two misleading images currently dominate organizational thinking about leadership: one the heroic champion with extraordinary stature and vision, the other the "policy wonk," the skilled analyst who solves pressing problems with information, programs, and policies. Both these images emphasize the hands and heads of leaders, neglecting deeper and more enduring elements of courage, spirit, and hope. (Bolman & Deal, 2001, p. 11)

Faith emphasizes the "heart" of leadership and works in concert with the hands and head. In the end, it is characterized by the leader's certitude and attitude that students will be placed in the forefront.

Conclusion

CUT proposes a road map for positive change of African American education experiences in urban schools. It pragmatically combines Afrocentric thinking with multidimensional ethics. CUT does not suggest radical financial investment, nor does it hide itself in paradigmatic complexity. To a large measure, CUT combines both individual and collective concerns to guide urban school leaders. It fuses scholarly insight and ethical decision making with principles that are common sense, if not common knowledge. CUT's value becomes apparent when considering the African American experience and the educational context. Thus, CUT is a vehicle for the assertion of political will, teacher collaboration, professional collegiality, group planning and strategizing, and empowerment. It is important to focus on how to educate all learners, including those who have been traditionally disfranchised. In the words of Obiakor et al. (2002):

> If we can work together in our classrooms, families, communities, and governments we can work together in our world. Shifting paradigms and powers can be a painstaking process, and as educators, we have to be willing to step outside our comfort zones to take risks. (p. 13)

References

Ackerman, D. B. (2003). Taproots for a new century: Tapping the best of traditional and progressive education. *Phi Delta Kappan 84*(5), 344–349.

Alston, J. A. (2002). *Multi-leadership in urban schools: Shifting paradigms for administration and supervision in the new millennium.* Lanham, MD: University Press of America.

Asante, M. K. (2003). *Erasing racism: The survival of the American nation.* Amherst, NY: Prometheus Books.

Ayers, W. (1994). Can city schools be saved? *Educational Leadership 51*(8), 60–63.

Bolman, L. G., & Deal, T. E. (2001). *Leading with soul: An uncommon journey of spirit.* New York: Jossey-Bass.

Bryant, B., & Jones, A. H. (1993). *Seeking effective schools for African American children.* San Francisco: Caddo Gap Press.

Cunningham, W. G., & Cordeiro, P. A. (2003). *Educational leadership: A problem-based approach* (2nd ed.). Boston: Allyn Bacon.

Decker, L. (1997). Is parent involvement your job? *NEA Today 16,* 6–7.

Dumas, J., & Mills, R. (1999). *24 reasons why African Americans suffer: A critical analysis of an African American teenage subculture.* Chicago: African American Images.

Dyson, M. E. (1997). *Race rules: Navigating the color line.* New York: Vintage Books.

Karenga, M. (1989). *The African-American holiday of Kwanzaa: A celebration of family, community, and culture.* Los Angeles: University of Sankore Press.

Kohn, A. (1997). How not to teach values. *Phi Delta Kappan 78*(6), 429–439.

Kunjufu, J. (2002). *Black students—middle class teachers.* Chicago: African American Images.

Noddings, N. (1992). *The challenge to care in schools: An alternate approach to education.* New York: Teachers College Press.

Obiakor, F. E. (2001). *It even happens in "good" schools: Responding to culturally diversity in today's classrooms.* Thousand Oaks, CA: Corwin Press.

Obiakor, F. E., Grant, P. A., & Dooley, E. A. (2002). *Educating all learners: Refocusing the comprehensive support model.* Springfield, IL: Charles C. Thomas.

Owens, R. G. (2001). *Organizational behavior in education: Instructional leadership and reform.* Boston: Allyn Bacon.

Rogers, W. G. (2000). The power in our community: Finding solutions to our problems. In S. F. Battle & R. Hornung (Eds.), *The state of Black Milwaukee* (pp. 121–138). Milwaukee, WI: The Milwaukee Urban League.

Sanders, E. T. W. (1999). *Urban school leadership: Issues and strategies.* Larchmont, NY: Eye on Education.

Sergiovanni, T. J. (1992). *Moral leadership: Getting to the heart of school improvement.* San Francisco: Jossey-Bass.

Sergiovanni, T. J., Burlingame, M., Coombs, F. S., & Thurston, P. W. (1999). *Educational governance and administration.* Needham Heights, MA: Allyn and Bacon.

Starratt, R. (1991). Building an ethical school: A theory of practice in educational leadership. *Educational Administration Quarterly 27*(2), 185–202.

Strike, K. A., Haller, E. J., & Soltis, J. F. (1998). *The ethics of school administration* (2nd ed.). New York: Teachers College Press.

Tatum, B. D. (1997). *Why are all the Black kids sitting together in the cafeteria? And other conversations about race.* New York: Basic Books.

Vance, B. (2001). *From ghetto to community: The resurrection of African American institutions.* Chicago: African American Images.

Weiner, L. (1999). *Urban teaching: The essentials.* New York: Teachers College Press.

West, C. (1994). *Race matters.* New York: Vintage Books.

CHAPTER TWENTY

Mentoring Across Social Class Boundaries

Empirical Lessons

FRED MUSKAL

The problem of communicating across class boundaries has long vexed educators and other social scientists, notably B. Bernstein (1971, 1975) and M. Kohn (1977). The literature on low-income youth in the 1960s and 1970s identified a broad range of problems that impeded middle-class messages from reaching working-class youth in ways that mentored them to do better in school. Even though low-income persons share the same aspirations as the middle class, there is no sense of how to make one's way up the social ladder (Han, 1969). Since the appearance of Levinson et al.'s *The Seasons of a Man's Life* (1978) sparked a resurgence in the topic of mentoring, a number of empirical studies have tried to come to grips with the problem of communicating across class boundaries through mentoring. These include a range of studies focusing on the upward mobility of people of color and low-income youth.

This chapter draws from several of these studies (Ogbu, 1978; Carlquist-Hernandez, 1987; Chairez, 1990; Gándara, 1995) and the author's own inquiries over the years to examine the concept of mentoring and the process of communicating across class boundaries to promote upward mobility. In reconciling differences between various studies, this chapter will address the definition and nature of mentoring, the social-psychological context of working class life, and the documented steps that enable mentors to communicate across class boundaries. The variations across studies suggest that a closer examination of the concept of mentoring is necessary to clarify the full range of issues involved in the process of communicating across class boundaries.

The Concept of Mentoring

The *Shorter Oxford English Dictionary* notes that the noun *mentor* entered the English language around 1750 with the meaning of "an experienced and trusted counselor." Mentor was the name of a guide and adviser to a young Greek, Telemachus, in Homer's *Ulysses*. The core of the concept has remained the notion of the experienced, trusted counselor. Traditionally, mentoring involves extended exposure between the "mentor" and "mentee," as with a dissertation adviser and doctoral student. Recent studies have suggested that, while the original meaning is still at the core, this meaning is inadequate to describe clearly the kind of mentoring relationship that promotes upward mobility. Thus, it is necessary to examine the concept of mentoring empirically.

The core of mentoring remains the extraordinary interest of a person of higher status, knowledge, or occupational experience in someone of lesser knowledge, experience, and lower status. Often the first interest and connection is made because of some shared characteristic like culture, neighborhood (social class position and/or physical location), or even some common personal or personality trait. *The core of mentoring, as it emerges in recent literature, is a form of advising that has fateful consequences for the life of the mentee.* That is, successful mentoring, including that which successfully crosses class boundaries, has a genuine impact on the life of the mentee. This may mean that a young person accepts the counsel of the mentor and, for example, commits to going to college and follows through, regardless of the intervening contingencies of life. This definition preserves the original meaning, but focuses more acutely on the process of mentoring successfully. As the next section demonstrates, the key to mentoring lies not in the length of a mentoring relationship, but in the quality of its communication.

Types of Mentoring

Long-term mentoring is what Mentor did in Homer's *Ulysses*. He provided extended exposure and some consistent relationship between two or more people of unequal status: himself and Telemachus. In this type of mentoring, long-term exposure is implemented, whether as a doctoral student and dissertation adviser, a supervisor and worker, or an experienced person dealing with someone new to a particular status, as a new school principal or manager. Mentoring generally involves advising, showing the newcomer "the ropes," and helping another person negotiate some bureaucratic career.

A second kind of mentoring has been noted with many low-income, upwardly mobile youngsters. In this type of mentoring, the exposure of mentor to mentee was limited to a single incident. As one informant named Marco related the story of his life:

> My father was dying and I was the oldest son. My family has fourteen children. I was walking down the street in [town in Mexico] and this man came up to me. I didn't know him, but I think he knew my father. He said to me, "Marco, your father is dying. How will the family survive?" I was eighteen and had no answer. He told me, "Marco, you must go to the United States and study to become a teacher. Then you can send money back to your mother."
>
> Q. What did you do?
>
> A. I went to the United States, studied and became a teacher. Now I send $800 a month back to Mexico.
>
> Q. Why did you do what the man said?
>
> A. I don't know. I just did it. It made sense and there was nothing in it for him, so I just did it. (M. Valdez, Personal communication, Stockton, CA, Spring, 1988)

Marco never met this stranger again, yet the stranger made a fateful, positive impact on his future. Incidental mentoring occurred with some frequency in Chairez's 1990 study. Gándara also confirms the existence of this type of mentoring in her sample (P. C. Gándara, Personal conversation, Sociology of Education Association Annual Meeting, 1995). The essence of this kind of mentoring was the ability to communicate clearly across class boundaries, even though the conversation may have lasted no more than a minute or two.

The Structure of Mentoring

Two basic components make up mentoring: (1) making a personal connection and (2) giving guidance that communicates effectively across class boundaries and assures personal survival. The personal connection is a reason that two people find some natural affinity for each other. The connection may be based on culture, ethnicity, class background (e.g., coming from a similar neighborhood or the same neighborhood), looks, personal reminiscence of one's youth, or an acquaintance with the family of the mentee.

The connection is significant in two fundamental ways. First, it draws the mentor to reach out or volunteer some form of commitment. Second, often in an unaware fashion, it prepares the mentee to accept the counsel of the mentor. This is a crucial element in legitimating the mentor. Once the connection is made (i.e., the mentor is accepted), then the superior knowledge, status, and experience of the mentor are accepted with trust.

The last component is the guidance offered by the mentor. To be effective (i.e., to mentor in a way that has fateful consequences), the mentor must understand how to cross class boundaries in a way that communicates some perceived benefit. The benefit may be a matter of fulfilling or strengthening the connection and sometimes is not understood clearly or fully by the mentee. For example, some informants report that youngsters who were encouraged to work hard in school ended up facing the opportunity to go to "college," often without clearly understanding the meaning of the word *college*. Others have clear-cut direction from a mentor that evades the limitations discovered in early research (Kohn, Bernstein) that impede cross-class communication. There are many social barriers to making a mentoring connection, some of which appear attributable to the limitations imposed by class status. The basic understanding needed to mentor across class boundaries is the grounding of a student's perspective in the social psychology of working-class life.

Working-Class Life

The term "working class" emerged in the early nineteenth century to identify a group of persons impoverished by the emergence of the industrial revolution and the economic dislocations generated by the changes needed to create a modern, capitalist economy. This group was created by the impact of social change in the form of extreme poverty. The working class became a more or less permanent feature of industrial societies, its isolation cemented by the severe social class segregation developed at that time. It was detached from traditional sources of community and values, or felt betrayed by them. The capitalist and middle classes could and did ignore the poor, who were left to their own devices and in their own places (Hobsbawm, 1996). Within the severe constraints imposed by poverty, the working class adapted to their situation of limited opportunity, low income, and segregation.

One outcome of working-class segregation was that social scientific research tended to ignore this group. As a result, a good deal of the knowledge of working-class life is of recent origin and, at best, fragmentary. One theoretical approach is Durkheim's construct of mechanical solidarity. This position would argue that the severity of social conditions imposes a solidarity, or shared sense of hardship and community. The young group members reinforce this because they tend to live within the narrow boundaries of the neighborhood and, in fact, create a framework that affects how people see the world for the rest of their lives (Karp, 1986). There is, through the imposition of social constraints and the sense of shared conditions, a powerful sense of loyalty to the community. This loyalty may have an impact on the willingness to become upwardly mobile and ways in which young people approach school (Sennett & Cobb, 1972; Willis, 1977). Another form of loyalty is that the responsibilities for raising children are shared by the entire community (Heath, 1983). *Understanding how these factors impact a student's perspective is essential to the communication process.* The most coherent examinations of the social psychology of working class life have been developed by Kohn (1977) and Valentine (1978).

Kohn (1977) argues that the social constraints of working-class life lead to a style of child rearing that emphasizes how to survive at the bottom of the occupational structure. The argument is that in a situation of highly supervised work, typically of low skill requirements, the need to survive places an emphasis on conformity and chance, in which the immediate consequences of one's behavior are fateful. This generates a powerful orientation and sensitivity toward the present time. The contrast with a middle-class parental orientation is profound. The middle class typically engages in work that is more complex, less supervised, and in which there is an emphasis on self-direction and individual control of one's fate. Long-term consequences are fateful, not things that occur in the present. Working-class youngsters, in this explanation, are socialized to help their survival under a range of social pressures that have an immediate impact on their lives. As a later section of this chapter shows, this emphasis on a present-time orientation may be long lasting.

Valentine (1978) and her family lived on a welfare budget in a low-income area of a large US city for a period of 5 years. She determined that dignity and respect were significant issues in the community. The respect of one's neighbors was determined by the way in which one earned money. There are three ways to earn money: (1) welfare, (2) unreliable, low-paid work, and (3) hustling. Respect is earned when one uses two of the three money sources to survive. If a person survives only on welfare, they are likely to be cheating. *Hustling* means some form of illicit activity; if one survives (or prospers) solely through illicit activities, they are likely to be exploiting the community and earn no respect. However, if one accepts welfare and hustles a little bit, one earns understanding and respect. Jobs held by community members tend to be unreliable; that is, they do not afford steady income. For example, whatever the merits of one's work, when it rains in the summer, the car wash closes. Few car washes remain open in the winter, so there are few reliable jobs in this line of work. Those who hold low-reliability jobs generally must pursue one of the other revenue sources to survive.

Others have observed the impact of increased income on working-class life. Steele (1989) identifies one group as "Blue Collar Respectables," persons of relatively low income who seek ways to win respectability. Their homes or apartments are decorated through the accumulation of things, and a serious illness will wipe out the family. This makes respectability something of a consolation prize. Respectability is won through living a life based on order. One follows rules, has a place for everything, and puts everything in its place. Heath (1983) identifies a similar group as the residents of Roadville. The children of the Blue Collar Respectables do work under instruction and seek approval from teachers to find out if they have done their work properly. As Kohn (1977) might predict, there is no emphasis on self-direction or long-term consequences, just on finding out if the job has been done right (Heath, 1983).

The context of working-class life includes: the significant impact of one's neighborhood as a social framework that grounds one's worldview, a limited way to achieve dignity and respectability, and a socialization style that emphasizes survival through a sensitivity to the immediate consequences of social situations. The social pressures of the neighborhood have a powerful impact on one's life, an impact that is enhanced through the traditional isolation and segregation of working class communities. In the less poverty-stricken elements of the working-class, respectability is won through following rules and, for children, following orders. The literature on this group indicates no sense of self-direction or future orientation. Rather, the emphasis on conformity and immediate consequences is still apparent, although some of the environmental pressure seems mitigated by higher income. The area of working-class life that has drawn the most attention in the literature is the impact of social class on language, a crucial point in mentoring and communicating across class boundaries.

Social Class and Language

A range of scholars have sought to assess the impact of working class life on the language of the poor (Bernstein, 1971, 1975; Heath, 1983). Bernstein's early work asserted that social class is an independent variable that mediates between intelligence and language. From this posit, he argues that working class language is, in one fundamental way, nonverbal (i.e., that it presumes the social actors and social relationships of a conversation are implicit). Much of the meaning of a conversation is derived from the knowledge implicit in the social setting. Moreover, the assumption of a social relationship in working class speech inhibits one's cognitive ability to isolate oneself as an individual. In contrast, middle-class speech is characterized by this ability to conceptualize one's individuality, which also involves some sense of personal power and responsibility. The significant point for our purposes is that Bernstein's construction of working class language as somewhat divergent from middle-class language emphasizes the significance of mentors making a powerful connection to help them communicate across class boundaries.

In *Ways With Words*, S. B. Heath (1983) works empirically to study language in three groups. The people of Trackton are working class, while those of Roadville qualify as Blue Collar Respectables. Last, there is a middle-class group who live in town. Heath's ethnographic approach documents a good deal of Bernstein's (1971, 1975) theorizing. The Trackton youngsters are accepted as part of the environment; that is, there is an implicit social relationship that lends significant meaning to the simplest language. This nonverbal quality is enhanced by a language game in the home, where young males are encouraged to generate as many meanings as possible to a single word, further emphasizing the nonverbal subtleties of everyday language.

The Roadville families make order a primary principle of life and are comfortable giving instructions to their young, or teaching them to follow orders. Steele (1989) notes that this leads to some emphasis on hard work which is a basic requirement of upward mobility. Blue Collar Respectables, particularly women who have had responsibility thrust on them by the circumstances of life, discover the benefits of mobility incidentally. Some of the examples cited in the following sections of this chapter testify to the need for mentoring across class boundaries because the discovery of a valid principle still offered no vision of the future. That is one function of the mentor.

The middle-class youngsters noted by Heath (1983) were reared as conversation partners. They were treated as adults in many ways, as a means of socializing them for their future. The autonomous group studied by Chairez (1990) reported that their most significant mentoring was done by parents. Teachers, counselors, and friends were all subordinate to parents as mentors.

The issue of school achievement as a contest to establish one's dignity, which places the teacher in the role of a passive arbiter of personal worth, has been raised in a number of ways. Sennett and Cobb (1972) specifically depict this situation, while a body of literature on academic self-concept supports their position by noting that school does not play a role in the self-concept of many working class youth. In effect, the purposes of school have not navigated the barriers of class boundaries, which is why there are important lessons in successful mentoring.

The area of language and social class has created much heat, mostly in the useless debate over the alleged relationship between language and mental ability. This debate seems moot, at best, as there is substantial agreement that language varies by social class. These social class distinctions, as has been widely noted in the literature, impact school performance and the prospects for social mobility through education. The social class variations in language socialization further impact the ability of teachers and others to mentor working-class youth.

The Social Dimension: Sources of Mentoring and Inhibitors to Mobility

One's social class has an impact on the number of mentors available. Chairez (1990) reports that the lowest-income students encounter the fewest mentors and the greatest number of persons who tend to depress aspirations. At the lowest-income levels, parents, peers, and siblings tend to react negatively or competitively to achievement, or to otherwise discourage aspirations. Ogbu and Fordham (1987) report this same phenomenon. Chairez (1990) found that teachers were the only accessible source of mentors in her small sample of very low-income students.

Occasionally, upwardly mobile low-income youngsters of high ability may conceptualize or recognize the significance of school in their future, through counter-identification with their current circumstances, those of their families, or simply as a way to improve their life chances. The persistence of inhibitors, whether peers or parents, seems associated with the decision of many youngsters to isolate themselves from peers and community. As one informant, matter-of-factly put it, "I don't have friends; I have a career" (M. Chairez, Personal communication, 1989, Sacramento, CA, videotape #2). Those who chose some form of isolation or early adulthood reported that their peers were "a drag" (M. Chairez, Personal communication, 1989, Sacramento, CA, videotape #2) on their opportunity and therefore to be avoided. Others in the same circumstances are able to maintain social relationships and, in a fashion, win permission from friends: "My friends think it's cool that I'm going to college, but they tell me, 'Maria, it's OK to get pregnant and stay in the neighborhood. We'll still love you" (M. Chairez, Personal communication, 1989, Sacramento, CA, videotape #3). The same informant added, "I can't share any of my success with my sisters or my parents. They don't want to hear it. The only person I can share my success with is my teacher" (M. Chairez, Personal communication, 1989, Sacramento, CA, videotape #3).

Bilingual education programs tended to perform what Arivizu (Chairez, 1990) terms *cultural brokerage*, or managing the transition to a new social system while maintaining the connection of a common language and, often, culture. Within bilingual programs, many students attempted to mentor their peers because they had become convinced that educational achievement was a key to upward mobility (Chairez, 1990). Not all of their efforts were successful, so many immigrant youngsters tended to fall into a caste status. Students report that Jesse Jackson's exhortation, "You can be somebody," was useful in convincing them to pursue the educational path to mobility (Chairez, 1990).

Luck plays a role in getting mentoring and continuing one's upward mobility. Carlquist-Hernandez (1987) reports that some high-achieving Latinos flounder or get lost when mentorship disappears, while other high achievers encounter many mentors who guide them as they negotiate a successful academic career. Another phenomenon that occurs within the social psychology of the upwardly mobile is that they sometimes call a halt to pursuing higher positions and stop at a certain occupational level (Karp, 1986). These persons voluntarily call a halt to mobility because of the strangeness (to them) of the social terrain of greater opportunity. Basically, they feel like both strangers and impostors in the new social class. Their feelings of unworthiness may be related to a sense of detachment from their working-class roots.

Sennett and Cobb (1972) describe this phenomenon from another perspective in factory workers who refuse promotion into management positions, noting a sense of betrayal of their class peers as a reason for their reluctance. The comforts, familiarity, and acceptance of one's social class group and the sense of "imposterhood" can drain aspirations and limit the desire for further mobility. Carlquist-Hernandez (1987) also finds that high achievers reconcile the pull of the community with their upward mobility by trying to maintain some connection with their origins. This generally takes the form of choosing a profession or specialty that allows them to retain some connection with their origins, whether defined by culture, social class, or some self-defined primary community. For example, most of Carlquist-Hernandez's (1987) sample chose careers that retained some symbolic membership in their communities of origin.

Mobility and Working-Class Life: A Summary

The decision to become upwardly mobile is significantly more complex than simply wanting more money, although that is one obvious reason to pursue an education at any age. In some cases, financial desire causes personal decisions to lead a person toward becoming upwardly mobile, but this group appears to be relatively small in size. The detrimental aspects of working-class communities—the dangers, deprivation, low-reliability work, and so on—are well known and well publicized. Less obvious are the social *costs* of upward mobility, beginning with its apparent appeal.

The social psychology of working-class life, or what researchers and theoreticians have identified as ways of thinking and communicating that make one functional within the community, sets a context of membership, security, and meaning. These perspectives include a sense of identity or solidarity with the group, including acceptance by one's community and a high level of shared meanings that impact the ways in which people communicate. Growing up in a working-class community tends to yield only a limited exposure to the world, as life tends to be lived largely within the neighborhood. This makes significant the impact of the community in how young people think about their lives and life chances.

Those who become upwardly mobile may counter-identify with poverty. Some counter-identifiers totally disidentify themselves with the community and choose isolation from peers as a useful and acceptable way to become upwardly mobile. The remainder of those who become upwardly mobile do so because of the intervention of others through mentoring. For whatever reason, mentors are able to make a meaningful connection with working-class youth (or adults) and give them guidance that gains compliance in the behavior of the mentee. This guidance overcomes the attractions of remaining in the community and of the community, although it does not alleviate the hazards of becoming upwardly mobile.

Connecting and Guiding

Bernstein's idea of language codes, the merits of which have been widely debated, clearly has an impact on communication across class boundaries. While mentor and mentee arguably both speak the same language, the idea of some linguistic code that limits meaning, or affects how messages are understood, seems operative in the examples studied here.

Carlquist-Hernandez began her exploration of upward mobility to tenured or administrative positions in higher education with a focus on examining the contributions of culture to mobility, but it became apparent very early on that the 12 sample members, all of whom were Hispanic in cultural origin, had begun life in poverty and lived very much within the social-psychological factors of social class examined by Kohn (1977) and Karp (1985), among many others. The "Twelve," as she termed them, also fit Ogbu's classification of an involuntary caste minority (Ogbu, 1978; Ogbu & Gibson, 1991). That is, they faced barriers to mobility typical of a group that has been in historical conflict with the public schools. These factors have typically been treated as constraints on mobility in the literature.

The lives of the Twelve fit comfortably within the dimensions established in the literature. They were raised in ways that Kohn (1977) discussed and lived present-oriented lives with perspectives shaped by their social environments. As Karp (1986) noted, this perspective stayed with them through their careers. None of this is surprising; their lives confirm the literature in all substantive ways. The Twelve had made their way through society with the help of numerous mentors. Given the research on mentoring since Levinson et al.'s *The Season's of a Man's Life* (1978), this is predictable. Levinson et al.'s sample generated a "dream," or future orientation, to motivate them to achieve. This sample differs from Levinson et al.'s findings in that the dream was vaguely formed in a few of the Twelve and not present at all in most of them. Some mentors were involved in relatively long-term relationships with a member of the Twelve, while others had an impact on the shape and direction of a life when the mentoring relationship was limited to a single conversation.

How is it possible that a few chance remarks had a significant impact on the lives of the Twelve? This question piqued interest and formed a focus for analysis. Essentially, many social-psychological factors of social class not only shaped a perspective on the world, but this perspective also functioned as a set of conditions, or limits, on communication. When messages were communicated in ways that accounted for this perspective, they had a fateful impact on the lives of the Twelve. In the interviews, they were seen as turning points that gave direction to their lives.

The Mentoring Process

The mentoring process that had such fateful consequences for the Twelve had three basic components, including the conditions necessary for a successful connection and two distinct rules for guidance. All components are essential for the mentoring process to work effectively.

A Nonracist, Interest-Based Connection

The first component of connection between mentor and mentee is that the mentor's communication had to be nonracist. This was recognized intuitively, rather than being the subject of conscious analysis. Most respondents could not say specifically why they trusted someone's statement: "Coming from a poverty background, the survival thing, you develop that sixth sense; that idea that this is the way it is" (Carlquist-Hernandez, 1987, p. 107). It was easier for respondents to recognize and reject racist mentoring when there was a cultural context. One respondent explained:

> . . . I was a good student. I was an honors student. I got perfect scores on my Spanish SATs, but the nuns gave me double messages. Some told me that they didn't think I'd make it through college, and some said I would, and those who said I would were Chicana. (Carlquist-Hernandez, 1987, p. 109)

Once the intuitive decision was made that the mentor was nonracist and his or her interest in the individual was genuine, the mentoring was accepted in an unqualified way. Mentoring was rejected unless the connection was made. This finding is an indirect way of saying that the mentoring has to be legitimate; that is, it must have the person's best interests in mind if it is to work. Once mentoring was accepted, the guidance had to meet the criterion of intelligibility. That is, it had to make sense to the person receiving mentoring.

Guidance Defined: The Next Step in Mobility

To be effective, the mentor's guidance had to set a direction for the mentee in a concrete, immediate way. The mentor defined the person's next step in the mobility process. This may have been to go to college, or in some cases, just to think about the benefits of education:

> I can think of one right off hand. . . . he was a Master Sergeant, which was the highest you could go in those days. He kind of adopted myself and this other guy from New Mexico, to the point where they were kind of like our parents. We'd even take our checks to his wife and she would give us like our allowance. . . . He was very influential. He was always telling us "Learn, go to school, because no matter what happens, they can never take that knowledge away from you." So I guess that was the beginning of getting motivated to go to school. (Carlquist-Hernandez, 1987, p. 108)

This mentee went through a career in the Air Force before going on to finish his Ph.D. Others were mentored within the family and guided on a long-term basis. Effective mentoring in the family still met the same criterion of defining the mentee's next step concretely:

> My oldest brother really was conscientious about giving me advice and guidance all the way through. At one point he told me, "Look, you'd better get your ass in school unless you're big enough to whip my ass." He weighed about 220 lbs. and I weighed about twelve lbs. wet. I don't think he would have done that, but he was pretty firm that since he had never gotten the chance to go to college, that somebody in our family needed to. And he recognized that I was good enough in school that I should, so he really pushed me. (Carlquist-Hernandez, 1987, p. 103)

These mentors were effective because they defined actions in clearly understood, concrete steps that the mentees could take to increase their mobility. In effect, the guidance gives a definable, understandable link between one's present position and what Levinson et al. (1978) call the "dream." In some cases, the mentor helped form the dream, whether it was defined as education, college, or a specific occupation like "world-famous researcher."

The majority of the Twelve did not have a dream early in life to motivate them, and several stated that they had not defined a dream yet. These persons indicated that they lived life as it came and expressed no concern about the future. They had no dream in the sense that Levinson et al. specify. Instead, they continued to rely on mentors to define the dream for them, while they focused on the mentor's guidance. One inference to be drawn from this is that it is possible to mentor someone positively and productively, even though the mentee has no clear conception of what the advice means or where he or she is headed in life. This highlights the significance of the first component of the mentoring process: If the connection is made in a nonracist way that recognizes the mentee's best interests, it will probably be accepted unquestioningly. This is what might be predicted for a person who lives mainly within the framework of conformity and a present-time orientation. The final element of effective guidance also respects the present-time orientation.

Career Decisions: The "Good Deal"

The second step in guidance is that the mentor's advice must make sense in terms of an immediate, personal advantage. To put it idiomatically, the mentor's advice had to be recognized as a "good deal." In this regard, money emerged as one way to judge the goodness of a deal:

> I was measuring them a pool to sell them a space heater . . . and the superintendent was there with me measuring the room, and somehow he found out that I had a teaching credential. So he came over and said to me, "I will pay you as much as you're making as a truck driver in a year for nine months of teaching at this school." I told him I may not be able to discipline kids. He said, "Well, I'll give you 30 days. If you can't do it I'll make you my gas and butane installation man for the school and the apartments and still pay you the same salary." So I couldn't refuse that. By that time my first wife had gotten her teaching credential and I said, "What about my wife?" and he said, "'I'll hire both of you. . . . . " (Carlquist-Hernandez, 1987, p. 110)

The good deal provided validation for a career decision. It offered an immediate, concrete advantage. The goodness of the deal might be understood in terms of time, money, or any other palpable advantage. The Air Force person quoted in the foregoing went to school earlier than planned because he found out he could get out of the service several months sooner if he were going to start school. He took the best deal and began college as quickly as he could. What he did was the essence of the good deal. He chose an alternative that affected his life immediately, within his present-time orientation.

Mentoring and the Constraints of Social Class

The Twelve taught us that mobility occurred because their mentors communicated effectively to them within the social-psychological constraints generated by their class position early in life. The point of this discussion is to show how the characteristics of effective mentoring respect these constraints. The constraint that has generated the most interest in the literature is the present-time orientation of working-class people. This issue has been identified as a major deficit in the educational literature and generally recognized as an impediment to attaining middle-class status.

Kohn (1977) attributes this characteristic to the way parents socialize their children to accommodate the parents' work world. He stresses that the nature of highly supervised work requires a significant amount of conformity to external social pressures and a powerful sensitivity to the events of the present. The conformity value identified by Kohn may be part of the reason mentoring is accepted so readily, even when given on a momentary basis. Even if one argues with Kohn's analysis of how a present-time orientation is generated, others have observed and verified the present-time orientation of working class people (Cohen et al., 1968; Bernstein, 1971, 1975) The lives of the Twelve show that it is possible to achieve upward mobility, even when the mentee lives within the constraint of a present-time orientation. If mentoring is done effectively and consistently, mobility is not only possible, but also likely.

This qualification of consistent mentoring points out another value mentioned by Kohn: luck and chance. Our data confirm that luck and chance indeed played a role in the lives of the Twelve. Mentors appeared and disappeared without pattern in their lives. Some of the Twelve lost their mentors and lost their way. Those of the Twelve who had the most mentors advanced the furthest. The number of mentors encountered by any one person was clearly a matter of luck and chance.

Karp (1986) makes the point that the experience of growing up in a working-class neighborhood bestows a particular frame of reference on a person. This framework is used to evaluate others throughout one's life. One element of this frame of reference is what can be termed "street smarts" or situational survival (Carlquist-Hernandez, 1987, p. 84). On the street, many situations present themselves that must be dealt with carefully and quickly if one is to survive. The basic elements of street smarts include exploiting any opportunity or advantage that presents itself in the immediate present. Another characteristic is that judgment of a situation or person must be made rapidly and accurately. This is typically a matter of responding to immediate environmental pressure. The possession of street smarts is consistent with the rapid judgment of nonracist intent when dealing with someone on a momentary basis and also facilitates quick judgment of what makes up a good deal.

One more point needs to be made about the impact of present-time orientation and mentoring. Mentees understood neither the significance nor the impact of mentoring when it occurred. They followed the mentoring and, to put it in terms of a present-time orientation, mysteriously found themselves in college, or teaching, or administration. There was no consciousness of the process, except in retrospect. In her study, Ruffner (1993) experimentally suggests that a sense of the past is a prerequisite to developing a sense of the future. The lives of the Twelve tend to confirm her point, specifically when they sought to mentor others after achieving upward mobility by becoming tenured faculty or university administrators.

A present-time orientation remains powerful in their lives even today. Several suggested that they do not worry about the future, because some opportunity will present itself, just as it always has in their lives. Some sense of the future was developed by observing personal history and recognizing someone else, usually a student or junior faculty member, in a familiar position. One way to gather some perspective on the impact of social class, culture, and mentoring on the lives of the Twelve is to examine their careers.

Making Their Way: The Careers of the Twelve

Once the Twelve found themselves in college or graduate school, most often as the result of a good deal, they had to decide on a career. The main step was to decide what constituted meaningful work. Work became meaningful when it helped retain some ties with one's primary community. This usually meant choosing a career dealing with the needs of the low-income, Mexican American community, which was conceived of as a way to retain a form of membership within this community. Eleven of the Twelve chose to enter bilingual education as a way to retain their ties to their community of origin. These eleven all mentioned encounters with racism as part of their lives. The twelfth, who felt that he had not encountered any racism, identified most strongly with his field, mathematics, and now teaches.

Meaningful work affected the individual's development of a professional identity within an institution of higher education. Eleven of the Twelve pursued forms of social activism within their institutions while following the rules to gain retention, promotion, and tenure. By the time tenure was attained, almost all had developed a sense of themselves as role models and actively sought to mentor others. The kinds of cultural mentoring they performed included recruiting Latinos into college, actively seeking other Latinos for higher education positions, and actively becoming role models in the local community. Once the faculty had attained senior membership; that is, attained tenure and/or full professorship, they actively mentored young faculty and advocated forcefully for their positions. By this time, they had developed a sharply defined sense of the rules for mobility and sought ways to use that vision to help others.

Getting mentored was a significant part of the success of the Twelve, or at least those who made it to senior membership. Various mentors actively defined the next step, whether it was achieving tenure or taking the next step in an administrative progression. When one of the Twelve lost a mentor, a career became stalled. When a person had abundant mentors, his or her career moved upward in an uninterrupted, rapid way.

Racism remained a factor in higher education. Occasionally, this meant extra pressure on a tenure decision; more often, the battle came during review for full professorship. One of the Twelve was reviewed so frequently and quickly that he attained full professorship in less time than any other faculty member in the history of the campus. When racism was perceived, the faculty member reached a turning point. Initially, each person confronted with racism or perceived racism in a promotion or tenure battle thought seriously about giving in to the pressure. In each case, the person waged and won their battle within the academic bureaucracy. At this point, he or she felt ready to mentor others and "repay the debt" fully. Until the last battle was won, mentoring was needed; afterward, it was not. At this point, too, some of the Twelve developed a sense of possible career goals that were invisible to them earlier.

A review of the careers of the Twelve makes it clear that the impact of social class remains strong, even when people are upwardly mobile. Achieving middle-class occupational status does not endow one with a future orientation. A sense of the future may develop partially or not at all, but it is never attained in the way middle-class parents instill it in their children. A sense of street smarts and sensitivity to racism worked as well in the bureaucratic maze of higher education as they did in the barrios of the southwestern United States. The stability of the social-psychological framework generated in their early experience only serves to point out the significance of mentoring that communicated across class boundaries to the Twelve.

Mentors took an honest, nonracist interest in their mentees, even though their interaction might be limited to a chance remark. That remark, or more extensive mentoring, defined the next step in mobility clearly and concretely, whether that step was taking high school math, going to college, or publishing enough to gain tenure. Mentees understood what to do in terms they could understand, and they followed through. It was not until they were established in professional careers, and often not until they had to stand and fight for themselves in those careers, that their own mobility process became clear to them. The history of their mobility path became a vision of possible futures for others. When this occurred, they were fully ready to pursue serious mentoring from the other side, as mentors.

Communicating Across Class Boundaries: The Rules

The keys to communicating across class boundaries begin with respecting the social psychology of working class life. This includes the boundaries within which communication takes place, as well as the significance of the values imparted by the community. Once these are accepted and respected, the person seeking to mentor must use this understanding and his or her own social resources to establish a genuine connection with the proposed mentee. It is significant that virtually none of the mentees covered in any of the studies appeared to respond to broad, general appeals to education and mobility. It was necessary to humanize and personalize the appeal by first making a connection.

The connection legitimates the message, but the guidance given must also respect the social psychology of working class life. The first rule of guidance is to define the next step in concrete, intelligible terms. The second rule is to make its appeal understandable within a present-time orientation, or in terms of a "good deal." The goodness of the deal may be a continuation of the connection with the mentor or a concrete demonstration of why the deal is a good one for the interests of the mentee. When these conditions are met, the middle-class message of mobility is translated and communicated across class boundaries. This kind of mentoring may not happen often, but when it does, it follows the rules dictated by the social psychology of working-class life. It is clear that the message of mobility is not lost on the working class, only it must be framed properly to be effective.

References

Bernstein, B. (1971). *Class codes and control: Vol. 1: Theoretical studies towards a sociology of language.* London: Routledge, Kegan Paul.

———. (1975). *Class codes and control: Vol. 3: Towards a theory of educational transmissions.* London: Routledge, Kegan Paul.

Carlquist-Hernandez, K. (1987). *Twelve Mexican-Americans in higher education: Their mobility process.* Unpublished doctoral dissertation, University of the Pacific.

Chairez, M. (1990). *The mobility strategies of successful Hispanic high school students.* Unpublished doctoral dissertation, University of the Pacific.

Cohen, R., Fraenkel, G., & Brewer, J. (1968). The language of the hard-core poor: Implications for culture conflict. *The Sociological Quarterly 9*(1), 19–24.

Gándara, P., (1995). *Over the ivy walls: The educational mobility of low-income Chicanos.* Albany: State University of New York Press.

Han, W. S. (1969). Two conflicting themes: Common values vs. class differential values. *American Sociological Review 34,* 679–690.

Heath, S. B. (1983). *Ways with words.* Cambridge and New York: Cambridge University Press.

Hobsbawm, E. (1996). *The age of revolution.* New York: Vintage Books.

Karp, D. A. (1986). You can take the boy out of Dorchester, but you can't take Dorchester out of the boy: Toward a social psychology of mobility. *Symbolic Interaction 9*(1), 19–36.

Kohn, M. L. (1977). *Class and conformity: A study in values.* Chicago: University of Chicago Press.

Levinson, D. J. et al. (1978). *The seasons of a man's life.* New York: Ballantine.

Mc Laren, P. (1989). *Life in schools: An introduction to critical pedagogy in the foundations of education.* New York and London: Longman.

Ogbu, J. U. (1978). *Minority education and caste: The American system in perspective.* New York: Academic Press.

Ogbu J. U., & Fordham, S. (1987). Black students' school success: Coping with the burden of acting white. *The Urban Review, 18,* 176–206.

Ogbu, J. U., & Gibson, M. (1991). *Minority status and schooling: A comparative study of immigrant and involuntary minorities.* New York: Garland.

Ruffner, T. (1993). *A study of time orientation, temporal integration, and reading comprehension.* Unpublished doctoral dissertation, University of the Pacific.

Sennett, R., & Cobb, J. (1972). *The hidden injuries of class.* Englewood Cliffs, NJ: Prentice Hall.

Steele, W. M. (1989). *Blue collar ministry.* Washington, DC: Alban Institute.

Strauss, A., & Corbin, J. (1990). *Basics of qualitative research.* Newbury Park, CA: Sage.

Valentine, B. (1978). *Hustling and other hard work: Life styles in the ghetto.* New York: Free Press.

Willis, P. (1977). *Learning to labor.* Aldershot, UK: Gower.

CHAPTER TWENTY-ONE

Discourse(s) of Local Literacy Practices in Adolescent Jail Classrooms

Cultural Mediation Through Critical Race Theory

BRETT ELIZABETH BLAKE

> Can't be a lawyer if you're a nigger.
> (Terrell, personal communication, 1997)

Introduction

Terrell and I were talking about career choices. Terrell was excited about continuing his education at the local community college when he got out of jail, although he feared that there was not much available for young men "like him." I met Terrell the first day I came to the jail. He was standing in front of one of the classrooms, talking to the teacher, and when I came in, he moved immediately toward me with his hand, outstretched. Quite frankly, I was taken aback. I certainly did not expect "these" kids to have the wherewithal to walk right up to an adult (a White adult) extend his hand, and introduce himself. If I had closed my eyes, Terrell and I could have been playing out this scene in one of the affluent White schools nearby, where this kind of behavior, I thought, probably occurred on a regular basis.

Terrell had learned to play the game, a game he knew was a prerequisite for his attempts at entering "mainstream," White American society: to successfully engage with "schooled literacy" to receive his "General Educational

Development (GED)"; to have learned to speak to adults (teachers, guards) as politely and deferentially as possible; to have shown signs of rehabilitation and humility; and even to have tried out the use of what mainstream American society might describe as "impeccable" manners in welcoming a newcomer like me into the classroom.

The purpose of this chapter is to explore the "local literacies" (Street, 1995) of incarcerated youths by situating their lives through their "local" literacy practices (i.e., reading, writing, and speaking) in a methodological context/framework based on critical race theory. Analyses of how deeply and profoundly race, ethnicity, class, and gender shaped perceptions, assumptions, and expectations of these youths' engagements with these literacy activities offer one crucial way in which to narrate these youths' own experiences and to excavate their voices across a wide range of life's activities, giving both their lives and their subsequent local literacies value. In turn, I argue, that this excavation works toward offering important implications for both research and practice, and is guided by the following questions.

What can these youths' local literacies tell us about schools and society? How does a "critical race methodology" help to frame who these youths are and why they develop their own sets of literacy practices as they engage with the world? And, finally, what does an analysis of their literacies tell us about schools, about how to change the discourse(s) of the schools, and about how to affect change throughout the current educational discourse in a move toward a more diverse dialog?

Theoretical Perspectives

Incarcerated youths in the United States are a particular brand of adolescents—a group of kids who Ayers (1997) has aptly labeled, "multiply-marginalized." Of color, poor, often speakers of an urban dialect or another language, these are the adolescents who, feared by most yet described by few, have either dropped out of school, plan to drop out of school, or have been "dropped" from school, only to end up on the streets or in the jails. Ultimately, it is here that these multiply-marginalized youths develop their own lives and literacies within a cultural space far removed physically and psychologically from White, middle-class America and the "schooled literacy" practices of White, middle-class American schools.

Much research has been written on the prison population in general (e.g., funding, new sites for building, changing population, public awareness and opinion [*The New York Times*, August 8, 1997, p. A16]), and a significant, yet small, body of literature has been written on the positive correlation between youth school dropout rates and the incidence of incarceration (Fine,

1994; Ayers, 1997; Blake, 2004). Little, however, has been written to describe the potential magnitude of this correlation and its connection to, and the significance of, the learning experiences of these youths.

This is a crucial area for educational research, particularly for youths of color. In 1995, one out of every three Black men between the ages of 18 and 30 was either incarcerated or caught up in the criminal justice system in some way. The homicide rate for Black youths ages 15–24 was seven to eight times higher than that of White youths of comparable ages. At the turn of the twenty-first century, two-thirds of the US prison population are persons of color, with the adolescent population showing the most growth. More adolescents of color in jails, of course, translates into fewer adolescents of color in schools.

This chapter begins by situating Terrell's and fellow inmates' local literacies within the framework of Street's (1995, 2001) notion of an "ideological" model for literacy. The author then describes how the tenets of "critical race theory" lay a solid theoretical foundation for a "critical race methodology" that in its most simplistic form "offers space to conduct and present research grounded in the experiences and knowledge of people of color" (Solorzano & Yosso, 2002, p. 23). Finally, the author presents the local literacies of the youths themselves, using critical race methodology to explore more deeply the stories and narratives, to analyze them more honestly, and to offer implications for both research and practice, as these youths' lives and literacies are excavated through their own stories and narratives, moving toward what, it is hoped, are opportunities for a more diverse dialog.

Local Versus Schooled Literacies: A Move Toward an "Ideological" Literacy

Literacy is associated with the status quo. Among the multiply-marginalized youths with whom I have worked, schooled literacy practices actually work *against* their success. Many of these students have endured years of racism by being told they simply do not have the ability to become literate in today's technological society, and as a result, these students have eschewed the attainment of literacy altogether. Fueled in large part by a return to the assessment of literacy and literacy learning in discrete and decontextualized ways (that are tied inextricably to predetermined standards and teacher accountability and are couched in traditional kinds of educational discourse), advocating for local literacies as measures of success continues to be an uphill battle, one often fraught with bias and fear amidst a social climate in the United States that has become more guarded and more suspicious.

As literacy practices are being increasingly canonized around the world (see various accounts on standards and reform in the United States, literacy reform in South Africa, and national curriculum reform in the United Kingdom and the Czech Republic), however, fueling a backlash toward alternative, more holistic perspectives on teaching literacy, challenges are emerging from a body of international and critical literacy scholars whose work is based on theoretical frameworks based in sociolinguistics, ethnography, the ethnography of communication, and of course, the new literacy studies (Gee, 1990; Willinsky, 1990; Horn & Kincheloe, 2001).

Led philosophically by Brian Street (1995) and his work in South Africa, Iran, and the United Kingdom; Hornberger and Skilton-Sylvester (1998) with their work in Cambodia, Puerto Rico, the United States, and among indigenous populations in the Andes Mountains; and Kell (1997) in post-apartheid South Africa with her work among the settlement populations in Cape Town, researchers have fashioned an ideological approach to literacy that, as a critical perspective, repositions entirely the notion of what it means to become literate in today's world. Rather than solely reflecting the outcomes of "schooled literacy," their work emphasizes, simply yet eloquently, that throughout the world, literacy practices and behaviors are, regardless of the government or schools' efforts, in reality, grounded in the everyday lives and experiences of people in their homes and communities.

These scholars write about a crucial need for the synthesis of various definitions of literacy to include those that are deemed alternative and/or holistic in nature. Specifically, for example, Street (1995, 2001) puts forth an ideological model that subsumes rather than excludes the work of what he calls the "rational model"; Hornberger and Skilton-Sylvester (1998) envision a continuum where literacy learners are encouraged to journey along all points; and Kell (1997) calls for those in power to understand literacy as a two-way process in which, as those in power provide literacy access to those not in power, those in power learn, too, to "read . . . with [the] understanding of the discourses of those who have been marginalized" (p. 19).

Specifically, Street's (1995) notion of local literacies reconceptualizes the traditional/rational ideal of literacy, broadening its scope to include a strong, ideological base. That is, literacy becomes an *ideological* practice that is embedded in the everyday social and cultural lives of people—their local literacies—and reflects, therefore, not a lack of traditional skills but an addition, a complement to that which is most often taught in schools, and thereby reified by society and government.

In Street's (1995, 2001) view, the reification of schooled literacy occurs because schooled literacy is seen as something autonomous, universal, and neutral—a "gift" that a government or an educational system bestows upon a people in order to lead them to "good social practices" (p. 4). And schooled literacy, too, is seen as a civilizing agent, an equalizing factor that ameliorates the lack of social and economic opportunities that poor, Black, non-English-speaking students would otherwise experience.

In classrooms, then, schooled literacy practices are realized through the teaching of Standard English (exclusively) and the use of a Western canon that not only directs (again, see national and state mandates in the United States and in the United Kingdom) literacy and literary choices, but literacy discourse(s) and practices as well. Indeed, in Kell's (1997) words, schooled literacy goes so far as to offer only one interpretive framework for meaning and is therefore "sanctioned and . . . framed from within particular textual interpretative processes currently being canonized" (p. 242).

A move toward acknowledging and accepting the local literacies of many students indeed represents an important ideological and conceptual shift in how the processes of reading and writing are directed, interpreted, and assessed, and in turn how these practices are represented in the current educational discourse, helping to shape larger, more powerful policy decisions for multiply-marginalized students across the United States.

Critical Race Theory: Historical Roots

Critical race theory emerged as a bona fide body of scholarship due to the work of legal scholars like Derrick Bell. From a legal perspective, critical race theory was not only seen as a powerful tool to reflect critically on the racial order but also to develop new constructs and formulations from which to legally analyze important historical, social, and political events such as slavery, civil rights, and the continuation and entrenchment of racism throughout our society.

Importantly, this new discourse found its way into the education dialog, where there has evolved a framework that can analyze race as well as "define, expose, and address *educational* problems" (Parker & Lynn, 2002, p. 7) (italics added). This framework also seeks to:

> . . . identify, analyze, and transform those structural, cultural, and interpersonal aspects of education that maintain the marginal position and subordination of African American and Latino students. CRT [in education] asks such questions as: What role do schools, school processes, and school structures play in the maintenance of racial, ethnic, and gender subordination? (Lynn et al., 2002, p. 3)

Importantly, too, critical race theory not only prioritizes the social category of race, but also that of class and gender, as its epistemological base intersects with (and therefore is in part constructed by) feminist theory. For example, critical race theory (much like feminist theory) attempts through narrative to subvert the dominant discourse and highlight instead "other" stories within these social constructions. These social constructions, then, have the potential to become transformative categories of analysis that have *material effects on real people* (Fernandez, 2002, p. 46) (italics added).

Critical Race Methodology

In education research, critical race theory informs critical race methodology (CRM). CRM, in turn, offers the space from which to conduct, to write, and to present research grounded in the experiences and knowledge of the multiply-marginalized, rendering their experiences into narratives that can be analyzed as both sites of oppression and sites of resistance. Further, by exploring more closely these narratives (using CRM), the discourses of these students become public, and as they become public, they also become potential sources of strength, as well as critical sources of insight. Specifically, as a methodological tool, CRM:

1. focuses research on how students of color experience and respond to the US educational system;
2. contextualizes student-of-color experiences in the past, present, and future;
3. uses multiple methods; and
4. challenges cultural deficit stories.

Methodology and Data Source

A major concern of critical race theory is the failure of the educational system as a whole to educate equally the majority of multiply-marginalized students in today's classrooms across the United States. This becomes particularly crucial in twenty-first century America, where states are increasingly demanding higher standards and accountability for students and teachers based on prescriptive, one-size-fits-all curricular and assessment practices.

Advocating for the use of local literacies as a conceptual/educational framework becomes more powerful by using the tools of CRM not only as ways to uncover and explore the literacies of students' lives, but also as ways to reflect upon how these literacies can lead to a better understanding of language and literacy development in all classrooms, thereby leading students to "success" in meeting these higher standards and in challenging the status quo.

Data for this chapter were drawn from a larger study that explored and described the "culture of refusal" among multiply-marginalized adolescents in both prison and migrant-camp settings. The culture of refusal (Blake, 2004) operates on the premise that there is little possibility for youths in a society that disdains and distrusts the poor, especially if the poor are also persons of color. Poor youths of color realize this more acutely, as they are routinely marginalized both inside and outside of school. As a result, these marginalized adolescents "refuse," and this refusal is reflected throughout all aspects of their lives and experiences.

CRM has been used here to attempt to locate these experiences firmly at the "intersection of race, class, and gender . . . so as to decenter and complicate . . ." the underlying issues of race, while at the same time *making race the primary unit of analysis*. But more importantly, perhaps, the tools of CRM have provided an analytical tool for understanding *the imbalances* and hence *the inequity* in conducting research on/with those not from the "same critical plane." In other words, critical race theory puts forth the position that because deep inequity exists (in conducting any type of educational research among those who are multiply-marginalized) on both group and individual levels, researchers must "get at it," and in doing so, refuse not only the essentialisms of race, but also of class and gender, while recognizing that the *intersections* of these categories can lead to "important questions and generalizations" (Fine & Weis, 1998, p. 440).

From a methodological standpoint, critical race theory, too, allows us to see more clearly how language or discourse practices can be appropriated by educational institutions like schools as an antidemocratic force. Gee (1990) suggests that schools push educators to remain complicit in maintaining inequities and prejudices by allowing assumptions about multiply-marginalized students to go unexamined. Ideology is inextricably bound to language, and without an examination of language and an inclusion of certain individuals into the dominant discourse, schools perpetuate false stereotypes and dangerous conclusions about particular groups of people. Gee (1990) contends, therefore, that all educators need make explicit the power dynamics implicit in institutionalized language, particularly within the educational discourse so prevalent today.

Local Literacies: Stories From a Jail Classroom

Terrell

Terrell, it would seem, had shed the vestiges of the culture of refusal, successfully becoming the kind of adolescent society may some day label, "model." Prison personnel would say that they had "rehabilitated" Terrell and that the "change" that manifested itself both in his behavior and in his schoolwork was reflective of an effective prison program designed to do just that. And there was tangible proof, too: Terrell, they pointed out, began to write about his experience of finding "truth," something he could not have done without having had come to jail in the first place. In one of his final essays for his GED teacher, indeed, Terrell writes:

> I am most proud of getting a chance to learn more and coming to reality and finding out the truth about life. If I wouldn't have never came to jail, I would never found out the quality of life. And about school, one thing I'm proud of is taking my GED test and I feel real good to know that I accomplished one of my goals. Another thing I was proud to find out was knowledge is infinite.

Despite these outward appearances, however, Terrell was still acutely aware of who he was and how he would be received as he left the jail, GED in hand, to attend classes at the local community college. When I pressed him, privately, to tell me more about his career aspirations, he was quick to list off any number of jobs that he, as a Black male, would have difficulty getting. "Can't be a lawyer if you're a nigger," Terrell said matter-of-factly. To him, it was simply a statement of truth.

The Literacies of Rehabilitation

Victor

Like Terrell, many of the adolescents with whom I worked had found ways, when necessary, to fulfill the expectations of White, middle-class society, both in their behaviors and in their schooled literacies. For example, Victor Nunez, a 17-year-old English Language Learner (ELL), practicing writing an essay for an upcoming GED test in his jail classroom, wrote:

> "Why honesty is the best policy"
>
> I agree with being honest . . . Out in the world people lie about everything. Man cheating on girls, girls cheating on man. The only thing it leads up to is the girl or boyfriend finding out and that's when the fighting begins. People even lie about being married, having kids in their lives, or the crimes they committed . . .

Here, Victor makes clear the effects of rehabilitation on his life by asserting that honesty—a solid, American-mainstream virtue—is the best policy. And yet, still, Victor's voice and the experiences (i.e., the local literacies) of his life are still very much a part of how he expresses himself, how he relates to the concept of "honesty," and how he, therefore, relates to the world.

Like their lives, these adolescents' literacies were statements of truth that, when necessary, were neatly matched to and beautifully enmeshed in mainstream society's perceptions and expectations. Schooled literacy was a game these kids could play, a script that could be learned and repeated, when necessary. And yet, sadly, it was their local literacies that revealed the "truth" about them: the peripheral status of their lives and the diminished expectations they had about becoming "successful," happy adults and equal partners in a society that continues to see them as different, dangerous, and unreachable.

The Literacies of Resentment

The literacies of the adolescents in the jail classrooms revealed their resentment toward school. For example, many of the jailed adolescents admitted that they had actually liked school (i.e., during their public school experience prior to coming to jail) and that it had been a combination of outside factors (mostly gang and drug related) that contributed to their "failure" in school. In other words, the jail kids, for the most part, saw *themselves* as the failures.

Robert

I met Robert as he came straggling into the pre-GED classroom late one morning. The teacher later told me that he had originally refused to come (but was eventually "forced" to because school is required for jailed adolescents in New York State). This had really surprised the teacher because he always came to class "early and very enthusiastic." Robert, a 17-year-old African American, was "slow," she told me (his mother had been a crack addict and he had suffered the consequences), and probably had become discouraged because of their talk a few days before about how difficult college might be for him. Robert often got discouraged, the teacher told me. And he rarely got the extra help or attention he needed during his public school education. "He was just one of those Black, special needs kids who slipped through the cracks," she explained. And he knew it.

When I asked him about school, Robert told me that he had "done really well" and had "really liked school," and blamed himself for falling prey to the violent atmosphere of a tough, urban school:

> I didn't get in trouble till I went to the city, then I started fighting to protect myself. Then I just brought a gun everyday, but I got caught doing that. I liked my teachers there [names 3 of them] it wasn't their fault. Then I had to go to the other school [the alternate school for kids kicked out of the public system] and I still carried my gun and never got caught. There was this one teacher there who was always in my face, making fun of me. So, I called him "Gaymeister" and

I took him to the supply room and threatened to kill him and I pushed him. I paid my girlfriend to smash his hood and then I ended up here on a drug trafficking and gun charge.

Some of the other young men, too, talked and wrote about school:

Marlin: School's great, don't let anyone tell you it's school and all that. They try to pretend it's the school's fault. It's not.

Marcos: Just like he said, I liked school. I took ESL and the White teacher was good. School's fine, it's fun, but you gotta go through the streets to get to school.

Sal: It's a tough life. To fit in you have to be bad, to belong, to be like somebody. I really liked school. Every little thing they said. Here, you gotta be real forgiving.

Yet, even as these adolescent males wrote about their failures rather than the school's, they still resented what school represented: an institution that, for the most part, they had been denied access to; an institution that did not reflect their realties nor their lives; an institution, therefore, that they could easily resist and refuse altogether.

The Literacies of Refusal

"I only got three more chickens left before I don't have to listen to this shit anymore," Ben said. The young men in the jail marked the time until their "outdates" (the day they would actually leave jail) by the number of Sunday chicken dinners they had left. "Three more chickens" was a cause for celebration; with good behavior, Ben might actually avoid the red tape confusions and delays jails are notorious for and be released before having to eat a fourth chicken.

Ben was visibly unhappy as the GED teacher began class by having all the students take out a pencil to prepare to write. There were loud groans and a lot of cursing heard: "Fuck this class. We go on the streets and take this!" I figured Ben, like the rest of the students, who had begun a collective whine, must know something I didn't.

And they did. The GED teacher continued her monolog at the front of the room. Like dutiful inmates, however, most of the students settled down, having had sufficient time to vent, pencils poised to blank sheets of prison-issue lined paper. The teacher continued:

We're going to do a literature lesson today on style and structure, formal and informal. Now, pay attention because this is something you need to get on with your life—formal style and diction. So, on your paper, tell me what these mean:

1. style, 2. diction, 3. figurative language, and 4. tone.

"Fuck this," I hear coming from the young man who had said "fuck this class" just moments before, as he turns to me and asks, "Are *you* going to teach us anything?" "No, not today," I reply. "I'm just gonna hang out." "Cool," he says, " 'cause this is another dumb-ass question—fuck this school."

As much as these adolescents were astute at playing the game, matching the stories of their lives to the expectations of school and society, they were also very astute at rejecting the game entirely. After all, they knew that, in reality, the game was one in which they were not players. They stood alone, yet together, rejected as the "leftovers" that the captain of the team never picks as he chooses up sides.

Not all of the adolescents were as forthcoming as the young man who understood that "style" and "diction" really had no bearing on his life, and yet, they were still quite expressive. In fact, many of the students were very vocal about the mismatch between what they were expected to learn in school and their lives, both past and future, and their complaints indeed seemed to carry merit.

For example, when the GED teacher decided to incorporate the theme of "resume and essay writing" into her daily writing lessons, the young men questioned, once again, her insistence that these were skills that they needed in order to become successful in the world. In some very creative moments, in fact, rather than writing about the topic—"Do you feel education is the passport to the future?"—the boys debated not only the actual usefulness of the skill itself (i.e., essay writing), but also the relevance of the specific question she expected them to write about. Following are some of their reactions.

In response to the usefulness of resume and essay writing, Roger wrote:

> What good is writing an essay do for me out in the world? What would it accomplish for me?
>
> I'll buy me a resume . . . makes no difference.

And Jorge added,

> Don't need to write. I'll hire a secretary. She'll write what I say.

Interestingly, when asked, both Jorge and Roger told me that, in reality, having a well-written resume would make no difference in their prospects of getting "good" jobs, so learning the skill was "twice as useless."

The specific question that the GED teacher assigned, "Do you feel education is the passport to the future?" too, was met with resistance. In fact, an extensive conversation ensued among some of the adolescents, first around their reasons for not wanting to rewrite what they had already written (especially just to find something nice to say about education and its positive impact on their futures), and then around the idea that a different question altogether might be more appropriate:

> Why write it over? What's wrong with it? I'd rather change the question—like Malcolm X said, if you get an education, it's a *tool* for the future. If I had the education they had [e.g., Malcolm X and his followers], I sure wouldn't be sitting here writing this essay.

Here is a rare glimpse of these students attempting to change the educational discourse with which they were so familiar: first by swearing, resisting, and refusing, and then by (finally) promoting a different discourse altogether—a discourse in which they actually changed and reframed the question, altering, one might ultimately expect, the response.

As revealing as these adolescents' literacies of resentment and refusal were, other students' stories that made up their culture of refusal revealed a more troublesome twist: despair. Many of these adolescents' lives had simply been engulfed by despair, which, when unearthed, could alternately be seen as hopelessness, depression, withdrawal, anger or violence. The despair of their lives, revealed in their literacies, was simply pervasive.

The Literacies of Despair

Ramon

Like most of his jailed peers, 17-year-old Ramon was doing time for drug possession when asked to participate in one of the lessons on essay writing. Quietly, with his head down, he wrote:

> My mother jumped out the window when she was pregnant with me . . . don't want much to do with this . . . [writing].

Ramon was a deeply sensitive, thoughtful, yet frightened young man. More often than not, however, when I was at the jail to work and visit with the kids, Ramon was in "the box." "Ramon's in the box again. He had three fights over the weekend!" was frequently the explanation I was given by his peers when I asked why he was not in class. (Being in "the box" or being sick were the only valid excuses for missing school, as school was a required part of rehabilitation.)

I was never allowed near "the box," and despite descriptions from the other inmates about what the box was really like (solitary confinement to a cell that was separated from the pods or living areas of the other inmates), the only image I could conjure up was one similar to the "box" where the prisoners of war were kept in the movie, *The Bridge Over the River Kwai*. And in fact, after talking to both a prison guard and Ramon, I am not sure the differences were so stark.

Ramon was routinely put in the box and left there for entire weekends, and even though the fights were not always Ramon's fault, a guard confided in me, it was just easier to lock him up for the weekend. The guard explained: Getting "rid" of Ramon would entail fewer explanations, fewer reports to write up, and therefore, less work and fewer problems. Ramon was simply a liability to an "easy" shift, so he was often "punished" simply for the sake of it.

Ramon, showing little emotion, explained to me matter-of-factly his interpretation of one of the weekend incidents:

> Yea, if I had been out in the street, I would of shot 'em. Not killed them, but shot 'em, you know in self-defense. But they [the guards] won't report me and take time away [from his outdate—the day he is to get released]. They [guards] know it was their [other inmates'] fault. But, yea, so anyway, the sergeant brought me out and banged my head against the wall, then he used the handcuffs and all just to take me to the box.

Ramon had grown up being punished just for the sake of it. Living in a home with a father who was, according to Ramon, both "a woman beater and a kid beater," Ramon lived in constant fear that his father would actually come home from work on Friday nights, only to beat him, his mother, and his siblings. His mother, in a desperate attempt to get away from the abuse, jumped out of a two-story window, pregnant and terrified. Indeed, life had been very difficult for Ramon, his tutor explained (Ramon, like all other adolescent inmates, is provided with a tutor during the time he is in the box), and as a consequence, she believed, he had become clinically depressed, angry, and on occasion, extremely violent. Ramon had become so attuned to his own needs and capabilities, however, his tutor claimed, that he actually would volunteer to go into the box (for a weekend, for example) because he knew that, without his medication and proper treatment, he would be unable to control his temper. She continued:

> This is definitely not the place for him . . . because he just can't get what he needs here. He can't even get his meds, and the counseling available is, well, unavailable. He'll just get worse here.

Ramon's understanding of himself and of the family and world he had grown up in was indeed remarkable. As I got to know him better (he would not talk to me at first because he said I looked like a "narc"), his life unfolded through both his oral and written literacies in unbelievably sad and disturbing ways.

Ramon talked a lot about his upbringing, in disjointed, almost surreal ways. It was as if he was not even sure he had really been there, and he jumped around from incident to incident when he tried to describe just what had actually transpired. A sample follows:

> There were tons of us at home, I had six brothers and five sisters. My father got paid on Fridays and never came home from work. When he did, he talked shit all the time, what a punk. I needed my father as a role model, if a father says not to fight . . . that's why I got into all fights, 'cause my father wasn't there for me. I would just look at my mother like . . . I wouldn't listen . . . with a father, he'd kick your ass . . . hard for kids to say "you not with that."

Ramon related his upbringing to his own slow start in taking responsibility for his family:

> When I had my son, it changed my way of thinking—didn't want him, I was still in school, no job. My cousin, he helped me out, I was working at the car wash, and the mom was taking care of the clothes and school. But, yea, my cousin went upstate [to a maximum security prison] and he just had a baby and didn't even get to see him. He had got a paid lawyer, so he would have gotten worse. After two kids, I just started smoking cocaine. It had really hurted me when I had found out my mother smoked the pipe . . .

And yet, even in Ramon there was a glimmer of hope. Just before his release date, he talked to me about "learning to take care of his children" and of wanting to attend the School of the Arts, where a female cousin of his went and was very happy and successful. In fact, the last time we talked, Ramon presented me with his first (!) written piece titled, "My Life," adding verbally that going to the School of the Arts might be the best thing for him:

> Maybe I could stay out of trouble there—you know it's a school for art, cooking classes, and theatre.

Little did he know, however, that he would not be allowed in any public school in the city. The district had "banned" him—in essence reinforcing the culture of refusal that they, as an institution, created for him, a culture from which, effectively now, Ramon had no escape.

MJ

MJ, a 20-year-old young man, labeled "borderline mentally retarded" and often called "a big kid in a man's body," was another such student. But for him, jail, it seemed, had become a safe place—a place where he could talk about himself and his life, a place where he could be the "older brother," a place where he could reflect and even cry.

MJ's life story unfolded to me much like Ramon's did: in bits and pieces, with powerful images and reflections that sometimes intertwined and other times bumped up against one another, contradicting themselves in vivid ways. It was as if both adolescents had never spoken (nor written) about their lives and themselves before, and as they did, they found out things about themselves that I'm not sure they ever knew.

Like Ramon, MJ talked a lot about family, who he was now, and who he envisioned himself to be one day. And also like Ramon, he spoke and wrote about the deep sadness in his life:

> Everyone always told me how dumb I am. I was born in Ohio, we left there when I was one. Left my father behind. My mother always said I'd be just like him—he was a bad man, and I never see him. And so when she moved away [his mother moved south and left MJ when he was still in junior high school] I just got in lots of trouble. I'm not very smart.

MJ was very much a loner at the jail. He always sat by himself, tucked away at the furthest table in the back of the classroom. None of the other inmates ever sat with him, and I had figured that it was because he was so big and powerful-looking that the others were afraid of him. One day, however, as I walked into the classroom, MJ smiled at me, and I decided, nervously, to ask him if I could join him at his table. After that day, I always sat in the back with MJ, my most trusted "observer," watching the processes of teaching, learning, and life unfold around us.

MJ kept to himself because he claimed he preferred it that way, and none of the other inmates questioned that. Indeed, he was older and more powerful-looking than most of the other young men in the adolescent program, and he seemed, too, to be at a different place in his life. He was a "thinker," I learned, and he struggled on a daily basis with understanding the notions of "manhood" and "maturity," especially in a world where he had been constantly reminded of how "dumb" he was:

> Yea, I'm in for 6 months this time, 'cause I'm a follower not a leader and being with the wrong crowd. But this time in here has really changed my life, but I feel like I'm dumb, I'm going to be 21 . . . don't have the brains . . . I'd like to pick up my life, I have so much time . . . I feel like I'm mature, you know I'm going to be 21 . . . I'm not like some of these kids . . .

But, for MJ, like Ramon, the despair came in overwhelming waves. Even when he had moments or days of feeling "smart" and sure of himself, the effects of the abuse, the abandonment, and the victimization kept coming back in real and terrifying ways. When I asked him what he would do and where he would go when he reached his outdate (which occurred when I was there), he told me, with a smile so genuine and a laugh so endearing that he almost fooled me, "not to worry." He continued, as tears welled up in his eyes:

> Don't worry about me. I'm alone. I don't get visitors, and I don't worry about it . . . you're the first person who ever "visited" me . . . I'm alone and that's the way I want it to be . . . give me time to think.

The deeply disturbing part, once again, was that MJ was a smart, sensitive, and caring young man, who, like countless others who ended up in the jail classrooms, had been labeled and thrown away by family, school, and a society that perpetuated horrendous abuses against him, once again engulfing him in a culture of refusal.

Interrupting the Dominant Discourse: Local Literacies and "CRM"

As the educational discourse of the twenty-first century becomes increasingly encoded with language that seeks to exclude particular kinds of dialogue and discourse (see state standards and accountability measures throughout the country related to the No Child Left Behind Act), for example, a methodological model based on critical race theory may be one way educators can open up this dialogue to include those voices that have been both silenced and devalued. This standards-based, narrowly defined educational discourse strictly regulates the language students use—mandating skills and competencies, while dismissing the multiple-discourse practices with which these students, in reality, engage. CRM offers a solid framework from which both teachers and students can examine their fears around "troubling talk," as well as add insights to existing theoretical understandings of multiple-discourse patterns, schooled and local literacy practices, and hence, teaching and learning itself.

Opening up the discourses of the jail classrooms, in effect, allowed students the opportunity to describe their lives and experiences (i.e., their local literacies), which most often others have undertaken to describe for them. By contextualizing these life stories within the discourses shaped by CRM, these students revealed the shared, often challenging and frightening, threads in their life histories.

Framing the local literacies of incarcerated youths such as those who have spoken here has the potential to probe deeper into the ways in which current educational discourse excludes the dialogs of many of our students and how, then, these dialogues go unexamined, left to the assumptions and value-ladened mainstream discourse of today's schools. This deeper probing becomes essential, once again, in today's climate of standards and accountability, especially where literacy choices, literacy practices, and literacy "attainment" are achieved in rigidly prescribed and narrow ways.

Final Thoughts and Questions for Future Research and Teaching

How can critical race theory help researchers and teachers provide a theoretical grounding more appropriate to the local literacies of multiply-marginalized adolescents like those whose stories are shared in this chapter? How does using "race" as *the* unit of analysis help not only to build theories of race and racism in schools, but also to make those theories public? Ultimately, then, can educators work toward new discourses that challenge the status quo? Can diverse discourses become prevalent in the language of the standards, testing, and accountability movements of today? And if so, can it help not just in theory, but in practice, the actual subordination students like those in this chapter endure?

Educators need to reject the notion of an autonomous literacy as the only valid form of literacy and embrace the local literacies of the classroom. This, in turn, helps highlight and emphasize the centrality of the social nature of literacy in reflecting the multiple ways in which context, culture, and material conditions affect specific literacy practices and the discourses that are embedded in, and thereby surround and engulf, these literacy practices.

Further, however, and perhaps more crucially, it seems apparent that educational researchers must, if they are going to counter the current educational dialog—the dialog of standards, one-size-fits-all curricula, and accountability measures that only account for those privileged enough to speak and write within the dominant discourse—consider the potential of critical race theory both as a framework from which to explore diverse discourses in schools and as a tool for analysis, as they search for ways to bring such discourses into the mainstream. Indeed, according to Lynn et al. (2002), critical race theory has the ability to *unify* "existing critical explications of educational phenomena in education and to provide more theoretical grounding and direction for educators who are concerned with the issues of racial, ethnic, and gender inequality in the US educational system" (p. 5). And in this search, it is hoped that researchers are not afraid of the discourses that they help make public, because it is only in making such diverse discourses public, that we can truly interrupt the current, and potentially dangerous, educational discourse so prevalent in our schools.

References

Ayers, W. (1997). Foreword. In B. E. Blake (Ed.), *She say, he say: Urban girls write their lives.* Albany: State University of New York Press.

Blake, B. E. (2004). *A culture of refusal: The lives and literacies of out-of-school adolescents.* New York: Peter Lang.

Fernandez, L. (2002). Telling stories about school: Using critical race and Latino critical theories to document Latina/Latino education and resistance. *Qualitative Inquiry 8*, 45–66.

Fine, M. (1994). Working the hyphens: Reinventing self and other in qualitative research. In N. K. Denzin, & Y. S. Lincoln (Eds.), *Handbook of qualitative research.* Thousand Oaks, CA: Sage.

Fine, M., & Weis, L. (1998). Crime stories: A critical look through race, ethnicity, and gender. *Qualitative Studies in Education 11*, 435–460.

Gee, J. (1990). *Social linguistics and literacies: Ideology in discourse.* New York: Taylor & Francis.

Horn, R., & Kincheloe, J. (Eds.). (2001). *American standards: Quality education in a complex world.* New York: Peter Lang.

Hornberger, N., & Skilton-Sylvester (1998). *Revisiting the continua of biliteracy: International and critical perspectives.* Paper presented at the annual meeting of the American Education Research Association (AERA), San Diego, CA.

Kell, C. (1997). Literacy practices in an informal settlement. In M. Prinsloo & M. Breir (Eds.), *The social uses of literacy: Theory and practice in South Africa.* Amsterdam, The Netherlands: John Benjamins Publishing.

Lynn, M., Yosso, T. J., Solorzano, D. G., & Parker, L. (2002). Critical race theory and education: Qualitative research in the new millennium. *Qualitative Inquiry 8*, 3–7.

News Article (1997, August 8). *The New York Times*, National, A16.

Parker, L., & Lynn, M. (2002). What's race got to do with it? Critical race theory's conflicts with and connections to qualitative research methodology and epistemology. *Qualitative Inquiry 8*, 7–23.

Solorzano, D. G., & Yosso, T. J. (2002). Critical race methodology: Counter-storytelling as an analytical framework for education research. *Qualitative Inquiry 8*, 23–45.

Street, B. V. (1995). *Social literacies: Critical approaches to literacy in development, ethnography, and education.* London: Longman.

Street, B. V. (2001). Introduction. In B. V. Street (Ed.), *Literacy and development: Ethnographic perspectives.* London: Routledge.

Willinsky, J. (1990). *The new literacy: Redefining reading and writing in the schools.* New York: Routledge.

CHAPTER TWENTY-TWO

An Industry's Delight

The Messages, Implications, and Uses of Positive Rap and Hip-Hop Media

LISA D. HORTON AND RODNEY WASHINGTON

Abstract

In this chapter, the researchers discuss the impact of hip-hop on popular culture, societal norms, and educational settings, as well as hip-hop's viability, feasibility, and legitimacy in curriculum and instruction. The purpose of the research was to determine whether students recognize positive rap and hip-hop, to identify themes found in positive rap and hip-hop, and to determine whether positive rap and hip-hop were economically viable. To identify songs for analysis, the researchers interviewed 87 students, ages 13–16 years, attending an urban, public, alternative school in the Southeast. The study also draws attention to the instructional appropriateness of utilizing the hip-hop genre in educational settings. Its findings show that, as with any instructional approach, educators must make evaluative decisions about what is acceptable and valuable and critically explore the options available for facilitating academic success in their respective classrooms.

Introduction

At issue for many educators and leaders is the influence of rap and hip-hop on urban African American youths. In this chapter, the researchers substantively analyze the lyrics of specific songs to determine if rap and hip-hop culture might be used to promote positive affective domain behavior. The following explores, critically and in depth, the relationship of the hip-hop genre to the educational environment, reviewing popular culture and its impact on students, what messages students learn from the genre, and how educators can discern ways of teaching diverse student populations. The researchers wanted to determine if students believed hip-hop could have positive influences and to ascertain whether there were positive messages in rap and hip-hop songs. Students also attempted to ascertain whether songs with positive messages could be economically viable.

Typically, rap has been criticized and labeled negatively in the media (Koza, 1994) for its influence on youth culture (Blake, 2003). The researchers' interest stemmed from the emphasis on arts-based education and research on music's effects on the brain. The guiding questions for the study were: (a) Are hip-hop and rap appropriate music for the school environment? (b) Are educators using rap and hip-hop beyond the performing arts classroom, and how is the genre used in educational settings? (c) Do students identify positive rap and hip-hop music? (d) Beyond school knowledge, can rap and hip-hop be used to teach academic concepts and, if so, what could be taught? (e) Do students recognize rap or hip-hop as a positive genre? and (f) Is positive or socially responsible hip-hop economically viable and marketable?[2] In exploring the guiding questions, the researchers believed it was important to initially establish a premise for using any type of music to motivate or instruct students.

Gardner (1983) included musical intelligence as a part of his multiple intelligences theory. Of the eight intelligences he identifies, the traditional concept of intelligence focused on two types: mathematical/logical and linguistic. Aldridge and Goldman (2002) believe multiple intelligences theory is a promising practice for instruction of students who do not excel in mathematical or linguistic areas. Additionally, brain researchers have shown that creation of music can affect neural pathways that control spatial–temporal reasoning particularly prevalent with the young brain (Sousa, 2001). Many mathematical concepts, including patterns, counting, geometry, ratios, proportions, equivalent fractions, and sequencing, are related to music (Sousa, 2001). Thus, nurturing a student's musical intelligence could promote achievement.

Even in the early 1970s, advertising executive David McCall came up with the idea for creating *Schoolhouse Rock* out of concern for his child's academic progress. He recognized that his 11-year-old had difficulty memorizing multiplication tables, but could memorize the words to rock songs.

McCall's idea to use musical beats to accompany academic lessons was presented to George Newall and Tom Yohe (cocreators of *Schoolhouse Rock*) and gained widespread appeal (SchoolHouse Rock.com, 2004a, b, c). Teachers continue to use music to teach academic concepts.

Literature Review

Historical Overview of Rap and Hip-Hop

The influence of rap and hip-hop on today's mainstream culture is unmistakable. This genre of music, which was typically indicative of African American urban environments, is now listened to in White middle-class suburban neighborhoods (Anderman, 2003). Rap, or hip-hop, began some 30 years ago, originating in the Bronx, New York, where it was used to discuss issues facing minorities in their communities (Blake, 2003). Hip-hop was articulated through a rhythmic play on words by a person then called an *emcee*. The first hip-hop song to have a widespread following was "Rapper's Delight."

As a new style of musical expression, hip-hop initially received significant skepticism from the music industry. However, rap and hip-hop have continued to flourish and have influenced the direction of many of other musical genres, including pop (Anderman, 2003), rock, and heavy metal. *Billboard Magazine*, the music industry's trade publication, compiles charts of sales and airplay of music genres and publishes *The Billboard Hot 100*, which lists the popularity of songs, is compiled from a national sample of sales reports provided by SoundScan, radio play lists, and radio monitored by Broadcast Data Systems (Anderman, 2003). Geoff Mayfield, director of charts and senior analyst at *Billboard Magazine*, commented that in the last half decade hip-hop has transitioned from largely urban-format radio stations to Top 40 stations (Anderman, 2003). As evidence of the genre's success, during the week of October 11, 2003, all Top 10 songs on the Billboard charts were by African American hip-hop artists. This is significant because having all 10 positions held by African American artists in October 2003 was a first in the 50-year history of the Billboard charts. Beyond holding all 10 positions, hip-hop music could be found on the charts for several months, which last occurred more than 30 years ago when Black artists dominated the charts in May 1972 (Anderman, 2003).

The success of the genre is also evident in the increased airplay on Music Television (MTV). Due to the popularity of music videos, today's youths have constant exposure to hip-hop songs by their favorite artists. Also, as Anderman (2003) observes, hip-hop is played in malls as music for shoppers.

Perceptions of Rap Music

Although there is a considerable amount of rap music with negative lyrics, there is also rap music with positive lyrics. Hip-hop addresses not only issues facing the urban community, but also issues facing society in general. Even in its origin, rap lyrics for inner-city youths have been used to voice the opinions of urban minority populations (Blake, 2003), as heard in the music of the late 1980s and early 1990s rap group Public Enemy. Other artists who followed the group also used rap lyrics to bring issues of racism and other social issues to light. However, they did not receive as much media recognition as those artists who focused on some of the same social issues with a hardcore edge (Dyson, 2004). Further perpetuating negative perceptions of hip-hop, some rap concerts were plagued by violent incidents in cities across the country (Dyson, 2004).

Articles that label hip-hop and rap negatively can still be identified in popular media. Although negative coverage of artists and songs in other genres has occurred, it seems that the genre of hip-hop, specifically, has been attacked. Negative coverage of the genre in the media has been accused of creating and perpetuating violent behavior related to rap and hip-hop. Some believe the West Coast versus East Coast rap conflict (which involved intergroup rapper hatred based on their respective geographic locations) was created, advanced, and escalated by mainstream media. The murders of the lead rappers from each area, Tupac Shakur and Notorious B.I.G. (Christopher Wallace), marked the height of the conflict. In response to an article by Chuck Phillips that appeared in the *Los Angeles Times*, several prominent hip-hop producers and rappers and a former Los Angeles Police Department (LAPD) detective defended Christopher Wallace against allegations that Wallace paid $1 million to have Tupac Shakur executed by a Crips gang member (Moss et al., 2004). Wallace was murdered in the same fashion as Shakur—shot while riding in a vehicle with his producer. Some hip-hop artists, producers, and advocates alleged these acts of violence would not have occurred if the media had not created an environment of negativity.

Even before the West Coast and East Coast media coverage, Koza (1994) researched rap articles in *Newsweek*, *US News & World Report*, and *Time* (the most widely circulated articles at the time) over a 10-year period, from January 1983 to December 1992, and revealed how the media constructed the hip-hop genre using the themes of violence, obscenity, hatred, crime, gangs, and anger. Eighty-five percent of the *Time* and *Newsweek* and 100% of the *US News & World Report* articles contained those themes (Koza, 1994). Koza found very little coverage of rap music other than that which focused on the lyrics. Additionally, some minority-targeted news sources have presented both positive and negative information about rap and hip-hop. More recently, popular Black publications like *Black Issues in Higher Education* and *Ebony* magazine have included both positive and negative coverage.

In a study by *Ebony* magazine, 12 editors of newspapers from Black colleges in the United States (Bennett College, Grambling State University, Howard University, Johnson C. Smith University, LeMoyne-Owen College, Lincoln University, Livingstone College, Medgar Evers College, Morehouse College, Norfolk State University, Southern University, and Spelman College) participated in round robin interviews in June and July 2003 responding to an 18-item survey about political, rap, sex, and civil rights issues (Simon, 2003). Of the 12 editors, 8 believed rappers were either too vulgar, anti-women, or both. Two of the eight spoke positively about rappers of songs with positive messages. Eleven of the editors ranged in age from 19 to 24 years, with one editor being 32. Eight female students and four male students participated.

Bill O'Reilly, a popular talk show host for Fox News Channel made the following argument against rap music and its influence on youths:

> If those kids adopt vulgarity in their speech, an anti-white attitude, and an acceptance of dope and violence, the only way they're likely to leave the hood is on a stretcher or in the back of police cruiser. Hard work and discipline punch the ticket out of poverty. Thinking up rhymes about cocaine is not going far on a college application. (2001, p. 9)

O'Reilly (2001) also indicated that in 1999 alone 81 million rap albums were sold. However, Blake (2003) argued that hip-hop will always have a profound effect on young people, particularly African Americans, because it is a vehicle of self-expression, a rallying point of activism, and a positive means of youth development. He further commented that as long as rap is portrayed to global society in a negative manner, the youths of African American communities will be judged unfairly. How urban youths are portrayed is particularly relevant because some individuals with little or no interaction with minority youths may form stereotypical opinions based on media images. With the increased music video airplay, magazine coverage, and award show premieres, rap artists are accomplishing new milestones. The scope of their audience can range from urban to suburban, and with this mainstream exposure (Anderman, 2003), the music industry has learned that the rap and hip-hop can be very lucrative. It appears that the rap industry's mainstream success could facilitate the genre being a prime target for political and social activists who focus on the negatives rather than how the music might be used positively within urban communities.

Even when rappers have made efforts to use their public personas to promote socially acceptable causes, negative images have been publicized. Some hip-hop artists, like rapper Nelly and T-Boz from the group TLC, have been vocal in their support of medical causes. For instance, Nelly has a foundation that supports bone marrow donation and research, and he and other foundation members speak across the nation at educational institutions to promote bone marrow research (Stewart, 2004). Recently, however, Nelly canceled a trip to Spelman College due to students' intentions to demonstrate against and raise questions regarding the sexualized nature of women in music lyrics and the demoralization of women in popular culture, according to Dr. Zenobia Hikes, vice president for academic affairs at Spelman. Male students from Morehouse College also planned to participate in the demonstrations (Stewart, 2004).

On the other hand, rap has been used recently by Jewish leaders to teach about the Holocaust. Wu Tang Klan's White Jewish member, Remedy, mentions the struggle of the holocaust in lyrics of the song "Never Again." He writes, "Never again, shall we walk like sheep to the slaughter/Never again, shall we sit and take orders/Stripped of our culture, robbed of our names/Raped of our freedom and thrown into the flames" (Oshun, 2004, p. 5).

Blake (2003) asserts that although a substantive body of positive hip-hop music exists, majority-run organizations may facilitate negative images of hip-hop by focusing on themes like excess, materialism, promiscuity, and misogyny. According to Blake,

> Quintessentially, hip-hop is evolving. It is moving beyond, race, ethnicity, and language to create a new culture. However, this new amalgamation of cultures into one culture has its drawbacks. As the new culture forms, it may dilute the voices of black and Latino youth, especially when controlled by white corporate media. The control of hip-hop by corporate media may have dire consequences for black and Latino youth in that it tends to promote artists with messages lacking substance, those who perpetuate the myths surrounding black and Latino anti-intellectualism, those that epitomize sexual avarice, those lacking political awareness, and those that represent unbridled greed. (2003, p. 7)

Blake (2003) also contends that Black leaders failed to participate, support, and direct hip-hop during its beginning stages because Whites initially dismissed the genre. Also, Black leaders were accused of failing to nurture and develop the next generation of leaders. Since hip-hop has crossed social, economic, and cultural boundaries, Blake believes hip-hop can serve as a powerful venue for mobilizing the African American community to make positive changes through leadership and that these efforts could have taken place at the beginning of hip-hop's development.

More recently, in an effort to explore hip-hop and its influence on society, prominent African American leaders, ministers, elected officials, actors, hip-hop artists, and entertainers met in New York for the Hip-Hop Summit (Chappell, 2001) organized by Russell Simmons, a leading hip-hop entrepreneur and mogul who is considered to be the "Godfather of the hip-hop industry" (Chappell, 2003). Elected officials in attendance included US Representatives Cynthia McKinney (D-GA), Earl Hillard (D-AL), and Benny Thompson (D-MS) along with Minister Louis Farrakhan and Martin Luther King III, and Kweisi Mfume, president and CEO of the National Association for the Advancement of Colored People (NAACP) (Chappell, 2001). Hilary Rosen, then president of the Recording Industry Association of America, also participated and said, "This growing movement is ready and willing to work with both sides of the aisle to make a difference in communities across the country" (Chappell, 2001, p. 111). To further those ends, summit participants agreed on the following initiatives: (a) the creation of a uniform parental advisory label for print, television, Internet, and radio advertisements; (b) the establishment of hip-hop mentoring programs to assist artists with personal, professional, and career development; (c) the collaboration of the hip-hop community with civil-rights organizations for political empowerment; and (d) the establishment of a hip-hop think tank (Chappell, 2001). Reflecting on the first and second Hip-Hop Summits, Simmons indicated that society has misunderstood young people: "We judge them too much, instead of letting them be themselves. I feel this is our best generation, and our best opportunity to make a difference" (Chappell, 2003, p. 178).

Michael Eric Dyson (2004) argues that the reactions of some Americans toward hip-hop music are shallow because of their unwillingness to listen to rap music. Dyson, a Baptist minister, further explains how our society created the conditions that developed this genre of music. In the chapter "In the Culture of Hip-Hop" from *The Michael Eric Dyson Reader*, Dyson writes:

> Rap is a profound musical, cultural and social creativity. It expresses the desire of young black people to reclaim their history, reactive forms of radicalism and contest powers of despair and economic depression that presently besiege the black community. Besides being the most powerful forms of black musical expression today, rap projects a style into the world that generates forms of cultural resistance and transforms the ugly terrain of ghetto existence into a searing portrait of life as it must be lived by millions of voiceless people. For that reason, rap deserves attention and should be taken seriously, and for its productive and healthy moments, it should be promoted as a healthy form of artistic expression and cultural projection and the enabling source of black juvenile and communal solidarity. (2004, p. 410)

One method of promoting rap in a healthy form is its use in educational arenas.

Use of Rap in Educational Settings

An initial review of the literature and newsprint, revealed that rap and hip-hop were used in educational settings in a variety of formats, including: (a) students creating educational raps to learn academic concepts; (b) purchasable curriculum aids/manipulatives using rap to teach academic concepts; (c) teachers using existing rap and hip-hop songs to teach socially acceptable behaviors or public service messages; (d) rapper-endorsed food products with educational messages; (e) rapper and hip-hop artist endorsements of social causes; and (f) university courses on rap and hip-hop.

Regarding the use of rap and hip-hop used to teach socially acceptable behaviors, Bob Peterson (1994), a Milwaukee, Wisconsin, public school teacher, used a number of approaches in his efforts to facilitate a socially just classroom. He used songs from different music genres, related to a variety of social justice topics, including the R&B song "Happy Birthday, Martin Luther King" by Stevie Wonder, which was used to recognize the civil rights leader, and the rap song "Mr. Wendal" by Arrested Development, which was used to provide instruction on the plight of the homeless (Peterson, 1994). Hip-hop was also used to teach socially acceptable behaviors during the 2004 Community Day School Conference held in San Diego, California, where rapper Chris Robinson, known as "CMC," spoke to educators about delivering positive messages using rap. The Community Day School Network is a nonprofit educational organization in California that promotes quality education and resources for its members (CDS Network, 2004).

Another connection of rap to educational settings involves artists using their economic resources to support philanthropic causes, like funding educational scholarships. Mississippi-based rapper David Banner, who holds both bachelor's and master's degrees, donated a total of $50,000 to five fans who found game pieces in CDs sold from his *MTA2: Baptized in Dirty Water* album. Each winner receives $10,000 toward postsecondary education, either on the undergraduate or graduate level (RapStation.com, 2004). In the public service arena, producer Sean Puffy Combs has sponsored programs that benefit underprivileged children. Rapper and producer Missy Elliott has volunteered through a national domestic violence prevention program. Rapper Busta Rhymes has worked with the Make-A-Wish Foundation (Chappell, 2001).

Russell Simmons, chairman of the Hip-Hop Summit Action Network (HSAN), donated $100,000 to Dr. Benjamin Chavis, president and CEO of the HSAN and the Hip-Hop Research and Education Fund for promoting awareness of the Rockefeller Drug Laws and encouraging youths to become registered voters. HSAN, a nonprofit, nonpartisan coalition of hip-hop artists, entertainment industry leaders, education advocates, civil rights proponents, and youth leaders, was founded in 2001 to harness the cultural relevance of hip-hop music as a catalyst for educational advocacy and other societal concerns related to the well-being of at-risk youths in the United States. HSAN believes hip-hop can be used to facilitate social change and focus on poverty and injustice (HSAN, 2004).

Other uses of rap in educational settings pertain to health education. Harry Terrell, CEO of Common Ground USA, has developed a line of hip-hop condoms called "Jimmie Hatz" to target the hip-hop generation of consumers, in which "jimmy hat" is slang for the word *condom*. Terrell's interest in the concept evolved when he was a high school baseball coach and had a student who contracted human immunodeficiency virus (HIV). Initially, Terrell believed that HIV/AIDS (acquired immunodeficiency syndrome) was an issue primarily affecting the White community (Doty, 2003). Through research from the Centers for Disease Control and Prevention (CDC), he recognized that minorities were experiencing the highest numbers of new HIV/AIDS cases. In an effort to (a) support his student, (b) facilitate a grassroots campaign on AIDS outreach and awareness, and (c) make condoms appear *cool* (i.e., socially acceptable), Terrell removed all of the funds from his 401k plan and obtained additional funding from family and friends to actualize his desire to save the community. Additionally, he provides information and research about HIV and AIDS on his website (Doty, 2003).

The use of hip-hop in educational settings extends beyond K–12 education to higher education as well. On the university level, hip-hop culture is being taught for academic course credit. Dr. Finnie Coleman, an English professor at Texas A&M University, offered a course on hip-hop culture including the history and artists of the genre, as well as the musical components of hip-hop such as rap, soul, reggae, and house (*Black Issues in Higher Education*, 2001).

Hip-Hop and Rap as a Source of Knowledge

Koza (1994) asserts that by disregarding rap as an art form, educators may perpetuate dominant power relationships. Poignantly, Koza states,

> Educators who acknowledge that rap is a significant aesthetic experience for countless American students and who recognize the merits of understanding and valuing the cultural experiences students bring with them, call for a broadened

definition of legitimate school knowledge, one that recognizes rap as a significant cultural artifact. (1994, p. 171)

Additionally, Kevin Powell, a public speaker and former hip-hop journalist and reporter for *Vibe* magazine, has commented that a generational gap exists between educators and students because educators fail to comprehend the population they teach. Powell states,

> Part of the reason why there is such a generational gap is because so few educators make an effort to understand the times in which they live. You can't apply '60s and '70s methods to teaching in the new millennium. You can't apply a jazz aesthetic to hip-hop heads. . . . You have to meet the students where they are. That's the nature of education. That's pedagogy. (Evelyn, 2000, p. 29)

Dr. Scott Heath, Assistant Professor of English at Georgetown, offers additional insight:

> One of the reasons that hip-hop is such a vital mode of African American cultural expression is its immediacy and its insistence on lived experience as a requisite for authority to speak in and about the culture. If you listen to rappers, it's always about where they were, what they did, that they will never leave. I believe that makes hip-hop an area where we might see theory and practice coming together inside African American intellectualism, where we might see an attempt to develop innovative approaches to using hip-hop as a method for organizing African American youth around issues that are important to their survival. (Hamilton, 2004, p. 34)

Moreover, according to Dr. Beatrice Bridglall, assistant director for Columbia University's Institute for Urban and Minority Education, "At one level, we need to document the genre. On a more sophisticated level, we need to determine how African American and Latino students perceive their social identity with respect to hip-hop's content, expressions and context" (Roach, 2004, p. 30).

Theoretical Framework

The data were analyzed using critical race theory (CRT). "Critical race theory enacts an ethnic epistemology, arguing that ways of knowing and being are shaped by the individual's standpoint, or position in the world. This standpoint undoes the cultural, ethical, and epistemological logic (and racism) of the Eurocentric, Enlightenment paradigm" (Denzin & Lincoln, 2000, p. 159). Components of CRT include the unmasking of racism, the use of narrative rendering, critique of liberalism, and recognition of Eurocentric privilege in legislation (Ladson-Billings, 2000). That is, CRT focuses on the racism "enmeshed in the fabric of our social order," the use of storytelling to understand people's experiences, and the premise that Whites were the primary recipients of civil rights legislation (Ladson-Billings, 1999, pp. 212–213). As well, CRT provides a venue for giving voice to marginalized groups.

The researchers used CRT to analyze the data because many hip-hop artists cite an overall misunderstanding of the genre by many segments of society and assert that hip-hop critiques stem from racism. Initially, the genre was disregarded by Whites and by Black leadership because it stemmed from the urban poor (Blake, 2003). Hip-hop is now also critiqued along racial lines because it has attracted a suburban White following. CRT's attention to race and "giving voice," both of which are also elements of hip-hop culture, prompted the use of the theory to analyze the study data. It seemed that the premises of CRT related directly to the contentions of those studying or promoting hip-hop culture.

Methodology

In May 2004, the researchers surveyed 87 middle school students attending an urban public alternative school in the capital city of a Southeastern state. All students were African American. Each student was asked, "Can you identify the names of rap or hip-hop songs with a positive message? If so, what is the name of the song and who is the artist?" The students were given a one-slip survey asking them to identify rap or hip-hop songs with positive lyrics and to provide the names of three songs. The surveys were collected, coded, and put into SPSS for data analysis. Table 23.1 includes demographic data on the student population.

Table 23.1 Student Participant Demographic Data

Grade	Frequency	Percent	Valid percent	Cumulative percent
7th	31	35.6	35.6	35.6
8th	56	64.4	64.4	100.0
Age				
13	1	1.1	1.1	1.1
14	17	19.5	19.5	20.7
15	48	55.2	55.2	75.9
16	21	24.1	24.1	100.0
Gender				
Male	53	60.9	60.9	60.9
Female	34	39.1	39.1	100.0

After collecting the lists of songs, we obtained copies of the song lyrics and read through the lyrics using a CRT perspective to identify the following components: (a) overall message/theme, (b) social justice categories, (c) negative imagery (if any), (d) possible educational use, and (e) economic success. To determine sites for viewing and listening to lyrics, we contacted two retail stores of two large national CD chains, FYE (For Your Entertainment) and Sam Goody. We posed the question, "If parents or patrons wanted to preview lyrics prior to purchasing music, what Internet sites could they view to ascertain the information?" Sales representatives at FYE indicated that their website (www.fye.com) allowed browsers to hear 30-second segments of songs (and sometimes the full version of a song) and that lyrics could be viewed at lyrics.com. Sales representatives at Sam Goody said that patrons could listen to lyrics at VH1.com. The researchers used these websites and others to view the lyrics. Nine songs were analyzed, revealing themes related to the following character education and social justice categories: domestic violence awareness/prevention, self-esteem, promotion of education, antidrug, abstinence/safe sex. In addition, the researchers analyzed the songs for images related to race/ethnicity, gender, and socioeconomic status. The following chart includes the responses of 75 students out of 87 (Table 23.2). For the 12 responses not included in the chart, 4 provided no response and 8 listed songs that contained sexually graphic lyrics.

Table 23.2 Student Listing of Positive Hip-Hop and Rap Songs

Song selection and artist	Frequency	Percent	Valid percent	Cumulative percent
I Can—Nas	25	28.7	28.7	28.7
All Falls Down—Kanye West featuring Syleena Johnson	18	20.7	20.7	49.4
This Way—Dilated Peoples featuring Kanye West	20	23.0	23.0	72.4
Jesus Walks—Kanye West	8	9.2	9.2	81.6
Waterfalls—TLC	4	4.6	4.6	86.2
Others	8	9.2	9.2	95.4
No Response	4	4.6	4.6	100.0

Limitations

One limitation of the study was the paucity of scholarly research regarding hip-hop and rap. To compensate for the lack of research on the subject, periodical data was used in the literature review. Other data included information from authors who are considered experts or leaders in the hip-hop arena. Also, the youths interviewed were from the middle-level population of an alternative school. That population was of interest because the students who attended the school were placed at the site either because of failing 2 years in school or because of expulsion from their home school site. The site seemed appropriate because rap music has often been criticized as glorifying antisocial or violent behaviors (activities that would result in expulsion) and for its use of slang. Through data analysis, the researchers sought to examine themes and to compare the study group with perceptions about the typical rap consumer. It was not our intention to marginalize the study population or to facilitate stereotypes. An additional limitation relates to the number of songs listed by the participants as positive rap and hip-hop. However, the number of songs is not problematic, considering the purpose of the research.

Data Analysis and Discussion

I Can

Analysis of Nas' "I Can" from the 2002 album *God's Son* identified the following themes: career aspirations; spirituality (trust in God); negative affects of drug use; avoiding overly sexual appearances; positive views of African and African American culture; importance of schooling, education, and diligence; the colonization of many African and Middle Eastern countries; and admonitions against gangster lifestyles and prostitution. The chorus, which is actually sung by children, says:

> I know I can (I know I can)
> be what I wanna be (be what I wanna be).
> If I work hard at it (if I work hard at it),
> I'll be where I want to be (I'll be where I wanted to be).

Throughout the song, Nas emphasizes positive behaviors and the importance of avoiding negative lifestyles.

Educators can use the song to teach a variety of concepts. Beyond the affective domain, the song gives a history lesson regarding the colonization of African and Middle Eastern countries. The song also helps students learn about classical music, as its melody is derived from Beethoven's "Für Elise."

The song "I Can" was listed on the Top40-Charts.com for a total of 46 weeks, appearing in a total of 8 charts, with a total running period of 96 days. During its peak position, "I Can" ranked number 11 on the World RnB Top 30 Charts. Nas received a Heroes Award for the song at the 2003 Hip-Hop Summit in Detroit.

All Falls Down

In the song "All Falls Down" (track number 4 of Kanye West's 2004 *College Dropout* album) is a critique of prevalent social vices, including drug use, materialism, obsession with brand-name fashion, overspending in lieu of financial prioritizing, or competition for the latest and trendiest fashion novelty. In the song, West attributes these vices to self-esteem issues and self-devaluation stemming from the influence of the majority culture. The song implies that the White population has been responsible for self-devaluation in the Black community and that the White community encourages a desire for items typically or previously only available to its members. Moreover, the song transitions to an economic focus concerning drug use and excess spending by noting that White men profit from such vices. The chorus, sung by Syleena Johnson, states, "Oh when it all, it all falls down. I'm telling you ohh, it all falls down" (AZLyrics.com, 2004a). The chorus suggests that at some point, an obsession with excess will eventually result in a negative descent or "fall."

Negatives of the song include the use of expletives and a negative statement toward law enforcement. Tensions have been growing between hip-hop artists and law enforcement, as some believe police departments in major cities (specifically New York) have special teams or units (called "hip-hop cops") whose purpose is to monitor rap and hip-hop stars (Century & Oh, 2003). Although New York Police Department (NYPD) spokespersons have stated that such comments are false and that they do not have the fiscal resources to commit such activities, one former NYPD police officers contends that such units exist (Century & Oh, 2003). In addition, officers from the Miami Police Department acknowledge their attendance along with Los Angeles and Atlanta Police Departments at a "hip-hop training session" hosted by NYPD where a binder was presented with information on rappers and hip-hop artists, key radio stations to listen to, and how to understand rap lyrics. Negative discussion of law enforcement can be found in the lyrics of many rappers.

Many of these artists have the perception that police officers unnecessarily monitor and harass them. These rappers view the treatment as racial profiling. Other rappers believe that when artists glamorize and glorify illegal behavior in their songs, they should expect that kind of treatment from the police (Moss et al., 2004). Perhaps West's derogatory statement about police officers in "All Falls Down" stems from the widely held view that police officers intentionally harass hip-hop artists. With the use of school resource officers and school support officers in schools, teachers could carefully and critically discuss criticisms of law enforcement.

Another negative in the lyrics of "All Falls Down" is that they address the issue of attending college with the implication that college may not be an ideal option for everyone. In that same vein, it should be noted that the title of the album is *College Dropout*.

Educators would have to use excerpts from the song to avoid negative messages and profanity; emphasize that the classroom lecture would only focus on positive portions of the song; be careful not to offend certain populations within the classroom; ensure critical discussion of the race-related themes of the song; and complete a critical and poignant discussion of the effects of failing to attend college. For example, college degree recipients typically earn more than workers with only a secondary degree. The median weekly income of male college graduates was $1,089 versus the $421 earned by male high school graduates (Bureau of Labor Statistics, 2003). For women, the median weekly income of college graduates was $809, and the median weekly income of high school graduates was $441 (Bureau of Labor Statistics, 2002).

With so many minorities failing to attend college, some may question whether the song endorses avoiding college. The song did not seem to advocate failing to attend college, but it did not seem to strongly support college attendance either. Although West is himself a college dropout, he is the son of an English professor at Chicago State University, Dr. Donda West. Kanye West says, "It's entertainment. It's my past. I dropped out of school because I wasn't learning fast enough . . . I learned from real life better" (Davis, 2004, p. 94). Additionally, West believes that his life is *his life*, and others should pursue their own aspirations. He explains, "I talked to some girl and she was like, 'you don't know how bad I want to drop out of college' " . . ."And I said, 'what do you want to do.' She said, 'I don't know.' I was like, 'Well, you better stay yo' a** in school" (Davis, 2004, p. 94).

The song has had significant sales and popularity with music listeners, as evidenced by its position on a number of music charts. For the week of June 4, 2004, "All Falls Down" was positioned at number 14, four positions down from the previous week and five positions down from its peak position at number 9. As of the week of June 4, 2004, "All Falls Down" had been on the various charts for a total of 49 weeks with the total period running 69 days. In terms of being featured on all charts, the song ran for 45 weeks (Top40-Charts.com, 2004a).

On the Billboard Hot R&B/Hip-Hop Singles and Tracks chart for the week of June 19, 2004, the song was listed at number 9 and previous week at number 6, having been on the charts for a total of 18 weeks with a peak position of number 4 (Billboard Charts.com, 2004a). On the Billboard Hot Rap Tracks chart, for the week of June 19, 2004, the song was listed at position number 5 and the previous week at number 3, having been on the charts for a total of 15 weeks with a peak position of number 2 (Billboard Charts.com, 2004b). Additional information was discovered regarding the position on different music industry charts for the song's initial appearance, most recent appearance, and top appearance (Table 23.3).

Table 23.3 Chart Positions for "All Falls Down"

	Date	Position
First appearances		
USA Singles Top 40	03/04/2004	26
World RnB Top 30 Singles	03/04/2004	10
Top40-Charts.com Internet Sales	03/04/2004	12
USA Singles Top 40	10/04/2004	23
World RnB Top 30 Singles	10/04/2004	9
Latest appearances		
USA Singles Top 40	12/06/2004	14
Top40-Charts.com World Top 100	12/06/2004	32
Top40-Charts.com Airplay World Top 100	12/06/2004	26
UK Singles Top 40	06/06/2004	21
USA Singles Top 40	05/06/2004	10
Top40-Charts.com Airplay World Top 100	05/06/2004	37
Top40-Charts.com World Top 100	05/06/2004	53
Muchmusic Top 30	05/06/2004	23
USA Singles Top 40	05/29/2004	9
World RnB Top 30 Singles	05/29/2004	27
Top appearances		
World RnB Top 30 Singles	04/17/2004	4
World RnB Top 30 Singles	01/05/2004	4
Top40-Charts.com Internet Sales	04/24/2004	4
Top40-Charts.com Internet Sales	04/31/2004	4
Top40-Charts.com Internet Sales	04/17/2004	5

Source: Top40-Charts.com (2004a).

Jesus Walks

In "Jesus Walks," also by Kanye West (track number 8 on the 2004 *College Dropout* album), the lyrics propose that "we are at war" with society, racism, terrorism, and *ourselves*. West asks for God's divine intervention against devilish designs and explores the need for God in one's life. West also describes people who are unproductive or involved in petty theft as "niggaz." As in "All Falls Down," he expresses disappointment with law enforcement. He strongly comments on police brutality and harassment. In addition, the song's lyrics contain critiques of common hip-hop songs in which artists discuss guns, sex, and lies, yet are reluctant to discuss God. West questions the perception that discussing God in a hip-hop song will not be economically viable. (From a historical perspective, pioneering rap group Run DMC had success in 1993 with "Down With the King," a song about being a believer in God.) Other themes in "Jesus Walks" include: welfare recipients as victims and rappers as role models.

For the week of June 4, 2004, "Jesus Walks" was positioned at number 9. As of the week of June 4, 2004, "Jesus Walks" had been on the various charts for a total of 4 weeks with the total period running 20 days (Top40-Charts.com). On the Billboard Hot R&B/Hip-Hop Singles and Tracks chart, issue, the song was listed at number 10 for the week of June 19, 2004, and the same for the previous week, having been on the charts for a total of 18 weeks with a peak position of number 10 (BillboardCharts.com, 2004a). On the Billboard Hot Rap Tracks chart, the song was listed at position number 7 for the week June 19, 2004, and at number 8 the previous week, having been on the charts for a total of 10 weeks with a peak position of number 7 (Billboard Charts.com, 2004b). Additional information was found regarding the position on different music industry charts for the song's initial appearance, most recent appearance, and top appearance (Table 23.4).

This Way

Dilated Peoples' "This Way," featuring Kanye West, track number 13 on the group's 2004 *Neighborhood Watch* album, is a song about a person's decision to change a negative lifestyle that can no longer be sustained. The chorus states, "I can't live my. I, I can't live my. I can't live my. I, I can't live my. I can't live my. I, I can't live my. I can't live my life this way" (Lyrics Domain, 2004). The lyrics make reference to discontinuing negative behaviors such as drug use and having relationships with multiple partners, and promote the idea that a person must leave behind such behaviors in order to change. The song also criticizes the music industry for its economic and social control of artists' lives.

For the week of June 13, 2004, the "This Way" video was listed as number 5 on the MTV Top 20 Hip-Hop Count Down, a show where online voters can pick the top 20 videos and have those videos played on the show.

Table 23.4 Chart Positions for "Jesus Walks"

	Date	Position
First appearances		
World RnB Top 30 Singles	05/22/2004	11
USA Singles Top 40	05/29/2004	32
World RnB Top 30 Singles	05/29/2004	10
Top40-Charts.com Internet Sales	05/29/2004	30
Top40-Charts.com Web Top 100	05/31/2004	80
Latest appearances		
World RnB Top 30 Singles	12/06/2004	9
USA Singles Top 40	05/06/2004	40
World RnB Top 30 Singles	05/06/2004	7
Top40-Charts.com Internet Sales	05/06/2004	33
Top40-Charts.com Web Top 100	05/31/2004	80
USA Singles Top 40	05/29/2004	32
World RnB Top 30 Singles	05/29/2004	10
Top40-Charts.com Internet Sales	05/29/2004	30
World RnB Top 30 Singles	05/22/2004	11
Top appearances		
World RnB Top 30 Singles	05/06/2004	7
World RnB Top 30 Singles	12/06/2004	9
World RnB Top 30 Singles	05/29/2004	10
World RnB Top 30 Singles	05/22/2004	11
Top40-Charts.com Internet Sales	05/29/2004	30

Source: Top40-Charts.com (2004c).

Waterfalls

Analysis of TLC's "Waterfalls," track number 8 from their 1994 *CrazySexyCool* album, revealed the following themes related to social justice, character education, and religion: critique of gang/street life, promotion of safe sex, STD awareness, warnings about drug use, value of self-worth and responsibility, and the importance of spirituality. The chorus of the song states, "Don't go chasing waterfalls. Please stick to the rivers and the lakes that you're used to. I know that you're going to have it your way or nothing at all, but I think you're moving too fast."

Waterfalls are often fast-moving and dangerous, with the ability to carry a person over the edge. In the African American community, many elders admonish youths for "acting fast," which means assuming behaviors that are not appropriate for their age level. Through the use of the waterfall metaphor and the phrase "moving too fast," the song suggests listeners should avoid life situations that are dangerous or related to "fast living." The overall message of the song is to encourage individuals to avoid behaviors that are too fast or will cause them to fall.

No negative messages were identified in "Waterfalls," but the CrazySexyCool album contained other songs with mature lyrics. Although "Waterfalls" was 10 years old, the students in the study still identified it as a positive hip-hop song. Many of the students would have been toddlers, kindergartners, or first graders when the song was first released; however, the song still made a lasting impression on them.

Some 10 million copies of CrazySexyCool have been sold (MTV Networks, 2004a). The success of "Waterfalls" with its positive message seems to contradict the idea that only misogynistic, sexist, and violent hip-hop sells. For educators, "Waterfalls" has several positive themes that correlate with character education and social justice initiatives in schools, including DARE (Drug Abuse Resistance Education) programs and Project Goals (an abstinence education program).

Conclusions and Implications for Research and Practice

Labeling hip-hop as a negative genre would be inaccurate and stereotypical. There are many artists whose songs fit into the category of positive hip-hop. Although some rappers and hip-hop writers question the marketability of positive hip-hop, the genre has had high chart ratings and has generated significant profits. Since both positive and negative hip-hop sell, as evidenced by Top40-Charts.com and Billboard.com data, artists and record labels need not hesitate to produce more positive hip-hop.

Moreover, there is a place for the use of hip-hop and rap in educational settings. If teachers want to find ways to connect with their students, many of whom are hip-hop listeners and consumers, these teachers should consider finding ways to integrate the genre into their lessons. Rap and hip-hop have impacted youths in appearance, language, behaviors, and norms. Educators can shift those influences to educational purposes.

Teachers can use Lisa Delpit's concept of involving the students' world/environment in the educational setting to promote achievement. Delpit (1999) asks educators to "use familiar metaphors and experiences from the children's world to connect what they already know to school knowledge" (one of Delpit's "Ten Factors Essential to Success in Urban Classrooms"). Rap music can be a vehicle for making that connection. As Peterson asserts, teachers cannot build a community of learners unless the voices and lives of the students are an integral part of the curriculum. Children, of course, talk about their lives constantly. The challenge is for teachers to make the connections between what the students talk about and the curriculum and broader society. (Peterson, 1994, p. 30)

Peterson (1994) also articulates five elements of the critical/social-justice classroom, which include curriculum grounded in the lives of students, dialog, questioning and problem-posing approach, emphasis on critiquing attitudes and stereotypes, and teaching activism in social justice. If the curriculum is to be grounded in the lives of students, educators must use genres that greatly impact youth culture.

Many youths enter the school system with knowledge of lyrics by their favorite artists. Their retention of rap lyrics and stanzas is evidence of cognitive ability. Educators can help students navigate to higher academic outcomes by using familiar material to springboard them into other areas of interest.

For example, with Nas' "I Can" teachers could play Beethoven's "Für Elise" as an anticipatory set and solicit students' opinions about the originator of the melody. Some students would not be aware that Nas sampled the melody featured in "I Can" from Beethoven's "Für Elise." The discussion could serve as a springboard into listening to classical music. Other rappers have incorporated music from well known plays into their songs. Rapper Jay-Z used the melody of "It's the Hard Knock Life" from the play and movie *Annie* in his 1998 song "Hard Knock Life (Ghetto Anthem)." Not only can rap songs serve as anticipatory sets garnering students' interest in the lesson, but using music in the school setting also has positive academic benefits.

In an article by Dee Dickinson (2003), studies revealed that the schools producing the highest academic achievement in the United States are spending 20–30% of the day in the arts, with special emphasis on music. The same study cited St. Augustine Bronx Elementary School, which was about to fail in 1984 but implemented an intensive music program that resulted in 90% of the student population reading at or above grade level (Dickinson, 2003). In a study of the leadership of African American women principals in the urban Midwest, one participant commented that when she initially became principal of her school, it was performing poorly. Over the years, the school became one of the better schools in the district, a change the principal attributed to the school's becoming an expressive arts magnet (Hobson-Horton, 2000).

The implications for practice involve educators becoming more attuned to the populations they teach, becoming more aware of their students' interests, and using that knowledge to impact academic achievement. Educators often cite an inability to find methods to motivate their students. If students are interested in hip-hop and rap, teachers can capitalize on that interest.

There is a need for more empirical, statistical, and academic studies on the rap and hip-hop music. Most of the information on the genre comes from popular sources. More research needs to be done on the impact of the genre on education, including a long-term study of the positive and negative effects of rap music on students' behavior and achievement in school. To move beyond the popular belief that listening to rap and hip-hop causes students to adopt negative behaviors (O'Reilly, 2001), particularly minority students, educators must recognize that the genre's listeners include highly educated and highly productive members of society (medical doctors, pharmacists, attorneys, university professors, police officers, and so on). Researchers could conduct a comprehensive national study of urban and suburban youths who engage in negative behaviors, to determine if their behavior can be attributed to listening to rap and hip-hop.

The study presented in this chapter could be expanded to determine why students listed the songs they listed and whether or not the songs have impacted their lifestyles, to communicate with more youths about the genre, and to include interviews with teachers. The aim of this study was simply to determine what students viewed as positive songs within the genre. The study provides substantive information on the genre's positive potential in the educational arena and underscores the need for educators and researchers to critically discuss and learn from *and about* rap and hip-hop.

Endnotes

1. The height of hip-hop is evidenced by the fact that for the first time in the 50-year history of Billboard charts, the Top 10 slots during the week of October, 17, 2004, were held by African American hip-hop artists (Anderman, 2003).
2. We wanted to articulate that we recognized and acknowledged our own personal perspectives on the genre. Ultimately, we learned a lot about the genre and artists of the genre through the research. This research process helped confirm our stance that more critical, empirical, and objective scholarly coverage of hip-hop needs to occur.
3. For some reference citations found in the *Black Issues in Higher Education* website's article archives, we were not able to ascertain the paragraph number for the direct quotes.

References

Aldridge, J., & Goldman, R. (2002). Human development and learning. In J. Aldridge, *Current issues and trends in education*. Boston: Allyn & Bacon.

Anderman, J. (2003, October 4). Hip-hop setting the beat. *The Boston Globe*. Available: http://nl.newsbank.com

AZLyrics (2004a). Kanye West lyrics: All falls down. Retrieved June 11, 2004, from http://www.azlyrics.com/lyrics/kanyewest/allfallsdown.html

AZLyrics (2004b). Kanye West lyrics: Jesus walks. Retrieved June 11, 2004, from http://www.azlyrics.com/lyrics/kanyewest/jesuswalks.html

Billboard.com (2004a, June 19). Hot R&B and hip-hop singles and tracks. Retrieved June 14, 2004, from http://www.billboard.com/bb/charts/randb.jsp

Billboard.com (2004b, June 19). Hot rap tracks. Retrieved June 14, 2004, from http://www.billboard.com/bb/charts/airplay/rap.jsp

Black Issues in Higher Education (2001). Texas A&M offers course on hip-hop culture. *Black Issues in Higher Education, 18*(5).

Blake, R. N. (2003, February). Beyond the bling: A look at hip-hop, African American leadership and the Black church: Implications to African-American youth development. *Online Journal of Urban Youth Culture* (Institute for Children, Youth, and Families—Michigan State University).

Bureau of Labor Statistics (2002, June 26). *Women's earnings and education in 2001.* Retrieved February 16, 2004, from http://www.bls.gov/opub/ted/2002/jun/wk4/art01.htm

——— (2003, October 23). *Earnings by educational attainment and sex, 1979 and 2002.* Retrieved February 16, 2004, from http://www.bls.gov/opub/ted/2003/oct/wk3/art04.htm

Century, D., & Oh, M. (2003, February 18). Hip-hop cops: Is the NYPD at war with hip-hop? *MTV News Archives.* Retrieved 6/12/04, from http://www.mtv.com/bands/t/task_force/news_feature_020503/?_requestid=573833

Chappell, K. (2001, September). Hip-hop at the crossroads: Will lyrics and perceptions change? *Ebony,* 110–112, 114.

———. (2003, July). The half-billion dollar hip-hop empire of Russell Simmons. *Ebony,* 169, 172, 174, 178.

Community Day School Network (2004). Retrieved May 21, 2004, from http://www.cdsnetwork.org/Conference.html

Davis, K. (2004, June). The many faces of Kanye West. *Ebony,* 90, 92, 94.

Delpit, L. D. (1999). *Ten factors essential to success in urban classrooms.* Speech presented at the 1999 Fall Forum of the Coalition for Essential Schools. Retrieved June 15, 2004, from http://www.essentialschools.org/pub/ces_docs/fforum/1999/speeches/delpit_speech99.html

Denzin, N. K., & Lincoln, Y. S. (2000). Part II: Paradigms and perspectives in transition. In Norman K. Denzin, & Yvonna S. Lincoln (Eds.), *Handbook of Qualitative Research* (2nd ed., pp. 156–162). Thousand Oaks, CA: Sage Publications.

Dickinson, D. (2003). Music and the mind. Retrieved June 9, 2004, from http://childparenting.about.com/gi/dynamic/offsite/htm

Doty, M. (2003, July 11). Hip-hop condoms to hit stores. *CNN Health News Online.* Retrieved June 10, 2004, from http://www.cnn.com/2003/HEALTH/07/11/offbeat.hiphop.condom

Dyson, M. E. (2003). *The reflecting Black: African American cultural centrism.*

Minneapolis, MN: Minneapolis Press.
———. (2004). *The Michael Eric Dyson reader.* New York: Basic Civitas Books.
Evelyn, J. (2000, December 7). The miseducation of hip-hop: Are today's faculty and administrators simply out of touch? Or has today's popular music truly corrupted the minds of a whole generation? *Black Issues in Higher Education,* pp. 24–29.
Gardner, Howard. (1983). *Frames of mind: The theory of multiple intelligences.* New York: Basic Books.
Hamilton, K. (2004, April 22). Making some noise: The academy's hip-hop generation scholarship on the genre moves beyond a project of legitimization into a more self-critical, challenging realm. *Black Issues in Higher Education,* pp. 34–35.
Hip-Hop Summit Action Network (2004). Mission statement. Retrieved June 10, 2004, from http://hsan.org/content/main.aspx?pageid=7
Hobson-Horton (2000). *Black women principals: Examples of urban educational leadership.* Ann Arbor, MI: UMI Dissertation Services.
Koza, J. E. (1994). Rap music: The cultural politics of official representation. *Review of Education/Pedagogy/Cultural Studies 16*(2), 171–196.
Ladson-Billings, G. (1999). Preparing teachers for diverse student populations: A critical race theory perspective. In A. Iran-Nejad & P. D. Pearson (Eds.), *Review of Research in Education 24* (pp. 211–247). Washington, DC: American Educational Research Association.
———. (2000). Racialized discourses and ethnic epistemologies. In N. K. Denzin & Y. S. Lincoln (Eds.), *Handbook of qualitative research* (2nd ed., pp. 257–277). Thousand Oaks, CA: Sage Publications.
LyricsDomain (2004). This way lyrics. Retrieved June 11, 2004, from http://www.lyricsdomain.com/4/dilated_peoples/this_way.html
Moss, C., Downey, R. J., & Reid, S. (2004, March 22). FBI joins investigation into the murder of Notorious B.I.G. *MTV News Archives.* Retrieved June 12, 2004, from http://www.mtv.com/news/articles/1485912/03222004/notorious_big.jhtml
MTV Networks (2004a, June 13). MTV top 20 hip hop count down. Retrieved June 15, 2004, from http://www.mtv.com/onair/mtv2/hip_hop_countdown
MTV Networks (2004b). *VH1 behind the music: TLC.* Retrieved May 8, 2004, from http://scripts.clickmusic.co.uk/click/tourl?url=http://tlc.vh1.com&name=TLC:%20VH1%20Fan%20Club&-refer=http://www.clickmusic.co.uk/Clickmusic_Web_Guide/Bands_and_Artists/T/TLC
O'Reilly, B. (2001, October). The rap on rap. Retrieved June 14, 2004, from www.worldnetdaily.com/news/article
Oshun, I. (2004). Jewish education leaders turn to hip hop remedy. Retrieved May 17, 2004, from http://rap.about.com/library/news/blmay2004jewishhiphop.htm
Peterson, B. (1994). Teaching for social justice: One teacher's journey. In B. Bigelow

et al. (Eds.), *Rethinking our classrooms: Teaching for equity and justice: Vol. 1.* Milwaukee, WI: Rethinking Schools.

Rap Station.com (2004, June 1). David Banner—crank it up. Retrieved June 10, 2004, from http://www.rapstation.com/today_in_hiphop

Roach, R. (2004, April 22). Decoding hip-hop's cultural impact: Scholars are poised to take a close look at the influence of hip-hop on the social identity, values of today's youth. *Black Issues in Higher Education*, pp. 30–32.

SchoolHouse Rock.com (2004a). *Schoolhouse Rock*—the official guide. Retrieved June 14, 2004, from http://www.school-house-rock.com/guide.html

SchoolHouse Rock.com (2004b). The creators. Retrieved June 14, 2004, from http://www.school house-rock.com/creators.html

SchoolHouse Rock.com (2004c). The history of *Schoolhouse Rock*. Retrieved June 14, 2004, from http://www.school-house-rock.com/history.htm

Simon, D. A. (2003, September). What Black college students think about sex, money and civil rights. *Ebony*, 72, 73, 76, 78, 80, 82.

Sousa, D. A. (2001). *How the brain learns* (2nd ed.). Thousand Oaks, CA: Corwin Press.

Stewart, P. (2004, April 22). Who's playin' whom? Overwhelming influence of hip-hop culture, rap music on HBCU campuses concerns students, faculty. *Black Issues in Higher Education 21*(5).

Top40-Charts.com (2004a). All falls down: Kanye West featuring Syleena Johnson. Retrieved June 10, 2004, from http://top40-charts.com/song.php?sid=9734

Top40-Charts.com (2004b). I can: Nas. Retrieved June 15, 2004, from http://top40-charts.com/song.php?sid=6341&sort=chartid&string=Nas

Top40-Charts.com (2004c). Jesus walks: Kanye West. Retrieved June 10, 2004, from http://top40-charts.com/song.php?sid=10209&sort=chartid&string=Kanye

CHAPTER TWENTY-THREE

Still Unequal

A Critical Exploration of Early Literacy Instruction with Primary Teachers and Implications for Policy

DENEESE L. JONES, SHERRY POWERS, ANTONY NORMAN,
WILLIAM BINTZ, ANGELA COX, MARGARET DAVIS,
YVONNE GREENWALT, PATRICIA HIGGINS,
AND FAYE NEWSON

Abstract

Instructional features and intervention practices in literacy that are grounded in pedagogies that merely prepare students to "fit into society" and to experience social class mobility within existing structures are not helpful in building a democratic and just society. An education for equity enables students not only to acquire basic skills in literacy, but also to use those skills to become effective learners.

This study challenges the cultural and social structure of early reading intervention instructional practices as powerful determinants of how students learn to perceive themselves and the literacy process. Becoming aware of the relationship between the instructional intervention structures for diverse learners who are struggling as readers, the social structure of the classroom, and the deep structure of schools can heighten the teacher's level of efficacy for attributing student success.

Introduction

In 1998, the General Assembly in the Commonwealth of Kentucky passed

Senate Bill 186, which established the Early Reading Incentive Grant (ERIG) program and the Collaborative Center for Literacy Development (CCLD): early childhood through adulthood to promote literacy development throughout the state. One of the charges of the CCLD was to conduct a comprehensive research agenda and evaluate the early reading models implemented in elementary schools across Kentucky. The CCLD has funded three cohorts of ERIG projects, each of which lasted 2 years (1999–2001, 2000–2002, and 2001–2003). Analyses from the first 2-year cohort group (1999–2001) indicated five major findings:

1. Children who received services from the ERIG program did achieve, on average, in reading in all areas tested: letter recognition, phonic awareness, phonics, reading level, and strategic/metacognitive reading.
2. While children in these classrooms grew significantly in their reading, it was not possible to tell whether one particular model of instruction was more effective than another because the scores by model were not significantly different from one another.
3. There was great variability in implementation fidelity (e.g., how closely the teachers' implementation of the model matched the intended implementation by the author[s] of the model).
4. There are similarities and differences across teachers on the implementation of reading instruction for struggling readers across and within models.
5. The teachers who scored high on particular instructional features have students who achieve higher on test scores than other children with teachers who did not score high on these same instructional features.

This study focused on the partial analysis of data collected and the preliminary assertions during the first year of a new cohort. The following research questions were used to drive the 2-year grant-funded study's design:

1. What are some promising practices of instructional features that contribute to the effective reading instruction for diverse learners?
2. To what do primary-grade teachers attribute success in early literacy achievement for struggling readers of diverse backgrounds?
3. To what do primary-grade teachers attribute failure in early literacy achievement for struggling readers of diverse backgrounds?

The study's goals include the following:

1. To examine teacher usage of reading instructional features for their chosen early reading intervention models.
2. To describe teacher patterns of instructional practices for their chosen early reading intervention models.
3. To explore the levels of teacher efficacy for intervention models with diverse learners.

Although these preliminary results outline interesting assertions based on previous research implications and can be used to direct the focus for further ongoing research programs, final assertions and findings cannot be supported without total evaluation of all data, including scores on statewide tests.

Theoretical Framework

Since a major finding from the prior ERIG program's 2-year intensive study (1999–2001) indicated variability in instructional fidelity for the majority of the early literacy reading models, the primary goal of this study was the examination of the teachers' use of instructional features of the chosen models and descriptions of the teachers' sense of efficacy with these features. To a greater extent, the instructional practices used and valued by teachers determine what is learned and how learning takes place. This is helpful information for determining appropriate and effective instruction.

Broadly defined, equity pedagogy is a process of teaching that helps students form diverse racial, ethnic, and cultural groups attain the knowledge, skills, and attitudes needed to function effectively in society and achieve academic success in school. This definition suggests that it is not sufficient to help students learn to read and write within the dominant canon without learning also to question its assumptions, paradigms, and hegemonic characteristics. Helping students become reflective and active citizens is at the essence of our conception of academic achievement. Instructional features used by teachers who are grounded in pedagogies that merely prepare students to "fit" into society and to experience social class mobility within existing structures are not helpful in building a democratic and just society. An education for equity enables students not only to acquire basic skills in literacy, but also to use those skills to become effective learners.

This study seeks to challenge the cultural and social structures of early reading intervention instructional practices as powerful determinants of how students learn to perceive themselves and the literacy process. More importantly, this includes the social interactions that take place between students and teachers and among students in the classroom. Becoming aware of the relationship between the instructional intervention structures for diverse learners who are struggling as readers, the social structure of the classroom, and the deep structure of schools can heighten the teacher's level of efficacy in attributing student success.

The widespread misconceptions about diversity issues and multicultural education have slowed their implementation and contributed to the contentious debate about their nature and purposes. One of the most easily cited contentions is the integration of content about diverse cultural, ethnic, and racial groups into what is perceived as the mainstream curriculum. Thus, the debate has consistently focused on content integration while ignoring other important dimensions of instruction. Nevertheless, with the national focus on closing the academic achievement gap and the dream of "no child left behind" for diverse groups, a broader conceptualization and a more varied implementation must be delineated for teachers and teacher educators in order to begin to make a difference.

Equity pedagogy, as described earlier, is a dynamic instructional process that not only focuses on the identification and use of effective instructional techniques and methods (as those sought in these ERIG projects for struggling readers), but also on the context in which they are used. Cooperative learning, for example, can be an effective instructional technique. However, when it is used without an awareness of contextual issues such as status differences among students, it can reinforce stereotypes and inequality in the classroom. Equity pedagogy challenges teachers to use instructional practices that feature the facilitation of the learning process with a consideration of such cultural issues as status, race, class, and gender. It challenges instruction as transmission of facts, skills, and the image of the teacher as the "sage on the stage." Instead of rote memorization of knowledge constructed by authorities and the use of the mechanics of isolated skills, students in classrooms where equity pedagogy is used learn to generate knowledge and to create new understandings that add to their knowledge base, increase confidence in their literate abilities, and boost academic achievement (Jones, Powers, & Cox, 2004). More importantly, it alters the traditional power relationship between teachers and students. Like other dimensions of multicultural education, equity pedagogy provides a basis for addressing critical aspects of schools and for transforming curricula and schools for diverse groups.

Differences in early reading success reflect social variables such as ethnicity/race, social class, and even gender differences. When young children enter school, their ability to read has been influenced by these factors (Cohen, 1984). Effective teachers understand these variables and base their instructional practices on appropriate classroom engagement that has the best chance of achieving success for the learner (Delpit, 1988). Hence, there is contention that there exist two types of instructional features used in classrooms of specialized or intervention instruction: (1) directive formal or direct instruction and (2) supportive or scaffold instruction (Mehan, 1994). Each has its own structure as patterned by observable features, and each provides assistance to students in literacy learning. But the functions and forms of assistance may vary, as does the influence each has on students' understanding of the purposes, meaning, and possibilities for learning. This is particularly instructive for young children who come from diverse backgrounds and frames of reference who may exhibit characteristics that make them at-risk based on specific learning expectations.

Methodology

This study included 24 elementary schools with 63 teachers from 6 congressional districts that used 9 different early reading intervention models. All of the schools identified learners for intervention based on at-risk characteristics such as socioeconomic status, race/ethnicity differences, linguistic differences, preassessment reading readiness data, and other indicators of potential failure in early reading. Several instruments were used to determine the teachers' instructional practices using their chosen intervention reading models. These included a classroom observation instrument, an interview protocol, and an observational summary sheet. The major focus of the classroom observations was to understand the overall nature of instruction for each teacher and provide a "snapshot" of the instructional features of intervention for the observed lessons. An additional survey was administered at the close of the study period to explore and examine teachers' perceptions of self-efficacy with the use of the reading models. These all served as sources of analyses from the data collection process during a 27-month period. Using qualitative analysis code sheets and condensed summary sheets, assertions were developed to identify patterns of instructional features used by the teachers. Results from the survey tool were used to correlate the assertions from classroom observations and interviews about the teachers' perceived levels of self-efficacy.

Findings

Postsurvey Data

Postinstruction surveys of the 63 teachers with a return rate of 63% indicated that most of the teachers who responded had completed their master's degree (79%). Most were teaching in rural schools (41%), a few were in urban schools (31%), and fewer were in suburban schools (28%). Teachers reported diversity percentages related to race/ethnicity, socioeconomic status, and linguistic differences for their schools ranging from 0% to 99% with a mean percentage of 24%. They reported the free and reduced lunch percentages from 12% to 100% with a mean percentage of 65%. Regarding their grades for instruction, these ranged from kindergarten to grade 4; 8 reported kindergarten, 31 reported first grade, 9 reported second grade, 5 reported third grade, 1 reported fourth grade, and 8 reported multi-grades at the primary level.

Classification of the reading intervention models revealed that 32 participated in phonics-centered models, 13 participated in the Four Blocks model, 11 participated in the Reading Recovery model, and 6 participated in the Literacy Collaborative models. When reporting on their level of fidelity to the models (0 = low and 10 = high), teachers on the average reported high adherence ($M = 8.53$; $SD = 1.37$) with a range of 4–10.

Regarding the effect of the ERIG models, chosen by the school districts and funded by their grants, on their diverse students who were struggling readers, all participants either agreed or strongly agreed that the models provided positive changes in their instructional practices, provided instructional practices that have increased reading achievement, and provided a positive classroom environment for these students as demonstrated by students' scores on reading achievement tests and assessments. Using factor analysis, teachers were categorized into several groups: 13 (22%) were more literature-based; 21 (36%) were more skill-based; 13 (22%) used a combination of literature-based and skill-based; 11 (19%) identified themselves as not using either as a base; and 4 teachers were not classified. Literature-based teachers were those who reported their instruction to be more developmentally appropriate, culturally responsive, and whole language oriented. Skill-based teachers were those who reported their instruction to be more phonics focused with basal readers and direct instruction oriented. Teachers who classified themselves as using both approaches responded positively to all the instructional strategies, whereas teachers who classified themselves as using neither approach responded negatively to all the instructional strategies.

A look at differences among these groups in their instructional intervention format, beliefs about student failure and student success, organizational style, and the role of family involvement in their instructional model revealed only one significant difference in the areas of instructional intervention format. This was found with flexible groupings. Teachers who used either a literature-based strategy or both strategies were significantly more likely to report using flexible grouping than those who were skill-based or used neither strategy. Due to the lack of significant differences across these groups, the aggregated results are provided in Tables 24.1–25.7.

In Table 24.1, results demonstrate that teachers in this survey reported using small groups as a primary instructional format. Family involvement was perceived as a major focus along with a combination of one-on-one instructional practices and whole-group instructional practices. A large portion reported using ability grouping and pull-out programs. Fewer teachers reported using computer-assisted groups as a part of their instructional formats.

Table 24.1 Teacher Post-Intervention Survey Results for Instructional Format in Early Reading Intervention

Percentages of teachers who strongly agree or agree to the following statements		
The instructional intervention format that would *most* characterize what was implemented in my classroom is …	%	Question rank
Small groups	82	1
Family involvement	59	2
One-on-one instructional practices	56	3
Whole groups	56	3
Ability groups	43	4
Pull-out groups	34	5
Computer-assisted groups	33	6

In Table 24.2, teachers in this study reported that they perceive the greatest factor that contributes to their students' failure in early reading intervention is poor family involvement. This is an important finding, considering the prior table that indicates family involvement as being a major focus of their instructional intervention format. Additionally, low parental literacy and low family income or resources were considered by these teachers as high contributors to diverse primary students' failure in early reading achievement.

It is interesting to note that teachers report the success of diverse students in early reading instruction is highly attributed to effective classroom instruction and high teacher expectations (Table 24.3). These findings seem to indicate that teachers, who are implementing district-chosen reading models with high-fidelity professional development preparation, believe that they do make a difference in the success of diverse learners in reading achievement. More importantly, these levels of high self-efficacy are not indicated to be affected by high family income or resources and traditional family structure. Critical to the findings from Tables 24.3 and 25.4, teachers seem to take credit for students' success but attribute student failure to ascribed characteristics (e.g., student IQ, family resources, and parental literacy) rather than their own instructional intervention.

Table 24.2 Teacher Post-Intervention Survey Results for Diverse Student Failure in Early Reading Intervention

Percentages of teachers who strongly agree or agree to the following statements on student failure		
The primary reason that diverse students in my classroom are *failing* to thrive in reading achievement is ...	%	Question rank
Poor family involvement	81	1
Low parental literacy	70	2
Low family income or resources	57	3
Poor school attendance	38	4
Low student IQ	36	5
Language differences or dialect	21	6
Low teacher expectations	3	7
Poor or mediocre classroom instruction	2	8

Further analysis from the survey data indicate that although the teachers had received specialized and monitored professional development and preparation for the use of the models, they perceived such ascribed characteristics as socioeconomic status and student IQ as having the greatest effect on academic achievement or failure. This was maintained even to the detriment of their implementation of the reading intervention models.

Table 24.3 Teacher Post-Intervention Survey Results for Diverse Student Success in Early Reading Instruction

Percentages of teachers who strongly agree or agree to the following statements on student success		
The primary reason that diverse students in my classroom are *successful* in reading achievement ...	%	Question rank
Effective classroom instruction	98	1
High teacher expectations	97	2
Good school attendance	93	3
High family involvement	78	4
Student use of standard English	66	5
High parental literacy	55	6
High student IQ	54	7
Family structure (e.g., traditional two-parent family)	39	8
High family income or resources	20	9

Table 24.3 continued

Percentages of teachers who strongly agree or agree to the following statements on student failure		
The primary reason that diverse students in my classroom are *failing* to thrive in reading achievement is …	%	Question rank
Poor family involvement	81	1
Low parental literacy	70	2
Low family income or resources	57	3
Poor school attendance	38	4
Low student IQ	36	5
Language differences or dialect	21	6
Low teacher expectations	3	7
Poor or mediocre classroom instruction	2	8

Table 24.4 ERIG Teacher Instructional Activities and Goals for Early Reading Models for Intervention

Reading models observed	Consistently observed activities	Teachers' goals for the observed lesson
Breakthrough to literacy	Unison read aloud Phonics (e.g., word families) IRE discourse Writing words Word recognition Low-level questioning Computer-based practice	Learn sight vocabulary Integrating of reading/drama Matching words Comprehend a particular text
Carbo learning styles	Task questions for comprehension Spelling/word recognition Oral reading, re-reading with student selected books Listening to leveled taped books Sight words (e.g., Dolch list)	Decode particular words Learn sight words Read fluently Comprehend a particular text
Direct instruction	Reading aloud Phonics (e.g., published manual) Explicit instruction from the manual Writing (e.g., copying) Mixed-level questioning IRE discourse Standardized assessments/tests	Decode particular words Comprehend a particular text Learn phonic correspondences Hear/understand phonemic aspects Practice skills (e.g., decoding strategies)

Table 24.4 continued

Four blocks/building blocks	Unison reading aloud Guided reading Phonics (e.g., mini-lessons) Partner reading Worksheet practice IRE discourse Standardized assessments/tests	Learn comprehension strategies Practice skills/strategies Read fluently Meaning vocabulary Identify text features Hear/understand phonemic aspects
Four blocks	Unison reading aloud Guided reading Phonics (e.g., mini-lessons) Independent reading Worksheet practice IRE discourse Informal and standardized assessments/tests	*Identify text features* Practice skills/strategies Learn comprehension strategies Read fluently
Literacy collaborative	Guided reading Shared reading Independent reading Read aloud Writing (e.g., shared, independent, interactive) Assessment (e.g., miscue analysis, teacher observation)	Read fluently Practice skills/strategies Learn comprehension strategies Reading/writing connections
Reading recovery	Explicit phonics instruction Oral reading Focus on accuracy in decoding Sight words Assessment (e.g., miscue analysis, record of books read, sight word lists) Writing	*Practice skills/strategies* Read fluently Learn decoding strategies Decode a particular word Decode a particular text Learn sight words
SRA/direct instruction	Direct instruction (e.g., published manual) IRE discourse Silent reading	Practice skills Decode a particular text Decode a particular word Comprehend a particular text
Success for all	Reading aloud Silent reading Accelerated reader (e.g., computer-based comprehension questions)	Learn comprehension strategies Practice skills Read fluently

Observational Data

Some of these differences, taken from transcribed observations and interview data, seemed to be based, in part on the teacher's sense of efficacy for the learner and the model of implementation and, in part, on the teacher's professional understanding of each model for the needs of the diverse learners. Qualitative analyses of constructivist grounded theory indicate that the patterns of instructional features observed were consistent for all of the intervention models, but the ways in which they were used were different depending on variables such as amount of room space, amount of time for instruction, and even the number of students per classroom (see Table 24.4).

Over the course of the school year, the teachers were observed four times with an average of 1 hour and 35 minutes per observation. Observers used an observation instrument to code instructional features, the percentage of time certain activities were observed, and the overall focus during reading instruction. From an instructional viewpoint, the most formal reading model of classroom interaction, and by far the most prevalent, parallels the direct instruction or skills-emphasis model of instruction (Pressley, 1998). It presumes that the teacher's primary job is knowledge transmission and assessment (Cazden, 1988) and uses the IRE discourse of initiate, respond, and evaluate, which can be found in traditional comprehension instruction (Cherry, 1978; Durkin, 1978–1979; Lemke, 1985; Panagos & Bliss, 1990). Instruction is defined by teacher control mechanisms and is designed to assess students' content knowledge in accord with a predetermined standard for acceptable participation (Gillimore & Tharp, 1990).

Supportive reading models provide instructional features that assess learning as a search for understanding, providing opportunities for responsive feedback with the reading process seen as occurring within a community of learners (Bransford et al., 1999). Such instruction allows for the integration of assessment with teaching, so that evaluation can be immediate and ongoing, while permitting the level and type of support to be modified "on the spot" (Pressley & Woloshyn, 1995). The basic form of instructional features of these practices integrates listening, speaking, reading, and writing as tools of inquiry serving multiple communicative purposes, with students acquiring the cultural tools needed to understand, remember, and express their perspectives in diverse literate ways. More importantly, instructional practices are grounded in culturally meaningful experiences that assist students in transferring classroom learning to nonschool settings (Brown & Campione, 1994; Pressley et al., 1998; Bransford et al., 1999). Many researchers have studied instructional conversations as features for formal or supportive reading models as central mechanisms for sustaining active, strategic learning in literacy for diverse groups (Brown & Campione, 1994; Goldenberg, 1996).

To analyze whether teachers were implementing a more formal or supportive feature for reading instruction, items within the above named areas were categorized as characterizing tenets of these two-type units of instruction. Tables 24.5–25.7 indicate how items were classified followed by comparisons between teachers who practice the formal and supportive features in their instruction.

Table 24.5 Instructional Features for Activity Settings With Formal and Supportive Items (Observers Could Choose Up to Four Items)

Formal items	Supportive items
• Teacher reading silently • Teacher directing students' attention to print • Skill instruction • Talk about text features	• Teacher reading aloud to children • Strategy instruction • Talk about text ideas • Metacognitive talk • Teacher scaffolding student discussion • Writing • Arts

Regardless of the professional development for the models, the instructional features in the activity settings were slightly, but not significantly, more likely to be supportive than formal. Teachers who used more supportive reading features averaged 1.56 ($SD = 0.60$) supportive items versus 1.44 ($SD = 0.56$) formal features for the activity settings. With the teachers who used more formal reading features, the average was 1.68 ($SD = 0.83$) supportive items versus 1.57 ($SD = 0.50$) formal features.

Table 24.6 Instructional Features for Teacher Activity With Formal and Supportive Items (Observers Could Choose Up to Three Items)

Formal items	Supportive items
• Telling • Explaining • Disciplining/managing	• Demonstrating (including thinking aloud) • Questioning • Listening • Guiding

Regardless of teacher training, teacher activities were significantly more likely to be supportive ($M = 1.64$, $SD = 58$) than formal ($M = 0.94$, $SD = 0.56$).

Regardless of the professional development for a particular model, student activities were significantly more likely to be supportive ($M = 2.34$, $SD = 1.16$) than to be formal ($M = 0.73$, $SD = 0.44$). On the other hand, teachers were significantly more likely to use formal skill instruction (e.g., phonemic awareness, phonics, sight words, vocabulary development, and print convention) as an instruction feature ($M = 0.45$, $SD = 0.22$) than the more supportive strategy instruction (e.g., comprehension, using context, decoding, study skills, and tracking print) ($M = 0.34$, $SD = 0.18$).

Table 24.7 Instructional Features for Student Activity With Formal and Supportive Items (Observers Could Choose Up to Five Items)

Formal items	Supportive items
• Reading silently • Kids reading orally for instructional purposes • Observing • Questioning • Copying	• Reading orally individually (e.g., assessment or celebration) • Reading in partners or groups without the teacher • Choral reading • Echo reading • Participating in reader response activities • Practicing strategies • Dialoguing about meaning without teacher • Dialoguing about meaning with teacher • Doing metacognitive talk • Writing (e.g., authentic, interactive)

And although observers recorded more features of more supportive instructional practices, this trend did not continue when it came to percentage of time observed. Across several activities, observers recorded the amount of time devoted to supportive and formal activities on a scale that balanced:

1 = 0–25%
2 = 26–50%
3 = 51–70%
4 = 71–100%

For the more formal items of children visually focused on print and children working on isolated skills, regardless of the reading model used, the percentage of time observed was significantly more heavily devoted to these items ($M = 2.55$, $SD = 0.65$) as opposed to the supportive items of children working on skills in context, children working on strategies, children reading connected text, and children talking about text ($M = 2.13$, $SD = 0.79$). However, indicative of a teacher's more supportive teaching style, students were slightly, but not significantly, more likely to do more reading and talking than teachers.

In summary, regardless of the chosen reading models, teachers were observed as demonstrating instructional features that were more supportive than formal in their instructional setting (i.e., not significantly), teacher activities (i.e., significantly), student activities (i.e., significantly), and balance of student reading and talking (i.e., not significantly). And regardless of the chosen reading models, teachers were observed as more formal than supportive in their use of skill instruction versus strategy instruction (significantly) and the percentage of time observed for formal activities versus supportive activities (significantly).

Conclusions

Few studies in reading instruction for diverse learners in the primary grades include instructional feature analysis to determine similarities and differences among teachers in their application of practices with particular reading models for intervention instruction. Fewer studies account for cultural differences in responsiveness to learning for academic achievement. This makes a case for the compelling need to critically examine teachers' own sense of efficacy with young, struggling readers from diverse backgrounds.

The findings from this study seem to indicate that some promising practices of instructional features that contribute to effective reading instruction for diverse learners include supportive organizational units that integrate formal assessment with teaching and more interpersonal behaviors that use a variety of activities. In the area of teacher efficacy, the surveyed responses indicate that these teachers believe the greatest factor that contributes to their students' failure in early reading is poor family involvement, while the most beneficial factor toward success in early reading is effective classroom instruction. The gap between our own experiences as educators and our personal identities compared to those of our students may be small or it may be tremendous. But there is a gap, and it will continue to grow as the student population becomes more diverse.

The intent of this study is not to create alarm but to signal a need to examine the academic achievement gap with a different lens. As we move forward beyond the legacy of *Brown v. Board of Education*, we invite more critical examination of the intersection of race, class, and gender in working with struggling readers at all levels. We have observed teachers who are willing to examine their own practices while attempting to learn from their students. As "students of their students," these teachers can begin to do a better job of building instruction around their students' cultural needs, interests, and perspectives. Instructional practices using the business-as-usual approach are easy to implement—teachers talk, and students sit and listen, or read and complete worksheets. Grouping during these types of instructional practices tends to reproduce the social stratification patterns in the larger society, or students are taught in ways that help them become increasingly different over the years. But when teachers become aware of the relationship between the instructional intervention structure for diverse learners who are struggling as readers, the social structure of the classroom, and the deep structure of schools, this can heighten the teacher's level of efficacy in attributing student success, while providing students with experience of not just acquiring basic skills but using those skills to become effective learners.

References

Bransford, J. D., Brown, A. L., & Cocking, R. R. (Eds.) (1999). *How people learn: Brain, mind, experience and school.* Washington, DC: National Academy Press.

Brown, A. L., & Campione, J. C. (1994). Guided discovery in a community of learners. In K. McGilly (Ed.), *Classroom lessons: Integrating cognitive theory and classroom practice* (pp. 229–270). Cambridge, MA: MIT Press.

Cazden, C. B. (1988). *Classroom discourse: The language of teaching and learning.* Portsmouth, NH: Heinemann.

Cherry, L. (1978). Teacher–student interaction and teacher expectations of students' communicative competence. In R. Shuy & P. Griffin (Eds.), *The study of children's functional language and education in the early years* (Final Report to the Carnegie Corporation). New York and Arlington, VA: Center for Applied Linguistics.

Cohen, E. (1984). Talking and working together: Status, interaction and learning. In P. Peterson, L. Wilkinson, & M. Hallin (Eds.), *The social context of instruction* (pp. 171–189). Orlando, FL: Academic.

Delpit, L. D. (1988). The silenced dialogue: Power and pedagogy in educating other people's children. *Harvard Educational Review 58,* 280–298.

Durkin, D. (1978–1979). What classroom observations reveal about reading comprehension instruction. *Reading Research Quarterly 15,* 481–533.

Gillimore, R., & Tharp, R. (1990). Teaching mind in society: Teaching, schooling, and literate discourse. In L. C. Moll (Ed.), *Vygotsky and education: Instructional implications and applications of socio-historical psychology* (pp. 175–205). New York: Cambridge University Press.

Goldenberg, C. (1996). Latin American immigration and US schools. *Social Policy Report of the Society for Research in Child Development 10*(1), 1–29.

Jones, D. L., Powers, S., & Cox, A. (2004). An examination of early reading intervention instructional practices with diverse groups for the primary grades. *International Journal of Learning 10*(1), 721–742.

Lemke, J. L. (1985). Using language in classroom knowledge: Reading lessons. *Curriculum Inquiry 15,* 247–279.

Mehan, H. (1994). The role of discourse in learning, schooling, and reform. In B. McLeod (Ed.), *Language and learning: Educating linguistically diverse students* (pp. 71–95). Albany: State University of New York Press.

Panagos, J. M., & Bliss, L. S. (1990). Clinical presuppositions for speech therapy lessons. *Journal of Childhood Communication Disorders 13*, 19–28.

Pressley, M. (1998). *Reading instruction that works: The case for balanced teaching.* New York: Guilford.

Pressley, M., & Woloshyn, V. (Eds.) (1995). *Cognitive strategy instruction that really improves children's academic performance* (2nd ed.). Cambridge, MA: Brookline.

Pressley, M., Wharton-McDonald, R., & Mistretta, J. (1998). Effective beginning literacy instruction: Dialectical, scaffolded, and contextualized. In J. L. Metsala & L. C. Ehri (Eds.), *Word recognition in beginning literacy* (pp. 357–373). Mahwah, NJ: Erlbaum.

CHAPTER TWENTY-FOUR

A Thing Most Brutish

The Calibanization of the African American Male

JAMES RICHARDSON

One need only turn on the television, listen to the radio, or open the newspaper to hear the latest negative prospects for Black males in America. As a response to these naysayers and doomsdayers, this chapter seeks to raise some pertinent, perhaps provocative questions: Why is it that academic, socioeconomic, interpersonal, and even sexual prospects seem to bode especially poorly for many Black males? Is there a system that pathologizes dark male bodies?[1] If so, what is it; how does it function; and how does it manifest itself in the realities of dark male bodies? If such a system exists, then how does its presence warp or mitigate how dark male bodies come to participate as humans in the current social paradigm? If this system negatively impacts dark male bodies, then how do its repercussions play themselves out when these same bodies enter the larger society as racialized, gendered, sexualized, and socioeconomically classed beings?

The process of using language to maintain Black male bodies in visibly dehumanizing, innocuous positions as a means of perpetuating a racist patriarchy, one that privileges White, usually male, bodies is what I call *calibanization*.[2] And in our society, a systematic, institutionalized calibanization daily and relentlessly slaughters the creative human psyches of men of color—particularly African American males, a group which, for historical, racial, even genetic reasons, is positioned as this White patriarchal hegemony's antithesis, its greatest bête noir. Moreover, an internalized calibanization—one that has been inculcated to, or culturally imbibed by, these same oppressed Black male bodies—evinces itself as Black men, in the process of trying to access and imitate White, capitalist patriarchy, often participate in a self-dehumanization that leaves in its wake oppressed bodies, oppressive relationships, and damaged psyches. The term *calibanization* is used to specifically name those peculiar, debilitating dynamics that occur among Black men and between Black male bodies and White patriarchy in this country. And although females (Black and non-Black) and males (non-White and non-Black) also are oppressed in brutal ways under this system, the dynamics in which their oppressions occur differ from how Black men encounter, learn, and ultimately reproduce oppression.

In her introduction to Jacques Lacan's *Feminine Sexuality*, Juliet Mitchell (1982) elucidates Lacan's idea of the role that language plays in how humans come to exist as complex, sentient beings:

> The human animal is born into language and *it is within the terms of language that the human subject is constructed.* Language does not arise from within the individual, it is always out there in the world outside, lying in wait for the neonate. Language always 'belongs' to another person. *The human subject is created from a general law that comes to it from outside itself and through the speech of other people* . . . (p. 5, italics added)

If this Lacanian rubric is used to reread *The Tempest*, how do Prospero, Miranda, Caliban, and language configure themselves? As Miranda and Caliban's teacher, Prospero constructs and heads this island hierarchy as its patriarch. Prospero consciously and unconsciously imposes on the island a phallologocentric order, as it is he who brings its finite creatures (Miranda and Caliban) into human consciousness via language and "art."[3] Prospero's mastery of language and manipulation of art and magic ensconces daughter Miranda in a quasi-privileged position as his fawning minion. Yet this same language imprisons her (at least initially) in a one-dimensional existence as chaste virgin and obedient daughter. The consciousness into which Prospero's language brings Caliban, however, pinions Caliban with servitude, restriction, and ultimately ostracization. For through heated exchanges in which father taunts servant with epithets like "poisonous slave," in which daughter labels servant "abhorréd slave," and in which servant curses both father and daughter and laments Prospero's usurpation of his island, it is revealed that Caliban, having arrived into Prospero's linguistic realm as a discursive subject, is rendered subhuman, lesser, dispossessed of both land and personal autonomy.

In true Lacanian fashion, then, Caliban comes into human consciousness—albeit an inferior one—through forces that exist outside of his body, "through the speech of other people"—namely through Prospero and Miranda. In fact, it is Miranda who, in a heated repartee, reminds Caliban of this:

> I pitied thee,
> Took pains to make thee speak, taught thee each hour
> One thing or other: *when thou did'st not, savage,*
> *Know thine own meaning,* but would'st gabble like
> A thing most brutish, I endowed thy purposes
> With words that made them known. (1.2.353–358, italics added)

Clearly, Miranda's connecting language with human consciousness concurs with Lacan's concept of speech as reifier of the human subject: For not until Caliban acquires language is he able to become human, to "know [his] own meaning."[4]

But *why* does Caliban respond to Prospero and Miranda's seeming magnanimities with curses, even a violent attempt to use Miranda to "[people] else/[t]his isle with Calibans?" (1.2.350–351) In an essay that introduces this play, Northrop Frye explains Caliban's desires to kill Prospero and rape Miranda as "eminently natural" (1977, p. 1369). Essentializing Caliban as a pure, uncorrupted being prone to evil, Frye deems him to be "*mere* nature, nature without nurture . . . nature that manifests itself more as an instinctive propensity to evil" (p. 1369). Echoing the optimistic humanism of the Renaissance, Frye further posits that Caliban's predilection for evil can be tempered, lured to "an upper level" via "education, obedience to law, and the habit of virtue" (p. 1369). In other words, Caliban, if only immersed in liberal learning, if only nurtured with knowledge, could mitigate his mean nature, becoming in the process a human being in the fullest sense.

But can Caliban's violent temperament be, as Frye implies, the result of deficient "nurturing?" Not according to Caliban; for though he rails against being cozened out of his island, Caliban acknowledges the attention that Prospero, as teacher and nurturer, initially lavishes on him:

> When thou cam'st first,
> Thou strok'st me and made much of me: would'st give me
> Water with berries in't; and teach me how
> To name the bigger light, and how the less
> That burn by day and night. (I. Ii. 332–336)

Prospero's proffered kindness, his "nurturing," elicits from Caliban love, as the son of Sycorax gives of himself wholly and freely: " . . . and then I loved thee/And showed thee all the qualities o' th'isle/The fresh springs, brine-pits, barren place and fertile" (I. ii. 336–338).

Exception, then, must be taken to Frye's assertion that Caliban is but unnurtured nature inclined to evil. On the contrary, he *has* been nurtured; but more precisely, however, he has been sociolinguistically conditioned. Indeed, Caliban's movement from the prelinguistic imaginary to the language-determined realm of the symbolic is fraught with not only the usual trauma that Lacan associates with the splitting and concomitant alienation of a being entering the realm of language as a human (Lacan, 1985, pp. 79, 81), but also Caliban must subject himself to this language as fellow humans unconsciously and consciously manipulate it, linguistically and physically fixing him as a racial, gendered, sexual, and socioeconomic other.

To Prospero and Miranda's angry protests (they deem him an ungrateful monster who audaciously disdains two who gave him language and learning) Caliban angrily retorts: "You taught me language, and my profit on't/Is, I know how to curse. The red plague rid you/For learning me your language!" (1.2.363–365) Caliban's violent behavior results from how he perceives and attempts to construct himself in relation to the other two humans on the island. His self, his ego, is defined by seeing a mirror image of himself as reflected (and projected) back on to him by Prospero and Miranda. As he invests Prospero with an omnipotence that can potentially rival his own ego, an ego incipiently violent and volatile because it is rooted in fantasy or what Lacan calls *méconnaissance* or faulty perception, Caliban is, by turns, awed and threatened by his master (Clark, 1994, p. 450). The precariousness of Caliban's ego is further heightened by the presence of Prospero and Miranda, who possess language and participate in a linguistic system that "others" Caliban. Caliban realizes that the language he has acquired denies him the privilege with which he associates Miranda and the power and privilege with which he associates Prospero. Try as he might, he is never able to realize himself as anything other than what Prospero and Miranda call him: "hagseed," "savage," "darkly deformed," "slave," "violator," and "wood fetcher." Try as he might, he is unable to appreciably challenge the unfordable chasm that exists between Prospero and Miranda and himself: In contrast to the "brave forms" of beings like Miranda and Ferdinand, Caliban's body is ascribed "villain," one that Miranda "[does] not like to look on" (1.2.310). Unlike Prospero and Miranda, who live in dwellings blessed with "humane care," Caliban, deemed categorically lesser and incorrigibly lustful, is "[d]eservedly confined into this rock . . . [and] hadst/Deserved more than a prison" (1.2.361–362). As a result of such a dehumanizing exclusion, the frustration

Caliban feels manifests itself in verbal and physical rebellion. Due to the logocentric order that has privileged Prospero and Miranda, the reader sees a hopelessly trapped Caliban who "yet . . . needs must curse" (2.1.4). Ironically, language cripples Caliban's ability to "logically" progress in a "rational" world. He creates idealized images of White males, *imagoes*, wherever he goes: To White male Prospero, he initially proffers the realm of his natural world; to White male and drunkard Stephano, he happily seeks vassalage as consummate bootlicker. Caliban, rather than seek autonomy, can only see himself in servile positions to White male imagoes, and this inability to even move toward self-determination defines a dehumanized, crippled Caliban, a being made hapless by language and humans who deny him humanity. This lack manifests itself in a being who hates self and others, is hated by others, and yet is unable to effectively challenge those who hate and abuse him.

Like Caliban, African American males historically have been victimized by a White, patriarchal, capitalist system in which language and people keep them subordinate, servile, lesser. And like Caliban, the social forces that keep Black men harmless yet feared, needful yet dispensable, "romanticized yet vilified" (hooks's *Black Looks: Race and Representation*, 1992, p. 96) serve several purposes. Keeping Black male bodies innocuous and dependent allows for the perpetuation of a capitalist system that exploits them. Keeping them feared creates the need for a White masculine response reified as a police/policing force that *ostensibly* "protects" White bodies (especially White women) and White-owned property. Keeping them vilified mitigates the horrific reality of calibanization; it even justifies its perpetuation as a necessary thing.

My argument, that the peculiar positioning of Black men in this country allows the current social paradigm to remain intact, is hardly a new one. In fact, sociologists, in trying to account for the stratification that results when racialized, gendered, sexualized, and/or socioeconomically classed bodies of people become either superordinate or subordinate, theorize similar conclusions, often employing a functionalist perspective, which emphasizes "the way in which parts of a society are structured in the interest of maintaining the system as a whole"; a conflict perspective, which analyzes the conflict and tension that arise among competing groups; or a labeling perspective, which "attempts to explain why certain people are viewed as deviants and others engaging in the same behavior are not" (Schaefer, 1993, p. 34). As I argue that calibanization consciously and unconsciously, overtly and latently, serves to perpetuate White supremacy and, more specifically, a capitalist, White male supremacy, I propose that analyzing and critiquing this process can be best achieved via a functionalist approach.

"If an aspect of social life," asserts sociologist Richard T. Schaefer, "does not contribute to society's stability or survival—if it does not serve some identifiably useful function—it will not be passed on from one generation to the next" (1993, p. 15). Assuming that calibanization's ability to survive generational and social changes proves that it has an "identifiably useful" function—a function I assert is the perpetuation of a system that mostly privileges humans who are what Black poet Audre Lorde called "white, thin, male, young, heterosexual, Christian and financially secure" (Ferguson, 1990, p. 9)—how does one name and critique how calibanization serves the interests of the current White capitalist patriarchy? An assessment of how Black male bodies are racialized, gendered, sexualized, and socioeconomically classed reveals how calibanization reinscribes the current social paradigm.

The initial (perhaps even overriding) factor that keeps Black male bodies in inferior and exploited positions, I propose, is language and the manipulation of language; and, as Caliban haplessly learns and Lacan enigmatically asserts, it is language, it is "the speech of others" by which people realize and are realized. Perhaps it is ironic how readily a Lacanian rubric is applicable to how African American filmmaker Spike Lee (1982) illustrates the effects language has on bodies—particularly Black male bodies in urban America. Somewhat initially skeptical of the scene in Spike Lee's *Malcolm X* where a member of the Nation of Islam moves Malcolm to epiphany and a burgeoning Black consciousness by having him compare the dictionary entries for *black* and *white*, I, armed with an integrationist's optimism and an eighties edition of *The American Heritage Dictionary of the English Language*, looked up the dictionary entry for *black*:

1. Being of the darkest achromatic visual value; producing or reflecting comparatively little light and having no predominant hue.
    a. Having no light whatsoever: a black cave.
    b. Belonging to an ethnic group having dark skin; especially, Negroid . . .
    c. Soiled, as from soot.
    d. Evil; sinister: black deeds.
    e. Cheerless and depressing; gloomy.
    f. Angered; sullen . . .
    g. Of or designating a form of humor dealing with the abnormal grotesque aspects of life and society and evoking a sense of human despair and failure.
    h. Indicating or incurring censure or dishonor . . .
    i. Any member of a Negroid people; a Negro. (p. 183)

The dictionary definitions for this term are overwhelmingly negative, and if, as Lacan asserts, language ushers the body into reality, allowing it to know its own meaning, then Black bodies, negatively impacted as soon as they are perceived as "black" (at birth), know themselves and are known in ways that, like Caliban's ways of self-knowing, are counterproductive, antihuman, and fraught with frustration.

Since its late-seventeenth-century origins, race as a static, biologically determined "reality" has become the guiding rubric under which Europeans explain physical differences between themselves and that mass of darker others encountered when Whites "discovered" these inhabitants of sub-Saharan Africa and the New World (Omi & Winant, 1992, p. 27). The concomitant exploitation of these people and their resources was justified by imaginative reinterpretations of the Bible, and in England and its colonies, the criterion by which one was deemed human shifted from whether or not one was *Christian*, to whether or not one was *English* and *free* to whether or not one was *white* (p. 31, authors' and my emphases).

By the end of the nineteenth century, when most of the globe was in the throes of European and American imperialism, the discourse of race and the propoganda of White supremacy were merged with social Darwinism—itself a capitalistic adulteration of Charles Darwin's theory of species evolution—and under the guise of eugenics, racism was made legitimate by a dubious "science." However, countering this reading of race as an essentialist/biological fact and its implications that the formation of dominant and oppressed groups along the lines of race is a natural, even normal phenomenon, W. E. B. DuBois compellingly argued (long before the advent of postmodernism's championing of sophistic discourse and poststructuralist "identity politics") that race is really a construct, mere human invention:

> The discovery of personal whiteness among the world's peoples is a very modern thing—a nineteenth and twentieth century matter, indeed. The ancient world would have laughed at such a distinction. The Middle Age regarded skin color with mild curiosity; and even up into the eighteenth century we were hammering our national manikins into one, great, Universal Man, with fine frenzy which ignored color and race even more than birth. Today we have all forgotten all that, and the world in a sudden emotional conversion has discovered that it is white and by that token, wonderful! (p. 176)

If, as DuBois asserts, race is a socially constructed phenomenon, more mythic than factual, then how does one explain its persistence? Who or what benefits from the continued oppressive presence of race and racism? An answer, perhaps, is implicitly given in sociologists Michael Omi and Harold Winant's (1992) definition of the term *racial formation*:

> We use the term racial formation to refer to the process by which social, economic and political forces determine the content and importance of racial categories, and by which they are in turn shaped by racial meanings. Crucial to this formulation is the treatment of race as a central axis of social relations which cannot be subsumed under or reduced to some broader category or conception. (p. 29)

Applying Omi and Winant's (1992) definition, the racialization of dark male bodies, which "evolved with the consolidation of racial slavery" (p. 31), served then and serves today to keep Black males "in offices that profit" the White supremacist patriarchy and capitalism, both of which, I assert, are symbiotically joined in a system that maintains itself by resisting being named and critiqued, and is thereby able to confound modes of resistance by oppressed bodies.

In tracing the labor movement in the United States, Alexander Saxton notes that a racism that vilifies non-White bodies in America is ironically served by a capitalism that valorizes these same bodies as a cheap labor supply. Realizing this seeming paradox between racism and capitalism, Saxton calls these non-White and poor-White bodies caught between this ostensible contradiction "indispensable enemies"[5]:

> North Americans of European background have experienced three great racial confrontations: with the Indian, with the African, and with the Oriental. Central to each transaction has been a totally one-sided preponderance of power, exerted for the exploitation of nonwhites by the dominant white society. In each case (but especially in the two that began with systems of enforced labor), white workingmen have played a crucial, yet ambivalent, role. They have been exploited and exploiters. On the one hand, thrown into competition with non-whites as enslaved or "cheap" labor, they suffered economically; on the other hand, being white, they benefited by that very exploitation which was compelling the nonwhites to work for low wages or for nothing. Ideologically they were drawn in opposite directions. Racial identification cut at angles to class consciousness. (1971, p. 1)

More specifically, then, systemic racism/calibanization keeps Black males powerless and dehumanized, marked as "enemies"; simultaneously, these dehumanized bodies, relegated to positions of inexpensive servitude, are also marked by a capitalist economics as "indispensable."

In *Yearning: Race, Gender, and Cultural Politics*, bell hooks (1990) asserts that masculinity is realized in the male body that is best able to acquire power, dominate bodies, colonize lands, exploit resources, and (in this country) achieve the "American Dream." How then does institutionalized racism, discrimination, and *de facto* second-class citizenship all serve to strap Black males economically, socially, politically, and linguistically, denying them in the process access to patriarchy. Robert Staples (1991) graphically illustrates in *Black Male Genocide: A Final Solution to the Race Problem in America* how government-sanctioned calibanization cripples Black men:

1. While Black men account for only 6% of the population in the US, they make up half of its male prisoners in local, state, and federal jails.
2. The majority of the 20,000 Americans killed in crime-related incidents each year are Black men.
3. Over 35% of all Black men in American cities are drug and alcohol abusers.
4. Over 50% of Black men under the age of 21 are unemployed.
5. 25% of the victims of AIDS are Black men.
6. 45% of Black men between the ages of 16–62 are not in the labor force.
7. About 32% of Black men have income levels below the officially defined poverty level. (p. 91)

Although Staples is meticulous in listing the many calibanizing factors that prohibit Black men from achieving the patriarchal ideal, bell hooks notes that:

> implicit in his [Staples's] analysis is the assumption that black men could only internalize this norm [patriarchal ideal] and be victimized by it. Like many black men, he assumes that patriarchy and male domination is not a socially constructed social order but a "natural" fact of life. (1992, p. 97)

Like Caliban, who attempts rebellion against his master but fails to rebel against or even question the very system that maintains him in a servile position, Staples and like-minded Black males are quick to challenge—or so hooks asserts—racist and classist forces that deny Black males access to patriarchy without questioning patriarchy itself. Thus, both Caliban and calibanized Black males are mired in a system in which they can never achieve ideal patriarchy and ideal masculinity. As they assume that patriarchy is a preexisting ideal, "a 'natural' fact of life," they miss the opportunity to "assert meaningful agency by repudiating the norms white culture impose[s]" (p. 97). A primary factor that perpetuates the calibanization of Black male bodies is their inability to critique the system that oppresses them. Such calibanized bodies will bemoan their inability to access patriarchy rather than challenge the normative order that valorizes patriarchy in the first place. Like the hapless Caliban who "needs must curse," calibanized Black males attempt rebellion in counterproductive ways.

Consciously and unconsciously dependent on a linguistic order and a racist, capitalist system to validate their "maleness," calibanized Black male bodies, investing all in a phallocracy that refuses to privilege or even humanize them, often vent their frustrations in futile, destructive ways. In abusive relationships with spouses, in violent melees with each other, and in debilitating intrapersonal experiences, Black male bodies, like Caliban, act out "upon those that are close in physical proximity as opposed to the real source of frustration" (The Wester Influence, 1993, p. 5). In other words, rather than confront the bodies and systems that are complicit agents in the suffering and dehumanization that African American males daily endure, these same Black men lash out not against racism and discrimination, but against other marginalized bodies, bodies likewise brutally oppressed.

If, as I assert, the root cause of calibanization is language, and a racist, capitalist, White supremacist patriarchy is the system through which such oppressive, excluding, and labeling discourse is realized and perpetuated, what are these modern-day Calibans, these "things most brutish" to do? First, oppressed bodies must name and critique the system that privileges Whiteness, White maleness, and wealth. The very act of naming power relationships that develop in a stratified society is potentially liberating. "Discourse," proposes Foucault,

> transmits and produces power; it reinforces it, but also undermines and exposes it, renders it fragile and makes it possible to thwart it. In like manner, silence and secrecy are a shelter for power, anchoring its prohibitions; but they also loosen its holds and provide for relatively obscure areas of tolerance. (1990, p. 101)

Inversely, as Black male bodies relentlessly insist on the ultimate, inherent humanity of their bodies, they, by exposing White supremacy and calibanization as it manifests itself in privileged and oppressed bodies, force the invisible power center that overtly and latently challenges their humanity to unmask itself. Cultural critic Russell Ferguson complements Foucault's assessment of how discourse can subvert and resist oppressive power paradigms:

> As historically marginalized groups insist on their own identity, the deeper, structural invisibility of the so-called center becomes harder to sustain. *The power of the center depends on a relatively unchallenged authority.* If that authority breaks down, then there remains no point relative to which others can be defined as marginal. The perceived threat lies partly in the very process of becoming visible. It becomes increasingly obvious, for example, that white American men have their own specificity, and that it is from there that their power is exercised. No longer can whiteness, maleness or heterosexuality be taken as the ubiquitous par-

adigm, simultaneously center and boundary. (1990, p. 10, italics added)

Perhaps not the principal step and certainly not the only step, using language to expose, critique, and make visible the system that calibanizes African American males is, however, an important first step in decentering and deconstructing a Eurocentric Western civilization that insists on valorizing Whiteness as inherently superior, beautiful, and better. "The center cannot hold," wrote W. B. Yeats, and perchance our critiquing and bringing into public discourse this thing, this system, that usually privileges White skin and categorically debases Black male bodies will usher in not an ominous second coming, nor even a panacean Parousia, but maybe a system that affirms all humanity.

Notes

1. I use the term "dark male body" in this chapter as a type of tabula rasa, to indicate the potential/ideal/unmarked/unspecified body. This term (I hope) reads differently from terms like "Black male body," "African American male," or "Black male human in the United States"—terms for which racial, gendered, sexual, and class markers are more apparent. However, throughout the rest of this chapter, terms like "African American male," "Black male," etc., are used interchangeably.
2. I expect that some may find problematic my attempts to use the term *calibanization* to explain a racial/racist phenomenon, especially since the idea of race is generally thought to be a late-eighteenth- or nineteenth-century construction, coming into vogue at least a century after Shakespeare (1611) wrote *The Tempest*. Nonetheless, however, race, racism, racialism, etc., did exist *avant la lettre*.
3. I anticipate some reaction to my use of problematic terms like *construct* and *impose*; it is as if I am implying that Prospero has somehow accessed *la langue* (Saussure's term for the symbolic realm of language) and, via *la parole* or actual speech, he has consciously designed a system that will privilege him with power over the island and its inhabitants.
4. I grant that Lacan's linguistic theory is far more complex than I have presented it; however, I am much more interested in attempting to name the power dynamics that arise when Caliban is dubiously "humanized" by a linguistic order that arbitrarily and categorically relegates him to an "other-ed" status.
5. Saxton's reading of the seemingly paradoxical relationship between racism and capitalism is—in light of the controversy in California between "illegal aliens" and proponents of Proposition 187—especially prescient.

References

Clark, M. P. (1994). Lacan, Jacques. *The Johns Hopkins guide to literary theory and criticism*. Baltimore: Johns Hopkins University Press.

DuBois, W. E. B. (1991). The souls of White folk from *Darkwater*. In A. Richard

(Ed.), *Afro-American writing: An anthology of prose and poetry* (pp. 176–185). University Park: Pennsylvania State University Press.

Ferguson, R. (1990). Introduction: Invisible center. In Russell Ferguson et al. (Eds.), *Out there: Marginalization and contemporary cultures* (pp. 9–14). New York: The New Museum of Contemporary Art and MIT Press.

Foucault, M. (1990). *The history of sexuality: An introduction* (Vol. 1). Trans. Robert Hurley. New York: Vintage Books.

Frye, N. (1977). Introduction. In W. Shakespeare, *The tempest* (pp. 1369–1372). New York: Viking.

hooks, b. (1990). *Yearning: Race, gender, and cultural politics.* Boston: South End Press.

———. (1992). *Black looks: Race and representation.* Boston: South End Press.

Lacan, J. (1985). *Feminine sexuality.* Trans. Jacqueline Rose. New York: Pantheon Books.

Lee, S. (1992). *Malcolm X.* New York: Fireside.

Mitchell, J. (1982). Introduction. In J. Lacan (Ed.), *Feminine sexuality* (pp. 1–26). New York: Pantheon Books.

Omi, M., & Winant, H. (1992). Racial formations. In P. S. Rothenberg (Ed.), *Race, class, and gender in the United States* (pp. 26–36). New York: St. Martin's Press.

Saxton, A. (1971). *The indispensable enemy: Labor and the anti-Chinese movement in California.* Berkeley and Los Angeles: University of California Press.

Schaefer, R. T. (1993). *Racial and ethnic groups.* New York: HarperCollins College Publishers.

Shakespeare, W. (1611). *The tempest.* In A. Harbage (Ed.) (1979), *The complete Pelican Shakespeare.* New York: Viking.

Staples, R. (1991). Black male genocide: A final solution to the race problem in America. *The Black family: Essays and studies.* Belmont, CA: Hadsworth Publishing.

The American heritage dictionary of the English language (Second College Edition) (1982). Boston: Houghton Mifflin Company.

The Western influence on African male/female relationships: Interview with Delores P. Aldridge. *The GaitherReporter,* December 1993, 1, 5.

CHAPTER TWENTY-FIVE

African American College Students' Attitudes Toward Mental Health Treatment

MAVIS MITCHELL, MALCOLM CORT, GEORGE YOUNG, AND LORNA ROBERTS

Introduction

African Americans are facing daily challenges to excel in American society. Many of these challenges are directly related to a history laden with prejudices and discrimination, which persists in the form of economic and health disparities. As African Americans continue to overcome such a history, emotional and environmental stresses affect their lives on a daily basis. Many of these stresses are common to all Americans regardless of their ethnic background. However, it appears that African Americans choose to ignore mental health treatment as an option for assistance in relieving their distress. The utilization of mental health treatment among African Americans is significantly low in comparison to the amount of psychiatric distress that appears to be in existence within the Black community.

This study evaluates the attitudes and beliefs of African American college students regarding mental health treatment. We utilize items from the General Social Survey (GSS) questionnaire on beliefs about mental illness. The GSS questionnaire was developed by the National Research Center affiliated with the University of Chicago. First, we examine the help-seeking behavior of the sample with regard to the person or persons from whom they would seek help in times of a mental health crisis. Second, we examine attitudes toward the use of psychotropic medication. Third, with the use of a qualitative approach, we explore some of the reasons respondents advance as explanations for their attitudes and practices with regard to mental health treatment.

Literature Review

A large body of literature advances descriptions of help-seeking behaviors of African Americans with regard to mental health. While many studies examine these behaviors in specific contexts, the most prominent descriptions are presented in this literature review. Matthew and Hughes (2001), for example, report that although there is evidence of significant emotional distress, African American women are less likely to seek out mental health assistance. Matthew and Hughes (2001) also state that there are many system barriers that hinder African Americans from accessing services, as well as negative attitudes and belief systems that influence the decision to decline mental health treatment.

Thorn and Sarata (1998), on the other hand, examine the mental health needs of African American men. They argue that the environmental and societal stresses that African American men experience appear to contribute to the difficulties they experience on a psychological level. In addition, African American men are more likely to be incarcerated or die from violent crimes. Educational and occupational opportunities are less available for African American men as well. Drug use and alcoholism are also factors that lead to mental distress in African American men. Thorn and Sarata (1998) further state that mental health treatment for African American men tends to be more often involuntary and initiated by systems outside of their primary family of origin.

Another prominent study by Schnittker et al. (2000) postulates that differences between Whites versus Blacks in beliefs regarding mental health etiology play a significant role in Blacks' negative perceptions of the mental health system. They believe that there is a fundamental difference between Black and White Americans in their belief systems concerning the origins of mental illness. Blacks disregard the notion of mental health problems being affiliated with genetic or biological disorders. They believe that society has always attempted to claim that Black people are genetically inferior to Whites; therefore, any theory that advances genetic reasons for mental ill health meets with much skepticism among Blacks. They see this belief system as a continued attempt by society to criticize Blacks and look at them in an inferior context. White Americans, on the other hand, are more likely to view mental health problems as being related to biological or genetic factors, and more willing to seek assistance from the mental health community. They tend to trust the professional community and believe that they can be assisted by its expertise.

Among African Americans, however, the issue of trust has a very interesting dynamic. Garretson (1993) reports that there is a mistrust of the mental health community due to a history of what appeared to be an ongoing practice of unequal treatment of African American patients at the hands of the healthcare community. Singleton-Bowie (1995) reports that many African Americans claim that they are diagnosed with more severe disorders than are their White counterparts and are given poorer prognoses for recovery. In mental health settings, cultural mistrust, when present in Black mental health patients, is believed to be responsible for a disproportionate number of schizophrenia diagnoses of African Americans by White clinicians. These diagnoses are believed to be the result of African American patients' perceptions of White clinicians as part of a distrusted, White-dominated power structure within the wider society in general, and within medicine in particular (Mouton, 2000; Whaley, 2001).

Although African Americans have attained substantial educational and economic gains over the past few decades, many health and economic disparities still exist. Psychological distress from various societal and familial issues contributes to an increase in mental health needs in the African American community. These needs, however, do not translate into an increase in the utilization of mental health services. On the contrary, African Americans choose to remain in the psychological distress rather than seek out mental health services.

This practice of avoiding mental health treatment translates into increasing suicide rates, marital distress, involuntary commitments, increased substance abuse, and increased crime and homicide rates. This situation only makes more evident the need for more mental health interventions in the African American community. For such interventions to take place, African Americans must utilize the available mental health treatments. The gap between need and utilization cries out for investigation of the barriers to mental health help-seeking that exist in the African American community.

Method

Subjects

The participants in this study were all African American college students from two traditionally Black colleges in Alabama. The sample consisted of 223 participants with an age range from 16 to 47 years, standard deviation of 4.8 years, and a mean of 20.8 years. Table 26.1 shows the distribution of demographic characteristics.

Table 26.1 Characteristics of Sample

Characteristic	N	%
Family income ($)		
Below 19,999	24	11.1
20,000–49,900	44	20.3
50,000–99,000	55	25.3
Over 100,000	32	14.7
DK	62	28.6
College classification		
Freshmen	74	33.5
Sophomore	38	17.2
Junior	47	21.3
Senior	60	27.1
Graduate	2	0.9
Father's education		
Elementary school	10	4.6
High school	56	25.8
Some college	54	24.9
Undergraduate degree	52	24.0
Graduate degree	45	27.1

As indicated in Table 26.1, the demographic characteristics under examination are fairly evenly distributed among the sample, indicating a wide variety of backgrounds among the student populations.

Procedures

The sample was collected on a convenience basis. Professors at two universities were asked to facilitate the study by requesting that the students in their classes participate in the study. All students who were present on the days when the data were collected participated in the study.

The questionnaire consisted of demographic variables, questions taken from the mental health module of the 1996 GSS. These scales measured individuals' religiousness, reliance on God, reliance on their religion, attitudes toward mental health treatment, and intention to use psychotropic medication in the event of a mental health crisis. For this study, scales measuring attitudes toward psychotropic medication were chosen for the dependent variable.

Measures

Dependent variable

The dependent variable for this study is an additive scale consisting of five variables. Each variable is a five-point Likert scale (1: strongly agree; 2: agree; 3: neither; 4: disagree; and 5: strongly disagree). The variables are as follows:

1. Taking these medications helps people deal with day-to-day stress.
2. Taking these medications makes things easier in relations with family and friends.
3. These medications help people control their symptoms.
4. Psychiatric medicine is harmful to the body.
5. If symptoms are no longer present, people should stop taking these medications.

Items 1, 2, and 3 were recoded to be conceptually consistent with items 4 and 5, so that higher scores on the scale reflect more positive attitudes toward psychiatric medication. The internal consistency of this scale (Cronbach's alpha), based on estimations using reliability analysis in SPSS, was 0.68.

Independent Variables

Strength and Comfort

This is an ordinal variable measuring the extent, in terms of frequency, that the respondent claims to find strength and comfort in religion. The responses are 1: many times a day to 6: never or almost never. The coding of this variable was reversed to indicate that higher scores reflect greater frequency of finding strength and comfort in one's religion.

Reliance on God as a Help for Coping

This is an additive scale measuring the extent to which respondents think of God as a help in coping with life's challenges. The scale consists of five Likert-type variables with responses from 1: a great deal to 4: not at all. These variables are as follows:

1. I think about my life as a part of a larger spiritual force.
2. I work together with God as partners.
3. I look to God for strength, support, and guidance.
4. I try to make sense of a situation and decide what to do without relying on God.
5. I wonder if God has abandoned me.

The coding of items 1, 2, and 3 was reversed so that higher scores on the scale reflect a greater perception of God as a help in coping with life's problems. The internal consistency of this scale using Cronbach's alpha was 0.54.

Undergone counseling

This is a dichotomous variable showing whether the respondent had ever undergone counseling for mental or emotional problems. Dummy coding indicated 1: yes or 0: no. Three demographic variables tested in the model were: father's education, used as a measure of social class. Measurements reflected 1: elementary school and 5: graduate degree. College classification was used as a measure of educational maturity and age (there was a high correlation between college classification and age). Higher scores reflect higher college classification.

Results

Quantitative Analysis

First, we investigated the pattern of help-seeking in the case of a mental health episode. In response to the question: Suppose you feel just a bit down or depressed, and you wanted to talk about it, whom would you turn to first? Table 26.2 gives the pattern of responses for categories of persons whom the respondents would speak to first, and those whom they would speak to second.

The pattern of persons who would be chosen as confidants for the first and second choice in cases of mental health episodes is similar. Less than 20% would choose an intimate partner, approximately 40% would choose a relative on both occasions, and between 31% and 36% would choose to turn to a friend. However, on both occasions, less than 5% would choose to tell either a member of the clergy or a health professional.

In order to investigate the effects of selected predictors on attitude toward psychotropic medication, a multiple regression analysis was performed. The analysis first entered reliance on God, and finding strength and comfort in one's religion, into the equation (step 1). Next, two demographic predictors—father's education and college classification—were added (step 2), and finally the variable "having gone to counseling" was added (step 3). This technique was carried out in order to determine the amount of variance accounted for by each cluster of variables, as each step in the analysis was undertaken. Table 26.3 shows the effects of each cluster at each stage of the analysis.

Table 26.2 Pattern of Help-Seeking

Category	First choice		Second choice	
	N	%	N	%
Intimate partner	32	15.1	26	11.9
Relative	84	39.6	86	39.4
Friend	66	31.1	78	35.8
Clergy	6	2.8	8	3.5
Health professional/counselor	2	0.9	4	1.8
Other	22	10.4	16	7.3

As indicated in Table 26.3, those who rely on God for help in life have a more negative attitude toward psychotropic medication than those who do not ($R = 0.4$, $F(2,131) = 12.6$, $p < 0.01$). Those who reported finding strength and comfort in their religion, on the other hand, have a more positive attitude toward psychotropic medication than those who do not report such reliance on their religion ($R = 0.53$, $F(4,131) = 12.37$, $p < 0.01$). Father's education, used here as a proxy measure for socioeconomic status, and college classification, used as a measure of educational maturity, are both positively related to attitude toward psychotropic medication in that those whose fathers have more education and those who have higher college standing are more positive toward psychotropic medication. Those who have gone to counseling for a mental health problem are significantly more negative than those who have not ($R = 0.58$, $F(5,131) = 12.76$, $p < 0.01$).

Qualitative Analysis

With the use of focus groups, the qualitative analysis illuminates and extends the results of the quantitative section of this chapter. The findings of those issues, which are reinvestigated by the focus group methodology, are also consistent with the results of the quantitative analysis. Participants expressed significant distrust for the mental health system overall. The majority of the participants believed that the mental health system overdiagnosed African American clients and tended to pathologize behaviors that are minimized in nonminority clients.

Table 26.3 Regression Analysis Showing Predictors of Attitude Toward Psychotropic Medication

Predictor	Step 1			Step 2			Step 3		
	β	t	p	β	t	p	β	t	p
Reliance on God	−0.20	−2.48	0.01	−0.22	−2.8	<0.01	−0.30	−3.78	<0.01
Strength and comfort	0.40	4.83	<0.01	0.39	4.96	<0.01	0.43	5.64	<0.01
Father's education	—	—	—	0.25	3.31	<0.01	0.20	2.69	<0.01
College classification	—	—	—	0.20	2.57	0.01	0.20	2.69	<0.01
Gone to counseling	—	—	—	—	—	—	−2.7	−3.25	<0.01

Note: Adjusted R^2 for step 1 = 0.15; step 2 = 0.26; and step 3 = 0.31.

During the discussion, many students indicated that they do not believe mental health treatment is a viable option for assistance with problems, except for the most severe of disorders that might incapacitate their ability to function. Additionally, the students did not trust medication and felt that it was too mind-altering to consider using, except again, in the most severe cases. Furthermore, they believed that even if their child were diagnosed with a common disorder such as attention deficit disorder, they would not consider using traditional medications such as Ritalin for treatment. They believed that this was an unnecessary crutch for children and could also be harmful to them physically. Instead, good old-fashioned discipline appeared to be the consensus among the group in dealing with behaviors in children such as attention deficit disorder.

A common theme throughout the discussion was the importance of maintaining family confidentiality. The thought of telling a stranger (mental health professional) about personal and private family matters was seen as a serious breach of the family system. Students reflected on the overtly angry response they would possibly receive from their parents or grandparents if they knew anyone in their family was seeking mental health treatment.

Interestingly, the majority of the students who participated in the focus groups were being trained in "helping professions," either social work or psychology, yet they overwhelmingly had beliefs that were contrary to the professions for which they were training.

Another common theme was that of belief in God. The students unanimously believed that faith in God should be sufficient for dealing with life's problems and circumstances. Furthermore, it was the overwhelming opinion of the participants that the use of a mental health professional or psychotropic medication would indicate a lack of faith in God. Moreover, the shame, humiliation, or embarrassment that the students would feel if their friends, church members, or family knew that they underwent mental health treatment or consented to taking psychotropic medication would be unbearable. Most students felt that it was important for them to handle their problems themselves and not depend on professional help to solve problems. To seek professional help was seen as a weakness. It appeared that presenting oneself as competent and in control of life and its problems was an essential theme.

Discussion and Conclusion

The high level of religiousness among African Americans is a phenomenon that saturates the social science literature and holds no surprise when research of this nature is undertaken. It would seem that higher levels of religiousness would lead people to more readily confide in religious leaders about crises such as failing mental health. This has not been the case, however, in the sample of African American college students under study. There is in evidence a consistent reluctance to confide in anyone outside of the friend-and-kin circle. Help-seeking behaviors bear out the notion that Blacks remain unwilling to approach professional helpers in the field of mental health and, more surprising, even their religious leaders. Since it is fair to conclude that most religious leaders in the Black community are Black, it is also fair to conclude that the most prominent barrier to help-seeking in mental health for African Americans is not cultural mistrust, but some yet-unknown cultural pattern that research in African American attitudes toward mental health has failed to identify.

What raises more questions are the findings that those who rely more intensely on God for help in coping with life stresses are more negative to psychotropic medication than those who do not, as compared to those who more often find strength and comfort in their religion, who are more positive to psychotropic medication. The difference in attitudes between these two groupings raises the question of whether reliance on *God* is sufficiently different from reliance on *religion* to drive a difference in attitude toward psychotropic medication. The evidence produced in this study suggests that this is the case. However, this difference needs further study before a definitive assertion can be made. It would appear, though, that among people in this sample, the perception is that reliance on God demands a commitment of faith that God and God alone should be able to help one through a mental crisis, and to seek other help is evidence of lack of faith in God.

An adherence to organized religion, on the other hand, may lead the believer to put confidence in the healthcare system. In fact, many religions own and operate hospitals, and as a result encourage among their believers the notion that there is a value to placing a certain level of confidence in modern medical treatments, which include the use of psychotropic medication. It is not surprising that those who show evidence of higher social standing, as indicated by the level of their fathers' education, are more positive toward psychotropic medication. It is also more consistent with commonsense thinking that those who are more educationally mature, as evidenced by their class standing, are more positive toward psychotropic medication. Both social class and the institution of education embrace the medical model; therefore, it is reasonable to think that persons of higher social class and those who are more educationally sophisticated will be more accepting of psychotropic mediation.

This study indicates that in this sample those who have undergone counseling for a mental health problem are more negative to psychotropic medication. This finding needs further study before a definitive explanation can be advanced. Should this result be replicated, then the question of whether the counseling experience may trigger more negative attitudes toward psychotropic medication needs to be confronted. The qualitative data indicate that many African Americans believe that the mental health system often overdiagnoses African American clients and tends to pathologize behaviors that are minimized in nonminority clients. If after a counseling experience drug treatment has been prescribed for a Black patient, then that patient may consciously or unconsciously rebel against the idea that he or she is considered so mentally ill that there is need for drug treatment. The consequence could well be that persons who have had this experience adopt a negative attitude toward psychotropic medication out of a feeling that their ethnic group is under attack by the "White" healthcare system.

Implications for Social Work Practice

The implications for social work practice are significant. Providing services in the usual traditional manner primarily based on Eurocentric modalities has proven to be ineffective. Additionally, providing services in settings such as agency buildings or counseling/therapy offices may be another factor that inhibits prospective African American clients in seeking services. African American communities may be more receptive to services that are provided in arenas in which they already feel safe and comforted: for instance, through programs within their neighborhood church and other nontraditional modalities.

In addition, because of the high regard for spirituality and religion within the African American community, change in the perception of mental health treatment must come from the pulpit. Religious leaders may be the first line of intervention in the quest to broaden the perception of mental health treatment and counter the notion that seeking help equates with lack of faith in God. Instead, the recognition that help from God may reveal itself through varying avenues, including professional assistance similar to that of going to the doctor for a medical issue, may influence a change in attitudes.

Moreover, education regarding the benefits of mental health treatment is paramount if social work practitioners expect the African American community to begin to consider mental health intervention as a viable option in dealing with emotional crises. It appears that some African Americans believe that even if they sought mental health treatment, it would not offer much help.

The issue of trust is one of the most difficult obstacles to treatment that social workers must overcome. Unfortunately, social work practitioners are seen as a part of the overall societal system that has historically mistreated and discriminated against the African American community. Current societal conditions continue to contribute to the perpetuation of the societal ills within African American communities. Social workers must acknowledge the impact of these societal conditions as an impetus to mental health problems among African Americans instead of focusing only on the medical model, which attributes the etiology of mental illness to genetic or biological factors. A change in this approach may begin to bridge the gap between the practitioner and the community, allowing trust to eventually develop.

It also appears that the training African American social work practitioners receive has little impact on changing attitudes toward mental health treatment on a personal level. In other words, practitioners are being prepared to provide a service they distrust and would not use themselves. This issue must be vehemently addressed in the classroom, allowing for active discussion about fears, values, and belief systems so that negative perceptions can be challenged and addressed before practioners enter the field of social work.

References

Garretson, D. J. (1993). Psychological misdiagnosis of African Americans. *Journal of Multicultural Counseling and Development 21*(2), 119–127.

Matthew, A., & Hughes, T. (2001). Mental health service use by African American women exploration of sub-population differences. *Department of Health and Administrative Nursing University of Illinois at Chicago 7*(1), 75–87.

Mouton, C. P. (2000). Cultural and religious issues for African Americans. In K. L. Braun, J. H. J. Pietsch, & P. L. Blanchette (Eds.), *Cultural issues in end-of-life decision making*. Thousand Oaks, CA: Sage.

Schnittker, J., Freese, J., & Powell, B. (2000). Nature, nurture, neither: Black–White differences in beliefs about the causes and appropriate treatment of mental illness. *Social Forces 78*(3), 1101–1131.

Singleton-Bowie, S. (1995). The effect of mental health practitioners' racial sensitivity on African Americans' perceptions of mental health services in the United States. *Social Work Research 19*(4), 238–245.

Thorn, G., & Sarata, P. V. (1998). Psychotherapy with African American men: What we know and what we need to know. *Journal of Multicultural Counseling and Development 26*(4), 240–254.

Whaley, A. L. (2001). Cultural mistrust of White mental health clinicians among African Americans with severe mental illness. *American Journal of Orthopsychiatry Special Issue 71*(2), 252–256.

Part Five
Global Perspectives

CHAPTER TWENTY-SIX

Education Enhances Equality and Fairness

Where Do People of Color Fit in Global Educational Systems?

JAMES MBUVA

Abstract

The purpose of this chapter is to examine how education enhances equality and fairness and to demonstrate where people of color fit in global educational systems, and the implications for the competitive twenty-first century job market. This chapter investigates the meaning of equality and fairness; the symbolic meaning of *Animal Farm*, *Things Fall Apart*, and "survival of the fittest"; the key factors that demonstrate where people of color fit in global educational systems; the ways education enhances equality and fairness; and implications for the competitive twenty-first century job market. The material presented in this chapter demonstrates that *equality* means all people must have a level playing field. People can never be equal if the gap between them continues to widen. Although education for students in poor communities has fallen, and the survival of students in wealthy communities is assured in the capitalistic education system, educating students of color remains the only instrument for enhancing equality and fairness. Thus, education is the only viable key that has the ability to open doors of access and opportunity to African American youths.

Introduction

The purpose of this chapter is to demonstrate that education enhances equality and fairness, and to ask where people of color fit in global educational systems. The 2004 Patterson Research Conference's theme, "Still Not Equal," merits a high degree of consideration today because surely, as Orwell (1945) contends, "All animals are equal but some are more equal than others"; *Things Fall Apart* every day (Achebe, 1958); and the Darwinian (1859) ideology of natural selection, also known as "survival of the fittest" (Spencer, 1864) still reigns in everyday educational, social, cultural, professional, and political contexts. Consequently, it is necessary to be educated about how the world works and how to navigate it in order to survive as a people. This chapter examines the following key questions:

1. What are equality and fairness?
2. What is the symbolic meaning of *Animal Farm*, *Things Fall Apart*, and "survival of the fittest"?
3. What are the key factors that demonstrate where people of color fit in global educational systems?
4. What are the implications for the competitive twenty-first century job market?

Equality and Fairness

Equality

What is equality? *Equal* means, "same in number, size, merit; fit, or qualified; [and] evenly balanced" (*Webster's New Dictionary*, 1994, p. 133). Hence, Black people are equal to White people. *The Merriam-Webster Dictionary* (1997) adds to the meaning of *equal* by demonstrating that *equal* means "of the same measure, quantity, value, quality, number, degree, or status as another; impartial, [and] free from extremes" (p. 257). However, the playing field must be the same to claim equality.

What does *equal opportunity* mean? Equal opportunity is a "theory and practice of employment opportunity unbiased because of race, color, religion, gender, age, national origin, or mental or physical handicap" (*Webster's New Dictionary*, 1994, p. 133). However, if some people in a society are more privileged than others in acquiring jobs, education, and resources, then equal opportunity is not available to all.

Fairness

What is fairness? *Fair* means, "beautiful, ample, unblemished, of moderate quality or amount, just, honest, [and] favorable" (*Webster's New Dictionary*, 1994, p. 143; *The Merriam-Webster Dictionary*, 1997). Fairness can only mean what it stands for if all people are treated justly, honestly, and favorably. All people are beautiful and merit equal treatment that is free from guile and malice.

The Symbolic Meaning of Animal Farm, Things Fall Apart, *and "Survival of the Fittest"*

Animal Farm

The key question is: Is our society immune from *Animal Farm* syndrome? According to Jones (2004), George Orwell's "classic allegory in 1945, his portrait of Mr. Jones' humble farm that becomes paradise when the animals overthrow the humans and establish the commandment, 'All animals are created equal' struck a vibrant chord in a world sick of war." Jones contends that George Orwell:

> . . . had Russian leaders in mind with his depiction of the conniving pigs Snowball, Squealer, and Napoleon. But his exciting tale stands the test of time because still today in some civilizations leaders believe 'some animals are more equal than others' and get away with it. (Jones, 2004)

If the pigs of the animal world represent the governed people who are considered unequal, then the leaders, the privileged, the rich, the elite, and the affluent are the "more equal" people of the world. Unfortunately, this divide has permeated everyday life, and as with the pigs in *Animal Farm*, it is the people's responsibility to speak against the evils of inequality and unfairness. It was thought that democracy "by the people, of the people, and for the people" would be sufficient, but it has failed radically. The divide is widening every day, and the remedy is not yet known because instead of providing a way out, leaders and policy makers perpetuate inequality through the uneven distribution of resources to children in the nation's school districts (especially poor schools), thus limiting children's right to learn (Darling-Hammond, 1997). The poor school districts' unfavorable educational policies and unfunded school programs designed to help all children learn equitably are signs of the widening gap of inequality and unfairness in the educational system.

Things Fall Apart

Things Fall Apart was written by Chinua Achebe in 1958. Born to a Nigerian family in Ogidi village in 1930, Achebe was acquainted with Anglican missionary work. Through the exposure to the work of missionaries, the start and the growth of Christianity, and the colonization of the British government, Achebe had a lot to say about how his world suddenly changed. Missionaries, Christianity, and British colonialism had disrupted the Ibo culture. Hence, Achebe's novel *Things Fall Apart* takes place in the Nigerian village of Umuofia in the late 1880s, before missionaries and other outsiders arrive. The Ibo clan practices common tribal traditions—worship of gods, sacrifice, communal living, war, and magic. Leadership is based on a man's personal worth and his contribution to the good of the tribe. Okonkwo stands out as a great leader of the Ibo tribe. Tribesmen respect Okonkwo for his many achievements (Perino, 2004).

However, Okonkwo had to face "punishment for his accidental shooting of a young tribesman," and due to this, "The Ibo banned Okonkwo from the clan for 7 years. Upon his return to the village, Okonkwo finds a tribe divided by the influence of missionaries and English bureaucrats who have interrupted the routine of tradition" (Brians, 2002; Perino, 2004).

Unquestionably, Chinua Achebe "uses his characters and their unique language to portray the double tragedies that occur in the story." Readers not only "identify with Okonkwo and his personal hardships, but also with the Ibo culture and its disintegration." For this reason, Achebe wrote, "not for his fellow Nigerians, but for people beyond his native country. . . . He wanted to explain the truth about the effects of losing one's culture" (Brian, 2002; Perino, 2004). Hence, Chinua Achebe was stripped of his culture and the world he knew so well by the invasion of the missionaries and the British colonialists. When people are ruled and oppressed by foreign forces or a dominant culture, they can only feel out of place, and like Achebe, they can say things have indeed fallen apart on their watch.

Survival of the Fittest

"Survival of the fittest" is based on Charles Darwin's Theory of Evolution (University of California Museum of Paleontology [UCMP], 2004). While Darwin's Theory of Evolution, is "a relatively young archetype, the evolutionary world view itself is as old as antiquity. Ancient Greek philosophers such as Anaximander postulated the development of life from non-life and the evolutionary descent of man from animal" (UCMP, 2004). Unlike the Greek philosophy of the origin of life, "Charles Darwin simply brought something new to the old philosophy—a plausible mechanism called 'natural selection' "(UCMP, 2004). The key questions concerning Darwin's Theory of Evolution are: How does natural selection work? What are the long-lasting implications of natural selection?

Natural selection acts to preserve and accumulate minor advantageous genetic mutations. Suppose a member of a species developed a functional advantage (it grew wings and learned to fly). Its offspring would inherit that advantage and pass it on to their offspring. The inferior (disadvantaged) members of the same species would gradually die out, leaving only the superior (advantaged) members of the species. Natural selection is the preservation of a functional advantage that enables a species to compete better in the wild. It is the naturalistic equivalent to domestic breeding. Over the centuries, human breeders have produced dramatic changes in domestic animal populations by selecting individuals to breed. Breeders eliminate undesirable traits gradually over time. Similarly, natural selection eliminates inferior species gradually over time (UCMP, 2004).

In natural selection, the very idea that stronger species might have supremacy over weaker ones and that their chances of survival are greater than those of the feeble suggests there is uneven distribution of power, resources, and authority in the natural order of things. This would imply that no matter how much a society speaks of equality and fairness in education and justice for all, there will always be injustice for the economically and socially "weak." Consequently, the rhetoric for justice becomes "a mask for injustice and leaves those who are weak to be preyed upon, those who are defeated to be abused, and those in a position of disadvantage in fear that their disadvantage will be exploited to their destruction" (Keyes, 2001). The symbolic meaning of this theory also implies that the poor will always be poor, the rich will always be rich, and students with low socioeconomic status will "naturally" suffer diminished learning and employment opportunities every day they wake up.

Where Students of Color Fit in Global Educational Systems

Factors Contributing to the Poor Academic Achievement of Students Of Color

Across US schools, African American students are not experiencing academic success due to various factors such as unfavorable support policies, low income, poor preschool programs, failure to engage African American parents in the school life of their children, mothers raising school children alone because the children's fathers are in prison, low self-esteem, lack of motivation, absenteeism, and so on (AAC & U, 2004; Crockett, 2004; Fagan et al., 1995; Keller, 2004; Kusimo, 1999; Mandara & Murry, 2000; Nolan et al.,

2001; Pong, n.d.; Railsback, 2004; Redd, 2003; Shokraii, 1998; Strydom & Strydom, 2004). While it is very easy to blame "the enemy out there" due to "a propensity to find someone or something outside ourselves to blame when things go wrong" or for our failures, it is very important to be involved in the search for solutions and especially to try to do what one can afford (Senge, 1990, p. 19).

The Remedy

The key questions here are: What is the remedy for the African American students' low academic achievement? What should be done to enhance academic and personal success of African American male students? It should be noted that African American female students tend to do well inside and outside the classroom (Wheat, 1997). However, "the shortage of positive African American male role models, the perceptions of societal racism and victimization, and existing African American male subculture work against academic achievement" (Davis & Muhlhausen, 2000; Reglin, 2004). Reglin's recommendations to schools seeking to remedy the problem are worthy of consideration. He suggests that schools focus on the following:

1. High but realistic expectations.
2. Parent and family involvement.
3. Parent centers.
4. Emphasis on the whole child.
5. Building self-esteem.
6. Cooperative learning.
7. Cross-age and peer tutoring.
8. Learning styles instruction.
9. Prevention and assessment of unfavorable classroom environments.
10. Integration of African males in classroom activities.
11. African American role models.

Moreover, schools, curriculum developers, and policy makers should think on how to teach all children by taking "antiracist education seriously," "rethinking the curriculum" to reflect students of color, examining the significance of standardized testing, and creating contextual learning environments where teachers, students, and parents can work together for the common good of students' academic achievement (Levine et al., 1995; Reeves, 1998).

A Meeting of the Minds

On a trip to San Diego, California, for the National University Faculty Spring

Symposium, I met and got to know Mr. Clarence Mason Weaver, who was staying at the Mission Valley Marriott, San Diego. Mr. Weaver's eyes were fixated on me when I stepped off the hotel's elevator. Walking toward him, I asked myself, "I wonder why this Black man is looking at me so intently?" With no hesitation, he asked me why I was at the Marriott, and I told him that the faculty members of National University meet during Spring Symposium to enhance their educational mission and to discuss educational issues, especially how to teach and make a difference in the diverse communities across California.

Mr. Weaver seemed interested in the subject, and we started a long conversation on Black culture and education, slavery, and "the master's farm." Through his witty stories about Black people on the plantations, Mr. Weaver touched my heart and mind. Then he delivered an uppercut punch: "I want you to know that I am concerned about my Black people's well-being, and for that matter, I have written a book, *It's OK to Leave the Plantation: The New Underground Railroad* (1998). Being a Black man from Kenya myself, I said to Mr. Weaver, "That is interesting. I have been looking for a Black man to share about the situation of the African brothers who were brought to the United States of America involuntarily by way of slavery." Mr. Weaver immediately said, "I will give you my book tomorrow morning." With deep appreciation for his offer, I went to bed happy that night because I finally met a fellow African with whom to share information about people and students of color. Little did I know that Mr. Weaver had written immensely about how African Americans should leave "the master's plantation."

Lessons Learned From Mr. Weaver

The more I read Mr. Weaver's book, the more I discerned that for people and students of color to succeed in global education systems and economies, they need to take responsibility. Certainly, people may lack resources and support, but it takes personal initiative to overcome systemic inequality. It takes courage to challenge the status quo of *Animal Farm* syndrome. It takes tenacity to overcome the challenges posed by the social, cultural, and political capital of the dominant culture. It takes determination to repudiate the implications of the "survival of the fittest" theory. Mr. Weaver's book, *It's OK to Leave the Plantation: The New Underground Railroad* (2000), presents the following recommendations to help African American men and women, African American youths, and those throughout the diaspora to succeed in global educational systems:

- *Avoid being enemies of one another.* It is important to support one another instead of being enemies. Whether we become actors, come-

dians, professors, doctors, CEOs, or family technicians, Black people must support one another to survive academically, socially, and economically.
- *Forgive one another at all times.* Forgiveness is the remedy to hatred, fear, and despondency. It provides therapy for adults and children alike.
- *Accept yourself.* It is vital to be confident, creative, resourceful, able, strong, leaders instead of followers, designers, free—liberated from slavery as well as mental, emotional, social, economic, psychological, and intellectual imprisonment.
- *Authentic education is necessary.* Climb the academic ladder by going to school and reading the right books. Develop a network of well-educated communities of men and women who are optimistic about life and are ready to liberate the human race from economic, cultural, social, and political domination.
- *Aim at success.* Black people must rise up from where they have fallen in order to stand up, walk, and succeed.
- *Lift up your brothers and sisters.* Develop a habit of lifting one another up from ignorance and poverty. Be proud of being Black people and maintain the beauty that there is in Blackness. Black people must pull together for survival's sake.
- *Final call.* Ultimately, Mr. Weaver calls on Black people to realize that it is OK to leave the master's plantation.

Conclusions and Implications for the Twenty-First-Century Job Market

This chapter has revealed the significance of understanding equality and fairness in our everyday life experiences. It is difficult for equality and fairness to take place in a social environment where "some animals are more equal than others," where things have fallen apart, and where "survival of the fittest" has become society's educational, social, cultural, economic, and political norm. Nevertheless, people of color can work hard to make steady movement toward equality and fairness through education.

It is necessary for Black people in the United States and in the global villages, to care about the education of the youth. Parental involvement in the everyday processes of children's education is as important as the jobs where parents spend most of their time. Educating children successfully is the only way to create leverage in the pursuit of equality, fairness, and opportunity in the competitive twenty-first-century job market. Mr. Weaver's work brings to our daily thinking clarity and vision for tomorrow through the realization that Black people need to leave the plantation and, with dignity and confidence, establish themselves in society through the instrument of education—because education opens doors.

References

AAC & U. (2004). Achievement gap continues to challenge ideal of equal educational opportunity. Retrieved October 22, 2004, from http://www.aacu-edu.org/aacu_news/AACUNews04/March04/facts_figures.cfm

Achebe, C. (1958). *Things fall apart*. London: Heinemann.

Brians, P. (2002). Chinua Achebe: Things Fall Apart study guide. Retrieved September 23, 2004, from http://www.wsu.edu:8000/?brians/anglophone/achebe.html#gyre

Crockett, O. R. (2004). Why African Americans are shying away from top colleges: After blows to affirmative action, black applications are off. Retrieved October 22, 2004, from http://www.businessweek.com/magazine/content/04_25/b3888051_mz011.htm\

Darling-Hammond, L. (1997). *The right to learn: A blueprint for creating schools that work*. San Francisco: Jossey-Bass.

Darwin, C. (1859). *The origin of species by means of natural selection, or the preservation of favored races in the struggle for life* (1st ed.). Retrieved October 20, 2004, from http://www.talkorigins.org/faqs/origin/chapter1.html

Davis, D. G., & Muhlhausen, D. B. (2000). Young African-American males: Continuing victims of high homicide rates in urban communities. Retrieved October 22, 2004, from http://www.heritage.org/Research/Crime/CDA00--05.cfm

Fagan, P. F., Rector, R. E., & Johnson, K. A. (1995). The positive effects of marriage: A book of charts. Retrieved October 22, 2004, from http://www.heritage.org/Research/Features/Marriage/index.cfm

Jones, K. (2004). Bailiwick Rep has musical Animal Farm plus First Lady Suite and Jewish Christmas in 2004–05. *PlayBill*. Retrieved September 23, 2004, from http://www.playbill.com/news/article/88044.html

Keller, E. (2004). Strategies for teaching science to African American students. Retrieved October 22, 2004, from http://www.as.wvu.edu/~equity/african.html

Keyes, A. (2001). God vs. Darwin: Survival of the fittest? Retrieved September 23, 2004, from http://www.freerepublic.com/forum/a3b4936eb0a36.htm

Kusimo, P. (1999). Rural African Americans and education: The legacy of the Brown decision. *ERIC Digest*. ERIC Clearinghouse on Rural Education and Small Schools, Charleston, WV. Retrieved October 22, 2004, from http://ericadr.piccard.csc.com/extra/ericdigests/ed425050.html

Levine, D., Lowe, R., Peterson, B., & Rita, T. (1995). *Rethinking schools: An agenda for change*. New York: The New York Press.

Mandara, J., & Murray, C. B. (2000). Effects of parental marital status, income, and family functioning on African American adolescent self-esteem. Retrieved October 22, 2004, from http://www.apa.org/journals/fam/fam143475.html

Marcon, R. A. (2004). Moving up the grades: Relationship between preschool model and later success. Retrieved October 22, 2004, from http://ecrp.uiuc.edu/v4n1/marcon.html

Nolan, R. F., Dai, Y., & Smith, J. N. (2001). Self-esteem reported by African-American students in southern middle schools. Retrieved October 22, 2004, from http://www.education.nsula.edu/lmsa/selfesteem.htm

Orwell, G. (1945). *Animal farm.* London: Secker & Warburg.

Perino, K. (2004). BookRags: Book notes on Things Fall Apart. Retrieved September 23, 2004, from http://www.boorags.com/notes/tfa

Pong, S.-L. (n.d.). The educational success of children in nonintact families: Do ethnicity and the school matter? Retrieved October 22, 2004, from http://www.aera.net/grantsprogram/abstract_list/Abstracts/Abs-RG-00000032.html

Railsback, J. (2004). Increasing student attendance: Strategies from research and practice. Retrieved October 22, 2004, from http://www.nwrel.org/request/2004june/index.html

Redd, K. E. (2003, February 27). Do state academic merit scholarships discriminate against African Americans? *Black Issues in Higher Education.* Retrieved October 22, 2004, from http://www.findarticles.com/p/articles/mi_m0DXK/is_1_20/ai_98539926

Reeves, D. B. (1998). *Making standards work: How to implement standards-based assessments in classroom, schools, and district* (2nd ed.). Denver, CO: Center for Performance Assessment.

Reglin, G. (2004). *Promoting success for the African American male students: A blue print for action. A series of solutions and strategies, Number 8. ERIC NO: ED371065.* Retrieved September 23, 2004, from http://www.education.ky.gov/KDE/Instructional+Resources/Closing+the+Gap/Equity/Acguevenebt+Gap/Annotated+Bibliography+on+Minority+Achievement.htm

Senge, P. M. (1990). *The fifth discipline: The art and practice of learning organization.* New York: Currency Doubleday.

Shokraii, N. H. (1998). The self-esteem fraud: Why feel-good education does not lead to academic success. Retrieved October 22, 2004, from http://www.ceousa.org/READ/self.html

Spencer, H. (1864). *Principles of Biology.* New York: Appleton.

Strydom, J., & Strydom, B. (2004). Early learning—the key to success in life. Retrieved October 22, 2004, from http://specialchildren.about.com/cs/education/a/learning.htm

University of California Museum of Paleontology. (2004). *Evolution: Theory and science.* Retrieved September 23, 2004, from http://www.ucmp.berkeley.edu/history/evotheory.html

Weaver, C. M. (2000). *It's OK to leave the plantation: The new underground railroad* (3rd ed.). Fallbrook, CA: Reeder.

Webster's New Dictionary (1994). Los Angeles, CA: Deluxe Books.

Wheat, C. (1997). Differences in education achievement for low income Black males and females. Retrieved October 26, 2004, from http://www.wjh.harvard.edu/~cwheat/malefemale.html

CHAPTER TWENTY-SEVEN

Obstacles to Equal Opportunity for African Refugees in the United States

ELAVIE NDURA AND OMIUNOTA NELLY UKPOKODU

We want to learn their customs, to take them as they are without laughing at them because in the end we have to behave like them in order to be allowed to live with them in their society easily. This requires intelligence, looking without looking, talking without talking, without pointing fingers.

(Burundian refugee)

Introduction

This sample statement by one of this study's participants, a Burundian refugee in his mid-50s, whose family of 11 had been living in the United States for only 12 months when he was interviewed for the study that generated the data for this chapter, highlights the complexity of acculturation and the urgency that most newcomers feel to fit into American society. Todd's family is part of the over 3 million African refugees and the 15 million refugees worldwide who fled to different countries in 2001 to escape persecution based on personal or group characteristics such as race, ethnicity, religion, nationality, social group, political opinion, or armed conflict, and the often resulting lack of a durable solution (US Committee for Refugees, 2001, 2002). The civil war that erupted in 1993 between the Tutsi and the

Hutu in the small landlocked country of Burundi in central-eastern Africa, for instance, has forced more than half a million refugees to seek shelter in Europe, the United States, and other African countries (United Nations High Commissioner for Refugees [UNHCR], 2000).

Any discussion of equal opportunity for African refugees and all African immigrants in the United States must begin with a full investigation and understanding of their perceptions of and experiences in the new culture in order to delineate factors that may facilitate or impede their acculturation process. The adjustment process of refugees and all other immigrants, in general, is influenced by a host of individual and societal factors (Kent, 1953; Haines, 1985; Arthur, 2000; Suárez-Orozco & Suárez-Orozco, 2001). This chapter focuses on the experiences of African immigrants in the United States.

Historically, the African immigrant experience has been twofold: (1) they were forcibly brought to the new world or (2) they immigrated to pursue educational aspirations but planned to return home to contribute to the task of nation building (Takougang, 1995). However, in recent years, because of political, economic, and religious instability, and threatening conditions such as warfare and persecution, many Africans are immigrating and resettling in the United States and other parts of the world. Data from the Immigration and Naturalization Services (INS), for example, indicate that the number of African immigrants and refugees to the United States has increased tremendously.

Africans, like all other immigrants, experience a number of acculturation situations as they encounter and are exposed to the traditions, values, norms, and interaction and communication styles of the dominant society. What is *acculturation*? Basically, *acculturation* refers to the transitions and related issues that occur as a function of continuous contact between two differing cultures. Generally, acculturation has been defined as an ethnic socialization process by which developing individuals acquire the host of cultural and psychological qualities that are necessary to function as a member of one's group (Berry, 1991, 1998; Roysircai-Sodowsky & Maestas, 2000). Others have viewed acculturation as the adaptation of minority groups to the culture of the dominant culture. Theoretically, two perspectives have evolved to frame the acculturation of immigrants (Liu et al., 1999). Four subacculturation processes and types have also been proposed (Berry, 1991; 1998, Kitano, 1989; Kitano & Maki, 1996). Type A (assimilation) is the case where the individual chooses to identify with mainstream culture and so rejects the minority culture. In Type B (integration), the individual seeks to retain his or her own ethnic culture but finds ways to adapt to the mainstream/dominant culture. Type C (separation) involves the individual identifying with his or her ethnic culture but rejecting the majority norms and values. Type D (marginality) is the lack of involvement and identification with one's ethnic culture as well as dominant culture.

In addition, research suggests that refugees undergo patterns of adjustment. In the initial period, they experience the reality of loss of occupational and social status—from professional to menial, from elite to an impoverished minority (Rogg, 1974; Weiermiair, 1971). As Doheny (1981) puts it, "a highly educated person with professional competence becomes a non-entity overnight." With loss of culture—their identity and habits—they have to carefully examine every action or routine that used to be familiar and habitual (Eitinger, 1960). Family strains are caused by the shift in power between husband and wife and the children's cultural conflict and disrespect for cultural and family values and practices (Hoff, 1968). Finally, nostalgia and other types of psychological anguish arise. The second adjustment stage occurs between the first and second years when the refugees work to rebuild their lives (Keller, 1975) as they experience language improvement, retraining programs, hard work, and determination. During this period, it is suggested that in most cases refugees tend to reflect and capitalize on the qualities that facilitated their upward mobility in their homeland (Rogg, 1974; Stein, 1979) and the determination to rise above their present circumstances (Keller, 1975). The third adjustment stage is marked by increased problems within the family due to refugees changing jobs, attending schools, and relocating. The fourth pattern of adjustment occurs between the fourth and fifth years of immigration, a period marked by survival and feelings of being acculturated enough to function but far from assimilated or integrated (Department of Health, Education and Welfare, 1979). Further, research has identified refugees as "at risk" or "adjusted." For example, single refugees such as those from separated families, divorced or widowed women as household heads, those in rural areas, or isolated communities have been identified as at high risk (Gordon, 1964; Rogg, 1974), while those with an intact family, homeowners, young children, and a community support system tend do well. Research suggests that the state and nature of the host–refugee relationship affects the extent and quality of refugee adjustment—whether the host community is welcoming, tolerant, hostile, or indifferent (Stein, 1981). For example, in the United States, Stein (1981) indicates that despite the use of sponsorship programs, few meaningful friendships are formed: the refugee is aided out of duty.

African immigrants and refugees, like other immigrants, experience all the aforementioned acculturation issues and conflicts generated by individual as well as societal factors (Suárez-Orozco & Suárez-Orozco, 2001). However, African refugees and immigrants tend to experience other critical psychological distress such as racism. Despite their hard work, dedication, and determination to realize the American dream, African refugees and immigrants are faced with the reality of what Aman (2002) calls "innocence about race relations" as they encounter the same stereotypes as their African American counterparts and are perceived as lazy, criminals, and drug dealers, and experience profiling, harassment, intimidation, and so on. The internationally publicized incident of Amadou Diallo, an African immigrant from Guinea who was mercilessly beaten to death by White New York police officers, is a case in point. In addition, African immigrants and refugees experience a hostile relationship or horizontal racism from some of their counterparts—African Americans who perceive them to be responsible for their slavery experience.

Literature has also linked immigrant families' acculturation to children's educational attitudes and performance. M. M. Suárez-Orozco (1989) conducted a psychosocial study of motivation and achievement of Central American refugees in US high schools. He pointed out how real life in the American inner city changed their initial idealistic perception of the opportunities that America has to offer, such as educational opportunities and financial stability. C. Suárez-Orozco and M. M. Suárez-Orozco (2001) investigated children of immigrants in the United States and how they were faring in American society. They discovered that immigrant children's success in schools is dependent on the whole family's successful long-term cultural adaptation, which is in turn influenced by many factors like family cohesion, interpersonal relations, and socioeconomic and educational background. They raised the important question of whether immigrants who look, talk, dress, and move differently will be allowed to truly become members of their new societies.

This chapter presents a synthesis of the findings from a broader study that investigated the acculturation dreams and challenges of Burundian refugees who reside in the United States. This chapter focuses on the refugees' perceived acculturation challenges that impede their quest for equal opportunity in the pursuit of the American dream.

The Study

Purpose Statement and Research Questions

This qualitative, phenomenological case study (Wolcott, 1994; Yin, 1994; Creswell, 1998; Marshall & Rossman, 1999; Stake, 2000) was designed to investigate the factors that impact the successful acculturation of Burundian refugee families who have been resettled in a large metropolitan city in the

Southwestern United States. In this study, the acculturation process is defined as cultural adaptation or adjustment to American society and culture.

Burundian refugees, like all other refugees and immigrants, expect to experience the American dream as they settle into their new society. How does this expectation match with reality as they acculturate? The overarching question that guided this investigation was: What obstacles hinder Burundian refugees' access to equal opportunity and the successful attainment of the American dream? Specifically, three questions were designed to answer this central question: (1) How do Burundian refugees describe their experiences with regard to employment opportunities and sustainability in the United States? (2) How do they navigate the confining social and cultural contexts within the multicultural American society? (3) In what ways do previous life experiences in Burundi and transitional host countries influence their adjustment process?

Participants

Over 500 Burundi families were resettled in the United States from different refugee camps in Africa between 1997 and 2000 by Catholic Social Services (CSC) and the International Rescue Committee (IRC). Fifteen of those families were sent to the current research site. The researcher, working as a volunteer, became actively involved in the acclimation process of the newcomers.

The participants consisted of a convenience criterion sample (Creswell, 1998) of 14 Burundian refugees (11 adults and 3 high school students) who had been resettled in a large metropolitan city in the Southwestern United States since 1998. The convenience sample was limited to Burundian refugees who reside in the same metropolitan area, due to time and financial constraints. This chapter will report on the findings from the interviews with the 11 adult participants.

The participants consisted of five married couples and one divorced male. Three of the couples had three children each; one had nine children; and another couple had one child and a baby on the way. The divorced participant did not have children. The participants ranged in age between 26 and 56 years old. Five were females and six were males. The participants represented different levels of education from their countries of origin. Seven had a college education; two had a secondary vocational education (grades 1–13); one had a general secondary education (grades 1–13); and one had a seventh grade education. Six of the participants (two females and four males) held professional positions in Burundi, mostly in education; two (both males) were college students; and three females were housewives. Three of the five married couples already owned their home in the United States; two couples were still renting an apartment; and one participant was renting a room in a participating couple's home. The participants had been resettled from different African countries outside of their native Burundi into the United States between 1998 and 2002. All participants' names have been replaced with pseudonyms throughout this chapter.

Procedures and Data Sources

The study was conducted over the course of 1 year in 2002–2003. Initially, the researcher called the adult participants on the telephone to request their participation in the study, as well as the participation of their school-aged children (7–17 years old). As the participants' culture dictates, she spoke with the male head of household, wherever applicable, in this initial recruitment telephone conversation in which she explained the project and requested the family's participation. She also gave each family a hospitality gift (a food/fruit basket and soft beverages) at the time of her initial visit, a practice that is very highly valued and appreciated in the participants' customs. These personal telephone calls and the researcher's sensitivity to the participants' culture helped develop the affinity that is required to conduct culturally responsive research. Being a fellow Burundian immigrant who speaks the participants' first language also helped establish a sense of sameness, which allowed for the development of trust (Vásquez-Montilla et al., 2000), another prerequisite for credible qualitative data collection. However, as a future publication will discuss, this affinity still did not guarantee access to all desired information from all target participants.

Data for the study were collected from three sources: interviews, document analysis, and direct observation, in order to achieve triangulation, or to search for the convergence of information (Yin, 1994; Creswell, 1998; Marshall & Rossman, 1999; Stake, 2000). Most of the data were collected through semistructured open-ended interviews conducted in Kirundi, the participants' first and home language, or English (according to participants' preferences) often mixed with French. The participants were asked to share their experiences as refugees in the United States. They were prompted to talk about work, social services, social interactions, and schooling experiences. The researcher also recorded any information that the participants volunteered regarding their experiences before resettling in the United States. The interviews were scheduled to last 1–2 hours; however, they lasted at least 3–4 hours each. Six of the participants allowed the researcher to tape record their interviews. The other five participants only allowed the researcher to write down notes during the interviews. All the interviews were conducted at the participants' homes. A Burundian immigrant who is proficient in Kirundi, French, and English, transcribed the recorded interviews. The professional transcriptionist lives outside the United States, and she does not know any of the participants personally. Field notes from the researcher's direct observation were collected. Direct observation generated data about the participants' physical environment, family and community interactions, and the general atmosphere surrounding the interviews. Relevant documents were analyzed to help answer the research questions. The researcher also maintained a journal in which she recorded her data collection experiences.

Data Analysis and Interpretation

All data from interviews, documents, and direct observation were analyzed separately during and after the data collection phase, identifying generated themes with different colors from the beginning. The preliminary report reflecting the description and interpretation of the case was returned to select participants who read and verified its authenticity and accuracy (Asmussen & Creswell, 1995). The informants were asked three questions: (1) Is the researcher's description and interpretation of your experiences as Burundian refugees in the United States accurate? (2) Are the themes and constructs that the researcher identified consistent with your lived experiences? (3) Are there any themes or constructs that she missed? The informants supported the description and interpretation of the findings.

Findings

The obstacles that hinder equal opportunity for African refugees in the United States can be categorized into six broad themes, which will be discussed individually in this section: (1) professional integration, (2) social relations, (3) family dynamics, (4) cross-cultural differences, (5) language issues, and (6) nostalgic memories.

Professional Integration

Several of the participants came to the United States with academic credentials and many years of professional experience. Yet, upon their arrival, they were offered low-paying, manual labor, and back-breaking jobs, which were far removed from the kinds of positions they expected and felt qualified to assume. Boniface, for instance, who was a college graduate and worked as a high school principal in Burundi before being forced into exile, recounted how he was hired to load and unload trucks 8 hours a day while still having to endure condescending attitudes from his employer. He stated,

> I was working for example eight hours, waking up at four o'clock and going back home at 6–7 pm very tired and when you are waking up to go to work we were feeling you didn't have the trust to go . . . you were feeling scared of what is gonna happen the next day . . . besides you also could feel a kind of not discrimination but when people look at you and they think even that minimum salary job you have you don't know how to perform it.

The participants believed that they were given the worst jobs, the ones nobody else wants to perform. They are also not given credit for their prior academic and professional experiences, as Connie complained, " . . . You come here as a doctor, or with a Bachelor's degree, you start working in hotels, day care, where you work for $7.00 per hour, you work for $6.00, so they don't even give you the highest rate they have. . . ." This systemic inequity in professional integration was a major source of disappointment and frustration for the participants.

Social Relations

Another obstacle that the participants described was the social isolation that they experience within their communities in the United States, as their social relations drastically differed from what they were accustomed to in their country of origin. As Todd explained, "Where I lived [in Africa], people are more sociable, sharing in the festivities, in the get-togethers, we feel like close friends. Families are very close, which makes it easy to resolve a number of problems."

Angela elaborated on the issue of social isolation,

> In our native country we are used to visiting with one another, but here . . . its is different because some people tell you that they have a sister or brother that they haven't seen for five years . . . and this is confusing . . . but this is not how we live [in Africa] . . . you feel like you have done something wrong when you don't visit somebody . . . we are used to visiting with one another and exchanging gifts regularly . . . and this feels really good.

Participants experience social isolation in the workplace as well, as Boniface noted,

> If you are not lucky, you will never meet with the person who cares . . . they really do care in such a way that they are sometimes . . . good work mates, good colleagues; they can help you in whatever you want at work, but you will never have a chance to sit down, socialize; there is no time . . . for nobody actually . . . if you have the chance that they ask you where you are from . . . that is the end

... it looks like everybody is for himself [or] for herself ... They don't show you that they really don't have time for you, but you cannot feel this warmth you have ... we used to [have] over there in Africa.

Family Dynamics

A strong family is a major prerequisite for success in many societal contexts. The participants come from a culture where the roles and hierarchical position of each member within the family are clearly determined and respected. The man is socialized to be the head of his family while the woman is raised to be a respectful and supportive wife who is prepared to do whatever it takes to raise well-behaved children and keep her family together. The shift in family dynamics that occurs during the African refugees' acculturation process in the United States, therefore, poses a challenge to the quest of successful integration and equal socioeconomic opportunities.

The participants were very concerned about the American family structure and system that encourages and promotes women's and children's independence and empowerment. Even more aggravating to the situation is the fact that children acquire the English language and assimilate into the American way of life faster than their parents, which causes major communication problems within the families. Louis explained, "Children change when they arrive here. The way people tell them that here no one will ever again tell them what to do ... that parents have no right to punish their children. ..."

Bertha elaborated on the destructive power shift that occurs between parents and their children,

> They [the children] no longer listen to their parents, and they respond to them in English; they want to show that children are smarter than the parents, because they want to show that they understand legal issues better than the parents. When parents advise children not to go out without telling them or not dress in sagging pants that expose their body, children respond that they are free to do whatever they want. This causes parents who are quick to anger to slap the children. Then the children scream and call the police ... this causes hatred between parents and children. ... Parents become confused because in their home land, parents are responsible for their children's upbringing, yet here [in the United States] it seems like the government assumes more responsibility towards the children.

Jerry blamed his failed marriage on the American society that empowers women beyond what his culture allowed for. He shared, " ... I came with [a] wife. When we just came in, you know American freedom, she said, 'I don't need you no more.' Then, we decided to divorce."

Cross-Cultural Differences

The participants cited four main cross-cultural differences that pose challenges to their acculturation in the United Sates. The first is the difference in communication styles, as Angela explained,

> It is difficult for us who come from other countries because we have a way of showing respect for other people . . . you can't maintain eye contact with a person who is older than you . . . you have to get close to the person, looking down, in order to greet him . . . but in this country, they think that you have no manners [when you act like that]. They expect you to be boisterous in order to be heard.

Angela also noted the frequent misinterpretation of refugee children's behaviors by schools as a major problem. She stated,

> There are often problems with children playing. Because in our home country, we are accustomed to run as we play; children run, chat, hug each other, push each other; this is how we play where we come from . . . but it doesn't mean that they hate each other; but in this country . . . when you touch a child, they say that you have hit them . . . that you are a bad person. . . . Even in school, when a child falls down when another child pushes him, they send a letter saying that your child was involved in a fight . . . even if this did not happen on purpose . . . so you see, cultural issues are difficult.

The third cross-cultural difference that the participants observed is dress. Connie relates the culture shock that she experienced due to the way Americans dress:

> Another thing that has shocked me is the way people dress . . . when you look at the way an African woman dresses . . . and then you look at the way people here dress . . . especially in warm weather . . . they walk around almost naked . . . this really shocked me and still shocks me . . . to this day I don't understand . . . I would say that their body has no secret parts that they should hide . . . they expose [their body] . . . but we are not accustomed to this and I think that I will never get used to this.

The American individualistic tendencies are another cross-cultural difference that the participants find rather isolating and difficult to deal with, as Veronique explained, "Africans are really sociable; they get together, they help one another a lot. They are warm people. It's difficult to communicate with people who have different customs here. In this country, you can spend a long time without anyone visiting you—other than on the telephone."

Language Issues

The participants described their limited English proficiency as a major obstacle to full acculturation as it impedes communication and successful employment in the United States. Bertha explained,

> Because of language problems, many of us . . . have difficulty maintaining our jobs. . . . Many people lose their jobs because of language problems, and they remain unemployed for years . . . often those who have no educational background or who are moderately educated have serious problems with the language, and it takes them a long time to secure employment because being unable to make themselves understood remains a problem.

The acquisition of the English language also causes family discord since the children tend to acquire the language faster than their parents, thus complicating parent–child relationships and communication, as Angela noted,

> Often children go to school to learn English . . . when they ask parents questions, they don't understand each other, and this is difficult because parents cannot communicate with them. Often children forget our language, and this causes a lot of problems due to misunderstandings between parents and children . . . This can drive parents to despair.

English language proficiency was viewed as a major identity variable that determines the worth of an individual, as Jacques insisted, " . . . we are not used to English, and here, you are nothing if you do not speak English; you are not worth anything when you don't speak English. . . ."

Nostalgic Memories

Reflecting on their rushed, tiring American lifestyle, the participants expressed deep nostalgia for the more relaxed, communal lifestyle that they enjoyed in their African homeland. They missed the social interdependence that shapes the fabric of African society. Boniface related the sustaining impact of such interdependence,

> In Africa, you had time to go say hello to a neighbor. . . . We had time to sit down, time to rest, time to eat, time to do personal things that are not related to your job; this is really what I miss the most. . . . We had time to see friends, to speak to friends . . . we had time for our family . . . time to waste actually. I will give you an example of our children. When I wake up in the morning to go to work, I really worry . . . about this little guy, how I have to wake him up, to take him out in the rain, or . . . when it is freezing, taking him to . . . day care. . . . This wasn't a problem in Africa because the child was for everybody; everybody's child was like a prince and everybody was running to help.

This interdependence also had psychological benefits that the participants miss greatly as they struggle to acculturate into their new American society, as Bertha explained,

> Life in Africa was easy . . . people live together socially . . . especially when you are working, you don't have to worry about day care when you have children, or who is gonna clean my house, how am I gonna handle cooking . . . or doing any other kind of house work. . . . [This] was not a problem in Africa because family members and extended family members are very united and rely on each other. If you have a child, the child belongs to society; the child belongs to your family. And what you do is to take him or . . . her directly to your family member who is around, and the one who helps you today is gonna also have something to ask you . . . tomorrow . . . so it is like . . . helping . . . one another, and that system works very well and this reduces stress.

Commenting on the economic advantages of African interdependence, Bertha also stated,

> I really miss . . . the way of living in a family structure where . . . you depend on one another . . . where you share a lot. People in the village . . . grow rice, they grow beans, they grow potatoes and bananas, and you don't have to worry about how much money you need for food. Family members will bring you food, or you go for the weekend, you pick up whatever you need, and that's all. The salary you have even if it is small, it is gonna be enough because you share the food [which is grown in the countryside].

Discussion and Conclusions

Three focus questions guided the investigation of the obstacles that hinder Burundian refugees' quest for equal opportunity in the United States: (1) How do Burundian refugees describe their experiences with regard to employment opportunities and sustainability in the United States? (2) How do they navigate the confining social and cultural contexts within the multicultural American society? (3) In what ways do previous life experiences in Burundi and transitional host countries influence their adjustment process? Each of these questions will be addressed in this section in light of the findings outlined above.

As they strive to adapt to the American socioeconomic system where the prosperity and well-being of the individual and the family are determined by the nature of employment that they hold, the participants are confronted with challenges related to discriminatory practices in the workplace. While it is understandable that the refugees who have neither relevant US academic credentials nor relevant professional experiences are recruited into minimum wage, manual labor kinds of jobs, this reality presents a major source of frustration and feelings of powerlessness for those who believe they are qualified for highly skilled, professional jobs, and better quality employment opportunities. These systemic discriminatory employment practices, therefore, constitute a major obstacle to equal economic advancement for African refugees in the United States.

The findings showed that cross-cultural differences pose another major challenge in the participant's acculturation process. They related an important clash of values that result from the intersection between their familiar African culture and the new American culture. Differences in communication styles, dress, family dynamics, and language are particularly significant, as they pose problems and misunderstandings not only in the participants' relationships with their host American community, but also within the refugee families themselves.

An overwhelming sense of nostalgia for African culture and lifestyle emerged from the findings. The participants miss the interdependent, communal, and relaxed family and social relations that shaped their African experience. This lingering emotional attachment to the participants' motherland, her culture, and values may be an obstacle to their full acculturation (Arthur, 2000) and thus may weaken their drive to succeed in their new country and culture. Reflecting back to the four stages that characterize refugees' patterns of adjustment as described in the literature review earlier in this chapter, it can be concluded that the participants were navigating between the first three stages. They were all experiencing the reality of cultural, occupational, and social status loss, even though some of them had achieved remarkable language and economic improvement by capitalizing on the qualities of perseverance and hard work that facilitated their upward mobility in their homeland. At the same time, they were concerned with increasing problems within their families due to the shift in family dynamics that resulted from the intersection between their African culture and American mores and practices.

Analyzing and understanding the factors that impact African refugees' cultural and structural integration into their host country are prerequisites for achieving equal opportunity. A related publication outlines eight recommendations for facilitating the acculturation process of African refugees and other immigrants in the United States: design policies and programs that motivate and empower refugee families and their children to seek and pursue solid educational opportunities; establish programs to facilitate the accelerated professional integration of African refugees; develop and implement sustainable acclimation programs; organize activities that foster community interaction; expand refugee assistance programs to allow sufficient acculturation time; immerse refugee families into intensive English language programs upon arrival into the country; establish a higher education scholarship fund for children from African refugee families; and empower the refugee to acculturate in ways that sustain their family units (Ndura, 2006). These recommendations highlight the importance of empowering African refugee families to take charge of their destiny and to strive to succeed as supportive, contributing members of their families and host society.

Acknowledgment

This work was supported in full or in part by a grant from the University of Nevada Junior Faculty Research Grant Fund. This support does not imply endorsement by the university of the research conclusions.

*An earlier version of this chapter, titled "African Refugees' Voices in the Quest for Equal Opportunity in the United States," was presented at the 2004 Patterson Research Conference Frederick D. Patterson Research Institute of the United Negro College Fund Washington Hilton and Towers, Washington, DC, September 24–27, 2004.

References

Aman, M. (2002). Foreword in Obiakor, F. E., & Grant, P.A. (Eds.), *Foreign-born African silenced voices in the discourse on race.* New York: Nova Science Publishers.

Arthur, J. A. (2000). *Invisible sojourners: African immigrant diaspora in the United States.* Wesport, CT: Praeger.

Asmussen, K. L., & Creswell, J. W. (1998). Campus response to a student gunman. In J. W. Creswell (Ed.), *Qualitative inquiry and research design: Choosing among five traditions* (pp. 357–374). Thousand Oaks, CA: Sage Publications. (Reprinted from *Journal of Higher Education* 66, 575–591, Ohio State University Press, 1995.)

Berry, J. (1991). Understanding and managing multiculturalism: Some possible implications of research in Canada. *Psychology and Developing Societies 3*, 17–49.

———. (1998). Acculturation stress. In P. B. Organista, K. M. Chun, & G. Marin (Eds.), *Reading in ethnic psychology.* New York: Routledge.

Creswell, J. W. (1998). *Qualitative inquiry and research design: Choosing among five traditions.* Thousand Oaks, CA: Sage Publications.

Department of Health, Education and Welfare (September, 1979). *Secretarial report: Indochinese refugee assessment.* Washington, DC: HEW.

Doheny, K. (1981). The plight of refugee: A case in point—Africa. *Migration News* 1 January.

Eitinger, L. (1960). The symptomatology of mental disease among refugees in Norway. *Journal of Mental Science 106*, 947–966.

Gordon, M. M. (1964). *Assimilation in American life: The role of race, religion, and national origins*. New York: Oxford University Press.
Haines, D. W. (Ed.) (1985). *Refugees in the United States: A reference book*. Westport, CT: Greenwood Press.
Hoff, H. (1968). *Home and identity. In uprooting and resettlement*. London: World Federation for Mental Health.
Keller, S. L. (1975). *Uprooting and social change: The role of refugees in development*. Delhi: Manohar Book Services.
Kent, D. P. (1953). *The refugee intellectual: The Americanization of the immigrants of 1933*. New York: Columbia University Press.
Kitano, H. H. (1989). A model for counseling Asian Americans. In P. B. Pedersen, J. Draguns, W. Lonner, & J. Trimble (Eds.), *Counseling across cultures* (3rd ed.). Newberry Park, CA: Sage Publications.
Kitano, H. H., & Maki, M. T. (1996). Continuity, change, and diversity: Counseling Asian Americans. In P. B. Pedersen, J. Draguns, W. Lonner, & J. Trimble (Eds.), *Counseling across cultures* (4th ed.). Newberry Park, CA: Sage Publications.
Liu, W., Pope-Davis, D., Nevitt, J., & Toporek, R. (1999). Understanding the functions of acculturation and prejudicial attitudes among Asian Americans. *Cultural Diversity and Ethnic Minority Psychology 4*, 317–328.
Marshall, C., & Rossman, G. B. (1999). *Designing qualitative research* (3rd ed.). Thousand Oaks, CA: Sage Publications.
Ndura, E. (2006). Coming to America: Dashed hopes and uncertain futures. In C. C. Yeakey, J. Richardson, & J. Brooks (Eds.), *Suffer the little children: National and international dimensions of child poverty and public policy*. Oxford: Elsevier.
Rogg, E. M. (1974). *The assimilation of Cuban exiles: The role of community and class*. New York: Aberdeen Press.
Roysircai-Sodowsky, G. R., & Maestas, M. V. (2000). Acculturation, ethnic identity, and acculturative stress: Evidence and measurement. In R. H. Dana (Ed.), *Handbook of cross-cultural and multicultural assessment* (pp. 131–172). Mahwah, NJ: Lawrence Elbaum.
Stake, R. E. (2000). Case studies. In N. K. Denzin & Y. S. Lincoln (Eds.), *Handbook of qualitative research* (2nd ed., (pp. 435–454). Thousand Oaks, CA: Sage Publications.
Stein, B. N. (1979, Spring). Occupational adjustment of refugees: The Vietnamese in the United States. *International Migration Review 13*(1), 25–45.
———. (1981). The refugee experience: Defining the parameters of a study. *International Migration Review 15*, 1–2.
Suárez-Orozco, C., & Suárez-Orozco, M. M. (2001). *Children of immigration*. Cambridge, MA: Harvard University Press.
Suárez-Orozco, M. M. (1989). *Central American refugees and US schools: A psychosocial study of motivation and achievement*. Stanford, CA: Stanford University Press.
Takougang, J. (1995). Recent African immigrants to the United States: A historical perspective. *The Western Journal Black Studies 19*(1), 50–57.

United Nations High Commissioner for Refugees (2000, July). *Refugees and others of concern to UNHCR: 1999 statistical overview*. Geneva: United Nations High Commissioner for Refugees. Retrieved January 14, 2002, from http:/www.unhcr.ch

US Committee for Refugees (2001). *World refugee survey major findings*. US Committee for Refugees. Retrieved January 14, 2002, from http://www.refugees.org

——— (2002). *World refugee survey 2002*. US Committee for Refugees. Retrieved January 8, 2003, from http://www.refugees.org

Vásquez-Montilla, E., Reyes-Blanes, M. E., Hyun, E., & Brovelli, E. (2000). Practices for culturally responsive interviews and research with Hispanic families. *Multicultural Perspective* 2(3), 3–7.

Weiermiair, K. (1971). Economic adjustment of refugees in Canada: A case study. *International Migration*, 9, 5–35.

Wolcott, H. F. (1994). Posturing in qualitative research. In M. D. LeCompte, W. L. Millroy, & J. Preissle (Eds.), *The handbook of qualitative research in education* (pp. 3–52). San Diego, CA: Academic Press.

Yin, R. K. (1994). *Case study research: Design and methods* (2nd ed.). Thousand Oaks, CA: Sage Publications.

CHAPTER TWENTY-EIGHT

Counseling for Global Citizenship Education as Innovation in South Nations

RICHARD IRIKEFE OKORODUDU

Abstract

This chapter examines counseling for global citizenship education in South nations. The aim is to tackle educational and counseling inequality for the purpose of promoting international peace and development. The conceptualization model was based on eclectic counseling strategies. Counseling was examined as a veritable service for inculcating global citizenship traits in Nigeria. The consideration of the constraints and prospects led to the inescapable conclusion that the integration of counseling toward global citizenship education will enhance the expansion of quality educational opportunity in South nations.

Introduction

A global citizen is simply one of the members of the North and South nations who has awareness of the wider world, with a sense of his own role as a world citizen; respects and values diversity; understands how the world works economically, politically, socially, culturally, technologically, and environmentally; hates social injustice; and acts and takes responsibility for his actions, while contributing to make the world a sustainable place (Oxfam, 1997). This chapter posits that the expansion of equal counseling opportunity in global societies would help tremendously in the process of making good global citizens. Given that counseling is a process for bringing about meaningful behavioral changes in individuals, it could be geared toward promoting characteristics of global citizenship. Therefore, an educational system that is directed toward achieving this goal is seen as promoting global citizenship education.

What is global citizenship education? It is simply an expanded education and reorientation opportunity for making good citizens in global societies. It involves a conscious effort designed to teach the tenets of good global citizenship at all levels of education in every discipline in global societies (Federal Government of Nigeria, 1998). In these days of high moral decadence, crime, delinquent and corrupt attitudes, child abuse and neglect, child labor, drug abuse and alcoholism, destructive activities, violence, child trafficking, child poverty, examination malpractices, and cultism, there is the need for expanded global citizenship educational opportunity for international children and for reorientation of youths' and adults' warped values (Agusiobo, 2002; Maisamari, 2002; Okorodudu, 2004b). The main argument in this chapter, therefore, is that counseling activities could help facilitate the realization of global citizenship education in South nations. In other words, counseling for global citizenship education should be a major focus throughout the educational systems of global societies.

The era of globalization features tremendous changes in science, communication, and technology. These developments pose challenges to every member or citizen of the global society, whether they live in North countries such as the United States, Britain, Germany, Italy, Russia, Japan, and France, or South nations such as Nigeria, Ghana, Cameroon, Togo, Botswana, Central African Republic, Ethiopia, Liberia, and Swaziland. However, citizens of the North countries appear to be making the adjustment to globalization more easily than their counterparts from the South nations (Khor, 2000). The globalization goal cannot be achieved without providing equal educational opportunity for international children (Zakariya, 2002) and gaining mutually from the available human and material resources in global societies.

Despite the need to establish a symbiotic relationship between the North and South nations of the world, there appears to be a widening gap in terms of equality in curriculum innovations, counseling, women's education (Adugbo, 1999), science, technological and human advancement, and general quality of life or standard of living. For example, while counseling in developed countries focuses on enriching their national educational and societal development, its neglect in the South nations has been problematic. For instance, the Universal Basic Education (UBE) program has been seen to have neglected the area of guidance and counseling in the process of making international citizens (Alutu & Ochuba, 2000; Ubah, 2000; Okorodudu, 2002a). In line with the above observation, R. I. Okorodudu and G. N. Okorodudu (2003, p. 46) notes that:

> Considering the enormous importance of counseling services in the area of educational, socio-personal, informational, and career services in the educational system at all levels, its neglect as an integral part of the whole education program in Nigeria and other South nations . . . no doubt, makes the UBE curriculum deficient and the achievement of its goal partially elusive.

Guidance and counseling functions have not been properly integrated into the educational systems of South nations compared to the tremendous efforts made by the United States, United Kingdom, Germany, and so on. However, since counseling processes are capable of assisting children, adolescents, and adults in North and South nations with developing full self-realization for normal adjustment in a complex world, it should be integrated into global citizenship educational programs. It is expected that counseling activities in South nations could be geared toward promoting global citizenship education traits. Such traits include: good reasoning, honorable conduct, cooperation, courage, faithfulness, independence, charity, generosity, meaningful sensitivity, honesty, constructive and benevolent attitudes and habits, respecting and valuing diversity, and so on (Oxfam, 1997; Adugbo, 2002; R. I. Okorodudu, 2004a). This development could form a solid foundation for international peace, justice, and equity in the global distribution of human and material resources.

In short, educational globalization would no doubt continue to "snail-walk" in its mission if all stakeholders would not refocus their commitment to the promotion and integration of counseling as a hub or catalyst around which administrative and instructional functions in the global educational systems revolve in South nations. It is against this backdrop that this chapter examines the concept of global citizenship education as a foundation for international peace and development.

Today, the world seems to be losing confidence in people's ability to think and act rationally, basically due to ideological differences in religion, politics, economics, culture, spirituality, sociology and psychology. The impact of these differences on the ordinary citizen around the globe has led to various crises ranging from minor intertribal clashes at the national level to international wars: for example, Ijaw and Itsekiri conflicts and war, Urhobo and Itsekiri clashes and war, nationwide youth restiveness, intertribal and religious wars, as well as religious and political assassinations in Nigeria (Okorodudu & Okorodudu, 2003). Other examples include the acculturated oppositional forms, separations, divisions, and isolations that are common in divided societies like the Korean Peninsula, Moluccas, Northern Ireland, and the Middle East (Kitchen, 2003). It would appear that the world is in greater need of peace education in this era of globalization than it has ever been in the past.

What, then, should be the way forward? In an attempt to answer this question, this chapter advocates counseling toward global citizenship education and its integration into global curriculum and instruction processes. At present, counseling services are still not being equally provided in the educational systems of South nations. There is a need for the expansion of equal quality of educational opportunity through the integration of counseling services in global curriculum and instruction. In this way, counseling can contribute to the great search for solutions to cultural problems, with the ultimate goal of achieving oneness of spirit, equitable distribution of resources, cooperation, and world peace. The quest for global unity through diversity and respect for the sociocultural values of all people of all nations would be enhanced.

Counseling for global citizenship education, with all its merits, has implications for curriculum innovation in South nations. For instance, there would be a need to train adequate counseling personnel; to promote understanding and cooperation among principals, teachers, parents, and students, with counselors in and out of the school setting; to provide funds, offices, and equipment; to manage psychological tests and their applications; and to create awareness and build capacity for expanding equal counseling and educational opportunity.

Counseling toward global citizenship education in the educational systems in South nations is faced with the challenge of ignorance, as well as socioeconomic and political instability. It is needless to stress the problem of abject poverty in many communities in South nations. Indices of unequal counseling and educational opportunity in South nations include: poor educational facilities; insufficient classroom space; paucity of counseling personnel; low teacher quality (Achebe, 1990; Obanya, 1992); and an inadequate supply of learning materials, including modern counseling and educational textbooks and computer facilities. Although several international education conferences have been held, such as World Conference on Education For All (EFA), International Congress on Education for Human Rights and Democracy, World Conference on Higher Education, and Education for All (EFA) Forum (Obanya, 2002), none of these conferences actually addressed the issue of counseling, its role in facilitating global citizenship education, and its implications for educational innovation in South countries. Consequently, the major problem addressed in this study is: What is counseling for global citizenship education as an innovation in South nations? In order to solve this problem effectively, the following subthemes are discussed: conceptual framework; status of counseling in South nations; the case of the Nigerian educational system; counseling for global citizenship education as an innovation in South nations; and constraints and prospects of counseling for global citizenship education in South nations.

Conceptual Framework

The conceptualization model for this study is based on eclectic counseling strategies for building good citizens in global societies. According to the major proponent of the eclectic model, Frederick Thorne (1950), eclecticism requires evaluation of an individual with regard to past history, present situation, and future possibilities. These issues find relevance in the process of expanding opportunity for global citizenship education in South nations. Eclectic conceptualization, therefore, provides the opportunity for the reeducation and treatment of maladaptive behaviors of international children through the tenets of global citizenship education. Eclecticism involves the processes of selecting, reconciling, and choosing appropriate procedures, techniques, and concepts from the plethora of counseling models. It focuses on the client with the goal of educating international children about how to acquire skills for replacing compulsive emotional behaviors with deliberate, rational, and adaptive behaviors. Counseling for global citizenship education permits the highest utilization of intellectual resources for preventing maladaptive behaviors and promoting a proactive adjustment process. The eclectic model provides for consideration of cultural variations in terms of customs, traditions, norms, and values within and across the South nations during counseling activities. In other words, the eclectic approach allows practicing counselors to accommodate personality traits, educational status, family background, levels of national development, as well as socioeconomic, political, cultural, and religious or spiritual development among global citizens.

The eclectic counseling model, which aims at helping individuals make effective adjustments in every aspect of life in and out of the educational setting, takes into consideration all factors that tend to affect the client, both internal and external. This constitutes the main reason for the adoption of the eclectic approach or model of counseling toward global citizenship education in South nations. Clients or counselees are all entitled to survival, protection, and development regardless of age, sex, socioeconomic status, or level of national development.

Another justification for adopting an eclectic therapeutic model for this study is that educational innovations in relation to the expansion of national and international curricula have become complex and dynamic. Today, the desire for acquisition of knowledge and skills, population growth, poverty, illiteracy, the need for technology transfer, the sophistication of communication devices, and so on, have all generated serious demand for counseling toward global citizenship education in South nations. The social, cultural, spiritual, educational, and economic inequality of all nations constitutes a challenge in itself and highlights the need to enhance complete integration of counseling (as an integral part of the national curriculum) as an educational innovation in South nations. For instance, Adugbo (2002, p. 38) notes, "counseling as a third force in education orders and gives hierarchy to the various values involved in human existence. But the hierarchy should be loose impositions upon each student, so that the individual's moral right to choose is not unduly or unreasonably restricted." This shows that the concern for others, the pursuit of excellence in all things, the sovereignty of nationality, with its implications for national and international peace education, and the search for full humanity in South and North nations are indeed major areas of interest to guidance counselors. Promoting counseling activities toward global citizenship awareness as an integral part of the entire educational system would contribute immensely to closing the wide gap in the quality of education received by the children of rich versus poor parents, male versus female students, White children versus children of color (Nario-Galace, 2003) in societies worldwide.

Status of Counseling in South Nations: The Nigerian Educational System

Guidance or counseling has been identified as one of the three main educational functions most neglected in educational institutions throughout Nigeria and other South nations (Adugbo, 1983; Achebe, 1990). Adugbo noted that the failure to combine the instructional and administrative functions with the complementary function of guidance and counseling would make the individual fail to achieve the expected level of self-fulfillment and human development. This chapter posits that proper integration of guidance and counseling functions into the normal educational system of South nations would greatly help enhance the knowledge, skills, and competencies of global citizens. It is believed that the creation of international citizens in both North and South nations would be largely promoted through well-organized and integrated counseling toward good global citizenship education.

In Nigeria, the development of the guidance program began around

1959, when some religious sisters at St. Theresa's College, Ibadan, Oyo State, Nigeria, invited outsiders to advise them about how to assist 60 of their fifth-form girls into jobs or further their education (Adugbo 1983; Okobiah & Egbule, 2004). Since then, various forms of guidance activities have spread to other states like Edo, Delta, Anambra, Enugu, Kwara, Gongola, Borno, Bauchi, Kaduna, and Lagos. The general method of counseling approach was said to be through educational placement services and decentralized generalism in schools. Despite the fact that counseling began in the middle of the 20th century in Nigeria, such services are still very marginal and have not been practically integrated as a major force in the educational system (Achebe, 1990; Agbe, 2000; Uba, 2000). In other words, learners at virtually all levels of education—primary, secondary, and higher institutions, as well as parents, guardians, teachers, and school principals—are still ignorant of the main functions and benefits of counselors. For instance, Adugbo (1983, p. 85) notes that:

> General guidance services throughout the country comprise skeletal services and the number of services offered is not only small but careers Guidance is in most cases emphasized at the expense of other services. An attributable cause of this situation is the severe shortage of qualified guidance workers.

While some efforts have been made to train counselors and promote counseling activities through the National Counseling Association of Nigeria (CASSON) (Okobiah & Okorodudu, 2004), the status of counseling programs in Nigeria and other South nations such as Ghana, Sierra Leone, Togo, Malawi, Ethiopia, and Uganda still leaves much to be desired. Basically, it is this gap in the educational system that this chapter seeks to fill. It is believed that properly integrated functions of the counseling program toward good global citizenship education would be a major innovation in the educational systems in global societies. Such an effort would help to a great extent in facilitating the process of closing the wide gap between the educational development of children in the North nations and those of the South.

Counseling for Global Citizenship Education in South Nations

The conceptualization of counseling in this discourse refers generally to the process of helping clients honestly understand themselves, have consciousness of their potentialities and weaknesses, and be able to consider alternatives in light of existing information that would enable them to make their own decisions. It is in line with this viewpoint that the argument for counseling for global citizenship education as an educational innovation in South nations is sustained. Counseling that is well integrated into the school curriculum and instruction at the elementary, secondary, and tertiary institution would help enhance citizens' awareness of the current globalization challenges. It would help draw children's attention to the development of self-awareness, skills acquisition, personal values clarification, needs fulfillment, tolerance, and of course, appreciation of cultural values, traditions, customs, mores, and beliefs of people from within and other nations of the world (Mirici & Ozturk, 2003).

Therefore, this chapter advocates a new sense of commitment to the promotion of counseling services in the primary, secondary, and tertiary institutions of learning in South nations of the world. For instance, Shertzer and Van Hoose, in line with Peters (Adugbo, 1983; Mokwunye, 1991; Osakwe & Hedere, 1994; R. I. Okorodudu, 1995, 2004a), note the following 15 task areas for counselors:

1. early identification of each pupil's learning capacities;
2. the design of each pupil's achievement pattern in terms of learning capacities;
3. analysis of the child's responses about himself;
4. assembly of data on the child's self-concept;
5. a portrait of the child's habits of study and living in school;
6. interpretation of the child in home and cultural setting;
7. interpretation of the child's development progress against development norms;
8. follow-up with pupils in the later school years, mainly in the secondary school;
9. the use of guidance functions in other phases of the school program;
10. inculcation of love and tolerance for people of other cultures in the child;
11. inculcation of positive thinking toward fairness, justice, and equity into the child;
12. inculcation of the skills for acquiring societal norms, sentiments, values, and mores, as well as willingness to learn and appreciate those of other ethnic groups and nations;
13. inculcation of the right attitudes, habits, and affective and information services relating to the required global citizenship skills, traits, abilities, and competencies for dedicated performance of duties in global societies;
14. inculcation of the skills for resisting and shunning antisocial and unguided youthful exuberance, cultism, violence, and unwholesome conduct; and
15. inculcation of the knowledge and appreciation of peace education.

Essentially, the achievement of these objectives of counseling would lead international citizens into thinking and behaving in such ways as to reduce or extinguish many maladaptive behaviors that threaten world peace. Understanding people's thoughts and actions within their own cultural milieu would lead to meaningful interpretation and hence lay a good foundation for international peace and development. Behaviors are generally governed by values, which are environmentally determined. However, under the present dispensation of globalization, values, customs, mores, norms, and their impact on behaviors and choices can be made known to clients or individuals in global societies through computer-assisted counseling or Internet services. The counseling process can be used to systematically promote a level of awareness for the choice of peace, tolerance, diversity of cultures, values, and behavior of individuals as a primary prevention measure to reduce violence, conflicts, wars, and destructive acts. In this way, counseling as a veritable service would enhance the inculcation of global citizenship traits of acceptance of people as they are, irrespective of their color, mental capacity, education, age, sex, religion, and the general choices they make, provided that actions based on such choices are not destructive to global societies but peaceful and progressive.

Apparently, the need to promote global citizenship education poses a major challenge to the counselors, teachers, politicians, governments, international organizations, and nongovernmental organizations (NGOs) in North and South countries of the world. The success of making good global citizens would necessarily depend on all the concerted efforts of individuals, institutions such as schools, churches, mosques, societies, social clubs, guilds, associations, social and political organizations, families, and all professionals within and outside educational systems.

The counseling model for making good global citizens in South nations explains the goal, objectives, method, and evaluation of global citizenship education. In the model, the major goal of global citizenship education in South and North nations would be to channel counseling services toward creating competent global citizens capable of making wise decisions and to promote acceptable behaviors for the enhancement of personal growth as well as national and international peace.

The objectives of counseling toward global citizenship education would focus on the orientation and reorientation of child, adolescent, and adult behaviors and abilities in relation to their cognitive, affective, and instrumental dispositions. Apparently, counseling activities would focus on these main areas and are to be reflected in the national and international curriculum and instruction in South nations. It is also important that the right attitudes, beliefs, knowledge, understanding, skills, and competences to guide acceptable behaviors in the cognitive, affective, political, and social-personal interactions be channeled toward promoting individual, national, and international cooperation and peace.

Further in the model is the method of counseling toward the achievement of the goals of making good global citizens in South nations. The question of how counselors can achieve the goals of global citizenship education finds its answer in the need to focus on promoting understanding, values clarification, opportunity for professional practice, and remediation of antiglobal values. Injustice and inequality in socioeconomic, educational, political, cultural, scientific, and technological advancement should be addressed. Effective and efficient counseling measures for preventive and proactive intervention in global maladaptive behaviors in and out of educational settings should be promoted. For instance, in line with the principles of counseling for global citizenship education, the governments of South nations should restructure their educational philosophies (Abiodun, 2002; Osaat, 2004) so that their implementation would have practical or functional relevance to the needs of global societies.

According to Osaat (2004), Japan used education as an instrument—including cardinal virtues of the Shinto philosophy of filial piety such as benevolence, justice, propriety, fidelity, and intelligence—for its national development. Germany under Bismarck employed education as an instrument for unification of diverse stocks, while Britain used education in the training of character to consolidate the state of monarchical welfarism. On the other hand, the United States has employed education for the utilization of knowledge of nature (laws) for the development of the individual qualities necessary for good American citizenship and democratization (Osaat, 2004, p. 79).

Consequently, this chapter advocates counseling for global citizenship education based on some cherished global values that have implications for expanding national and international curriculum and instruction. Counseling toward global citizenship education should focus on the following appropriate values (Federal Government of Nigeria, 1998, p. 8):

- Respect for the worth and dignity of the individuals in global societies.
- Faith in man's ability to make rational decisions irrespective of nationality and culture.
- Moral and spiritual values in interpersonal and human relations.
- Respect for the dignity of labor, equity, and justice in global societies.
- Promote emotional, physical, and psychological health of all chil-

dren, irrespective of their sex, socioeconomic status, political beliefs, religion, family, or nationality.

The fourth and fifth steps in the model are the need to provide the right attitude and beliefs for directing global citizens' behavior in a complex and dynamic world. Counseling efforts must channel appropriate attitudes, beliefs, norms, and values that govern behaviors in global societies. Apparently, professional knowledge, skills and competencies to be acquired through national and international education processes (Odediran, 2000; Uba, 2000) should constitute a major focus in the making of good global citizens in South nations.

On the whole, the counseling process should focus on evaluation. The counseling process would determine the success of promoting global citizenship education through formative, summative, quantitative, and qualitative evaluation efforts. The ultimate expectation is to determine or observe the manifestation of changed behaviors in line with global ethos, beliefs, and attitudes that make for personal, national, and international adjustments to peace, equity, fairness, and justice in global societies.

Constraints and Prospects

So far, this chapter has maintained a sustained argument for the need to promote counseling for global citizenship education in South nations. A clarion call of this nature poses major challenges for revisiting curricula of North and South nations in order to determine the presence or the absence of counseling in global educational systems. While this effort is being identified as paramount and rewarding, its systematic networking would help set the pace for reducing educational and counseling inequality within and between North and South nations in an era of educational globalization. In spite of these benefits, there are numerous constraints facing the implementation of counseling for global citizenship education in the South nations.

Generally, the nations in Africa, Asia, and Latin America are known to be economically poor; politically unstable; technologically impoverished; highly dependent on the scientific products and services of developed (North) nations; and riddled with internal conflicts, child abuse, and the general consequences of inflation. Ultimately, as a result of the cumulative effects of the harsh socioeconomic, military, and political upheavals and deprivations, these nations under perennially frustrating environments are known to produce citizens whose behaviors often reflect corrupt attitudes and maladjustment. This enabling foundation for educational inequality and unfairness, which underlies national and international confusion, conflicts, and wars, should be reappraised. This can be done through preventive counseling of children toward acceptance of persons of diverse colors, ages, nations, languages, social statuses, religions, cultures and views. Proactive counseling toward adult reorientation of warped values that have implications for destruction, defrauding, degradation, denigration, and derogatory appraisal of humanity in global societies should be promoted. Counseling for global citizenship education must support a planned program of peace education in South and North nations.

Obviously, there are problems of ignorance and lack of support for counseling innovation in the educational systems of South nations. Given that the world adult literacy rate is relatively low, especially in South nations, it is not surprising that the acceptance of counseling as an integral part of the educational systems of these impoverished nations has been problematic. The 1990 literacy rates between male and female adults, according to Akpotu (2002), showed that Southern Asia and sub-Saharan Africa had the lowest rates in the world and that more than one-half of the population is illiterate. Nigeria, the popularly acclaimed giant of Africa, had 29 million illiterates. These figures, no matter how startling, are not inclusive of the 15 million children whose ages are between 6 and 15 years who are out of school in Nigeria (Obanya, 2002; Okorodudu, 2004b). With this kind of poor educational foundation in South nations, creating good global citizens must involve counseling as a helping profession. Its promotion would add value to education as a way of expanding equal quality educational opportunity in global societies.

Shortage of counseling personnel is another constraint. The implication of this is that there should be global training of professional counselors, as well as manpower exchanges within and across developed and developing nations. The Internet and other fast communication devices and interuniversity program exchanges should be promoted for the support of counselor production as a measure for expanding counseling opportunity in global societies.

Another very important obstacle is lack of funds (Ikegbuname, 2000; Odediran, 2000). It has been noted earlier that poverty, ignorance, and illiteracy characterize South nations. Therefore, lack of funds will hinder the role that counseling can play in expanding opportunity toward global citizenship education. Opportunity for exposure of global citizens, counselors, and teachers to cultures in other parts of the globe would enhance global citizenship education. As a result, significant funds are required for the optimum training and development of personnel, as well as to provide materials to enhance school settings in South nations. The governments of developed and developing nations, world organizations like UNESCO, NGOs, religious and social organizations, and individuals should engage in endowment funds for promoting counseling activities toward global citizenship education in South nations.

Inadequate electrical power constitutes another major obstacle for the expansion of counseling opportunity in South nations. It is commonly observed that the supply of electricity is inadequate in South nations. This implies that South nations would find it difficult to derive the maximum benefit from educational globalization, due to their inability to access computers, Internet services, and other fast electronic communication methods that would promote effective and efficient counseling processes. The process of implementing counseling for global citizenship education would require even distribution of knowledge, skills, and competencies, as well as funds for revitalizing education and counseling toward the scientific and technological foundations of the South nations.

Lack of administrative support for counseling toward global citizenship education is another problem. The awareness of educated men and women, teachers, children, students, parents, politicians, governments, and non-governmental agencies about the need to channel counseling toward global citizenship education is still not very sharp. This implies that global campaigns through world conferences, seminars, and workshops on counseling toward global citizenship education should be promoted. This would provide the systematic enlightenment needed for the expansion of equal counseling opportunity in global societies.

Conclusion

This chapter has examined the concept of counseling for global citizenship education in South nations. It specifically focused on the need to create good global citizens through counseling processes. Counseling services are still not equally integrated into global curriculum and instruction processes of South nations. In order to achieve the goal of counseling toward global citizenship education, a counseling model based on eclectic theoretical postulate was recommended. This chapter discussed the eclectic conceptualization as a reflection of reality, bearing in mind the place of biological and environmental bases of behavior and behavior modification paradigms in the creation of international citizens. With a focus on Nigeria, the status of counseling in South nations revealed neglect (still not equal) of guidance and counseling as a major force in educational programs. The conclusion was drawn that the integration of counseling for global citizenship education as an educational innovation in South countries will enhance the expansion of counseling services and promote equal quality educational opportunity in global societies.

Considering the enormous positive impact of effective counseling for global citizenship education on national and international education for peace, equity, and justice, this chapter recommends that governments of the North and South nations, world economic, social-educational, and political organizations, UNESCO, multinational organizations, and NGOs, private sectors, social and religious organizations, parents, teachers, students, primary, secondary and higher institutions of learning should support all efforts toward the expansion of equal counseling and educational opportunity in South nations.

References

Abiodun, A. A. (2002). Rebuilding the foundations of education in Nigeria. *The Nigeria Social Scientists* 5(2), 21–31.

Achebe, C. C. (1990). Teacher education, guidance and counselling and the 6-3.34 education system. In A. Aderalegbe (Ed.), *Education in Nigeria: Proceedings of the 1989 and 1990 conferences of the Nigeria Academy of Education* (pp. 72–76). Lagos: NERDC Press.

Adugbo, A. J. (1983). Aspect of guidance and counseling. In P. N. Okoh (Ed.), *Professional education: A book of readings*. Benin: Ethiope Publishing Corporation.

———. (1999). Women and development: Current states and counseling intervention for females. *Journal of Educational Research and Development* 1(1), 193–209.

Adugbo, A. J. (2002, September 11–12). *The role of guidance and counseling in education*. Paper presented at the Workshop on Effective Management of Nursery and Adult Education in Delta State, sponsored by Delta State Government Civil Service Commission, Asaba, Delta State of Nigeria.

Agbe, N. N. (2000). Counseling for effective human resource management for productivity. *The Counsellor* 18(1), 124–130.

Agusiobo, B. C. (2002). Child to child—A new approach to sustaining the primary education curriculum innovation. *WCCI Nigeria Chapter—A Journal of the World Council of Curriculum and Instruction* 3(2), 116–125.

Akpotu, N. E. (2002). Education for all: A critique of its implementation in Nigeria. *Nigerian Journal of Educational philosophy* 9(1), 57–64.

Alutu, A. N. G., & Ochuba, V. O. (2000). Effective organization and management of universal basic education: The need for collaborative efforts of school administrators, teachers, and guidance counsellors. In J. A. Aghenta & D. Awanbor (Eds.), *Academic publications 2000—the Nigeria Academy* (pp. 137–148). Benin: Ambik press.

Federal Government of Nigeria. (1998). *National Policy on Education*. Lagos: Federal Government Press.

Ikegbuname, C. I. (2000). Achievement motivation: A panacea for effective educational process in secondary schools in Nigeria. *The Counsellor* 18(1), 115–123.

Khor, M. (2000). *Globalization and the South: Some critical issues.* Ibadan: Spectrum Books.

Kitchen, A. (2003). Education for healing and solidarity "to renew the face of the earth." *International Journal of Curriculum and Instruction* 5(1), 53–64.

Maisamari, A. M. (2002). The place of effective communication in combating drug abuse and drug education in Nigeria. *WCCI Nigeria Chapter—A Journal of the World Council of Curriculum and Instruction* 3(2), 94–100.

Mirici, I. H., & Ozturk, Z. (2003). Some suggestions for global citizenship education. *International Journal of Curriculum and Instruction* 5(1), 87–95.

Mokwunye, C. A. U. (1991). Citizenship and citizenship education. In E. O. S. Iyamu, & L. O. N. Onyesom (Eds.), *Readings in social studies* (pp. 133–157). Benin City: Okilo Publishers.

Nario-Galace, J. (2003). Prejudice in the classroom and hopes for change. *International Journal of Curriculum and Instruction* 5(1), 19–34.

Obanya, A. (1992). Improving teacher quality in Nigeria. In S. O. Oriaifo & U. B. Gbenedio (Eds.), *Towards education in Nigeria for the 21st century* (pp. 218–225). Benin City: Institute of Education, University of Benin.

Obanya, P. (2002). *Revitalizing education in Africa.* Ibadan: Stirling-Horden Publishers (Nig.).

Odediran, N. O. (2000). Counseling for effective educational process in Nigeria: Problems and prospects. *The Counsellor* 18(1), 84–90.

Okobiah, O. C., & Egbule, J. F. (2004). Historical development of guidance and counselling in America and Nigeria. In O. C. Okobiah & R. I. Okorodudu (Eds.), *Issues, concepts, procedures, theories and techniques of guidance and counselling* (pp. 1–46). Benin City: Ethiope Publishing.

Okobiah, O. C., & Okorodudu, R. I. (2004). Guidance and counseling: A general overview. In O. C. Okobiah & R. I. Okorodudu (Eds.), *Issues, concepts, procedures, theories and techniques of guidance and counselling* (pp. 47–69). Benin City: Ethiope Publishing.

Okorodudu, R. I. (1995). *Citizenship education in Nigeria: With implications for counseling.* Benin City: Osasu Publishers.

———. (2002a, October 28–31). *Counseling the Nigerian youths in an era of globalization.* Paper presented at the International Conference of Faculty of Education held at Chinua Achebe Arts Theatre, University of Calabar, Calabar, Nigeria.

———. (2002b, August 20–24). Counseling and equality of access to quality education in Nigeria. In A. A. Adogoke (Ed.), *Conference Proceedings of the 26th Annual Conference of the Counseling Association of Nigeria, the University of Benin, Benin City* (pp. 89–98). Benin City: Counseling Association of Nigeria.

———. (2004a). *Education and reorientation for good citizenship in nation building counseling psychological approach* (2nd ed.). Benin City: Ethiope Publishing .

———. (2004b, June 16–17). *Counseling for child protection and family life in an era of globalization in Nigeria.* Paper presented at the National Conference on Social Problems Development and the Challenges of Globalization Organized by the Department of Sociology and Anthropology, Obafemi Awolowo

University, Ile-Ife, Nigeria.

Okorodudu, R. I., & Okorodudu, G. N. (2003). Universal basic education issues: Problems and prospects in South nations in a global society. *International Journal of Curriculum and Instruction* 5(I), 25–51.

Osaat, S. D. (2004). Nigerian educational philosophy and policy making: A new look at educational philosophy. *Nigerian Journal of Empirical Studies in Psychology and Education* 1(9), 77–84.

Osakwe, E., & Itedere, P. O. (1994). *Social studies for tertiary students in Nigeria.* Enugu: New Age Publishers.

Oxfam (1997). *Cool planet for teachers—What is global citizenship?* Available from http://www.oxfam.org.uk/coolplanet/teachers/globciti/whatis.htm

Thorne, F. C. (1950). *Principles of personality counseling.* Brandon, VT: Journal of Clinical Psychology.

Ubah, A. C. (2000). The counseling needs of youth and school drop-outs in non-formal education centre. *The Counsellor* 8(1), 30–40.

Zakariya, J. O. (2002). A use of child rights educations in Nigeria. WCCI Nigeria Chapter. *A Journal of the World Council of Curriculum and Instruction* 3(2), 76–93.

CHAPTER TWENTY-NINE

Provision of Sports Facilities and Coaching for University Undergraduates in Southern Africa

A Comparative Study of Students With and Without Disabilities

I. U. ONYEWADUME AND H. S. DHALIWAL

Abstract

This survey study compares the provision of recreational sports facilities and coaching for university undergraduates with or without disabilities, to ascertain whether inequality still exists in terms of provision of, and access to, quality recreational sports, some 50 years after *Brown v. Board of Education* (1954). A multistage cluster sampling technique was used to randomly select 120 students with and without disabilities from 20 universities in eight countries in the Southern African region. Colleagues gathered information on the nature of recreational and sporting programs offered to students with and without disabilities in the universities. Factors affecting the provision of adequate equipment, facilities, and coaching opportunities for all students, whether with disabilities or not, were examined. The study revealed the general consensus that some Southern African universities are still far behind in realizing the ideals of Public Laws 93–112 of 1973, 93–380 of 1974 and, in particular, 94–142 of 1975. There were still inequalities in some of the universities in the region in the implementation of university sports policies and the provision of sporting equipment, facilities, and qualified coaching staff. Vice-chancellors and directors of sports in the universities affected were urged to reverse the unequal practices and model universities in the Republic of South Africa that seemed to have more equitable practices.

Introduction

The ruling of equality under the law of all persons, whether Black or White, whether with or without disability, by the US Supreme Court in 1954 in the landmark case of *Brown v. Board of Education of Topeka, Kansas* (Winnick, 2000; Sherrill, 2003) not only pertained to children but to adults as well. Adults and children alike are entitled to equal treatment and opportunity as citizens of the same country, whether they have disabilities or not. They are supposed, by the laws and constitutions of their countries, to have equal opportunity for education, employment, financial assistance for setting up business enterprises, legal redresses, unhindered access to public facilities, and unimpeded participation in physical activities and sports. This is without prejudice to whether or not they have any form of disability.

Universities, around the world are noted for producing quality athletes who represent their countries, be they able-bodied athletes or those with disabilities. Such athletes represent their institutions first and are later called up to represent their countries at world championships like the Olympic Games, Special Olympics, or Paralympic Games. To enable them to achieve this great height, such universities have well-implemented sports programs in place. With adequate state-of-the-art facilities and equipment for undergraduates with or without disabilities, qualified coaches, including adapted physical activity professionals, are recruited to ensure the success of the programs. These actions are in keeping with the ideals of their national constitutions that aim at ensuring equal opportunities for their citizens.

Apart from the opportunity to have a crop of athletes who could be called up to perform for their countries, people with disabilities also have a need for adequate physical fitness and improved quality of life through well-designed sports programs. This need for well-designed programs of activity is widely supported by researchers (Rimmer et al., 1992; 1993; Pitetti et al., 1993; Horvat et al., 1996; Stadler & Pitetti, 1996; Frey et al., 1999) in the field of adapted physical activity and sports. In fact, everything should be done to engage them in daily physical activities since these activities also have the potential for improving their fitness levels. Supporting this view, Chanias et al. (1998), Pommering et al. (1994), and Suomi et al. (1995) found that people with disabilities have the ability to improve in various aspects of fitness if given the proper environment and training.

The national constitutions of most African countries, including those of the Southern African region—Angola, Botswana, Lesotho, Malawi, Mozambique, Namibia, South Africa, Swaziland, Zambia, and Zimbabwe—contain articles or clauses that guarantee equal rights and opportunities for all their citizens. They state that no citizen shall be discriminated against on the grounds of disability, among others. Whether or not these promises of equal rights, privileges, and opportunities extend to the provision of sports facilities and coaching for university undergraduates with disabilities remains to be seen among selected universities in Southern Africa.

This study, therefore, sought to investigate the equality or inequality in the provision of recreational sports facilities and coaching for undergraduates with or without disabilities in selected Southern African universities. Specifically, the purpose of this study was to ascertain if having a disability or not was a factor that influenced the attention given to university undergraduates on the issue of provision of sports facilities and coaching in selected Southern African universities. Four dependent variables were examined:

1. Availability of the university sports policies.
2. Implementation of the university sports policies.
3. Availability/provision of adequate facilities and equipment for recreation and competition.
4. Availability of qualified coaches, including adapted physical activity professionals.

To achieve these objectives, the following four hypotheses were tested for each dependent variable at the 0.05 alpha level. There is no significant relationship between having a disability or not and:

1. the availability of the sports policies for university undergraduates;
2. the implementation of the sports policies for university undergraduates;
3. the availability/provision of adequate facilities and equipment for recreation and competition for university undergraduates;
4. the availability of qualified coaches for training university undergraduates.

Method

This study was conducted using the survey research design. This is a technique of descriptive research that seeks to determine present practices or opinions of a specified population (Thomas & Nelson, 1996).

Target Population of the Study

The target population of this study included all university undergraduates, with and without disabilities, in all the Southern African universities.

Sample and Sampling Procedure

Preliminary investigations show that there are great variations in the number of universities in each of the countries in the Southern African region. With the Republic of South Africa having almost the same number of universities as the rest of the countries in the region put together, the researchers decided to create two clusters: the universities in the Republic of South Africa in one group and the universities in the other countries in the region in the other group. This was done to ensure adequate, proportionate representation of opinions from all the universities in the region. Also, in the second cluster, a proportionate sampling was carried out in line with the number of universities in the cluster. Of the 20 universities randomly selected for this study, therefore, 10 were drawn from the Republic of South Africa, 3 from Zimbabwe, 2 from Zambia, while the remaining 5 universities were from Botswana, Lesotho, Malawi, Namibia, and Swaziland. Six undergraduates (three each with and without disabilities) were randomly selected by the research coordinators in the universities to fill in the University Students' Equal Access to Sports Participation Questionnaire (USEASPQ). Hence, a total of 120 undergraduates fill in the final version of the questionnaire for the study. Sixty of them had some form of disability, while the remaining 60 had no disabilities. This multistage cluster sampling technique was recommended by Cochran (1977) and Thomas and Nelson (1996) for use when a sampling frame does not exist and the population is spread over a wide geographical area.

Again, to ensure the generalization of the results of this study to the rest of the countries in the region, and thus achieve external validation, the representative sample had to reflect the characteristics of the entire Southern African region. This position was supported by Russo (2003) noting that the representative sample of a study must reflect the characteristics of the entire population of the study to achieve external validation. According to Kline (1994), samples must not only be representative, but also must be of sufficient size to produce reliable factors. In a data with a clear factor structure, samples of 100 were quite sufficient. If factor analyses are carried out with factors smaller than these, all results need replication in other samples (Kline, 1994). This study therefore satisfies this criterion.

Participants

The 120 undergraduates who participated in the study gave their consent to fill in the questionnaire. The mean ± standard deviation and range of their ages were 23.42 ± 2.32 years and 20–28 years, respectively, for undergraduates without disabilities, and 24.05 ± 1.03 years and 20–26 years, respectively, for undergraduates with disabilities.

Instrumentation

Given that no statistical evidence is required for content validity (Thomas & Nelson, 1996), the content validity of the questionnaire was established through wide consultation with textbooks, journals, and the Internet in the relevant areas of the study. A 16-item closed- and open-ended questionnaire known as the USEASPQ was developed and distributed among 50 undergraduates with disabilities and 50 without disabilities randomly drawn from the University of Botswana, Botswana; University of the North, Thohoyandou; University of Venda for Science and Technology, Venda; University of Pretoria, Pretoria; University of Witwatersrand, Johannesburg; all in South Africa. These students were not included in the final survey.

Data from this pilot testing of the questionnaire were factor-analyzed using the SPSS version 11.5.2.1. The principal component analysis presented four main components extracted from the questionnaire. The data were further analyzed using Varimax rotation with Kaiser normalization. The rotated component matrix showed five converged iterations ranging from–0.161 to 0.905. A reliability statistic of the Cronbach's alpha was then computed on the 16-item questionnaire, yielding a correlation coefficient of 0.802. Kline (1994) observed that whenever an orthogonal simple structure rotation is desired, the Varimax technique aims at maximizing the sum of variances of squared loadings in the columns of the factor matrix, producing loadings that are either high or near zero. This is one of the critical features of simple structures. Kline noted that a clever feature of Varimax is that the procedure is applied to the loadings squared rather than the actual loadings. Supporting this decision, Thomas and Nelson (1996) agreed that an internal consistency reliability coefficient could be obtained using the coefficient alpha technique. Out of the 16 items that constituted the pilot questionnaire, 12 items were loaded across the five converged iterations. A careful study of the five iterations revealed the following subthemes, or underlying concepts, of the study:

1. The availability of university sports policies for undergraduates with or without disabilities.

2. The implementation of university sports policies for the benefit of undergraduates.
3. Availability/provision of sports facilities and equipment.
4. The availability of qualified coaches for training undergraduates.

It is pertinent to note that the factor analysis technique assists in the identification of the underlying concepts of the study (Norusis, 1991). With a high reliability coefficient of 0.802, the questionnaire could be said to have a high internal consistency, which according to Thomas and Nelson (1996), is an integral part of the wider validity issue as it reflects the degree to which the measuring instrument is free of error variance. A revised version of the questionnaire was then developed using the 12-item loading by the Varimax rotation. The remaining 4 items were dropped from the final questionnaire.

Data Collection Procedure

The final version of the questionnaire was sent by e-mail attachment to some professional colleagues in the randomly selected universities. They were selected as coordinators of the survey exercise in their countries based on their knowledge of questionnaire administration. They were requested to extract the e-mail attachment, print the required copies, and distribute them to the randomly selected students in their universities. Telephone follow-ups and e-mail communications with the coordinators were done intermittently to facilitate data collection. Completed questionnaire copies were retrieved from students and couriered back to the researchers.

Data Analysis

Retrieved questionnaires were analyzed using the Chi-square (x^2) statistics of the SPSS version 11.5.2.1.

Results

Results in Table 30.1 show significant differences ($p < 0.05$) in the x^2 analyses of all four items. This meant a significant difference in opinion between Southern African university students with disabilities and those without on the issue of their universities not having a sports policy—hence, a rejection of the first null hypothesis. While students with disabilities agreed that there was no university sports policy, as they could not sense any trace of it, those without disabilities believed that there was a university sports policy, since they were able to see the manifestations of it all around them. This is inequality of treatment on matters pertaining to all students of the same university. There is, therefore, a significant relationship between having a university sports policy that addresses the needs of all the students and the ability/disability factor. This could mean that when university sports policies are drafted, less attention is paid to aspects concerning students with disabilities.

Table 30.1 x^2 Statistics on the Relationship Between Equality and Inequality in the Availability of University Sports Policies for Students With and Without Disabilities in Selected Southern African Universities ($N = 120$)

Items	χ^2 value	df	Asymptomatic significance (two-sided)	Results
(a) No university policy on sports for undergraduates with or without disabilities	10.241	2	0.006	Significant relationship
(b) No university policy on provision of sports facilities and equipment	18.996	3	0.000	Significant relationship
(c) No university policy on the employment of specialized coaching staff	89.837	3	0.000	Significant relationship
(d) No university policy on specialized coaching programs for recreation and sports	32.690	3	0.000	Significant relationship

Table 30.2 also shows significant differences ($p < 0.5$) in the results of the x^2 analyses of all the items. These show significant differences in opinion between Southern African university students with disabilities and those without on the issue of their universities not showing a strong commitment in implementing sports policies. This also led to the rejection of the second null hypothesis. While most students with disabilities strongly shared this view, those without disabilities were strongly not in support of the view. They probably could see structures on campus to convince them that a well-structured university sports policy was being well implemented. This again is gross inequality as portrayed by the results of the study. This also shows that a significant relationship exists between the implementation of a university sports policy and the type of students for whom implementation is effected—a relationship that has favored students without disabilities more, in this study.

Table 30.2 x^2 Statistics on the Relationship Between Equality and Inequality in the Implementation of University Sport Policies for Students With and Without Disabilities in Selected Southern African Universities ($N = 120$)

Items	χ^2 value	df	Asymptomatic significance (two-sided)	Results
(a) No strong commitment, on the part of university administrators toward implementing their university sports policies	34.828	3	0.000	Significant relationship
(b) No firm commitment, on the part of university administrators, in implementing policies on the provision of sports and recreation facilities	91.768	3	0.000	Significant relationship
(c) No firm commitment, on the part of university administrators, toward the implementation of policies regarding the employment of specialized coaching staff	45.983	3	0.000	Significant relationship
(d) No strong commitment, on the part of university administrators, toward the implementation of policies on the development of specialized coaching programs for all students	34.385	3	0.000	Significant relationship

Results in Table 30.3 show significant differences ($p < 0.5$) in the x^2 computation of the three items. These indicate that there were significant differences in opinion between the Southern African university students with disabilities used in this study and their able-bodied counterparts on the question of the availability of architecturally accessible sports facilities and equipment. The third null hypothesis was therefore rejected. While students with disabilities strongly stated that there were no sports equipment and facilities specifically provided to meet their special needs, students without disabilities had no reason to complain, as they probably had enough equipment and facilities to run their competitive and recreational sporting endeavors. This is yet another case of unequal treatment of both groups of students in the universities studied. These results made it clear that there is a significant relationship between the provision of sports facilities and equipment and the type of students for whom such facilities are provided. Several factors are probably called into play by university administrators that eventually exclude the students with disabilities from benefiting from what is supposed to be their right.

Table 30.3 χ^2 Statistics on the Relationship Between Equality and Inequality in the Availability of University Architecturally Accessible Sports Facilities and Equipment for Students With and Without Disabilities in Selected Southern African Universities ($N = 120$)

Items	χ^2 value	df	Asymptomatic significance (two-sided)	Results
(a) Gross inadequacy of sports equipment and assistive devices necessary for sports participation	37.706	3	0.000	Significant relationship
(b) No conscientious effort at providing architecturally accessible sporting facilities for all students	26.675	3	0.000	Significant relationship
(c) No availability of university-based fitness testing centers	21.336	3	0.000	Significant relationship

Table 30.4 also shows a significant difference ($p < 0.05$) in the x^2 analysis of the only item loaded by the factor analysis computed on the study instrument. This also implies a significant difference in the opinion of the Southern African university students with disabilities used in this study and their able-bodied counterparts on the issue of inadequacy of qualified sports coaches. This led to the rejection of the fourth null hypothesis. While students with disabilities strongly agreed that the university was not doing enough to provide them with coaches who are well-trained adapted physical activity professionals, their able-bodied counterparts seemed to be happy with the existing state of affairs. Here again is inequality in the treatment of students with disabilities.

With the trend observed in this study, and the nature of the bias shown by university administrators on issues concerning sports, the researchers decided to further analyze the data to find out if universities in the selected Southern African region treated their students with disabilities alike. Since, of the 20 universities selected by the multistage cluster sampling technique, 10 were selected from the universities in South Africa while the remaining 10 were drawn from the other seven countries randomly selected for use in this study, the present situation among all the 10 universities included in this study from the Republic of South Africa was compared with their peers with disabilities at universities across the region. Tables 30.5–30.8 show comparisons in the results of the χ^2 statistics computed on the differences between the treatment of managements of the selected universities in the Republic of South Africa and those of other countries in the Southern African region on issues concerning sports for students with disabilities. Results revealed that there were significant differences between the opinions of students with disabilities from the selected universities in the Republic of South Africa and those of their counterparts from selected universities across the region.

Table 30.4 x^2 Statistics on the Relationship Between Equality and Inequality in the Availability of Qualified Sports Coaches for Students With and Without Disabilities in Selected Southern African Universities ($N = 120$)

Items	χ^2 value	df	Asymptomatic significance (two-sided)	Results
Inadequacy of competent sports coaches for university sports (recreation and competition)	46.708	3	0.000	Significant relationship

University students with disabilities from the other seven Southern African countries were of the strong opinion that:

a) Their universities' sports policies did not make provisions for the employment of specially trained adapted physical activity coaches that could take care of their special sporting needs and sporting facilities.
b) Their universities' sports administrators were not strongly committed to the issue of sports policy implementation.
c) Their universities' sports administrators inadequately provided architecturally accessible sporting facilities for their special conditions.
d) Their universities' sports administrators inadequately provided qualified special coaches for them.

However, students with disabilities from the Republic of South Africa held a contrary view. They were strongly of the view that the situation in their country (South Africa) was not as bad as it was for the rest of the students from the other universities in the Southern African region selected for the study. This clearly showed that, of the university managements in the region, the managements of most of the universities in the Republic of South Africa need to be congratulated and modeled for upholding the constitutional rights of equal opportunities for all students, particularly those with disabilities, in their country.

Table 30.5 x^2 Statistics on the Relationship Between Equality and Inequality in the Availability of University Sport Policies for Students With Disabilities in South African Universities Versus Their Peers in the Other Selected Southern African Universities ($N = 60$)

Items	χ^2 value	df	Asymptomatic significance (two-sided)	Results
(a) No university policy on provision of sports facilities for students with disabilities	60.000	3	0.000	Significant relationship
(b) No university policy on the employment of specially trained coaches for students with disabilities	7.772	2	0.021	Significant relationship

Table 30.6 x^2 Statistics on the Relationship Between Equality and Inequality in the Implementation of University Sport Policies for Students With Disabilities in South African Universities Versus Their Peers in the Other Selected Southern African Universities ($N = 60$)

Items	χ^2 value	df	Asymptomatic significance (two-sided)	Results
(a) No strong commitment, on part of university administrators, toward implementing their sports policies	46.061	3	0.000	Significant relationship
(b) No firm commitment, on the part of university administrators, toward implementing policies on employment of adapted physical activity professionals	50.118	3	0.000	Significant relationship
(c) No strong commitment, on the part of university administrators, toward developing special coaching programs for their students with disabilities	30.819	3	0.000	Significant relationship

Table 30.7 x^2 Statistics on the Relationship Between Equality and Inequality in the Availability of Adapted Physical Activity Facilities and Equipment for Students With Disabilities in Selected Southern African Universities and Their Peers in Universities in South Africa ($N = 60$)

Items	χ^2 value	df	Asymptomatic significance (two-sided)	Results
(a) Gross inadequacy in availability of assistive devices for sports	24.991	3	0.000	Significant relationship
(b) No conscientious effort at providing architecturally accessible sporting facilities	18.725	3	0.000	Significant relationship
(c) Nonavailability of university-based fitness testing centers for students with disabilities	32.097	3	0.000	Significant relationship

Table 30.8 x^2 Statistics on the Relationship Between Equality and Inequality in the Availability of Qualified Adapted Physical Activity Coaches for Students With Disabilities in Selected Southern African Universities and Their Peers in Universities in South Africa ($N = 60$)

Items	χ^2 value	df	Asymptomatic significance (two-sided)	Results
Gross inadequacy of qualified coaches for sports for students with disabilities	30.101	3	0.000	Significant relationship

Discussion

The results of the study presented in Tables 30.1–30.4 show significant differences in opinion between Southern African university students with disabilities and those without on the issue of their universities not having a sports policy and not showing a strong commitment in implementing any available sports policy. They also differed in opinion on the issue of the availability of architecturally accessible sports facilities and adequate sports equipment and the inadequacy of qualified sports coaches for recreational pursuits and competition. These disagreements bring to the fore the issue of inequality when matters pertaining to people with disabilities are tabled by most leaders, heads of governments, and chief executives of various establishments. The vice-chancellors of universities and directors of sports at most of the Southern African universities have proved to be no different. They probably have not seen this dichotomy as a matter that requires urgent correction.

It is proper to note here that almost all the national constitutions of the countries represented in this study (including Angola, South Africa, Zambia, and Zimbabwe) have sections that promise commitment to the ideal of equal opportunity for all their citizens, be they with or without disabilities. They promise conducive environments that would afford their citizens the opportunity of actualizing their potentials to the fullest. Apparently, this study has shown that the issue of actualization of potentials in sports and recreational pursuits was not on the agenda of the heads of the institutions studied.

Heads of state and governments and their monitoring organs for educational establishments in the countries studied have a share of the blame. They should be seen correcting or sanctioning, where necessary, chief executives of institutions who act against the constitutional provisions of their countries. This is especially true since all heads of governments in Africa, including those in the Southern African region, agreed with the nongovernmental community of Africa to declare 2000–2009 as the African Decade of Disabled Persons (ADDP). To add credibility to the agreement, the Assembly of Heads of State and Governments of the African Union (AU), then known as the Organization of African Unity (OAU), adopted the recommendations at a meeting held in Algiers July 12–14, 1999 (Ad-Hoc Committee, 2003). The action plan calls upon AU member states and governments to study the situation of persons with disabilities with a view toward formulating measures favoring equal opportunity, full participation, and their independence in their societies. All member states and governments were urged to formulate or reformulate policies and national programs that encourage the full participation of persons with disabilities in social and economic development; and to create or reinforce national disability coordination committees (Ad-Hoc Committee, 2003).

The time has now come for all heads of state and governments in the Southern African region to be alive to their responsibilities and take after the noble ideals of the developed world. Vice-chancellors of most of the universities studied must take responsibility for all students put under their care. Countries in the Southern African region must learn the principle of equity for children with disabilities and their nondisabled peers as a fundamental value upon which the United States built its current special education practice. Under the current US federal legislation, the Individuals with Disabilities Education Act (IDEA) is operationalized with the requirement that states must provide free and appropriate public education to qualified students;

that, to the maximum extent possible, an individual with disabilities must be educated in the least restrictive environment; and that education is to be individualized and appropriate to the individual's needs (Huber, 1995; Rueda et al., 2000; Rizzo et al., 2003). This is achievable if the heads of governments in the Southern African region and their university vice-chancellors are determined to remove the barriers that could hamper sports participation by students with disabilities, and uphold the tenets of their constitutions toward all their citizens, with or without disabilities. Some of the barriers possible, according to Rimmer et al. (2004), include those related to the built and natural environments, economic issues, emotional and psychological factors, and equipment. Other barriers include those related to the use and interpretation of guidelines, codes, regulations, and laws, and those stemming from perceptions and attitudes of persons without disabilities, including professionals. These obstacles can be removed.

Further analysis of the data (Tables 30.5–30.8) distinguished the universities in the Republic of South Africa as different from the rest of the universities in the Southern African region on all four dependent variables tested in this study. Undergraduates with disabilities in the universities in the Republic of South Africa agree that:

1. Their universities have and implement a university sports policy.
2. They have adequate equipment and architecturally accessible facilities for sports.
3. They have specialized coaches for their sporting and recreational needs.

This did not come as a surprise because in 1997 the Office of the Deputy President of South Africa developed a white paper on the Integrated National Disability Strategy with numerous monitoring structures, and it continues to oversee the program (Office of the Deputy President, 1997). The implementation of this program for all persons with disabilities is probably the reason South African athletes with disabilities are among the best in the world. For instance, one recalls the extraordinary world record performance of Natalie Du Toit, a South African freestyle swimmer with a disability (Jeffery, 2002; The Times, 2002), and the victory of the South African Special Olympics team over the South Korean team in a soccer match held at the Ninth Special Olympics World Summer Games in New Haven, Connecticut (Anderson, 1995).

Recommendations

From the results obtained in this study, the following recommendations are considered necessary to bring about equality in the actions taken by vice-chancellors and directors of sports in the various Southern African universities studied toward university undergraduates, whether or not they have disabilities:

1. Vice-chancellors and directors of sports in the Southern African universities should have a well-structured and properly implemented sports policy that caters to the sporting, coaching, and recreational needs of all students, irrespective of disabilities.
2. They must employ well-qualified coaches, including adapted physical activity coaching personnel to handle the sporting programs for all their students. Since many countries in Africa still lack professionally trained adapted physical educators that can plan/design and execute adapted physical education programs and can develop (through improvisation) and utilize adapted facilities and equipment (Onyewadume, 1999), vice-chancellors of universities in the Southern African region should source professionals from anywhere, including outside Africa, if necessary.
3. They must also provide adequate assistive devices and other sporting equipment and architecturally accessible facilities, including fitness centers, for their students.
4. Vice-chancellors and directors of sports from the universities in the Southern African region must emulate the practices of the vice-chancellors in the Republic of South Africa with regard to equitable implementation of sports programs for all their students.
5. Finally, governments of the countries in the Southern African region must make sure that their vice-chancellors provide equal opportunities for sports and recreation to all their students, irrespective of disabilities. Vice-chancellors should be sanctioned if they default in their responsibility in this regard.

References

Ad-Hoc Committee (2003, June 16–27). *Progress in equalization of opportunities by, for and with persons with disabilities: Report of the secretary-general.* Paper presented at the Ad-Hoc Committee on a Comprehensive and Integral International Convention on Protection and Promotion of the Rights and Dignity of Persons with Disabilities, New York. Retrieved September 10, 2004, from http://www.un.org/esa/socdev/enable/rights/a_ac265_z.htm

Anderson, D. (1995, July 4). Oh, by the way, we won. *New York Times 144*, 50112–50150. Retrieved September 16, 2004, from EBSCO HOST Research Databases.

Angola Constitution. *Angola Constitution*. Retrieved September 19, 2004, from http://www.oefre.unibe.ch/law/icl/ao00000_.html

Chanias, A. K., Reid, G., & Hoover, M. L. (1998). Exercise effects on health-related physical fitness of individuals with an intellectual disability: A meta-analysis. *Adapted Physical Activity Quarterly 15*, 119–140.

Cochran, W. G. (1977). *Sampling techniques* (p. 223). New York: John Wiley.

Frey, G. C., McCubbin, J. A., Hannigan-Downs, S., Kasser, S. L., & Skaggs, S. O. (1999). Physical fitness of trained runners with and without mild mental retardation. *Adapted Physical Activity Quarterly 16*, 126–137.

Horvat, M., Croce, R., Stadler, L., & Pitetti, K. H. (1996). Isokinetic strength characteristics in children with and without mental retardation. *Medicine and Science in Sports and Exercise 28*, S50 [Abstracts].

Huber, J. H. (1995). Equity in athletics: Full participation for all students. *The Journal of Physical Education, Recreation and Dance 66*(7), 4–5.

Jeffery, N. (2002, August 2). South African able to go the distance—Commonwealth Games 2002. *The Australian 33*. Retrieved September 16, 2004, from EBSCO HOST Research Databases.

Kline, P. (1994). *An easy guide to factor analysis*. London: Routledge.

Norusis, M. J. (1991). *The SPSS guide to data analysis for SPSS/PC+*™ (2nd ed.). Chicago: SPSS Inc.

Office of the Deputy President (1997). South Africa integrated national disability strategy white paper. Retrieved September 15, 2004, from http://www.gladnet.org/infobase/files/319.htm

Onyewadume, I. U. (1999). Perspectives of adapted physical education in Africa. In L. O. Amusa, A. L. Toriola, & I. U. Onyewadume (Eds.), *Physical education and sport in Africa* (pp. 141–156). Stellenbosch: University of Stellenbosch Printers.

Pitetti, K. H., Rimmer, J. H., & Fernhall, B. (1993). Physical fitness and adults with mental retardation: An overview of current research and future directions. *Sports Medicine 16*, 23–36.

Pommering, T. L., Brose, J. A., Randolph, E., Murray, T. F., Purdy, R. W., Cadamagnani, P. E., & Foglesong, J. E. (1994). Effects of an aerobic exercise program on community-based adults with mental retardation. *Mental Retardation 32*, 218–226.

Rimmer, J. H., Braddock, D., & Fujiura, G. (1992). Blood lipid and percent body fat levels in Down syndrome versus non-DS persons with mental retardation. *Adapted Physical Activity Quarterly 9*, 123–129.

———. (1993). Prevalence of obesity in adults with mental retardation: Implications for health promotion and disease prevention. *Mental Retardation 31*, 105–110.

Rimmer, J. H., Riley, B., Wang, E., Rauworth, A., & Jurkowski, J. (2004). Physical activity participation among persons with disabilities: Barriers and facilitators. *American Journal of Preventive Medicine 26*(5), 419–425.

Rizzo, T., Faison-Hodge, J., Woodard, R., & Sayers, K. (2003). Are public facilities accessible to individuals with disabling conditions? *Adapted Physical Activity Quarterly 20*(3), 319–320.

Rueda, R., Gallego, M. A., & Moll, L. C. (2000). The least restrictive environment: A place or a context? *Remedial and Special Education 21*(2), 70–78.

Russo, R. (2003). *Statistics for behavioural sciences: An introduction.* New York: Psychology Press, Taylor & Francis.

Sherrill, C. (2003). *Adapted physical activity, recreation and sport with power web blind-in passcard* (6th ed.). Dubuque, IA: McGraw-Hill.

Stadler, L. V., & Pitetti, K. H. (1996). Isometric and isokinetic leg strength of youths with and without mental retardation. *Medicine and Science in Sports and Exercise 28*, S49 [Abstract].

Suomi, R., Surburg, P. R., & Lecius, P. (1995). Effects of hydraulic resistance strength training on isokinetic measures of leg strength in men with mental retardation. *Adapted Physical Activity Quarterly 12*, 377–387.

The Times (2002, August). The swimmer who turns distress into sporting inspiration. *The Times*, 42–44. Retrieved September 16, 2004, from EBSCO HOST Research Databases.

Thomas, J. R., & Nelson, J. K. (1996). *Research methods in physical activity* (3rd ed.). Champaign, IL: Human Kinetics.

Winnick, J. P. (2000). An introduction of adapted physical education and sport. In J. P. Winnick (Ed.), *Adapted physical education and sport* (3rd ed.). Champaign, IL: Human Kinetics.

Zambia Constitution. *Zambia country profile.* Retrieved September 19, 2004, from http://www.bibl.u-szeged.hu/oseas_adsec/zambia.htm

———. *Draft Constitution of the Republic of Zimbabwe.* Retrieved September 20, 2004, from http://www.gta.gov.zw/Constitutional/Draft%20constitution/Contents.Draft.Const.htm

CHAPTER THIRTY

Equality or Inequality

Physical Education for the Children of Africa, Problems and Way Forward

I. U. ONYEWADUME

Abstract

This study compares the present status of physical education for the children of Africa, with or without disabilities, in terms of provision of, and access to, quality physical education programs. The aim is to ascertain whether or not inequality still exists in the provision and implementation of physical education programs, some 50 years after the outcome of *Brown v. Board of Education* (1954). Colleagues gathered information on various aspects of physical education, as structured for children with and without disabilities, in different African countries. The status of, problems facing, and future direction of, physical education in their countries were also examined. The general consensus was that Africa is still far behind in realizing the ideals of Public Laws 93–112 of 1973, 93–380 of 1974 and, in particular, 94–142 of 1975. Governments of most African countries still pay lip service to the education of people with disabilities. Results show that both children with and without disabilities have equal treatment in the provision of national policies that could promote the cause of physical education in the selected African schools. There were also physical education curricula in both types of schools, and physical activity classes were time-tabled. However, there were inequalities in funding, provision of equipment and architecturally accessible facilities, public support, and the implementation of relevant national policies that could promote physical education and sport.

Introduction

Literature on the nature of physical activities organized for the children of Africa with disabilities prior to the advent of the current adapted physical activity is nonexistent. Adapted physical activity, as it is presently constituted, can be rightly said to have emerged from the landmark decision of *Brown v. Board of Education* in 1954, in which, according to Sherrill (2003) and Winnick (2000), the US Supreme Court ruled that the doctrine of "separate but equal" in the field of public education was unconstitutional and deprived the segregated group (Blacks) of rights guaranteed by the Fourteenth Amendment. What is known about the general public attitude toward people with disabilities in Africa was handed down the generations by oral tradition and observation of current events as they unfold around the world. To a great extent, it is natural in Africa to view people with disabilities with sympathy rather than empathy. And the implication of this philosophy is that, to date, the people with disabilities are still pitied, assisted, provided for, accorded some acts of kindness, and even exempted from physically exhausting tasks by a great majority of the African populace. In fact, parents to a large extent, still protect their children with disabilities in Africa.

The infusion of the field of adapted physical activity into the curriculum of broader physical education in some higher institutions in Africa came in the early 1980s. Prior to that time, professionals in the field of physical education and recreation were trained to teach physical education and coach the various sports to only individuals without disabilities. At that time, people with disabilities were largely expected to remain at home. This was very unfortunate because, as has long been observed by various researchers (Rimmer et al., 1992; 1993; Pitetti et al., 1993; Horvat et al., 1996; Stadler & Pitetti, 1996; Frey et al., 1999), people with disabilities constitute the endangered species in terms of their lack of, and need for, the various components of physical fitness. Their poor level of fitness results from, among other things, physical inactivity; chronotropic insufficiency; and poor motivation, encouragement, and support (Pitetti et al., 1993; Frey et al., 1999; Onyewadume, 1999). This sedentary way of life should be reversed, and everything should be done to engage people with disabilities in daily physical activities since these individuals also have the potential to improve their fitness levels. Supporting this view, Chanias et al. (1998), Pommering et al. (1994) and Suomi et al. (1995) found that people with disabilities have the ability to improve in various aspects of fitness with training.

Adapted physical education, as it was called when it was introduced, was taught in departments of physical education at few universities across Africa, as one of the courses needed for obtaining the required credits for graduation. In most African countries, the course was offered only in very few higher institutions other than universities. For want of trained professionals in the area, at that time, the course was even sometimes relegated to the status of an elective, or an optional course. Even now, there is acute scarcity of adapted physical activity professionals in most African universities and other higher institutions of learning on the African continent. The implication of this scarcity is the inability to produce enough graduates who would eventually teach or coach in the schools as adapted physical activity professionals. The spiral effect of this shortfall in equalizing opportunities for children with disabilities with those of children without disabilities—at least in the realm of school physical education programs, recreational sports activities, physical fitness, and competitive sports training—is that of gross inadequacy of adapted physical activity specialists who could handle the various programs in the primary schools for children with disabilities in Africa (Onyewadume, 1999).

While the rest of the world celebrates 50 years of positive correction of the injustices that preceded the *Brown v. Board of Education* saga, most African governments are probably not very sure of what to do or are probably unwilling to redress the injustice. It is now time for Africa to look inward and find out if it benefited much from this landmark rejection of injustice toward people with disabilities by the US Supreme Court. It is also time to identify what problems face the people and governments of various African countries in their struggle toward empowering their citizens with disabilities to achieve equality with their counterparts who have no disabilities.

With this in mind, this researcher investigated some of the issues that affect the present practices in the field of physical education in selected primary schools for children with and without disabilities in selected African countries. The study aimed at finding out if there was equality or inequality in the treatment given to school children with disabilities, vis-à-vis their counterparts without disabilities, in the provision of viable physical education programs. Specifically, this study investigated whether having a disability or not was a factor that was mainly considered by the various African governments in the provision of an adequate physical education program to school children in the schools studied in African countries. In conducting this comparative study, the following six dependent variables were examined for equality or inequality of attention between schools for children with disabilities and those for children without:

a) the availability, or otherwise, of national policies that could affect the physical education practice in the selected African schools;
b) the implementation, or otherwise, of any existing relevant national policy in the selected African schools;
c) the provision, and sources, of funding for the schools' physical education facilities, equipment, and programs;
d) the availability of physical education equipment and facilities in the schools;
e) public attitude toward the children's participation in school sports programs;
f) physical education curriculum design and scheduling in the selected African schools.

To further direct the study, six hypotheses were tested at the 0.05 alpha level. There is no significant relationship between having disabilities or not and:

a) the availability of national policies that could affect the practice of physical education in the selected African schools;
b) the implementation of any existing, relevant, national policy in the selected African schools;
c) the provision/sources of funding for the physical education facilities, equipment, and programs in the selected African schools;
d) the availability of physical education facilities and equipment in the selected African schools;
e) the public attitude toward the children's participation in school sports programs in the selected African schools;
f) the physical education design and scheduling in the selected African schools.

Having uncovered the prevailing situation of affairs on the African continent, including the problem areas, this study proposes the way forward to enable future generations of African children with disabilities to benefit from previous and present legislation designed to provide equality with their peers without disabilities. Proposals were put forward to improve the situations that negatively impact the achievement of equal opportunity for pupils with disabilities in line with their peers with no disabilities.

Methods

This study was conducted using the survey research design. This is a technique of descriptive research that seeks to determine present practices or opinions of a specified population (Thomas & Nelson, 1996).

Target Population of the Study

The target population for this study included all physical educators, sports teachers, and games masters, with or without certification in physical education or adapted physical activity, in all the primary schools for children with or without disabilities in Africa.

Sample Size and Sampling Procedure

To ensure adequate coverage and representation of the study population from the entire continent of Africa, the multistage cluster sampling method was used to select the participants for the study. According to Cochran (1977), this sampling technique is recommended when there is no sampling frame and the population is scattered over a wide geographical area. A sample of 140 teachers was randomly selected from 140 randomly selected primary schools from 14 randomly selected African countries drawn from five regions. In each of the countries selected, five primary schools for children without disabilities and five for those with disabilities were randomly selected for the study. Seventy of these schools were special primary schools, while the remaining 70 schools trained children who had no disabilities.

To achieve external validation—that is, the ability to generalize the results of this study to similar situations in other African countries not included in this study—the representative sample had to reflect the characteristics of the entire African continent within the five regions: North African region (Egypt, Morocco); West African region (Ghana, Ivory Coast, Nigeria, Sierra Leone); Central African region (Cameroon, Congo); East African region (Kenya, Tanzania, Uganda); and South African region (Botswana, South Africa, Zimbabwe). Also, since ministries of education in each country oversee the implementation of national policies that are relevant to the educational system, there is every likelihood that the 10 schools randomly selected from each country would comply with directives from their ministries. It is therefore possible to have a general picture of what obtains in each of the countries from the 10 schools randomly selected. These positions were supported by Russo (2003), who notes that the representative sample of a study must reflect the characteristics of the entire population in order to achieve external validation. According to Kline (1994), samples must not only be representative but must be of sufficient size to produce reliable factors.

It should be noted that the terms *special primary schools*, *special schools*, or *primary school for children with disabilities* in this study refer to homes, rehabilitation centers, or primary schools exclusively established for children with disabilities. For instance, there are schools for children with hearing impairment, homes for children with mental retardation, and so on.

Participants

One hundred forty randomly selected physical educators, sports teachers, and games masters, with or without certification in physical education or adapted physical activity took part in the study. Seventy of the teachers were from special primary schools while the remaining 70 were from primary schools training children without disabilities. These gave their consent to fill in copies of the questionnaire. The mean ± standard deviation and range of their ages were 27.4 ± 4.8 years and 24–48 years, respectively, for teachers in the special primary schools, and 29.1 ± 5.8 years and 22–44 years, respectively, for teachers in the schools for children without disabilities.

Instrumentation

Given that no statistical evidence is required for content validity (Thomas & Nelson, 1996), the content validity of the questionnaire was established through extensive reference to textbooks, journal articles, and Internet sites in the relevant areas of the study. A 36-item closed- and open-ended questionnaire known as the African Children Equal Access to Physical Activity Questionnaire (ACEAPAQ) was developed and piloted among 100 physical educators, sports teachers, or games masters with or without certification in physical education. These were drawn from primary schools training children with or without disabilities in the central and southern districts of the Republic of Botswana. These schools were not included in the actual study. In any data with a clear factor structure, a sample of 100 participants was quite sufficient. If factor analyses are carried out with factors smaller than these, all results need replication in other samples (Kline, 1994). It is worthy of note that this study satisfies this criterion.

Data from the pilot run of the questionnaire were factor analyzed using the SPSS version 11.5.2.1. The resulting principal component analysis extracted six main components from the questionnaire. The data were further analyzed using the Varimax rotation with Kaiser normalization. The rotated component matrix revealed seven converged iterations ranging from–0.963 to 0.977. A reliability statistic of Cronbach's Alpha was then computed on the 36-item questionnaire, yielding a correlation coefficient of 0.822. Kline (1994) notes that whenever an orthogonal simple structure rotation is desired, the Varimax rotation should be applied. According to Kline, this is because the Varimax technique aims at maximizing the sum of variances of squared loadings in the columns of the factor matrix; producing loadings that are either high or near zero. This is one of the critical features of simple structures. Kline noted that a clever feature of the Varimax technique is that the procedure is applied to the loadings squared rather than the actual loadings. Supporting this action, Thomas and Nelson (1996) agreed that internal consistency reliability coefficient could be obtained using the Coefficient Alpha technique. Out of the 36 items that constituted the pilot questionnaire, 16 items were then loaded across the seven converged iterations. A careful look at the seven iterations revealed the following subthemes, or underlying concepts, of the study:

1. the question of the availability of national policies that could impact on the physical education program of children with or without disabilities in Africa if not made available;
2. the issue of the implementation of a relevant national policy by the various African governments for the benefit of the African children with or without disabilities;
3. the main sources of funding required for physical education equipment, facilities, and programs for African children with or without disabilities;
4. the availability/nonavailability of physical education facilities and equipment for children having or not having disabilities in Africa;
5. public attitude toward participation in sports by African children with or without disabilities; and
6. the structure and nature of the design and scheduling of physical activities in the school timetables of children with or without disabilities in Africa.

According to Norusis (1991), the factor analysis technique assists in the identification of the underlying concepts of a study. With a high reliability coefficient of 0.822, the questionnaire could be said to have a high internal consistency, which, according to Thomas and Nelson (1996), is an integral part of the wider validity issue, as it reflects the degree to which the measuring instrument is free of error variance. A revised version of the questionnaire was then developed using the 16 items loaded by the Varimax rotation. The remaining 20 items were dropped from the final questionnaire. A French version of the final questionnaire was developed and sent to colleagues in Francophone African countries for distribution to the randomly selected teachers used in the study.

Data Collection Procedure

The questionnaire was sent by e-mail attachment to some physical education colleagues in the countries selected for the study. Most of these colleagues were not adapted physical activity professionals. They were selected to coordinate the survey exercise in their countries because they were knowledgeable in questionnaire administration and able to communicate fluently. They were requested to extract the e-mail attachment, print out the required copies, and distribute them to the randomly selected participants in the selected schools. Telephone follow-ups and e-mail communications with the coordinators were done intermittently to facilitate the data collection. Completed questionnaire copies were retrieved and couriered back to the researcher.

Data Analysis

Data were analyzed using the chi-square (x^2) statistics and the column percentages within the cross tabulations menu of the SPSS version 11.5.2.1.

Results

In Table 31.1, x^2 analyses on the two items did not show any significant difference ($p < 0.05$) in the opinions of the physical education teachers in both special schools and schools for children without disabilities on the issue of the availability of a national policy that could promote the cause of physical education for children with and without disabilities. Both groups agreed that there was such a national policy. This shows that there was no significant relationship between having a disability or not and the availability of a national policy that could enhance the programs of physical education in the selected African schools.

Table 31.2(a) shows significant differences ($p < 0.05$) in the results of the x^2 analyses on both items, indicating a significant difference in opinion between physical education teachers, sports teachers, and games masters in the special schools and those in the normal schools on the issue of equality or inequality in the implementation of relevant national policies that could assist the cause of physical education in their schools. Teachers from special schools noted that such policies were not strongly implemented, while those from normal schools disagreed. This shows a significant relationship between having a disability or not and the implementation of any existing, relevant national policy in the selected African schools. This led to the rejection of the second null hypothesis.

Table 31.1 x^2 Statistics on the Relationship Between Equality and Inequality in the Availability of Relevant National Policies for Enhancing Physical Education Program for Children With and Without Disabilities in Selected African Schools ($N = 140$)

Items	χ^2 value	df	Asymptomatic Significance (two-sided)	Results
(a) No national policies in building schools (normal, special)	1.036	1	0.309	No significant relationship
(b) No national policies on the IEPs (early children admission to schools) and multidisciplinary cooperation/collaboration among personnel of related services	2.397	1	0.122	No significant relationship

Table 31.2(a) x^2 Statistics on the Relationship Between Equality and Inequality in Implementation of National Policies Relevant to Physical Education for Children With and Without Disabilities in Selected African Schools ($N = 140$)

Items	χ^2 value	df	Asymptomatic Significance (two-sided)	Results
(a) National policies on building schools (normal, special, mainstreamed) not strongly implemented	78.636	4	0.000	Significant relationship
(b) National policies on the IEPs (early childhood admission to schools) not strongly implemented	28.353	4	0.005	Significant relationship

When the column percentages of the data were further compared by regions (Table 31.2(b)), it was observed that only teachers of children with disabilities from the Southern African region had the same opinion as their counterparts from normal schools. The teachers of children with disabilities from the Southern African region noted that policies that promoted physical education were implemented in their schools. This they supported with their schools' implementation of the Individualized Education Programs (IEPs). This comparison shows clearly that through their ministries of education, there was a significant implementation of some national policies that promote physical education for children with disabilities by selected governments in the Southern African region as compared to the other regions in Africa.

The results in Table 31.3(a) show a significant difference ($p < 0.05$) on the issue of African governments' funding of physical education equipment, facilities, and programs, and what the main source of funding was. This significant difference meant that there was no consensus in their opinions about whether or not government funded school physical education programs, provided facilities and equipment, and where the main source of funding came from. While teachers from the normal schools agreed that their governments were the main sources of funding for physical activity programs, those from special schools reported that nongovernmental organizations (NGOs) were their main sources of funding. This again showed a significant relationship between having a disability or not and the provision/sources of funding for physical education facilities, equipment, and programs in the selected African schools. It was another evidence of African governments' unequal support for their citizens' welfare, particularly physical activity programs for people who need them most. The third null hypothesis of the study was therefore rejected.

Further comparison of funding by African governments among the various regions (Table 31.3(b)) revealed that only the Southern African teachers from special schools had opinions similar to those of their colleagues from the normal schools. This indicates that they received substantial funding for their physical education programs mainly from their governments. This shows equality of treatment and a lot of commitment in funding physical activity programs by some governments in the Southern African region compared to the attitude of governments in the rest of the continent.

Table 31.4(a) shows significant differences ($p < 0.05$) in the results of the $?^2$ analyses of the two items analyzed. The teachers from both types of schools did not agree on the issue of equality or inequality in having proper and adequate facilities and equipment for teaching physical activities to their pupils. Whereas teachers from schools for children without disabilities indicated that their governments provided their pupils with the proper and adequate physical education facilities and equipment, those from special schools reported that they had gross inadequacy in the provision of physical education facilities and equipment from their governments. They also reported gross insensitivity to their needs in the provision of architecturally compliant physical education facilities for their pupils. Here again, inequality of treatment by most African governments was obvious, indicating a significant relationship between having or not having a disability and the provision of physical education facilities and equipment. This meant the rejection of the fourth null hypothesis.

Questions and responses			North African region (%)	West African region (%)	Central African region (%)	East African region (%)	South African region (%)
Policy on building special/normal schools not strongly implemented	Teachers from special schools	SA	54	51	74	38	
		A	41	49	16	62	
		U	5		10		9
		D					36
		SD					55
	Teachers from normal schools	SA					
		A					
		U	21	5	39	9	
		D	49	15	61	41	54
		SD	30	70		50	46
Policies on IEP/early childhood admission not strongly implemented	Teachers from special schools	SA	61	33	33	38	5
		A	39	67	64	62	19
		U			4		52
		D					24
		SD					
	Teachers from normal schools	SA	11	44	61	33	
		A	68	56	39	67	
		U	21				
		D					47
		SD					53

Table 31.2(b) Cross-Tabulation of Relationship Between Equality and Inequality in Implementation of National Policy Relevant to Physical Education for Children With and Without Disabilities in Selected Regions of Africa ($N = 140$)

Table 31.3(a) x^2 Statistics on the Relationship Between Equality and Inequality in African Governments' Funding of Physical Education Equipment, Facilities and Programs for Children With and Without Disabilities in Selected African Schools ($N = 140$)

Items	χ^2 value	df	Asymptomatic Significance (two-sided)	Results
(a) Government is the main source of funding of physical education equipment, facilities and programs. Below are the sources of funding for physical education programs, facilities and equipments	75.285	4	0.000	Significant relationship
(b) Government as main source	140.000	4	0.000	Significant relationship
(c) NGOs as main source	136.133	4	0.000	Significant relationship
(d) Church organizations as main source	129.000	4	0.000	Significant relationship
(e) Parents as main source	0.457	1	0.499	No significant relationship

However, a further analysis by regions marks out the Southern African region from the injustice perpetrated by governments in the other regions of the continent (Table 31.4(b)). The study, once more, revealed that there was a commendable level of commitment in matters concerning people with disabilities by most Southern African governments in comparison with the rest of their peers on the continent. Teachers of children with disabilities in the Southern African region confirmed that they had adequate provision of physical education facilities and equipment.

Results in Table 31.5 also show significant differences ($p < 0.05$) in the opinions of both groups of teachers on the attitude of the public toward sports participation by the children. While teachers from schools without children with disabilities were happy about the public support they enjoyed from the general public during intramural and interscholastic sports programs, teachers handling children with disabilities were not pleased about the nonchalant attitude of the general public during their sports competitions and trainings, including even the parents of children with disabilities. There was therefore a significant relationship between public attitude and the ability/disability factor. This also boils down to inequality of treatment when the issue concerns children with disabilities. This led to the rejection of the fifth null hypothesis.

Questions and responses			North African region (%)	West African region (%)	Central African region (%)	East African region (%)	South African region (%)
Government as main source of funding for physical education facilities, equipment, and programs	Teachers from special schools	SA					47
		A					33
		U	6			4	10
		D	10	34	32	57	6
		SD	84	66	68	39	4
	Teachers from normal schools	SA	71	63	57	64	74
		A	29	35	43	36	26
		U		2			
		D					
		SD					

Table 31.3(b) Cross-Tabulation of Relationship Between Equality and Inequality in the Funding of School Physical Education Equipment, Facilities and Programs for Children With and Without Disabilities by Governments in Selected Schools From Different Regions of Africa ($N = 140$)

Table 31.4(a) x^2 Statistics on the Relationship Between Equality and Inequality in the Availability of Physical Education Equipment and Facilities for Children With and Without Disabilities in Selected African Schools ($N = 140$)

Items	χ^2 value	df	Asymptomatic Significance (two-sided)	Results
(a) Gross inadequacy of assistive physical education devices (ambulatory devices, orthotics, braces) equipment balls, rackets, etc., and facilities	54.483	4	0.000	Significant relationship
(b) No conscientious effort made by the government to provide architecturally accessible sporting facilities (least restrictive physical education environment)	65.978	4	0.000	Significant relationship

Table 31.6 shows the x^2 results on equality or inequality in the design and scheduling of physical education curricula for the children of Africa with and without disabilities. There was no significant difference ($p > 0.05$) in the opinions of the physical education teachers from special schools and schools for children without disabilities on the issues of not including physical education in the general school curriculum and the gross inadequacy of physical activity classes per week. Both groups denied these and reiterated that they were adequately provided for on the timetable and school curriculum. The sixth null hypothesis was therefore not rejected.

Questions and responses			North African region (%)	West African region (%)	Central African region (%)	East African region (%)	South African region (%)
Gross inadequacy of physical education equipment and facilities and assistive devices	Teachers from special schools	SA	42	59	62	32	19
		A	53	37	35	57	
		U	5	4	3	11	
		D					52
		SD					29
	Teachers from normal schools	SA					
		A					
		U	11	6	4	9	15
		D	61	71	17	71	85
		SD	28	23	79	20	5
No conscientious effort to provide architecturally accessible sports facilities	Teachers from special schools	SA	45	41	38	40	2
		A	48	59	58	53	13
		U	7		4	7	25
		D					55
		SD					
	Teachers from normal schools	SA					
		A					
		U	12	16	8	6	
		D	40	51	33	34	46
		SD	48	33	59	60	54

Table 31.4(b) Cross-Tabulation of Relationship Between Equality and Inequality in the Availability of Physical Education Facilities and Equipment for Children With and Without Disabilities in Selected Schools From Different Regions of Africa ($N = 140$)

Table 31.5 x^2 Statistics on the Relationship Between Equality and Inequality in Public Attitude Toward Participation in Sports by Children With and Without Disabilities in Selected African Schools ($N = 140$)

Items	χ^2 value	df	Asymptomatic Significance (two-sided)	Results
(a) Inadequate public attendance during intramural and interscholastic sports competitions	140.000	4	0.000	Significant relationship
(b) Nonchalant behavior by parents, if children improve in fitness	136.133	4	0.000	Significant relationship
(c) Inadequate parental concern and support for their children's participation in sporting activities	194.081	4	0.000	Significant relationship

Table 31.6 x^2 Statistics on the Relationship Between Equality and Inequality in Physical Education Curriculum Design and Scheduling for Children With and Without Disabilities in Selected African Schools ($N = 140$)

Items	χ^2 value	df	Asymptomatic Significance (two-sided)	Results
(a) Physical activities not included in the general school curriculum	0.029	1	0.866	No significant relationship
(b) Gross inadequacy in physical education periods per week	1.357	2	0.507	No significant relationship

Discussion

From the results of this study (Table 31.1), physical education teachers, sports teachers, and games masters of the special schools and schools for children without disabilities agreed that there were national policies that could promote physical education programs in their schools. There was, therefore, no significant relationship between governments' provision of national policies that could promote physical education programs and whether the children had disabilities or not. Both groups of respondents did not agree with the suggestion that there was no inclusion of physical activities in the general school curriculum. They also did not agree with the statement that physical education periods per week were grossly inadequate (Table 31.6). This was commendable on the part of the governments and probably their supervising ministries of education. However, the results in Table 31.2(a) reveal that the available relevant national policies that could assist the cause of physical education were unequally implemented. Also, results in Table 31.3(a) suggest that the governments did not equally fund the physical education programs in both types of schools. This inequality of treatment was also clear from the results in Table 31.4(a) on the availability of equipment and architecturally accessible facilities for physical education and sports in both types of schools.

Inequality of treatment, in these cases, shows that the governments of most African countries studied have not lived up to the sections of their national constitutions that speak of commitment to the provision of equal opportunities for their citizens. For instance, a look at the national constitutions of almost all the African nations included in this study (Angola, Congo, Egypt, Ghana, Kenya, Nigeria, Uganda, South Africa, Zambia, and Zimbabwe) shows that, on paper, they pledged to provide their citizens with the right environment for development and also to uphold and defend the equality of rights, opportunities, privileges, and benefits for all their citizens. Some, in fact, even go further to state that their citizens would not be discriminated against on the grounds of disabilities (see national constitutions of Nigeria, South Africa, and Uganda) and that they shall provide appropriate facilities for disabled persons (see national constitutions of Ghana, Nigeria, and South Africa). From the results of this study, one can most categorically say that most African governments are at a loss about what to do to equalize opportunities for people with disabilities in line with what they provide for their citizens without disabilities. According to Onyewadume (1999), some African governments still pay lip service to the education of their citizens with disabilities. African leaders must uphold the constitutions of their countries and make sure that all their citizens benefit from all the rights, privileges, and opportunities set forth therein. It is the duty of the state to protect its citizens from restrictions (Konczei, 1997).

It is worth mentioning here that all the governments of the countries in Africa agreed with the nongovernmental community of Africa to declare year 2000–2009 the African Decade of Disabled Persons (ADDP). This recommendation was adopted by the Assembly of Heads of State and Governments of the African Union (AU), then known as the Organisation of African Unity (OAU), at a meeting held in Algiers from July 12–14, 1999 (Ad-Hoc Committee, 2003). The action plan calls upon AU member states and governments to study the situation of persons with disabilities with a view to formulating measures favoring equal opportunity, full participation, and their independence in their societies. All member states and governments were urged to formulate or reformulate policies and national programs that encourage the full participation of persons with disabilities in social and economic development; and create or reinforce national disability coordination committees (Ad-Hoc Committee, 2003).

It is difficult to believe that all these documents are lying on dusty shelves while the responsible officers who are supposed to implement the noble ideas in the documents are receiving fat salaries for no good job done. It is time for all the heads of state and Governments in Africa to wake up from their slumber and imitate the noble ideals of the developed world. In the United States, for example, one of the fundamental values built into the current special education practice is the principle of equity for children with disabilities and their nondisabled peers. Under the current US federal legislation, the Individuals with Disabilities Education Act (IDEA) is operationalized with the requirement that states must provide free and appropriate public education to qualified students; that, to the maximum extent possible, a child with disabilities must be educated in the least restrictive environment; and that education is to be individualized and appropriate to each child's needs (Huber, 1995; Rueda et al., 2000; Rizzo et al., 2003). With the will to truly serve their citizens, African governments should be able to have a breakthrough in these areas.

The attempt to analyze certain variables by regions (Tables 31.2(b), 31.3(b), and 31.4(b)) clearly marked out the Southern African region as the best of all five regions on the continent in terms of providing for their children with disabilities. Teachers in this region agreed with their counterparts who teach children without disabilities that:

a) National policies that strengthen the physical education practice were being implemented in their schools.
b) Government was the main source of their funding.
c) Their governments and NGOs provided equipment and architecturally accessible facilities for their children.

In 1997, the Office of the Deputy President of South Africa developed a white paper on, and continues to oversee, the Integrated National Disability Strategy with numerous monitoring structures. It was therefore not surprising to find South African athletes with disabilities among the best in the world. For instance, one recalls the extraordinary world record performance of Natalie Du Toit, a South African freestyle swimmer with a disability (Jeffery, 2002; The Times, 2002), and the victory of the South African Special Olympics team over the South Korean team in a soccer match held at the Ninth Special Olympics World Summer Games in New Haven, Connecticut (Anderson, 1995). These, together with others (Angola Press Agency, 2004; Nampa, 2004), are very good examples of synergy between government and NGOs.

One shocking revelation of this study was that even parents of children with disabilities did not provide the much-needed support for their children's involvement in physical education and sports (Table 31.5). For the teachers, this must be a great disappointment, as they probably have tried very hard to find genuine reasons for the nonchalant attitude of the general public during their sporting competitions and trainings. This reality is probably why most scholars dealing with children with disabilities (Allen & Schwartz, 2001; Farrell, 2003; Fergusson & Duffield, 2003; Sherrill, 2003; Westwood, 2003; Vahid et al., 2004) advocate that the school must evolve the best approaches for getting the parents involved. In fact, Allen and Schwartz (2001) suggest that schools work toward developing mutual understanding with parents through an effective communication channel. They note that talking with parents, rather than to parents, should form the basis for effective communication.

The Way Forward

To guarantee persons with disabilities exercise or enjoyment of all the rights enshrined in the international covenants and other instruments of human rights, every obstacle must be removed that hinders their effective participation, in conditions of equality (Inter-Regional Expert Group, 2002). According to Rimmer et al. (2004), potential obstacles include the built and natural environments; emotional and psychological factors; equipment; the interpretation of guidelines, codes, regulations, and laws; perceptions and attitudes of persons who are not disabled, including some professionals; policies and procedures at facility, community, and government levels; and resource availability. For a change toward the direction of the developed world, African leaders must ensure that they look inward, closely and hard, at the above potential obstacles and resolve to tackle them with vigor for the benefit of all their peoples and to uphold the national constitutions to which they are sworn.

To properly focus on the issues of physical education and sports for all citizens, heads of state should ensure that their ministries of education and sports function efficiently and that there is collaboration between them. For countries without sports ministries, such should be created immediately to concentrate on issues pertaining to the sporting needs of all citizens, especially people with disabilities (Onyewadume, 1999). Governments must endeavor not to deprive such ministries of funds, as new technologies would be needed to enhance mobility during exercise and training (Kristiansen, 1988). These cost money.

It is important to categorically state here that a lot of children with disabilities must have died in the past of hypokinetic diseases due to the inadequate attention some governments have paid to matters concerning well-funded and implemented physical education and sports programs in schools. Such leaders have therefore contributed to the death of a large number of their citizens. There is not much difference between a leader who commits the crime of genocide or ethnic cleansing and one who looks on and allows their citizens with disabilities to die of hypokinetic ailments, conditions that they could have helped control if they were committed to the wellbeing of all their citizens. Such African heads of state who lack the moral will to equalize opportunities and promote wellness among all their citizens, as sworn to, must be made to face some sort of prosecution in an international court of justice. An international arm of the United Nations, similar to the genocide/war crimes tribunal at The Hague, should be created with the full powers to legally prosecute any such head of government. Since almost all countries signed up to the pledge to grant equity to all their citizens, such a body as prescribed above should be able to provide sanctions in the case of failure by a leader to provide such constitutional obligations to its citizens (Konczei, 1997).

Finally, since participation in physical activities improves the health of everybody, including people with disabilities, physical education should be made compulsory in primary schools throughout the African continent. To this end, governments must equip schools with architecturally accessible facilities to promote the principle of "least restrictive environment" for physical education and sports participation. Adapted physical activity professionals and other allied professionals taking care of people with disabilities should be encouraged to do their work through better conditions of service, particularly through increased salaries. Also, the general public must be educated about issues pertaining to people with disabilities. For cooperative actions, schools caring for children with disabilities must evolve an efficient channel of communication with parents of children with disabilities.

References

Ad-Hoc Committee (2003, June 16–27). *Progress in equalization of opportunities by, for and with persons with disabilities: Report of the secretary-general.* Paper presented at the Ad-Hoc Committee on a Comprehensive and Integral

International Convention on Protection and Promotion of the Rights and Dignity of Persons with Disabilities, New York. Retrieved September 10, 2004, from http://www.un.org/esa/socdev/enable/rights/a_ac265_z.htm

Allen, K. E., & Schwartz, I. S. (2001). *The exceptional child: Inclusion in early childhood education* (4th ed.). Albany, NY: Delmar Thomson Learning.

Anderson, D. (1995, July 4). Oh, by the way, we won. *New York Times 144*, 50112–50150. Retrieved September 16, 2004, from EBSCO HOST Research Databases.

Angola Constitution. *Angola Constitution.* Retrieved September 19, 2004, from http://www.oefre.unibe.ch/law/icl/aoooooo_.html

Angola Press Agency (2004, January 8). *War crippled association to implement training.* Retrieved September 16, 2004, from EBSCO HOST Research Databases.

Chanias, A. K., Reid, G., & Hoover, M. L. (1998). Exercise effects on health-related physical fitness of individuals with an intellectual disability: A meta-analysis. *Adapted Physical Activity Quarterly 15*, 119–140.

Cochran, W. G. (1977). *Sampling techniques.* New York: John Wiley.

Congo Constitution. *Congo Constitution.* Retrieved September 19, 2004, from http://www.oefre.unibe.ch/law/icl/cf00000_.html

Disability Rights, Education and Defense Fund (1992). *The Constitution of Ghana.* Retrieved September 15, 2004, from http://www.dredf.org/international/Ghanaconstitution.html

Egypt Constitution. *The Constitution of the Arab Republic of Egypt.* (After the ratified amendments at the May 22, 1980 referendum—partial reproduction.) Retrieved September 15, 2004, from http://www.uam.es/otroscentros/medina/egypt/egypolcon.htm

Farrell, M. (2003). *Understanding special educational needs: A guide for student teachers.* New York: RoutledgeFalmer.

Fergusson, A., & Duffield, T. (2003). Multicultural inclusion for pupils with severe or profound and multiple learning difficulties. In C. Tilstone & R. Rose (Eds.), *Strategies to promote inclusive practice* (pp. 34–47). New York: RoutledgeFalmer.

Frey, G. C., McCubbin, J. A., Hannigan-Downs, S., Kasser, S. L., & Skaggs, S. O. (1999). Physical fitness of trained runners with and without mild mental retardation. *Adapted Physical Activity Quarterly 16*, 126–137.

Horvat, M., Croce, R., Stadler, L., & Pitetti, K. H. (1996). Isokinetic strength characteristics in children with and without mental retardation. *Medicine and Science in Sports and Exercise 28*, S50 [Abstracts].

Huber, J. H. (1995). Equity in athletics: Full participation for all students. *The Journal of Physical Education, Recreation and Dance 66*(7), 4–5.

Inter-Regional Expert Group (2002). *Text of elements for a United Nations comprehensive and integral International Convention to promote and protect the rights and dignity of persons with disabilities.* Original draft of paper presented June 11–14, 2002 in Mexico City. Retrieved September 15, 2004, from http://www.sre.gob.mx/discapacidad/elements.htm

Jeffery, N. (2002, August 2). South African able to go the distance—Commonwealth Games 2002. *The Australian 33*. Retrieved September 16, 2004, from EBSCO HOST Research Databases.

Kline, P. (1994). *An easy guide to factor analysis*. London: Routledge.

Konczei, G. (1997). *Equalising opportunities—disability—discrimination: The choices of anti-discrimination legislation* (comparative study—draft). Paper presented at the Council of Europa Committee on the Rehabilitation and Integration of People with Disabilities; Working Group on Legislation against Discrimination of Persons with Disabilities (P-RR-LADI) 3rd Session, Strasbourg, December 1–3, 1997. Retrieved, September 17, 2004, from http://www.independent living.org/docs5/equalisingopps.html

Kristiansen, R. (1988). *The quantum leap in special education: New information and communication technologies. Their impact upon educational opportunities for disabled people, focusing on how integration in the ordinary educational system can be facilitated*. Draft document of the United Nations Education, Scientific, and Cultural Organization, Paris (IBG 88895). Retrieved September 16, 2004, from EBSCO HOST Research Databases.

Nampa, O. (2004, July 23). *Special Olympics national champs*. Retrieved September 16, 2004, from EBSCO HOST Research Databases.

Norusis, M. J. (1991). *The SPSS guide to data analysis for SPSS/PC+™* (2nd edn). Chicago: SPSS Inc.

Office of the Deputy President (1997). *South Africa integrated national disability strategy white paper*. Retrieved September 15, 2004, from http://www.gladnet.org/infobase/files/319.htm

Onyewadume, I. U. (1999). Perspectives of adapted physical education in Africa. In L. O. Amusa, A. L. Toriola, & I. U. Onyewadume (Eds.), *Physical education and sport in Africa* (pp. 141–156). Stellenbosch: University of Stellenbosch Printers.

Pitetti, K. H., Rimmer, J. H., & Fernhall, B. (1993). Physical fitness and adults with mental retardation: An overview of current research and future directions. *Sports Medicine 16*, 23–36.

Pommering, T. L., Brose, J. A., Randolph, E., Murray, T. F., Purdy, R. W., Cadamagnani, P. E., & Foglesong, J. E. (1994). Effects of an aerobic exercise program on community-based adults with mental retardation. *Mental Retardation 32*, 218–226.

Rimmer, J. H., Braddock, D., & Fujiura, G. (1992). Blood lipid and percent body fat levels in Down syndrome versus non-DS persons with mental retardation. *Adapted Physical Activity Quarterly 9*, 123–129.

Rimmer, J. H., Braddock, D., & Fujiura, G. (1993). Prevalence of obesity in adults with mental retardation: Implications for health promotion and disease prevention. *Mental Retardation 31*, 105–110.

Rimmer, J. H., Riley, B., Wang, E., Rauworth, A., & Jurkowski, J. (2004). Physical activity participation among persons with disabilities: Barriers and facilitators. *American Journal of Preventive Medicine 26*(5), 419–425.

Rizzo, T., Faison-Hodge, J., Woodard, R., & Sayers, K. (2003). Are public facilities accessible to individuals with disabling conditions? *Adapted Physical Activity*

Quarterly 20(3), 319–320.
Rueda, R., Gallego, M. A., & Moll, L. C. (2000). The least restrictive environment: A place or a context? *Remedial and Special Education 21*(2), 70–78.
Russo, R. (2003). *Statistics for behavioural sciences: An introduction.* New York: Psychology Press, Taylor & Francis.
Sherrill, C. (2003). *Adapted physical activity, recreation and sport with power web blind-in passcard* (6th ed.). Dubuque, IA: McGraw-Hill.
Stadler, L. V., & Pitetti, K. H. (1996). Isometric and isokinetic leg strength of youths with and without mental retardation. *Medicine and Science in Sports and Exercise 28*, S49 [Abstract].
Suomi, R., Surburg, P. R., & Lecius, P. (1995). Effects of hydraulic resistance strength training on isokinetic measures of leg strength in men with mental retardation. *Adapted Physical Activity Quarterly 12*, 377–387.
The Republic of Kenya (2002). *Draft bill: The Constitution of the Republic of Kenya.* Retrieved September 15, 2004, from http://www.kenya.rcbowen.com/government/draft_constitution_sep2002.html
The Republic of Uganda. *The Constitution of the Republic of Uganda: Chapter 4—Human rights and freedoms.* Retrieved September 15, 2004, from http://www.dredf.org/international/UgaConst.html
The Times (2002, August). The swimmer who turns distress into sporting inspiration. *The Times*, 42–44. Retrieved September 16, 2004, from EBSCO HOST Research Databases.
Thomas, J. R., & Nelson, J. K. (1996). *Research methods in physical activity* (3rd ed.). Champaign, IL: Human Kinetics.
Vahid, B., Harwood, S., & Brown, S. (2004). *500 tips for working with children with special needs.* New York: RoutledgeFalmer.
Westwood, P. (2003). *Commonsense methods for children with special educational needs: Strategies for the regular classroom* (4th ed.). New York: RoutledgeFalmer.
Winnick, J. P. (2000). An introduction of adapted physical education and sport. In J. P. Winnick (Ed.), *Adapted physical education and sport* (3rd ed.). Champaign, IL: Human Kinetics.
Zambia Constitution. *Zambia country profile.* Retrieved September 19, 2004, from http://www.bibl.u-szeged.hu/oseas_adsec/zambia.htm
Zimbabwe Constitution. *Draft Constitution of the Republic of Zimbabwe.* Retrieved September 20, 2004, from http://www.gta.gov.zw/Constitutional/Draft%-20constitution/Contents.Draft.Const.htm